UNDER THE COPE OF HEAVEN

UNDER THE COPE OF HEAVEN

Religion, Society, and Politics
in Colonial America

Updated Edition

PATRICIA U. BONOMI

OXFORD
UNIVERSITY PRESS
2003

OXFORD
UNIVERSITY PRESS

Oxford   New York
Auckland   Bangkok   Buenos Aires   Cape Town   Chennai
Dar es salaam   Delhi   Hong Kong   Istanbul   Karachi   Kolkata
Kuala Lumpur   Madrid   Melbourne   Mexico City   Mumbai   Nairobi
São Paulo   Shanghai   Taipei   Tokyo   Toronto

Copyright ©1986 Patricia U. Bonomi
Preface to the updated edition © 2003 by Patricia U. Bonomi

First published in 1986 by Oxford University Press, Inc.
198 Madison Avenue, New York, New York 10016

www.oup.com

Oxford is a registered trademark of Oxford University Press

Library of Congress Cataloging-in-Publication Data
Bonomi, Patricia U.
Under the cope of heaven.
Bibliography: p.
Includes index.
ISBN 0-19-516217-X; 0-19-516218-8 (pbk.)
1. United States—Religion—To 1800.   2. United States—History—
Revolution, 1607–1783—Religious aspects.   I. Title.
BL2525.B66   1986   277.3'07   86-8418

1   3   5   7   9   8   6   4   2

Printed in the United States of America
on acid-free paper

In memory of
Winston R. Updegraff
Kathryn Mathews Updegraff
Dorothy Schmidt Updegraff

Preface to the Updated Edition

The history of religion in colonial America, once the almost exclusive domain of intellectual and church historians, has in the past two decades become part of the larger story of early America. Since 1986, when this book was published, writers on colonial religious subjects have increasingly turned toward the study of popular religion. They have reached beyond Puritan New England to the Middle Colonies and the South. They have refocused attention on the religious lives of African Americans, Native Americans, and women. And they are beginning to place their work in the larger context of communities in Europe, Africa, and the Caribbean. This updated edition provides an occasion to review the former and current state of the literature and to consider possible future directions.

A particularly fertile area of the recent scholarship explores the religious practices of African Americans. If my earlier assumption that "only a tiny proportion of blacks were active Christians before the Revolution" (p. 126) has not yet been overthrown, the new work suggests that the subject is more complex than we once thought. An important breakthrough is the growing recognition that the quest for Christian influences on colonial blacks must begin not in America but in Africa.

A substantial number of the Africans forced into slavery had roots in the Angola colony and its neighbor the Kingdom of Kongo, where Portuguese Roman Catholic missionaries had worked from the late-fifteenth century to convert the native populations. Although the religious practice that emerged was often freighted with African traditions, the Portuguese church was more tolerant of such syncretic compromise than was, for example, the Spanish church. Apparently Portuguese clerics and Rome both accepted African converts as orthodox. Huge numbers of the inhabitants were baptized, and a tradition of training Africans to become lay practitioners and catechists continued into the late eighteenth century. Thus there is every reason to think that some portion of the slaves delivered to British America, possibly including the first Africans shipped to Virginia in 1619, had prior exposure to Christian beliefs. Slaves from West Central Africa also were sent to the colonies of New York and New Jersey; others went to Barbados and Savannah, Georgia. "About ten thousand Africans from Angola arrived in Carolina in the 1730s alone," and the Stono Rebellion may have been led by slaves from the Kingdom of Kongo.[1]

Did African Christianity survive the dolorous journey into slavery? If so, did this make slaves more susceptible than previously assumed to Christian, especially Anglican, missions in British America? Might there even have been Afro-Christian lay preachers scattered among slave communities from an early date? Such possibilities run up against the view, still widely held, that few blacks were touched by Christianity, that white slaveholders supported missionary efforts only insofar as they made slaves more docile, and that it was not until the revivals of the mid-eighteenth century that larger numbers of slaves, though still a minority, were exposed to Christianity and a few black preachers made their appearance.[2] Nonetheless it may be prudent to keep open the tantalizing possibility of an earlier and somewhat broader Christian knowledge among Africans in the Americas.

Recent studies also suggest that more clergy than previously credited, and even more southern planters, sought to encompass blacks within their religious communities. Scores of slaves on the Virginia plantations of the Carter and Burwell families were baptized in the Church of England from the 1720s to the 1760s, possibly with their owners' encouragement.[3] In other parts of Virginia, too, substantial numbers of slaves were baptized, apparently after receiving some form of instruction: 200 in Accomack Parish between 1709 and 1724, and 354 in North Farnham Parish from 1725 to 1732—of whom 103 were slaves of Colonel Robert Carter. The Huguenots of Manakin Town baptized more than 150 slaves between 1727 and 1754, and in some years as many blacks as whites. Between 1740 and 1775 in Albemarle Parish, 846 young blacks received baptism; and in Bruton Parish at least 980 slaves plus a few free blacks were baptized between 1746 and 1768.[4] South Carolina's Anglican ministers strove from the early eighteenth century onward to catechize slaves. Hundreds were baptized, many attended church services, and some became communicating members. These efforts were later supplemented by a network of southern evangelicals encouraged by George Whitefield. In 1740, the plantation-owning Bryan family opened a school for slaves in St. Helena Parish and three years later formed a Presbyterian congregation that included black as well as white members. The Moravians, active in the Caribbean and Georgia from the 1730s, and in Pennsylvania from 1740, founded a holy community in North Carolina in 1753. Slaves were baptized in these Moravian settlements and embraced as brethren, though black bondage itself was accepted as ordained by God.[5] New York City's Trinity Church had first supported the instruction of slaves in 1704, and thereafter slaves and free blacks were regularly catechized by Elias Neau and his successors on weeknights and Sunday afternoons, with thousands being baptized over the eighteenth century. Anglican missionaries active in New Jersey recorded baptizing some 350 African Americans between 1740 and 1782. In addition, a number of northern Lutheran and Moravian churches were open to black conversions and interracial congregations.[6]

If baptized African Americans seem to have been more numerous than we once thought, the effect the rite had on their inner spiritual lives remains in doubt. Still, accumulating evidence makes clear that some blacks embraced more than the exterior forms of Christianity. Of particular interest are the reports from schools established in a number of colonies to teach reading and church catechisms to slaves and free blacks. Certain slaves, presumably with the encouragement of their masters, eagerly grasped this opportunity, perhaps merely to ease their conditions of bondage. Yet we cannot exclude the possibility that some were motivated by genuine conviction.[7]

Blacks "flocked" to the classes offered by New York's Trinity Parish, where selected pupils assisted with the instruction. In Massachusetts, Cotton Mather and others worked to bring blacks within the fold.[8] A number of Virginia's Anglican clergy had long catechized slaves on Sunday afternoons, sometimes in company with white youths, and by 1750 three schools were apparently operating in Williamsburg. The Reverend Alexander Garden opened a school for blacks in Charleston, South Carolina, in 1743, personally training the slave Harry to serve as a Christian teacher. Harry in turn was expected to encourage his students to read the Bible along with various religious tracts to their fellow slaves.[9] After mid-century, the Anglican Associates of Dr. Bray, which had for years supplied books for the instruction of slaves, undertook to establish schools for them throughout British North America. Several were founded in the south, including Georgia, South Carolina, and Virginia; the Associates' school at Williamsburg was active from 1760 to 1774. Others were opened in Philadelphia (1758), New York (1760), and Newport (1762). In total, the Bray Associates offered Christian instruction to some two to three thousand blacks.[10] The Moravians educated slaves along with white children in their schools, and the Great Awakening prodded Philadelphia Anglicans to appoint a teacher for blacks in 1747. The Quaker Anthony Benezet tutored slaves himself until he gained enough support to open a school for them in 1773.[11]

These schools, a number of which predated the Great Awakening, may even have provided a foundation—or reinforced an existing foundation—for the black preachers occasionally mentioned in the eighteenth-century records. Most interesting in this regard are South Carolina minister Francis LeJau's references in 1710 to three or four slaves in his parish who were "born and baptized among the Portuguese," and thus were Roman Catholics. LeJau observed that the slaves were "well instructed," though he refused their request to join his church until they abjured such "Popish tenets" as praying to the saints. Might these men have been lay practitioners working among slaves in the quarters? In one telling incident, LeJau reports that the best scholar among them aroused fear in "all the negroes in this country" when he told of God's forthcoming chastisement of sinners. "It was publicly blazed abroad that an angel came and spake to the man. . . . he had heard voices, seen fires etc." After further instruction in the Anglican rite at least two of these slaves were received into communion. LeJau encouraged his literate students to carry the Christian message to their fellow slaves, and he reported in 1716 that those he had baptized "prayd and read some part of their Bibles in the field and in their Quarters in the hearing of those who could not read."[12] Here are early hints that Afro-Christian leaders were themselves giving shape to the religious understanding of their fellow bondsmen and -women.

Historians have long assumed that the first African-American preachers were a direct product of the Great Awakening, emerging only after 1740 in the north and not until the 1760s in the south. This suggests that black preachers were forged only in the fires of white revivalism, with their emotional appeals, oral forms, and rhythmic exhortations. But if some blacks had adopted Christianity in their African homelands, and if some of those trained as catechists and lay preachers continued their work in the Americas, the Christian experience of colonial blacks may be broader than we have previously acknowledged. Much more scholarly digging needs to be done. The examples noted here are no more than golden grains in a largely unexplored field. Yet to foreclose speculation—especially about the period before 1740—might confine and perhaps foreshorten the colonial foundation of what would within a few decades become an exuberant African American Christianity.

Native American history has in recent years become a lively field of study. One consequence of this growing interest has been to carry Indian history beyond its earlier polarities, which had much in common with the victim-resistance antipodes that once governed African American history. In the earlier literature, Indians were often cast either as culturally demoralized victims of European aggression or as self-actualizing resisters of white imperialism. While these contrasting approaches continue to set the outer boundaries of interpretation, the distance in between has become the arena of sophisticated ethnohistorical study.[13] Recent works explore, among other questions, the interaction between Indians and Christian missionaries. My previous understanding that native populations were strongly resistant to Protestant Christianity may, once again, require modification.

A focus on the spiritual realm offers rich opportunities for historians to observe and appraise the intersection of cultures. A number of studies have examined the middle ground on which Indians and Europeans met, mingled, and reached accommodations, giving to and taking from each others' cultures in a dynamic captured in the word *syncretism*. Elements of the Great Lakes tribes, the Iroquois, and the Delawares of western Pennsylvania assimilated aspects of Christian teaching, sometimes using them to revive and augment traditional values. Substantial numbers of Indians in seventeenth-century southern New England also proved receptive to Christianity as their own shamans' powers were called into question by rampaging European diseases and Anglo-Indian warfare. Yet the Christianity that resulted was "a selective blend of Indian and English ways." Even Samson Occom, the Connecticut Mohegan convert who preached Christianity to Native Americans for more than four decades, can be seen as a cultural broker who upon moving west to live among the Oneidas dispensed "a form of spiritual syncretism."[14]

A somewhat different perspective on Indian converts that looks beyond accommodation to questions of Indian identity and volition comes from new work on that most closely scrutinized subject, Massachusetts missionary John Eliot's praying towns. Recent studies acknowledge that the numbers are impressive—1,100 Indians settled in 14 praying towns, six churches with Indian elders, and 350 baptized natives by 1674—but find that the Indians' motives were both varied and as often secular as religious. Some sought shelter from native communities stripped by death and fractured by contesting cultures, while others looked for leverage in tribal power struggles, especially those that challenged the control of native priests or powwows. A number of Indians were motivated by the benefits of English technology or diplomatic alliance. Others may have been attracted by Eliot's oral culture of communal prayer and dialogue between minister and potential converts.[15] Many Native American women found Christianity a boon because it reshaped gender relationships, bringing men into agricultural production and promoting monogamous marriage.[16]

Another group of scholars sees evidence of authenticity in Native American conversions, noting that the power lost by Indian priests was often transferred to Christian clergymen. In addition, Christian communities extended material and spiritual comforts that many Indians, especially those living in closest proximity to Europeans, came to value. French Jesuits were particularly effective, baptizing countless members of the Great Lakes tribes and perhaps as many as 4,000 Iroquois by 1679, at which point, some 20 percent of the Iroquois peoples "may have become sincere Roman Catholics." Protestant missionaries seem to have been less successful, possibly because they set the bar for inclusion in their churches at a higher level. Still, Eliot's praying towns, the long-term conversions fostered by the Thomas Mayhews on Martha's Vineyard, and the later headway made by Moravian missions cannot be discounted. Even the Anglicans had occasional successes, as at one Mohawk village where in 1716 perhaps one-third of the Indians were practicing Christians.[17]

Some writers do not shy from attempts to gauge the quality of Native American religious beliefs, though they acknowledge the paucity of first-person accounts. Their efforts may in part reflect the wish to move beyond syncretism, which has limits as an explanatory device given that all religions assimilate elements of the cultures through which they move. One approach emphasizes revitalization, the process whereby Indian prophets in the western territories breathed new life into traditional beliefs, which were then molded into a platform for pan-nativist resistance to white encroachments. The cosmology of the Delaware prophet Neolin, for example, while incorporating certain Christian elements, was dominated by an Indian spirituality that later suffused the resistance struggle led by Pontiac.[18] Another study analyzes the theological structure of conversion statements offered by eight Indians and recorded by the Rev. John Eliot, comparing them over time and against the Puritan model. Differences were evident: the Indians could not work up the same "magnificent self-disgust" as the Puritans because their universe did not include the concept of sin; they also had difficulty "conceiving a god of love"; and they continued the native tradition of seeking an equilibrium with all of God's creatures.[19] A study of Moravian contact with Native Americans in Pennsylvania sees neither victimization nor resistance, affirming instead that the Indians had choices. Some established a dialogue with the missionaries (and perhaps 10 to 20 percent were baptized), some shunned Christianity, and others appropriated aspects of it to their own uses.[20]

The recent studies thus offer a fragmented picture of Native American Christianization, limited as they are by a narrow evidentiary base and interrogatory agenda. There are areas of agreement, such as the widely noted willingness of native groups to listen attentively to Christian proselytizers, and the often positive response of Indian women. Perhaps only when more data is gathered on the successes and failures of Christian missions will we be able to speak with confidence about the interaction between Indians and Europeans in the religious sphere.

A good deal has also been written about colonial women since 1986, though not as much as one might expect addresses issues of female religion. Yet, the soul equality implicit in church doctrine potentially offered women an arena for intellectual and moral leadership. That a number of them seized the opening is shown in a new study that compares the experiences of women in seventeenth-century Puritan New England, Dutch Reformed New York, and Anglican Virginia. As historians continue to extract the rich commentary on gender (as well as race and class) that lies in church archives, we can look forward to a fuller picture of the religious lives of colonial women.[21]

Recent research has added context and insight into a number of eighteenth-century female religious circles. Middle-Colony Quaker women, though they accepted a role gendered by traditional domestic expectations, exerted real influence within and sometimes beyond their local communities. The women's meetings in Pennsylvania and New Jersey, unlike those in England, functioned not only at monthly- and quarterly- but also at yearly-meeting levels, exercising authority over unruly women, the poor, and candidates for marriage. Moreover, when the Society of Friends debated pacifism in the 1750s, Quaker women participated and their issues often prevailed. The lives of itinerant female preachers, or "traveling Friends," have now been set more fully in a transatlantic context, an indispensable dimension given the frequency with which these women crossed the water. The itinerants apparently rose from a wide spectrum of social backgrounds, and if often single or widowed, married preachers with young children were granted leave from domestic duties by a closely knit community of caregivers that included husbands.[22]

New England Baptist women emerged in the 1740s as exhorters as well as vocal participants in church discipline and in choosing ministers. Southern Anglican women gained indirect authority as a stabilizing sex ratio strengthened family life in the eighteenth century. Although excluded from governance in a firmly patriarchal church, they participated equally as communicants and godparents, and through informal female networks exercised indirect but meaningful leadership in organizing baptisms, marriages, and funerals in their homes.[23]

A number of recent studies note that women's influence within their religious communities flowed and ebbed. New England was centerstage for charismatic women in the early seventeenth century, including not only the likes of Anne Hutchinson and Mary Dyer but also contemporaries such as Lady Deborah Moody, Anne Austin, and Mary Fisher, among others. In succeeding decades women were less visible (or perhaps still undiscovered), and their preponderance in the cohort of accused witches may indicate that they were especially beleaguered by the late seventeenth century.[24] The Great Awakening, however, ushered in a bold chorus of evangelical women. That many of them have recently been searched out and identified confirms that the Reverend Charles Chauncey's "FEMALE EXHORTERS" were more than figments of an ardent imagination (see p. 123). Baptist women were prominent among them; yet in the Revolutionary era Baptist men in New England and Virginia rapidly reclaimed power, as masculine values displaced the weakened hierarchies of a previously feminizing church.[25] Indeed, religious women may have possessed more real power during the colonial years, when they acted directly on churchmen in their congregations, than they held in the early republic, when they were assigned a moral sphere distinct from that of the men.[26]

The issue of female authority is also linked to questions about the feminization of churchgoing—the process whereby women came to outnumber men in some denominations, though not perhaps in others, as well as the timing of any shift in the male-female ratio. In New England's Congregational churches female members became the majority between 1650 and 1680, and though men joined in greater numbers during revivals, the movement toward feminization seems to have been inexorable. But as scholars look beyond New England, the pattern becomes clouded. Whereas Dutch Reformed women in New York City composed from 59 to 66 percent of the communicants between 1665 and 1730, in the rural Tappan church female members only slightly outnumbered the men.

Feminization in the Society of Friends also seems to have depended on time and place. The Moravian community at Bethlehem, Pennsylvania, attracted more women than men. But among the Baptists in Massachusetts men outnumbered women by two to one before 1740, while in Virginia Baptist women led in both attendance and membership. And as yet no study to my knowledge has discovered a significant sex differential among adherents of the colonial Church of England.[27] There is also conflicting evidence about whether a professionalizing clergy may have hastened men's turn from church governance and thus from membership (see the discussion on pp. 113–115).[28] Far more work is needed on these and other questions—including the roles that Indian and black women played in their religious cultures—to gain a more complete sense of women's religious experience.

On another front, the burgeoning field of Atlantic history has already left a significant impress on our conception of early American religion. Perhaps most important, the colonial revivals that once were viewed narrowly as local events are now being examined within a transatlantic evangelical tradition strongly shaped by Scottish and English practices. Further, the history of colonial Lutherans and of German and Dutch Reformed has in recent years been placed within the essential context of European pietism, opening many new areas of study.[29] Questions of slavery and race now encompass not only the Christian but also the Islamic worlds. The multiple efforts by Europeans to convert Indians to Christianity are increasingly being cast in the comparative framework of French, British, Spanish, and Portuguese proselytization among native populations in various parts of the Americas. And the perennial question in women's history of whether Catholic culture or Protestant was more empowering for women is currently being tested in colonial settings.[30]

This brief glance at the new and ongoing work in early religious studies suggests the variety of fruitful approaches that have been opened in recent years. Perhaps it is not too much to say that colonial religious history itself is experiencing a kind of awakening, as it becomes more fully incorporated into the broader stream of early American scholarship.

This resurgence points to perhaps the most striking change of all over the past two decades, that is, the much larger place that religion now occupies in the colonial story. To be sure, historians have always lavished attention on the Puritans. Yet when this book was published in 1986, it was still widely accepted that few early Americans in any region had much to do with churches. The eighteenth century was seen as a particularly low point, except for a brief spurt of piety during the Great Awakening. And the clergy outside of New England were regularly depicted as ne'er-do-wells who "babble in a pulpit [and] roar in a Tavern."[31]

By the 1980s, however, a shift of understanding was already glimmering on the horizon. With the ascent of social and cultural history many scholars turned their attention to detailed explorations of local communities, including church congregations. These disclosed a religious life far more vital in the South and the Middle Colonies than previously supposed. Further, it now seemed that a long post-Puritan decline was not the best way to characterize religion in New England. Close inspection showed that religious observance in the American provinces was often strong, with congregation formation matching population growth and church building proceeding at a vigorous pace throughout the colonial years.[32] This book, along with a preceding essay that questioned the notion of low church adherence,[33] caught the wave that has since crested in a more positive view of colonial religious life.

Why, we might ask, did the older version, with its emphasis on religious apathy and unfit clergy, dominate historians' perception of colonial religion for well over a century? The major role granted to Puritans in the founding narrative is perhaps understandable, given the exquisite intellect and spiritual commitment of many Puritan men and women, the drama of their clash with Quakers and other disrupters of Zion, and their high literacy with its consequent paper trail. Add to this the elegant writings of Perry Miller, his student Edmund S. Morgan, and their scholarly offspring.[34] Yet whatever "declension," to use Miller's word, may have occurred in New England religion over the colonial years was reflected not in numbers of churches or churchgoers—which continued to grow—but rather in the inevitable sense of falling short of the charter generation's sublime ideals.[35]

It is not so easy to account for the gloomy view of religious life in the southern and mid-Atlantic colonies. From the (hind)sight-lines of a new paradigm, however, it is apparent that a bias governed that literature—

one that arose from the dramatic success of evangelical religion in the nineteenth century and then was promoted by its chroniclers, especially Robert Baird, a Presbyterian missionary and proponent of the Atlantic-wide Evangelical Alliance. In 1844, Baird compiled a general history of American religion to that date, dividing the colonial period into four parts. From 1607 to 1660 religion flourished under Calvinist leaders in New England, New Netherland, and the Chesapeake; 1660 to 1720 was marked by the rise of Congregational and Anglican ecclesiastical structures, with an attendant "decline in vital Christianity"; from 1720 to 1750 revivals "infused a new life into the churches"; finally, from 1750 to 1775 wars and political commotions led to a "declension in spiritual life." However, with the rise of Methodists and Baptists in the early nation, as well as the growing evangelical branches of the Congregational, Presbyterian, and Episcopal churches, God rekindled the spark with a "great salvation," namely, the Second Great Awakening. For Baird, the most admirable element of religious life in the United States was its attachment to the principles of "evangelical Christianity."[36]

The next marker on the road to the "evangelical synthesis," as I have called the older historiography,[37] came from the work of William Meade, Episcopal bishop of Virginia from 1841 to 1862. In more detailed if less subtle strokes than those of Baird, Meade homed in on Virginia, tracing its religious development from 1607 to the 1850s in a parish by parish survey. Looking back on the history of his parent Church of England, Meade sketched a bleak picture. Colonial Anglicanism was not "even tolerably good," plagued as it was by vacant pulpits, minimal discipline, and "evil living among the clergy." Even worse was the post-Revolutionary Episcopal Church, where sermons inclined toward "the moral kind"—in other words, the church was infected with rationalism. Only with the rise of evangelical preaching in the antebellum years, and with the days-long revival meetings promoted by Meade, did the church shake off its lethargy and prosper.[38]

For the next 100 years and more historians of American religion, in particular those undertaking large syntheses drawn from secondary sources, followed the path blazed by Baird, Meade, and other evangelical church historians. The most influential were the works of William Warren Sweet, written from the 1930s to the 1950s, for Sweet converted the ostensibly desiccated religious landscape of colonial America into numbers. In the eighteenth century, he asserted, no more than 5 to 15 percent of the inhabitants were church members, with New England occupying the upper end of the spectrum and the other regions shading toward a religious wasteland. Successive historians repeated Sweet's undocumented statistics, while blurring the distinction between church members and churchgoers. They repeated as well his summary conclusion that the American colonies contained a greater proportion of unchurched people than existed "in any country in Christendom."[39] This was a convenient fiction for those comfortable with the notion that "real" religion arrived in America only with the rise of Methodist, Baptist, and other evangelical churches.

So things stood until the 1960s, when the conventions of the evangelical synthesis began to loosen. As the grand structural histories that had dominated post–World War II European scholarship gave way to more intimate explorations of early society, there ensued a fascination with historical demography, family reconstitution, and quantitative analysis. One consequence was that a number of historians narrowed their sights to subregions and even to single communities, which led them to comb local records—including church records—for vital statistics and other traces of the inarticulate. By 1970, a vanguard of American historians versed in the new techniques were producing deeply textured studies of New England towns, which began to reveal a religious vitality that contradicted earlier assumptions about declension.[40] Further insights came from psychology and sociology; and soon the microcosmic techniques of cultural anthropology were seized on as offering new approaches to popular history, including the careful analysis of supernatural beliefs and symbols.[41] As early as 1964 Henry May had haled the growing interest in American religious history ("The Recovery of American Religious History," *American Historical Review*, 70 [Oct. 1964], 79–92), though such interest was largely confined to intellectual historians and theologians. Only with the subsequent rise of social history did popular religious practice catch the eye of a broader range of historians.

These new social and cultural models, which emphasized the laity and popular religious practice, soon shouldered aside the old top-down, institutional view of colonial religion. And as church records were more fully exploited by social historians, it became increasingly evident that early Americans in all sections lived not in a spiritual desert but in a world where religion formed a key component of their mental landscape. Thus the older historiography, for all its accomplishments in laying out the basic institutional contours of parishes, denominations, and ecclesiastical networks, is being replaced by a new paradigm that works increasingly from the bottom up, and in the past decade within the framework of an Atlantic-wide history.

Moving beyond the evangelical synthesis has had the further advantage, as we have seen, of shifting attention to the religious lives of early Americans previously ignored. And this brings promise of a more rounded and satisfying history of colonial religion that will encompass that world in its totality—all races and ranks, women as well as men, the young and the old.

NOTES

1. John Thornton, "The Development of an African Catholic Church in the Kingdom of Kongo, 1491–1750," *Journal of African History*, 25 (1984), 147–167; and Thornton, "The African Experience of the '20s. And Odd Negroes' Arriving in Virginia in 1619," *William and Mary Quarterly* (hereafter *WMQ*), 3d Ser., 55 (July 1998), 421–434. "Portuguese law required all African slaves to be baptized and made Christian before their arrival in America" (ibid., 434). Graham Russell Hodges, *Root & Branch: African Americans in New York and East Jersey, 1613–1863* (Chapel Hill, 1999), 38; Philip D. Morgan, *Slave Counterpoint: Black Culture in the Eighteenth-Century Chesapeake & Lowcountry* (Chapel Hill, 1998), quotation on pp. 62–63. For slave trade patterns, see David Eltis, "The Volume and Structure of the Transatlantic Slave Trade: A Reassessment," *WMQ*, 3d Ser., 58 (January 2001), 17–46, esp. Table II; and Lorena S. Walsh, "The Chesapeake Slave Trade: Regional Patterns, African Origins, and Some Implications," ibid., 139–170. On Stono, see John Thornton, "African Dimensions of the Stono Rebellion," *American Historical Review*, 96 (October 1991), 1101–1113.

2. This standard interpretation is most recently reiterated in Sylvia R. Frey and Betty Wood, *Come Shouting to Zion: African American Protestantism in the American South and British Caribbean to 1830* (Chapel Hill, 1998). It follows a deft summary of religion in Africa, including references not only to Catholic but to Dutch Reformed, Moravian, and Anglican missions active in

Africa's west coastal regions (chap. 1), though the authors draw few connections between African and American Christianity. See also Ira Berlin, *Many Thousands Gone: The First Two Centuries of Slavery in North America* (Cambridge, Mass., 1998).

3. Lorena S. Walsh, *From Calabar to Carter's Grove: The History of a Virginia Slave Community* (Charlottesville, Va., 1997), 153–155; figures for the five plantations examined total 248. Although it may be impossible ever to gauge the depth of the slaves' Christian commitment, Walsh suggests that "the sheer numbers involved at least raise the possibility that these slaves were adopting and adapting Christian religiosity at a relatively early date" (p. 224).

4. John K. Nelson, *A Blessed Company: Parishes, Parsons, and Parishioners in Anglican Virginia, 1690–1776* (Chapel Hill, 2001), 264–265, 267, 304; R. A. Brock, comp., *Documents, Chiefly Unpublished, Relating to the Huguenot Emigration to Virginia* (1886; reprint, Baltimore, 1995), 79–110; Thad W. Tate, *The Negro in Eighteenth-Century Williamsburg* (Charlottesville, Va., 1965), 128, 131.

5. Annette Laing, "'Heathens and Infidels'? African Christianization and Anglicanism in the South Carolina Low Country, 1700–1750," *Religion and American Culture: A Journal of Interpretation*, 12, no. 2 (2002), 197–228; Alan Gallay, "The Origins of Slaveholders' Paternalism, George Whitefield, the Bryan Family, and the Great Awakening in the South," *Journal of Southern History*, 53 (August 1987), 369–394; Jon F. Sensbach, *A Separate Canaan: The Making of an Afro-Moravian World in North Carolina, 1763–1840* (Chapel Hill, 1998), 29–47, chaps. 3–4.

6. Hodges, *Root & Branch*, 54–63, 84–88, 119–121. For a report on related, if preliminary, findings from the African Burial Ground project in New York City, see Anne-Marie Cantwell and Diana deZerega Wall, *Unearthing Gotham* (New Haven, 2001), chap. 16. For information on Trinity's catechization of blacks in the first half of the eighteenth century, see the New York correspondence, Records of the Society for the Propagation of the Gospel in Foreign Parts, Letterbooks A (Micro Methods, Ltd.).

7. A sample of 158 South Carolina slaves baptized between 1736 and 1768 was disproportionately mulatto, creole, adult, skilled, and English speaking. That is, the most literate and assimilated slaves were more likely to become Christians. Robert Olwell, *Masters, Slaves, & Subjects: The Culture of Power in the South Carolina Low Country, 1740–1790* (Ithaca, N.Y., 1998), 119, 125, 127–129. See also Walsh, *From Calabar to Carter's Grove*, 155–157.

8. Hodges, *Root & Branch*, 60, 84–88, 119; John Hope Franklin, *From Slav-ery to Freedom: A History of Negro Americans* (1947; New York, 1967), 108.

9. Tate, *The Negro in Eighteenth-Century Virginia*, 135; Robert Olwell, *Masters, Slaves, & Subjects*, 121; Nelson, *A Blessed Company*, 263–268, 270.

Starting with 30 children, Alexander Garden's school had doubled in size a year later; 70 pupils were enrolled in 1755. Harry was so important to the school that it closed after his death in 1764. Frank J. Klingberg, *An Appraisal of the Negro in Colonial South Carolina: A Study in Americanization* (Washington, D.C., 1941), chap. 5.

10. John C. Van Horne, ed., *Religious Philanthropy and Colonial Slavery: The American Correspondence of the Associates of Dr. Bray, 1717–1777* (Urbana, Ill., 1985), 20–24, 38; Nelson, *A Blessed Company*, 269–270; Tate, *The Negro in Eighteenth-Century Virginia*, 140–151.

11. Sensbach, *A Separate Canaan*, 124, 135–136; Gary B. Nash, *Forging Freedom: The Formation of Philadelphia's Black Community, 1720–1840* (Cambridge, Mass., 1988), 18–31.

12. Klingberg, *An Appraisal of the Negro in Colonial South Carolina*, 16, 18, 23. Among other apparent Catholics, a black woman from Guadalupe also wished to abjure and become an Anglican (p. 24). For instruction in the quarters, see Frank J. Klingberg, ed., *The Carolina Chronicle of Dr. Francis Le-Jau, 1706–1717*, in *University of California Publications in History*, 53 (Berkeley, 1956), 120, 174.

13. The works of Francis Jennings set the terms of the earlier model. Studies that introduced a more ethnologically balanced reading include Neal Salisbury, *Manitou and Providence: Indians, Europeans, and the Making of New England, 1500–1643* (New York, 1982) and James Axtell, *The Invasion Within: The Contest of Cultures in Colonial North America* (New York, 1985).

14. Richard White, *The Middle Ground: Indians, Empires, and Republics in the Great Lakes Region, 1650–1815* (Cambridge, 1991), see, for example, 279–280, 336–339; Neal Salisbury, "'I Loved the Place of My Dwelling': Puritan Missionaries and Native Americans in Seventeenth-Century Southern New England," in Carla Gardina Pestana and Sharon V. Salinger, eds., *Inequality in Early America* (Hanover, N.H., 1999), 111–133, quotation on p. 128; Margaret Connell Szasz, "Samson Occom: Mohegan as Spiritual Intermediary," in Szasz, ed., *Between Indian and White Worlds: The Cultural Broker* (Norman, Okla., 1994), quotation on p. 77.

15. Robert James Naeher, "Dialogue in the Wilderness: John Eliot and the Indian Exploration of Puritanism as a Source of Meaning, Comfort, and Ethnic Survival, *The New England Quarterly*, 62 (Sept. 1989), 346–368; Harold W. Van Lonkhuysen, "A Reappraisal of the Praying Indians at Natick, Massachusetts, 1646–1730," ibid., 63 (Sept. 1990), 396–428.

16. Van Lonkhuysen, "A Reappraisal of the Praying Indians," 413; see also Ann Marie Plane, *Colonial Intimacies: Indian Marriage in Early New England* (Ithaca, N.Y., 2000).

17. James Axtell, "Were Indian Conversions *Bona Fide*?" in Axtell, *After*

Columbus: Essays in the Ethnohistory of Colonial North America (New York, 1988), chap. 7; Daniel K. Richter, *The Ordeal of the Longhouse: The Peoples of the Iroquois League in the Era of European Colonization* (Chapel Hill, 1992), chap. 5, 231; quotation on p. 116; David Silverman, "Deposing the Sachem to Defend the Sachemship: Land Sales and Native Political Structure on Martha's Vineyard, 1680–1740," in *Explorations in Early American Culture*, 5 (2001), 12.

18. Gregory Evans Dowd, *A Spirited Resistance: The North American Indian Struggle for Unity, 1745–1815* (Baltimore, 1992); Alfred A. Cave, "The Delaware Prophet Neolin: A Reappraisal," *Ethnohistory*, 46 (Spring 1999), 265–290.

19. Charles L. Cohen, "Conversion Among Puritans and Amerindians: A Theological Perspective," in Francis J. Bremer, ed., *Puritanism: Transatlantic Perspectives on a Seventeenth-Century Anglo-American Faith* (Boston, 1993), 233–256; quotations on 252, 256.

20. Jane T. Merritt, "Dreaming of the Savior's Blood: Moravians and the Indian Great Awakening in Pennsylvania," *WMQ*, 3d Ser., 54 (Oct. 1997), 723–746. On this same theme, see Karen Ordahl Kupperman, *Indians and English: Facing Off in Early America* (Ithaca, N.Y., 2000), chap. 5. See also Russell Bourne, *Gods of War, Gods of Peace: How the Meeting of Native and Colonial Religions Shaped Early America* (New York, 2002).

21. Leslie J. Lindenaueur, *Piety and Power: Gender and Religious Culture in the American Colonies, 1630–1700* (New York, 2002). The letters and journals of the Society for the Propagation of the Gospel in Foreign Parts and correspondence in the Fulham Papers, Lambeth Palace Library (cited on p. 231 [nn.12–13]), exemplify the sources on a variety of social and ethnocultural topics in denominational archives, including those in Scotland, Germany, and the Netherlands. There seems to be little information available on the practices of colonial Jewish women, though the importance of religion to their lives is evident in Edith B. Gelles, ed., *The Letters of Abigaill Levy Franks, 1733–1748* (forthcoming).

22. Jean R. Soderlund, "Women's Authority in Pennsylvania and New Jersey Quaker Meetings, 1680–1760," *WMQ*, 3d Ser., 44 (Oct. 1987), 722–749; Rebecca Larson, *Daughters of Light: Quaker Women Preaching and Prophesying in the Colonies and Abroad, 1700–1775* (New York, 1999).

23. Susan Juster, *Disorderly Women: Sexual Politics & Evangelicalism in Revolutionary New England* (Ithaca, N.Y., 1994); Nelson, *A Blessed Company*, 253–258; Joan R. Gundersen, *To Be Useful to the World: Women in Revolutionary America, 1740–1790* (New York, 1996), 97, 101–111.

24. Marilyn J. Westerkamp, *Women and Religion in Early America, 1600–1850* (London, 1999), chap. 3; Carol F. Karlsen, *The Devil in the Shape of a Woman: Witchcraft in Colonial New England* (New York, 1987).

xxiv   *Preface to the Updated Edition*

25. Catherine A. Brekus, *Strangers and Pilgrims: Female Preaching in America, 1740–1845* (Chapel Hill, 1998), part I, esp. p. 52; Juster, *Disorderly Women*; Janet Moore Lindman, "Acting the Manly Christian: White Evangelical Masculinity in Revolutionary Virginia," *WMQ*, 3d Ser., 57 (April 2000), 393–416.

26. See Amanda Porterfield, *Female Piety in Puritan New England: The Emergence of Religious Humanism* (New York, 1992), 9–10, chap. 4.

27. For New England, see Harry S. Stout and Catherine A. Brekus, "Declension, Gender, and the 'New Religious History'" in Philip R. Vandermeer and Robert P. Swierenga, eds., *Belief and Behaviour: Essays in the New Religious History* (New Brunswick, N.J., 1991), 15–37; and Porterfield, *Female Piety in Puritan New England*, 9–10. For the Dutch Reformed, see Joyce D. Goodfriend, "The Social Dimensions of Congregational Life in Colonial New York City," *WMQ*, 3d Ser., 46 (April 1989), 252–278, and Firth Haring Fabend, *A Dutch Family in the Middle Colonies, 1660–1800* (New Brunswick, N.J., 1991), 146–147. Beverly Prior Smaby, *The Transformation of Moravian Bethlehem: From Communal Mission to Family Economy* (Philadelphia, 1988). Quakers are discussed in Carla Gardina Pestana, *Quakers and Baptists in Colonial Massachusetts* (Cambridge, 1991), 72. For Baptists, see ibid., 71 (n26), and Lindman, "Acting the Manly Christian," 398 (n.13).

28. For contrasting views, see Fabend, *A Dutch Family in the Middle Colonies*, 147, and Westerkamp, *Women and Religion in Early America*, 79–81. See also Charles L. Cohen, "The Post-Puritan Paradigm of Early American Religious History," *WMQ*, 3d Ser., 54 (Oct. 1997), 719–721.

29. Leigh Eric Schmidt, *Holy Fairs: Scotland and the Making of American Revivalism* (Princeton, 1989); Michael J. Crawford, *Seasons of Grace: Colonial New England's Revival Tradition in Its British Context* (New York, 1991); Frank Lambert, *"Pedlar in Divinity": George Whitefield and the Transatlantic Revivals* (Princeton, N.J., 1994); A. G. Roeber, *Palatines, Liberty, and Property: German Lutherans in Colonial British America* (Baltimore, 1993); David William Voorhees, "The 'fervent Zeale' of Jacob Leisler," *WMQ*, 3d Ser., 51 (July 1994), 447–472.

30. David Brion Davis, "Constructing Race: A Reflection," *WMQ*, 3d Ser., 54 (Jan. 1997), 7–18; Michael Angelo Gomez, *Exchanging Our Country Marks: The Transformation of African Identities in the Colonial and Antebellum South* (Chapel Hill, 1998); Nicholas Griffiths and Fernando Cervantes, eds., *Spiritual Encounters: Interactions Between Christianity and Native Religions in Colonial America* (Lincoln, Neb., 1999); Emily Clark, "'By All the Conduct of Their Lives': A Laywomen's Confraternity in New Orleans, 1730–1744," *WMQ*, 3d Ser., 54 (Oct. 1997), 769–794.

31. The quotation, a favorite of the earlier historiography, is from John Hammond's *Leah and Rachel* (London, 1656), in *Tracts and Other Papers*,

Relating Principally to the Origin, Settlement, and Progress of the Colonies of North America, Peter Force, coll. (Washington, D.C., 1844), 3, no. 14, p. 9. And see note 39 below.

32. Representative studies include Goodfriend, "The Social Dimensions of Congregational Life in Colonial New York City"; Richard W. Pointer, *Protestant Pluralism and the New York Experience* (Bloomington, Ind., 1988); Stout and Brekus, "Declension, Gender, and the 'New Religious History'"; and most recently, John K. Nelson, *A Blessed Company: Parishes, Parsons, and Parishioners in Anglican Virginia, 1690–1776.* Jon Butler has estimated that eighteenth-century congregation formation and church building "outpaced the colonies' population growth"; *Becoming America: The Revolution Before 1776* (Cambridge, Mass., 2000), 186. But see also Butler, *Awash in a Sea of Faith: Christianizing the American People* (Cambridge, Mass., 1990).

33. Patricia U. Bonomi and Peter R. Eisenstadt, "Church Adherence in the Eighteenth-Century British American Colonies," *WMQ,* 3d Ser., 39 (April 1982), 245–286.

34. A recent example of the last is David D. Hall, *Worlds of Wonder; Days of Judgment: Popular Religious Belief in Early New England* (New York, 1989). In former years, the Puritan focus led to a belief, firmly embedded in countless textbooks, that American culture was primarily shaped by New England Puritanism, with its accent on morality and holy mission (Sacvan Bercovitch, *The American Jeremiad* [Madison, Wis., 1978])—an extremely serviceable notion as settlement flowed west in the nineteenth century to meet its "manifest destiny."

35. On the "myth" of declension, see Stephen Foster, *The Long Argument: English Puritanism and the Shaping of New England Culture, 1570–1700* (Chapel Hill, 1991), xiii, 213–220, 312–313, 357 (n.77).

36. Robert Baird, *Religion in America: or, An Account of The Origin, Progress, Relation to the State, and Present Condition of The Evangelical Churches in the United States, with Notices of the Unevangelical Denominations* (New York, 1844), 100–102, 292. Baird includes among the "unevangelicals" Roman Catholics, Jews, Mormons, Shakers, and—lumped together in their own ninth circle—Unitarians, Atheists, and Deists; ibid., 289. For all his evangelical fervor, Baird was an industrious researcher who usually presented his findings in moderate language, while his spacious mind linked American religious developments to happenings in Britain and Europe. For Baird's career see John A. Garraty and Mark C. Carnes, eds., *American National Biography* (New York, 1999), 1, 909–910.

37. Review of Butler, *Awash in a Sea of Faith,* in *WMQ,* 3d Ser., 48 (Jan. 1991), 118–124.

38. William Meade, *Old Churches, Ministers, and Families of Virginia,* 2 vols. (1857; reprint, Baltimore, 1966), I, 14, 15, 16, 25ff; Garraty and Carnes, *American National Biography,* 15, pp. 219–220.

39. A representative work is William Warren Sweet, *The Story of Religions in America* (New York, 1930), quotation on pp. 7–8. For Sweet's estimate of church membership—1 in 7 in New England; 1 in 15 or 18 in the Middle Colonies; and 1 in 20 in the South—see "The American Colonial Environment and Religious Liberty," *Church History*, 4 (1935), 53. The Methodist Sweet's negative view of colonial religion influenced, among others, Sidney E. Mead, *The Lively Experiment: The Shaping of Christianity in America* (New York, 1963), 30, 122; Richard Hofstadter, *America at 1750: A Social Portrait* (New York, 1971), xv-xvi, 181–182; and Sydney E. Ahlstrom, *A Religious History of the American People* (New Haven, 1972), 4, 189–190, 199.

40. For the importance of historical demography and the social sciences to New England community studies, see Philip J. Greven, Jr., *Four Generations: Population, Land, and Family in Colonial Andover, Massachusetts* (Ithaca, N.Y., 1970), chap. 1; and John Demos, *A Little Commonwealth: Family Life in Plymouth Colony* (New York, 1970), Foreword. The use of church records is illustrated in Philip J. Greven, Jr., "Youth, Maturity, and Religious Conversion: A Note on the Ages of Converts in Andover, Massachusetts, 1711–1749," *Essex Institute Historical Collections*, 108 (1972), 119–134. For the English model see E. A. Wrigley, ed., *An Introduction to English Historical Demography from the Sixteenth to the Nineteenth Century* (New York, 1966).

41. For cultural anthropology, see "Religion as a Cultural System," in Clifford Geertz, *The Interpretation of Culture* (New York, 1973), 87–125. Influential micro-historical studies include Emanuel LeRoy Ladurie, *Montaillou: The Promised Land of Error* (1975; New York, 1978), and Carlo Ginzburg, *The Cheese and the Worms: The Cosmos of a Sixteenth-Century Miller* (1976; Baltimore, 1980).

Preface

In a sense this book began during an informal conversation I had with Richard Hofstadter a year or so before his death. At the time I was working on politics in colonial New York, whose factions, I then supposed, were strongly influenced by ethnic sensibilities. Professor Hofstadter was skeptical, and he suggested instead that if there was a single determinant of the colonists' political responses more important than any other, it might have been religion. Once this notion was implanted in my mind it continued to grow, in part because so much of what I read thereafter seemed to bear it out. Whereas ethnic identity was actually a somewhat abstract notion to most colonials—except as it operated in certain specific local controversies—religious loyalties were well developed in all sections by the 1730s, and were continuously reinforced from the 1740s onward as intensifying denominational rivalries expressed themselves in provincial politics.

Soon I was launched on a new undertaking whose initial purpose was to test Professor Hofstadter's idea by exploring the connections between religion and politics in early America. But how could religion exert real influence on an aspect of colonial life so central as politics when, according to almost every book I read, some 80 to 90 percent of the provincials were "unchurched" and anticlericalism was a visible influence throughout the colonies? Even the church historians, whose specialized denominational studies contained much evidence of an active congregational life and clergymen of considerable accomplishment and dedication, almost invariably observed in passing that the great majority of colonials were not churchgoers at all.

I concluded that the only way to resolve these disjunctions would be to examine the religious sociology of all the colonies over a very extended period of time. This meant focusing less on theology—which in any case has received plenty of attention from historians—than on popular religious attitudes, the character of the provincial clergy, and prevailing churchgoing practices. When my investigation began to reveal a far more vital religious culture than that portrayed by conventional historiography, I returned to the initial question about the interrelationship of religion and politics.

Though this book considers American religious life from 1607 to 1776 in all thirteen colonies, its approach is selective and thematic rather than comprehensive. I have excluded many denominational details and local variations, choosing instead to concentrate on episodes or transitions in the history of this or that denomination or region which illuminate developments elsewhere, either through typicality or contrast. When it seemed pertinent I have also incorporated findings from recent research in religious and social history. My objective is to offer an interpretive reading that may disentangle a number of contradictions in the present literature and suggest some alternative ways of thinking about the functions of religion in early American culture.

I gratefully acknowledge fellowship support for this book from the American Council of Learned Societies, the John Simon Guggenheim Memorial Foundation, and the Rockefeller Foundation. The American Philosophical Society and the Graduate School of Arts and Science at New York University kindly provided grants for travel and book preparation. I also wish to thank the Shelby Cullom Davis Center for Historical Studies at Princeton University, where I was a Visiting Fellow in 1979–80, and especially its Director, Professor Lawrence Stone. Research assistance was given unstintingly by the staffs of Bobst Library (New York University), Butler Library (Columbia University), The New York Public Library, The New-York Historical Society, Widener Library and Houghton Library (Harvard University), Firestone Library (Princeton University), Princeton Theological Seminary, Union Theological Seminary, The Presbyterian

Historical Society, The Historical Society of Pennsylvania, The American Philosophical Society, and the Huntington Library and Art Gallery; also Lambeth Palace Library, the United S.P.G. Archives, and Dr. Williams's Library, all of London, and the Bodleian Library (Oxford University).

A portion of Chapter 3 was published previously as "'Watchful Against the Sects': Religious Renewal in Pennsylvania's German Congregations, 1720–1750," *Pennsylvania History*, 50 (1983), 273–83. Parts of Chapter 5 appeared in somewhat different form as "'Stewards of the Mysteries of God': Clerical Authority and the Great Awakening in the Middle Colonies," in *Professions and Professional Ideologies in America*, ed. Gerald L. Geison (Chapel Hill, 1983), chap. 3; and as "'A Just Opposition': The Great Awakening as a Radical Model," in *The Origins of Anglo-American Radicalism*, eds. Margaret Jacob and James Jacob (London, 1984), chap. 14. I wish to thank *Pennsylvania History*, the University of North Carolina Press, and George Allen & Unwin for permission to reprint portions of these essays.

I am especially grateful to friends and colleagues who have responded to my queries, shared findings from their own research, and directed me to obscure sources: Jon Butler, Elaine Crane, Donald F. Durnbaugh, Edwin Gaustad, Joan Gundersen, Margaret Jacob, the Reverend John McNab, Jack Marietta, John Murrin, Mary Murrin, Elizabeth Nybakken, Richard Pointer, Eugene Sheridan, Kenneth Silverman, and Caroline Stifel. My greatest debt is to Lois Green Carr, David D. Hall, and Margaret Hunt, who agreed to read and criticize parts of the manuscript, and especially to Christine Heyrman, who read it all. They, as well as my editors at Oxford University Press, Sam Tanenhaus, Leona Capeless, and Sheldon Meyer, have improved the book in countless ways. Finally, my immediate family has offered infinite good will and patience throughout the enterprise.

Irvington, New York   Patricia Updegraff Bonomi
March 1986

Contents

Chapter 1. The Religious Prospect 3

PART I.   RELIGION AND SOCIETY

Chapter 2.   The New Heavens and the New Earth 13
  The "forlorne" State of Religion, 15
  A Grudging Toleration, 21
  *The Restoration Colonies and the Growth
    of Toleration,* 30
  Religious Liberty on-Principle, 33

Chapter 3.   The Clergymen 39
  *"The precariousness of their Livings":
    The Colonial Anglican Clergy,* 41
  The Rectors' Daily Rounds, 54
  *The "clean Air" of New England:
    Congregational Clergymen,* 61
  *Diversity and Renewal: The German
    Church Clergy,* 72

Chapter 4.   The Churchgoers 87
  A Word about Numbers, 87
  Churchgoing and Social Rank, 92
  A Gentleman's Religion, 97
  "Daughters of Zion," 105
  More Godly Women Than Men, 111
  Young and Old, 115
  Blacks, Indians, and Indentured Servants, 119
  *The Great Awakening and Church
    Membership,* 123

PART II.   RELIGION AND POLITICS

Chapter 5. "The Hosannas of the Multitude": The Great
            Awakening in America 131
            Presbyterian Beginnings, 133
            New Sides vs. Old Sides, 139
            The "divine fire" Kindled in New England, 149
            *Minority Rights and Divided Sovereignty: The Great
            Awakening as a Radical Model,* 152
            "Who is upon GOD's Side?", 157

Chapter 6. The Political Awakening 161
            From Religion to Politics in Connecticut, 162
            Denominational Politics in Pennsylvania, 168
            Dissenters vs. Anglicans in Virginia, 181

Chapter 7. Religion and the American Revolution 187
            The Ideology of Dissent, 189
            *The "infernal confederacy": Controversy
            over an American Bishop,* 199
            The Clergy, the People, and the Patriot Cause, 209

Chapter 8. The Formation of American Religious
            Culture 217

Notes   223
Index   281

UNDER THE COPE OF HEAVEN

Woodblock of a stylized New York City Skyline (1771)
(New-York Historical Society)

CHAPTER 1

The Religious Prospect

The skylines of our eastern cities in, say, 1760 were in their way just as striking as they are now, perhaps more so. But what drew the eye then, and gave the horizon its definition, was a very different sort of edifice from those that mark it today—not skyscrapers but church spires—and beneath that contrast lies a fundamental shift in the spiritual perspective of the American population during the more than two centuries that have intervened. The seaboard cities of colonial America, though relatively small, were amply supplied with places of worship. You walked no distance at all, in any of them, without passing a meetinghouse, and you were never beyond earshot of church bells. The sights and sounds of today's cities are not primarily symbolic of religion. But in eighteenth-century America—in city, village, and countryside—the idiom of religion penetrated all discourse, underlay all thought, marked all observances, gave meaning to every public and private crisis. There was hardly a day of the week, to say nothing of the Sabbath, when colonial Americans could not repair to their churches for some occasion or other, all of which gave a certain tone to everything they did in their collective and communal capacity.

The quintessential form of public edification was not the spectacle

but the Word. The expression "popular entertainment" had not yet
come into being, but in any case the term does faint justice to the
satisfactions universally derived from the well-aimed and roundly
delivered sermon. A renowned preacher could draw hundreds,
sometimes thousands, and it was not only the George Whitefields
and other revivalists of the 1740s who attracted such crowds.
Ministers of every denomination, settled or itinerant, who were
touched by the spirit and by an oratorical flair could expect an
appreciative following. A variation was the theological debate, held
between preachers of rival denominations. Such occasions, especially in rural areas, could bring in people from many miles to fill
tents and wilderness clearings. The hanging of a notable criminal, it
might be said, could accomplish much the same thing. And yet it
was the accompanying execution sermon, with its solemn reminder
of last things and of men's reaping what they sowed, that both reknit
the multitude and sent it home edified.[1]

When not listening to their preachers' words the provincials were
reading them. Thousands of sermons were printed in the course of
the eighteenth century, many at the urging of congregations convinced that what their ministers had told them deserved a larger audience. The sermons of such British clerics as John Tillotson, Samuel
Clarke, and Philip Doddridge were widely circulated in America, as
were Foxe's *Book of Martyrs*, Bunyan's *Pilgrim's Progress*, and Isaac
Watts's hymns and instructional writings. Lay readers in congregations not yet supplied with permanent ministers resorted regularly
to printed collections of sermons, among the most popular Flavel's
devotional tracts and Robert Russel's *Seven Sermons*.[2]

Indeed, sermons, devotional writings, catechisms, pious legends,
and theological treatises formed by far the biggest category of printed
matter in colonial America. Up to 1765 more literature of this sort
was published than were writings on political science, history, and
law combined, and even during the Revolutionary era devotional
works comprised the largest single classification.[3] Moreover, this
reflected the reading of all ranks. Religious books dominated the
libraries of such southern gentlemen as Edmund Berkeley, William
Fitzhugh, Richard Lee II, and many others. The Pennsylvania

Quaker James Logan owned thirty versions of the Bible. Among commoner readers the variety may not have been so great, but the degree of specialization was even more striking. It is true that by the time of the Revolution there was a considerable awareness in America of the writings of British libertarian political theorists. Nevertheless, when one farmer who had fought at Concord Bridge was asked years later whether he was defending the ideas of such liberal writers, he declared that for his part he had never heard of Locke or Sidney, his reading having been limited to the Bible, the Catechism, Watts's Psalms and Hymns, and the Almanac.[4]

The style and atmosphere of the Sabbath of course varied considerably throughout the colonies, depending to a large degree on how the population was concentrated or dispersed. The Virginia gentry typically rode some distance to attend divine worship. Landon Carter did so "with a devout heart," and took communion "to Commemorate the love and Passion of my divine redeemer." But they seem to have used the occasion, understandably, for other purposes as well. The Virginia tutor Philip Fithian referred to Sunday services as "a useful weekly resort to do business," and described churchyards filled with "beaux chatting . . . on Gallantry." It appears that the women, meanwhile, were showing off the latest silks and brocades from London.[5] In backwoods parishes, on the other hand—of which some had no western boundaries and many were still served only by itinerant preachers—people sometimes traveled as far as fifteen or twenty miles to attend services, and came without much finery, often barefoot, the men in shirts and breeches and the women wearing such thin shifts in hot weather that, according to one clergyman, they might as well have been "Puri Naturalibus." Yet it was this same class of people whose minister, in a remote South Carolina parish, found them so starved for spiritual comfort that they appeared "ready to devour Me."[6]

The regulated Sabbath as a feature of colonial life was confined to those towns and cities, principally in the North, that had the settled character and compactness, and thus the resources of community will, to establish and maintain it. There, regulation was encompassing and purposeful. The selectmen of Boston, to the astonishment of an English midshipman in 1768, were known to "parade the Streets and oblige everyone to go to Church or Meeting . . . on pain of being put in the Stocks or otherwise confined."[7] Drinking and gambling on the Lord's Day were tolerated virtually nowhere. Quaker magistrates imposed fines for working or carrying guns on the Sabbath. The churchgoers of New York were reputed to be less solemn and more sociable on Sundays than the Calvinists of Boston. Yet New York, like Boston, had its laws forbidding traffic through the city on that day, "unless it be to or from church or other urgent and lawful occasions." Gilbert Livingston, a member of one of the colony's most powerful families, was once indicted for being out driving his wagon on the Sabbath.[8]

Still, it is not the primary aim of this book simply to multiply, or to expand upon, such random observations as those just introduced. It is more to my point that they are all drawn from the religious life of the eighteenth century—from the final seventy-five years or so of America's colonial existence; for it is the state of American religious practice and religious institutions in the eighteenth century that I have come to see as a particular historical problem. There is a very pervasive impression, given weight by a number of learned authorities, that American religion was by the eighteenth century already in a state of decline. My own impressions point in a distinctly different direction. To me the same era presents itself as one of rising vitality in religious life, an era not of decline but the reverse—of proliferation and growth.

Of course, one ought not to be too free and easy about presuming to bring down prevailing generalizations. There are always reasons for them, more often than not legitimate ones, and that in itself is part of the problem: one must discover what they are, and take due account of them. In the present case, the attention that has been given to Puritan New England stands as a leading difficulty. The very scope and extent of modern writing on that subject, as well as the quantity of documentary materials on which it is based, have somehow preempted most of the categories in which one even ventures to think about religion anywhere in colonial America.

Casting a shadow over the entire history of colonial religion is the dark theme of declension, as the utterances of New England ministers were for many years read as one long lament over apostasy and falling off. Yet all the while congregations grew, more were gathered, old churches were enlarged and new ones built as the population increased and stabilized.[9] It was not religion, in any measurable sense, that had declined and paled, but something else, something perhaps even loftier: a veritable utopia—or rather, a utopian vision, one that had shone brightest at the very moment of the Puritan exodus from Old England to New.

The illusion of decline—and I do believe it an illusion—has been fed in many smaller ways as well. The accounts of travelers from more populous regions to thinly settled parts of the colonies are full of a sense of falling off as they describe the folk beliefs and improvisational practices of an underchurched frontier. The very increase in denominational variety gave a different cause for gloom, especially in the journals of ministers, of which a fair number have survived. An Anglican, for example, could see wherever he looked "heretics" and "infidels"—people who turn out to have been simply adherents of rival denominations. Shortages of ministers almost everywhere (except in New England) were a perennial complaint. It was only to be expected that appeals for more should be rendered more urgent by descriptions of the lax morals and impious habits that threatened to overflow all bounds if nothing were done to curb them.[10] Even the words used—among them many that have since changed meaning—are often carelessly construed by modern writers. "Indifferent," which appears again and again in the early accounts, is a prime example. In eighteenth-century religious commentary "indifferent" usually referred not to loss of interest, as it does today; it simply pointed to the latitudinarian practices that resulted whenever diverse religious groups were obliged to share church buildings and even ministers.[11]

All such accounts, moreover, have a static quality, being necessarily tied to the observer's time and place, whereas a primary concern of this book is movement, and the movement I see is on the whole upward. Mostly overlooked by the "declension" paradigm is the rising level of religious intensity in the Middle Colonies and the backcountry South as Quakers, pietistic sects, and church-centered communities of Lutherans, Reformed, and Presbyterians entered the colonies from the late seventeenth century onward. This book will follow populations that were both increasing and in motion, as well as chronically undersupplied in the facilities of formal religion. It will chart the slow but steady process whereby these deficiencies were remedied. As the supply of clergymen in the eighteenth century rose, facilitating the emergence of the church as a basic institution of provincial life, folk religion receded,[12] ecclesiastical structures stabilized, and churchgoing became more regular. A variety of dependable contemporary reports, used systematically, shed new light on eighteenth-century religious practices. To interpret them I shall resort not only to words but also to numbers, and even, when appropriate, to physical measurements—numbers of people, as well as measurements of the church buildings erected to accommodate them.

This study has other objectives besides charting growth. I am not prepared to claim that the ascending vitality I see in colonial religion included an increase in doctrinal rigor. If a certain rounding-off in sharpness of doctrine be construed as an aspect of "declension," then something obviously has to be conceded. But vitality may be looked for, and I believe found, in all other aspects of religion in eighteenth-century America. It is to be found in the very tensions generated by territorial and demographic growth—tensions between the parallel processes of denominational competition, on the one hand and, on the other, simply of reaching a degree of mutual accommodation. There were problems, moreover, within denominations as well as between them. These also were brought about by growth, and were not to be resolved without further kinds of strain. There was the matter of imposing internal denominational order, and of agreeing upon acceptable professional standards for clerical training, recruitment, and practice—issues that were at the heart of the division of churches during the Great Awakening.

Another process has impressed me at least as much as anything else I have observed in the life of colonial America: the increasing interpenetration of religion and politics. Reflexes generated by the schisms of the Great Awakening and by the colonists' denominational rivalries made for a contentiousness that pervaded the entire realm of the provincials' public behavior, and eventually the categories in which they framed political and religious issues became almost interchangeable. Indeed, what Clarendon said of England at the time of the Civil War might also be said of the American colonies by the mid-eighteenth century: "the ecclesiastical and civil state . . . [are so] interwoven together, and in truth so incorporated in each other, that like Hippocrates' twins they cannot but laugh and cry together."[13] I do not believe it necessary to postulate, as some writers have done, a close connection between the ideology of the Revolution and the main currents of millennial and evangelical thought. My own emphasis in this respect falls more directly on the ways in which religious rationalists employed the dissenting tradition to advance the Revolutionary cause. I will also suggest that at the immediate instrumental level—for instance in the use of denominational and congregational networks as devices for political instruction and propaganda—the connections between religion and politics are everywhere discernible. Thus Vernon L. Parrington's separation of the colonial period into a seventeenth-century *saeculum theologicum* and an eighteenth-century *saeculum politicum* will no longer quite do, even as an epigram.[14] For Americans, the eighteenth century came more and more to be an intermixture of both.

The advantage of studying American religious practice in all of the colonies over many decades, in this case from 1607 to 1776, is not only that regional and denominational variations gain new meaning when viewed comparatively but also that the rhythms and direction of religious culture are more easily discoverable when the various currents are allowed a more or less uninterrupted chronological course. It was only in contrast with the disorder and volatility of seventeenth-century religious life that I came fully to appreciate the more stable character and growing influence of religion in the eighteenth. It was only in contrast with those colonies possessing established churches that I was able to gauge the significance of middle-colony pluralism, with all its challenges and opportunities. And only after describing in Part I of this book how from 1607 to about 1750 a number of Old World churches and clergy gradually built ecclesiastical structures, gained influence among the people, and expanded their power in public life could I assert, as I do in Part II, the indispensable role that religion played in politics between the Great Awakening and the Revolution. Rather than treating colonial religion as a patchwork of discrete events and unrelated developments in individual denominations or specific provinces, I have tried to thread the story of religion into the fabric of early American history. Thus religious change is dealt with here as a process, one that in my view is more or less equivalent to processes in the economic and political realms as an influence on the formation of early American culture.

PART I

RELIGION AND SOCIETY

CHAPTER 2

The New Heavens and the New Earth

There have emerged two fairly distinct ways of looking at religious developments in the seventeenth-century American colonies. The older approach explores religious life and institutions from the traditional perspective of the civil magistrates and churchmen who provided leadership for the early colonies. The newer scholarship takes a more popular position, seeking to understand the religious perceptions and practices of men and women at every level of colonial society. Because the two approaches start from different points on the social scale, each contributes important insights about our religious beginnings, but they do so in terms not always easy to reconcile or combine.

According to traditional history, colonial leaders were concerned above all with creating stable New World communities, and it was an axiom of early seventeenth-century political thought that a strong church was the handmaiden and bulwark of a stable state. The church's guardianship of morality and public behavior made it an ally of orderly government, an interdependence that statesmen acknowledged by granting official status to one church only. Every colony founded in the western hemisphere before the mid-seventeenth century, except Maryland, reproduced the Old

World model of a single, established church. The English in
Virginia, Swedes on the Delaware, and Dutch in New Netherland
transferred their state churches to the New World as a matter of
course, as did Catholic France, Spain, and Portugal to their western
provinces. The Puritans established Congregationalism throughout
New England. The privileged position of these churches was
protected by laws restricting the religious and political rights of
dissenters from the official establishment. Only through such an
arrangement, so the leaders believed, might the colonists ward off
the evils of religious strife and achieve the civic harmony essential
to the survival of those imperial outposts situated so precariously on
the rim of the civilized world.[1]

From the contrasting viewpoint of popular religion, the elite's
assumptions about the mutually reinforcing character of church and
state implied a consensus on spiritual matters that was not always
present among the people at large. Indeed, the early English
colonists have recently been depicted as remarkably unsettled in
religious belief and practice. Many, to be sure, adhered to the
Anglican church or followed some form of Puritan Calvinism, which
itself was divided into a number of factions at this time. But a
sizable part of the population, it seems, was split into radical sects
of Anabaptist or mystical origins as varied and unruly as their
counterparts in Civil-War England. Some colonists may actually
have been pre-Christian in belief, or at least only superficially
Christian, their perception of the supernatural being rooted in
folkways that partook of magic and the occult. Even those historians
who argue that magic was in decline by the seventeenth century
hardly claim that a formal churchly religion had completely
displaced folk practices—witness the presence of "wise women"
and "cunning persons" in the colonies, to say nothing of the
continuing belief, among both high and low, in witchcraft.[2]

Wherever one stands on questions about the true nature of early
American religious culture, it seems clear that a tension existed
between colonial leaders devoted to building an orderly and
reverent society, and a people of variant backgrounds, lesser status,
and multiform as well as passionate religious convictions. We may

never know what proportion of the seventeenth-century settlers shared the religious attitudes of their leaders, but we do know that certain features of the resettlement process itself obstructed efforts by the elite to foster religious uniformity and exacerbated conflicts between leaders and people. Disease, hunger, and Indian wars threatened the survival of the first settlements, diverting attention from spiritual to material needs. Later, when inhabitants ventured out into the countryside, it was more difficult for the newly transplanted sanctions of church and religion to assert their authority. Many colonists scrambled to acquire land and goods, often at the expense of pious habits. Successful colonies attracted new settlers, leading to an ever increasing diversity of population and belief. And perhaps the greatest challenge of all to church establishments was the severe shortage of ordained clergymen.

Recent findings by historians of popular religion run parallel with this book's questioning of religious "declension," since the apparent volatility of early seventeenth-century religious practice makes it unlikely that by about 1650 the colonists possessed sufficiently stable church establishments from which to decline. Instead, we might better view the seventeenth century as a time of strain and conflict, as religious expectations and practices at all points on the social scale were being reshaped to fit colonial realities. One of the most striking products of that age of diversity and experimentation—a growing toleration for the beliefs of every sect and denomination—would later become a cherished American principle. But none of this was even imaginable to the first pioneers who sank to their knees in thanks to God for carrying them safely to the New World.

The "forlorne" State of Religion

As the first permanent colony, Virginia experienced a number of false starts in organizing the institutions she eventually found so serviceable. The Virginia Company charter instructed the colony's founders to settle the "true [church as] established within our realme of England,"[3] and an Anglican chaplain was sent over with the first ships. As earnest Christians and Englishmen, the company leaders looked to the church not only for spiritual solace but as a civilizing agent among a people far removed from traditional social restraints. Yet in the absence of churchwardens and ecclesiastical courts the church depended on the government to enforce its moral authority. In the colony's second governor, Sir Thomas Dale, religion found a firm ally, for Dale had a vision of Virginia as "the new Jerusalem." The first section of Dale's 1611 code of laws ordered that all officials "have a care that the Almightie God bee duly and daily served." Any employee failing to attend church twice a day or neglecting to appear for catechizing was to be punished with fines, whippings, or a six-month stint in the galleys. For repeatedly breaking the Sabbath the offender was to "suffer death." Furthermore, the initial session of the House of Burgesses in 1619 made provision for financial support of the Anglican clergy, and soon thereafter erected a system of parish government under locally elected vestries.[4]

At first glance religion appears to have been well planted in early Virginia, but in reality its hold was tenuous. Warfare between settlers and Indians, economic instability, and political disruption plagued the fragile colony, impeding the growth of all institutions including the church. Nor did the turbulent character of the company's employees bode well for religion. The second minister to reach Virginia almost despaired of bringing God to the former "Murtherers, Theeves, Adulterers, [and] idle persons" who in his view constituted much of the work force. Drunkenness, gambling, brawling, and abuse of servants were so common that the government was almost helpless to stop them. With women composing less than one-quarter of the population and with mortality high, family life—a mainstay of religion in all societies—was slow to develop. Most damaging of all was the scarcity of ministers in early Virginia; by 1662 only ten were in residence to serve over forty-five parishes.[5] No wonder Virginia's early leaders described the unruly multitude they were trying to govern as brutes inhabiting a barbarous country.

The formation of a cohesive ecclesiastical structure was retarded, as well, by geographic and economic factors. By the second decade of settlement an expanding plantation economy encouraged dispersed homesteads and large parishes (some measured sixty to a hundred miles long), weakening lines of communication and undermining central church authority. When the Virginia Company failed, its land was parceled out to private owners who claimed the right to select ministers for their own parishes. A 1643 act granted local vestries the power to choose rectors and present them to the governor for induction. As time passed many parishes ignored the governor altogether; in others presentation became a mere formality. The Commonwealth period saw a further growth of local control, since the more orthodox Anglican vestrymen had no intention of giving Cromwell or any of his lieutenants authority over the Church of England in Virginia.[6] Finally, though the first generation of gentlemen leaders had warmly supported the church and its stabilizing influence, the second generation—some of them risen from less than gentle circumstances and therefore lacking the aristocracy's long-standing attachment to the Church of England— were often too busy acquiring economic and political power to think much about strengthening religion. In a report to the Bishop of London on the "forlorne" state of the Anglican church in mid-seventeenth-century Virginia, one visitor located the cause in the low origins and "private worldly interest" of Virginia's leaders: "these are usually such as went over Servants thither, and though by time and industry, they may have attained competent Estates; yet by reason of their poor and mean education they are unskillful in judging of a good Estate either of Church or Commonwealth, or of the means of procuring it."[7]

The religious scene to the north has usually been painted in brighter hues. It is a common assumption that the Puritan commitment to build a New World commonwealth on religious principles fortified New Englanders against many of the hazards of resettlement. Yet they, like other seventeenth-century pioneers, knew that "many unconceivable perills and dangers" awaited them in the North American wilderness. One such peril, eminently conceivable, was that sinful men and women might mistake liberty for license, throw off authority, and become "worse than brute beasts"—an image that sprang readily to mind when contemplating America.[8] Only if church and state were firmly fixed in a mutually reinforcing relationship, it was thought, might the Puritan band fulfill its errand in the wilderness.

John Winthrop and other leading laymen of the Massachusetts Bay General Court promised the establishment of a firm political structure in their colony, as did Governor William Bradford in Plymouth Plantation. The settlement of the church was less easily accomplished. Plymouth Colony was without an ordained minister for the first nine years of its existence, during which time a lay elder conducted services on the Sabbath. As for Massachusetts Bay, when the Reverend Francis Higginson of Salem died in August of 1630, the rapidly growing colony was left with only five ministers. Four others, including Roger Williams, arrived within the next two years, but the colony was receiving such a flood of immigrants that several congregations were required to share the services of neighboring clergymen. As settlement spread out from Boston the regulation of religious life loosened further, and soon lay preachers and prophesiers made their appearance. As one inhabitant objected in late 1632, "fellowes which keepe hogges all weeke preach on the Saboth." Things looked up considerably in 1633 with the arrival of Thomas Hooker and John Cotton, though it might be noted that Cotton was followed by Anne Hutchinson within the year whereas it was not until 1635 that such founding eminences of Massachusetts Puritanism as Thomas Shepard, Hugh Peter, and Richard Mather made their way to the Bay.[9]

Roger Williams, Anne Hutchinson, and other "radical spiritists" of the age may have gained the followings they did in Massachusetts because of opportunities opened to them by the disarray of the early Puritan establishment. Owing to the initial shortage of ministers, Williams was able to shop around for a church until he found one sympathetic to his radical theological tendencies. Mrs. Hutchinson's success in drawing a crowd to her

Tuesday devotional meetings may have resulted in part from an insufficiency of regular preaching and a consequent restlessness of spirit among the more zealous Puritans. In no time at all the radicals had split the colony into factions, reminding Winthrop of nothing so much as the religious frenzies of sixteenth-century Münster.[10] Even after the General Court cast Hutchinson out as "unsavory salt," the disturbances continued. Now it was the Presbyterians, and then, according to the Reverend Nathaniel Ward, "Familists, Antinomians, Anabaptists, and other Enthusaists" whom he urged "to be gone as fast as they can, the sooner the better." The first public questioning of infant baptism occurred at about this time; in 1654 the president of Harvard College, Henry Dunster, refused to present his newborn child for baptism and was forced to resign.[11]

"Earnest fanatics everywhere," as Samuel Eliot Morison has put it, "were discovering some little bit of truth in the Bible and organizing a church or fierce little sect around it."[12] Add to this a variety of whimsical necromancers and speculators in the occult, and it is understandable why Puritan congregations undertook scrupulously to screen all candidates seeking admission to their churches. This narrowing of the gateway to church membership may also have reflected a new assertiveness among Puritan leaders as their authority was augmented by an influx of ministers in the later 1630s. By the second decade of settlement, the high ratio of ministers to inhabitants was one of the most striking features of New England society. Indeed, with the graduation of the first class from Harvard in 1642 the region actually found itself with a surplus, though the less desirable pulpits in remote towns could go unfilled for years.[13]

Religious life certainly attained a degree of stability earlier in New England than elsewhere. Yet the turbulent scenes of the first years, as well as continuing tensions over church membership, and rising challenges after mid-century to Puritan hegemony, attest that even the highly motivated Puritans had much to overcome in order to plant their garden in the wilderness.

For chaotic beginnings no colony matched Rhode Island, which to orthodox minds fully earned its title as the "latrina of New England."[14] The Narragansett settlements were so beset by the disintegrative forces of religious and civil contention that their early extinction was widely predicted. True, Roger Williams's community at Providence, Anne Hutchinson's Portsmouth group, and William Coddington's settlement at Newport (which broke off from Portsmouth in 1639) each drew up community compacts. But these provided only loose forms of local government, and either granted liberty of conscience or were silent about religion. Whether any of the early settlers consciously envisioned Rhode Island as a haven for the otherwise-minded is unclear, but when "all the scume [and] the runne awayes of the country" descended upon them, the colony's leaders knew that "a heavy burden [was] upon the land."[15]

Representative of the colorful types attracted to the Narragansett was Samuel Gorton, an English mystic whose theology resembled that of the Seekers and Ranters in England. Gorton's first landfall in America was at Boston in 1637. Like the Hutchinsonians and others of Antinomian tendency, Gorton seemed to claim a direct communion with God that threatened the rule of law and civil authority. Thus Boston's leaders viewed him with alarm, and Gorton soon moved on to Plymouth. There he held devotional meetings at his house and engaged in lay preaching, arousing the fears of Plymouth magistrates, who in 1639 banished him for religious and civil insubordination. Settling next at Portsmouth, Rhode Island, Gorton fashioned his own sect from the materials so abundantly present in that colony. The Gortonists opposed the sacraments and all church rituals and distrusted a learned ministry, for as Gorton put it, God's word is "a thing too sublime to be congealed into ink . . . [or] piled up in libraries." Gorton soon proved too extreme even for Portsmouth, which sent him on his way after a public whipping. When next heard from Gorton was "bewitching and bemadding poor Providence," as Roger Williams reported in dismay to John Winthrop.[16] Soon ejected from Williams's bailiwick, Gorton and his followers finally established their own town at Warwick in 1643. The Gortonites, along with subsequent infusions of Anabaptists and

Quakers, did much to convince the Puritan elite that Rhode Island was a colony of madcaps and fanatics.

One consequence of this confusion was that in a remarkably short time freedom of conscience became an accepted principle in early Rhode Island. Elsewhere, too, the Old World traditions of a single church establishment and intolerance toward dissenters were being eroded, though in most cases such changes had far more to do with force of circumstance than with principle.

A Grudging Toleration

Among the early colonies Maryland alone established no official church, an oddity of its proprietorship by English Catholics that did much to set the stage for a troubled history. The Catholic Church was never specifically mentioned in the charter that Charles I granted to Cecilius Calvert in 1632, since neither patron nor patentee wished to arouse anti-Catholic sentiment in England. The king simply noted that Calvert was "animated with a laudable, and pious Zeal for extending the Christian Religion" in America. Nonetheless, when "private plotts" threatened to prevent the voyage of the first colonists to Maryland in 1634, Calvert moved to quiet Protestant fears. He instructed his brother, designated as the first resident governor, to "suffer no scandall nor offence to be given to any of the Protestants," and to "cause all acts of Romane Catholique Religion to be done as privately as may be." So much was only prudent, since Catholics would never constitute other than a minority in the colony. With no established church to reinforce government authority, Calvert sought alternative ways to settle his colony on a stable foundation. Early settlers were required to take an oath of allegiance and to receive training in military discipline; moreover, a manorial system of land development was designed to support a hierarchical pattern of social and political relationships.[17]

True to Calvert's expectations Protestants formed a numerical majority in Maryland from the start, outnumbering Catholics by about ten to one. Most of the colony's early leaders were Catholic, however, and the power to implement proprietary policies was in their hands. Faithful to Calvert's injunction "to do justice to every man without partiality." Maryland welcomed a number of displaced groups, including Puritans and other nonconformists from Virginia whose ministers had been proscribed by a 1643 law against dissenters. [18] None of this saved Maryland from the assaults of an aggressive Protestant faction that intermittently gained political power during the Civil War. In 1645 the Catholic government was forced to flee the colony and two Jesuit priests were seized and sent to England in chains. Despite the restoration of proprietary control in 1646, Catholic services were subjected to harassment throughout much of the decade. [19]

Viewing this turbulent scene from England, Lord Baltimore foresaw the destruction of his fragile colony by the forces of intolerance and religious factionalism unless order could be restored. In 1648 he appointed a Protestant, William Stone, as governor and submitted a new code of laws, which he urged the Maryland assembly to adopt without alteration. This the legislators would not promise to do. The assembly which met in April 1649 apparently had a slight Catholic majority. Seizing the moment, it wrote a number of new laws, foremost among them the "Act Concerning Religion." [20] The act incorporated a statement on religious toleration—very likely taken from Lord Baltimore's code—that completely inverted the traditional formula for social stability. Instead of finding stability in a single established church, it noted that "the inforceing of the conscience in matters of Religion hath frequently fallen out to be of dangerous Consequence" to peaceable government. Therefore, no Christian in Maryland was any longer to be "troubled, Molested, or discountenanced" because of religious belief, or forced to participate in religious observances "against his or her consent." [21]

No more should be read into this legislation than was intended by its colonial authors. The Maryland assembly might have taken any number of opportunities to pass such a law before 1649, yet only when the liberties of the Catholic elite were in danger of being snuffed out did it act. Maryland's Catholic leaders, facing a precarious political future, decided to safeguard their own religious privileges while they still had the political leverage to do so. To be sure, the legislation benefited other Christian groups as well. The Act of Toleration, as it came to be known, included prohibitions not only against "reproachfull words or Speeches" concerning the Virgin Mary, but forbade Marylanders to label any inhabitant a "heretick, Scismatick, Idolator, puritan, Independant, Prespiterian [,] popish pr[i]est, Jesuite, Jesuited papist, Lutheran, Calvenist, Anabaptist, Brownist, Antinomian, Barrowist, Roundhead, Sep[ar]atist, or any other name" on pain of fines and whippings, unless a public apology was given. Such a specific and detailed proscription was unique for that time. Still, nothing in the contemporary record suggests that Maryland Catholics intended to fashion a new principle of religious liberty. Indeed, their seventeenth-century orthodoxy is evident in the clause prescribing death or loss of all property for anyone denying the Trinity. It also becomes apparent when Maryland's law is compared with that of Rhode Island, where not only Christians but Jews and "Turks" were theoretically included within the grant of religious freedom. Taking Marylanders at their word, we can assume that the Act of Toleration grew out of their need "to preserve mutuall love and unity amongst the inhabitants here."²² Feeble New World institutions and a diverse population had proved a volatile combination, forcing Marylanders to move beyond the old formulas for maintaining community order.

One consequence of this early religious turmoil was that Maryland church life was somewhat aimless and disordered during much of the seventeenth century. A shortage of clergymen and disruptions connected with the Civil War caused many settlers to lose touch with an organized church. The Quakers, who entered the colony in sizable numbers after 1657, may have possessed the strongest religious structure in Maryland at this time, held together in part by their identity as a "peculiar" people. In 1676 Lord Baltimore reported that Maryland's population "doe consist of Presbyterians, Independents, Anabaptists and Quakers, those of the Church of England as well as those of the Romish being the fewest."[23] But if their religious institutions were weak and their leaders divided, Maryland's Protestants shared a number of grievances around which they could unite. Their inherent anti-Catholicism was intensified by the Calverts' reluctance to grant land in fee simple, that family's notorious preference for Catholics and close relatives in posts of authority, and by high taxes. Protestant-led disturbances in 1645, 1660, 1676, and 1681 expressed the majority's chronic restlessness under Catholic rule, which culminated during the Glorious Revolution in Coode's Rebellion and the overthrow of the proprietary regime.[24] The fall of the Catholic King James II and the support given by William and Mary to a more coherent colonial policy brought Maryland's conversion to a royal colony in 1691, while agitation in both Maryland and London led to the formal establishment of the Church of England in 1692. With Protestants in the seat of power at last, a flurry of legislation over the next twenty years sharply contracted the political and religious rights of Maryland Catholics. Even when the colony reverted to Calvert proprietorship in 1715 the Anglican establishment was unaffected, for the Calvert heirs had converted to the Church of England in 1713.[25] Thus the Glorious Revolution marks an end to Maryland's bold experiment in toleration and the beginning of an Anglican era in which the colony's religious life, if never exactly traditional, would at least stabilize and conform more closely to that of its neighbor to the south.

The Dutch colony of New Netherland provides another example of how religious diversity and unsettled conditions combined to force a grudging toleration on New World leaders. The West India Company was concerned primarily with commerce and profits, but to strengthen order and uphold religion it also had pledged to establish and support the Dutch Reformed Church. The first church-trained *ziekentrooster*, or visitor of the sick, was sent out in 1624, but no ordained clergyman arrived until 1628. In accordance with the mild religious policies of the mother country, dissenters were allowed to meet for worship, though only in private. By the late 1640s Indian wars, growing religious and cultural diversity, and ferocious economic competition fostered severe social stresses, prompting the West India Company in 1647 to dispatch Peter Stuyvesant, a seasoned and resolute administrator, as Director General. Stuyvesant found the colony in shocking disorder, the people "wild and loose in their morals. . . . drinking to excess, quarreling, fighting and smiting, even on the Lord's day."[26]

Stuyvesant, the son of a clergyman and an elder of the Reformed Church, believed strongly in the Old World axiom that the combined forces of church and state were the best promoters of morality and social harmony. Thus he moved decisively to bolster the Reformed establishment by dealing firmly with dissenters and other unruly types. Lutherans were denied a charter for their church, subjected to fines, and imprisoned for organizing public services.[27] When twenty-three Jews arrived from Brazil in 1654, with the promise of more to come, the two Reformed ministers then in the colony wrote anxiously to the Classis of Amsterdam urging "that these godless rascals . . . may be sent away from here." And Stuyvesant asked the Dutch West India Company to rule that no more Jews be allowed "to infect and trouble this new colony." The Jews, however, posed an especially delicate problem for the Company directors. Weighing private prejudices against business interests, the directors' reply was shaped by the time-honored leaven of self-interest. Noting that they "would have liked to agree" with Stuyvesant and deny the Jews entry, the directors had decided that such a course would be "unreasonable and unfair" in view of the Jews' sufferings in Brazil. And besides, there was that "large amount of capital, which . . . [Dutch Jews] have invested in shares of this Company." By such leverage did the colony's Jews— though initially denied the right to worship, or to become citizens, or to operate public businesses—gain within half a dozen years all privileges but that of holding public services in their own synagogue.[28]

At their first appearance in 1657 the Quakers, with their private source of law in the inner light, alarmed not only Stuyvesant and the Reformed ministers but other residents of the colony. When two young women "began to quake and go into a frenzy," crying out in

the middle of the street that the day of judgment was at hand, the
New Netherlanders, "not knowing what was the matter, ran to and
fro, while one cried 'Fire,' and another something else." The
women were arrested, cast into a dank prison for eight days, and
then, their arms tied to rods, were placed on a boat to Rhode Island.
Other Friends soon returned, however, to make substantial inroads
among the English settlements on Long Island. Stuyvesant, his
official dignity possibly bruised by the Quakers' refusal to remove
their hats in his presence, did everything in his power to root out
the "abominable heresy." But as Quakers and other dissidents
continued to press for religious toleration, the West India
Company's fear that harsh treatment might discourage immigration,
"which must be favored at so tender a stage of the country's
existence," finally led to a change of policy if not of heart.
Stuyvesant was instructed in 1663 to "shut your eyes" to the
activities of dissident sects so long as they did not disrupt government. Acknowledging that his first duty was to the company that
employed him, the chastened Director General ended his harrass-
ment and pursued a more moderate course in the short time
remaining to his administration.[29]

By the second half of the seventeenth century a number of colonials,
realizing that religious diversity could not be stamped out, adopted
a new approach. The best way to discourage dissent, they counseled, was to ignore it. To the Puritan leaders of New England such
advice was the counsel of Satan. The Massachusetts and Connecticut magistrates had managed by mid-century to isolate and contain
the most strident dissenting voices. But with the arrival of the
Quakers after 1656 the Puritan saints met their match. Here was a
sect that not only rejected absorption and scorned exile but
disdained compromise of any sort, a sect that gloried in adversity
and employed martyrdom as the early Christians had done—to gain
sympathy, and then adherents, for their cause. Quakers would
neither back down nor stay away, forcing Puritan leaders to confront
the full implications of their refusal to grant religious toleration to an
increasingly diverse population.

The history of Quaker–Puritan conflict is usually told from the Quaker perspective, and a doleful chronicle it is. But the conflict that arose between these two anointed societies in a theological age makes little sense unless we take into account the Puritans' profound commitment to social order as a prerequisite for the coming of God's kingdom. Governor John Endicott of Massachusetts never doubted who the Quakers were: "open and capital Blasphemers, open Seducers from the glorious Trinity . . . open Enemies to Government itself . . . malignant and assiduous Promoters of Doctrines directly tending to subvert both our Churches and State."[30]

The Quaker belief in Divine Light, an inner radiance shed by God directly on the souls of individual men and women, struck Puritan leaders as a dire threat to the secular authority of law and magistracy.[31] More alarming still, Quakers were not content to practice their religion in corners, especially after public collision was shown to be their most effective tactic. Thus did Quakers make scenes with a purpose. When arrested for crying out in the streets or invading Congregational churches, they stoically accepted whippings and ear croppings, inviting a martyrdom that further publicized their beliefs. The Quakers' determination seemed to grow in proportion to the obstacles raised against them. Exiled from Boston, they decided that Massachusetts Bay was the very place where they ought most to be. Thus throughout 1656 and 1657 the Quakers continued their "presumptuous and incorrigible contempt of authority." Finally, in October 1658 the General Court, observing that members of the "pernitious sect" continued to undermine the authority of civil government, declared them subject thereafter to the death penalty.[32]

For all this, the magistrates were growing uneasy about the effect that repeated public punishments were having on popular opinion, as the Quakers' physical courage and humble forbearance attracted widening sympathy. In Barnstable townspeople cried out against the whipping of a Quaker in 1658, one woman lamenting: "Did I ever think that New England would come to this?" When Horred Gardiner, the young mother of a nursing infant, suffered ten lashes at Weymouth and then publicly forgave her whipper, a woman in the crowd commented, "Surely if she had not the spirit of the Lord she could not do this thing." When the Boston magistrates selected four of ten Quakers in the town jail for a biweekly whipping, "the cry against cruelty increased . . . Blood at that season, they had sufficient."[33] Still, the values of the community required the civil authority to see religious diversity as leading to social chaos, and the dilemma of duty remained. Faced with the extreme provocations of Quaker exiles who returned to Massachusetts time and again to stir up trouble, the magistrates believed they had no choice but to invoke the ultimate penalty.

That penalty—death—was exacted on four occasions. Marmaduke Stevenson, William Robinson, and Mary Dyer, who refused to accept repeated sentences of exile, were finally ordered to be hanged on October 27, 1659. When they were led through the streets of Boston toward the place of execution, over one hundred soldiers were required to keep order, "as if they were afraid that some of the people would have rescued the prisoners." Whenever the condemned tried to address the crowd a drummer beat a tattoo to drown out their words. A witness reported that the doomed Quakers walked to the gallows "Hand in Hand, all three of them, as to a Weding-day, with great cheerfulness of Heart." After executing the sentence against Stevenson and Robinson, the magistrates relented and reduced Mary Dyer's punishment to exile. Six months later when Mrs. Dyer returned once again to Massachusetts, the original sentence was carried out.[34]

The executions aroused such public dismay that the magistrates were impelled to publish a defense against those who would "calumniate us, and render us bloody Persecutors." Declaring that milder laws had been of no avail against the Quakers' "impetuous and fanatick Fury," the magistrates explained that they had been left no alternative. Governor Endicott concurred, noting that when the Quakers' desperate turbulency threatened "the Estate Civil and Ecclesiastical" the magistrates were forced to point the sword outward in self-defense. The Quakers "willingly rushing themselves thereupon was their own act."[35]

A small though growing number of New Englanders seem not to have been persuaded by this logic. As early as 1658 it had been reported that the Quakers had many meetings and adherents, with almost the whole town of Sandwich, for example, adhering toward them.[36] In 1662 the General Court heard that Quakers abounded, especially in the eastern parts. One year later many inhabitants were refusing to go to church or bear arms, and in some towns Quakers were making "parties suitable to theire designes in election of such persons according to theire ends."[37] When at last the king himself, pressed by Quakers in England, demanded an explanation, the General Court managed to get itself off by means of an analogy. The Quakers, declared the Court, were not put to death in Massachusetts for their religious beliefs any more than were the Jesuits and priests in the time of Elizabeth and James I; in both instances the culprits were punished "for their breach and contempt of his majesties lawes."[38]

Still, after 1660 it was becoming more evident that the costs of building a pure commonwealth were greater than many New Englanders were willing to bear. Thus the Quaker incidents denote a crisis and a turning point in New England's attitude toward religious toleration. The contrast between the gentle stoicism of the Friends and the severity of the magistrates—who themselves could hardly have been free from inner conflict over what they believed they had to do—aggrieved the hearts of many Puritans. By the later 1660s, moreover, it was no longer so clear in either Old or New England that the extirpation of religious dissent at any price brought peace and stability to the state. New England society was in any case more settled now, with requirements for church membership eased and Puritan values having been passed on to a second generation. Conditions were now present in which a community containing some diversity of views was at least thinkable. Even so, it was no more than a beginning. True, the first Baptist church was founded in 1665, but no other gained a foothold until the 1730s. Nor was any Quaker meeting allowed officially until 1697.[39] Though the facade of orthodoxy had been pierced, the Puritan temple remained a strong bastion against true religious toleration for many years to come.

The Restoration Colonies and the Growth of Toleration

Charles II was welcomed back to England in 1660 as a symbol of continuity and stability. For similar reasons the Church of England was restored to its accustomed place in the established order. Logically this impulse for establishment and regularity should have carried outward to the colonies, and in some places it did. Yet it was in these very years that religious dissent made striking gains in North America.

Next to matters of political accommodation, one of the most urgent questions facing the Restoration government was what to do about Britain's sizable population of religious dissenters. As might be expected, opinion was divided. One side favored "comprehension"—a scheme whereby both Anglicans and Presbyterians would have been included within the established church, making it a strong national institution that encompassed most of the British population. This would have isolated Independents and other dissenting groups on the fringes of British religious life. The other side preferred "toleration"—allowing only Anglicans into the church but granting to Presbyterians, Independents, and other dissenters the right to exist as tolerated minorities. Supporting the second plan were the orthodox Anglican clergy, for obvious reasons, and Charles II, for reasons more subtle and more suspect: he hoped to smuggle in Catholics under cover of a general toleration. In the end the Toleration Act of 1689 embraced the second alternative. But in view of the ambiguous motives behind it, as well as earlier restrictions placed on dissenters by the so-called Clarendon Code and the Test Act, religious toleration seems to have meant something decidedly more limited in the late seventeenth century than it would to liberals a hundred years later.[40]

On the face of it, then, there was little cause to assume that toleration would be welcome in the Restoration colonies, and indeed there was substantial support for the mother Church of England. In the Carolinas and later Georgia, Anglicans ranked prominently among the founding proprietors and trustees. There was even talk in the later seventeenth century of settling an

Anglican bishop in America, and schemes to encourage the immigration of Anglican clergymen included university fellowships with seven-year colonial service clauses, government subsidies for transportation, and a form of clerical "impressment" that would have sent ministers abroad for five-year stints.[41] Despite these tremors of Anglican resurgence, all colonies founded after the Restoration made fairly generous provision for dissenters. Only in Georgia and Carolina did the effort, halfhearted at best, to establish the Church of England meet with partial success.

The Anglican leaders' plans to build a strong colonial church in the thirty years after the Restoration—perhaps the most propitious time of the entire colonial period—were thwarted by a number of counter currents that kept the church overseas from acquiring the kind of exclusive authority they had in mind. One was that Charles II used colonial lands to reward his English supporters, leading him to patent all post-Restoration colonies under proprietary charters that conferred broad powers upon the recipients. The proprietors' first concern was to populate their domains, yet this was a time when few Englishmen (except dissenters) desired to move to the New World. Proprietors thus sought out new sources of immigration in Europe and Scotland. In all Restoration colonies, then, dissenters formed the majority of the seventeenth-century population, making toleration the only feasible policy for the proprietors. Another difficulty was the mercantilist character of Restoration England, where the impulse for economic regulation led to the formation of the Lords of Trade and the passage of a series of Navigation Acts. Inevitably the mercantilist program came into conflict with the established church, for merchants could not encourage an environment hostile to dissenters in colonies whose economic success depended on persuading a diversity of peoples, holding a variety of religious beliefs, to settle there. In these circumstances, imperial interests often took precedence over religious ones.[42] The Anglican Church nonetheless had tradition and a resurgent missionary spirit on its side and conceded nothing as Charles II handed out his proprietary grants.

Carolina faced the French and Spanish on its southern flanks,

making prompt settlement crucial to the colony's stability. Therefore the original Carolina proprietors, while establishing the Anglican church on paper, granted liberty of conscience to the Baptists,
Huguenots, Quakers, and Presbyterians who offered the likeliest
prospects as settlers. Dissenting churches usually had to be char-
tered and were expected to hold services in private, but in the early
decades the government placed no restrictions on suffrage or
officeholding by dissenters. That this liberal religious foundation
achieved its purpose is evident. Of the approximately 4000 white
inhabitants of southern Carolina in 1700, some 500 were Huguenots, 1300 Presbyterians, 400 Baptists, and 100 Quakers, while
another 1700 adhered to the mother Church of England.[43] Jewish
immigration to Carolina had specifically been encouraged in the
Fundamental Constitutions. Though that document never became
law, it reflected not only the proprietors' need for settlers but also
their belief that Jews would make reliable citizens in a colony which
shared a border with Catholic Spain, whose Inquisition had made
emigrants of so many Jews in the first place. The northern part of
Carolina rapidly became a haven for Quakers and other dissenters
forced out of Virginia. Dissenters soon formed the majority in both
parts of early Carolina, where no significant religious prohibitions
existed in the early years, save for restrictions against Catholics,
who took the hint and stayed away. The colony-wide Anglican
establishment in southern Carolina was not delineated by law until
1706, several decades after the colony was settled. And though
northern Carolina began passing legislation to establish the Church
of England in 1701, the acts either were not approved in England or
were effectively resisted by the province's dissenters until 1765.[44]

By the time Georgia was founded in 1732 the tide of non-English
immigration to America was at a peak. With German Lutherans,
Scottish Presbyterians, Moravians, French Huguenots, and various
others making their way to the colony, the grant of religious
privileges was necessarily broad. Not that religious toleration was an
accepted principle even by the 1730s; rather the need for settlers
and the peculiar circumstances of each colony's history determined
how dissident sects would fare. A sizable community of Moravians,

for example, was forced out of Georgia after 1738 because their pacifist principles and refusal of conscription made them a liability in that buffer colony as war with Spain approached. Similarly, the proximity of Spanish and French settlements led the trustees to discourage Catholic settlers by denying them the right to hold property.[45]

Over forty Jews, the largest such group to enter any colony at one time, landed at Savannah on July 11, 1733 while the trustees were in the midst of a debate about whether they should allow Jews into the new colony at all. The arrival of this contingent caused alarm and consternation, one trustee grumbling that Georgia would soon become a Jewish colony which "the needy Protestants for whom it was designed would desert as leaves from a tree in autumn." But James Oglethorpe was not inclined to expel the Jews, and the Protestants were in no condition to go anywhere owing to a raging epidemic that had already taken twenty lives. Fortunately, among the new arrivals was Dr. Samuel Nunez, a Portuguese Jew, and at that moment the only physician in Georgia. Nunez's valuable role in controlling the epidemic earned for him and his companions a permanent place in the community and very possibly eased the entry of subsequent Jewish immigrants. When Georgia was made a royal colony in 1752, such a high proportion of dissenters resided in the province that establishment of the Church of England was successfully resisted until 1758, when a mild establishment that generally tolerated all denominations except Roman Catholics was agreed upon.[46]

Religious Liberty on Principle

In only two places in seventeenth-century America—Rhode Island and the Quaker colonies on the Delaware—did a religious freedom fixed in principle take root. The Quaker doctrine on freedom of conscience developed out of the sect's interpretation of the divine word and its experiences in England. Religious liberty in Rhode Island was born of experience and grew into principle, as can be seen by glancing back at the founding era.

As religious zealots, political misfits, and "some notorious Delinkquents [looking to] avoid the stroake of Justice" set their sights on Rhode Island in the 1640s, Roger Williams and a few others feared the loss of their own freedom and religious individualism unless civil order could be achieved. Rhode Islanders had "drunck of ye cup of as great liberties as any people," wrote Williams, and it "hath rendered many of us wanton and too active." Thus Williams took ship for England, where in 1644 he obtained from Parliament a patent that brought Providence, Portsmouth, and Newport under one charter. In 1647 these three towns and Warwick drew up a common charter that established a representative legislature and, in accordance with existing realities, affirmed that "all men may walk as their consciences persuade them, every one in the name of his god."[47]

Roger Williams, chosen Chief Officer of the colony, now faced a dilemma. The logic of his religious beliefs required him to place no restraints on diverse theological opinions, but his responsibilities as magistrate required that he support a common code of law and conduct in political life. The effort to reconcile these two interests seems to have stimulated in him an immensely creative tension. In *The Bloudy Tenent of Persecution* (1644) he had already broached the novel idea that an enforced uniformity of religious belief, instead of preserving peace, itself offered "the greatest occasion of civill Warre" throughout history. But when one critic subsequently charged that the *Bloudy Tenent* promoted sedition by interpreting the gospel as forbidding prosecution of transgressors against the common good, Williams moved instantly to dissociate himself from such a misrepresentation of his views. "That I ever should speak or write a tittle, that tends to such an infinite liberty of conscience, is a mistake," he declared, "and which I have ever disclaimed and abhorred." To clarify his position, Williams offered his famous ship analogy: in a commonwealth, as aboard a ship, all seamen and passengers had to perform their duties, pay their freight, and obey the common laws of the community, or be punished for failing to do so.[48]

In the furnace of such debate did Williams refine his conceptions of religious liberty and political order. A man of the seventeenth-century, possessed of an ardent nature, Williams might have preferred a colony in which his own religious views were embraced by all. But his unswerving commitment to the separation of church and state forbade coercion in matters of the soul. Over the years his conviction grew. By 1670 he was writing that God had "provided this country and this corner as a shelter for the poor and persecuted, according to their several persuasions"; Rhode Islanders would give up "lands and lives before we part with such a jewel." He offered to debate publicly the proposition that "forced worship stinks in God's nostrils," and to defend the political corollary that "there is no other prudent, Christian way of preserving peace in the world, but by permission of differing consciences." Surely the severest test for Williams was posed by the Quakers, whose doctrine of the inner light he viewed as a direct challenge to the laws and peace of the commonwealth.[49] Yet neither Roger Williams nor other seventeenth-century leaders of Rhode Island ever placed restrictions on Quaker practices. Instead, with increasing conviction they affirmed what had become the central principle of their "lively experiment": that a "flourishing civil state may stand and best be maintained . . . with a full liberty in religious concernments."[50]

The complaisant religious climate of Pennsylvania and New Jersey can be traced in significant part to the Quaker leadership of those colonies. A number of Friends were proprietors of West and East Jersey, where the Quaker experiment in colonial government received its first test. West Jersey's charter of 1677, which incorporated many of William Penn's ideas, included the statement that "no men, nor number of men upon earth, hath power or authority to rule over men's consciences in religious matters." By 1681 over 1400 Quakers had settled in the Jersies.[51] With the early addition of Baptists, Congregationalists, Scots-Presbyterians, Anglicans, and others, the sheer diversity of religious faiths made it unlikely that any single church could achieve hegemony, nor indeed was the Church of England established when New Jersey was made a royal colony in 1702.

William Penn meantime had transferred his colonizing interests to Pennsylvania, receiving a charter for that territory from Charles II in 1681. Penn's "Holy Experiment" was inspired by a utopian idealism no less sublime than that of the Puritans, but the Quaker tenets of humility and pacifism had convinced him that "force makes hypocrites; 'tis persuasion only that makes converts."[52] Penn's 1682 Frame of Government, the first constitution of Pennsylvania, declared that all who believed in one God and agreed to live in civil peace would "in no ways be molested or prejudiced for their religious persuasion or practice," nor be compelled to contribute to the support of any church. As for political rights, the first assembly required only a belief in Jesus Christ, making Pennsylvania one of the few colonies prepared to admit Catholics to full citizenship.[53] The governments of both William and Mary and Queen Anne refused, however, to allow such inclusive political participation. Despite the resistance of Penn and other Quaker leaders, the Pennsylvania assembly finally capitulated and in 1705 passed a law excluding Catholics along with Jews and non-believers from political life, a law that if often disregarded would remain on the books until 1776.[54] Nonetheless, Pennsylvania's contribution to seventeenth-century colonial religious development is noteworthy in that the Quaker colony had granted religious liberty on the basis of principle rather than expediency.

The transplantation of orderly religious institutions to America was hampered at every turn by the settlers' diversity of belief, the requirements of physical survival, and the vast spaces that encouraged a dispersion of settlement and fragmentation of power. Once survival was assured, some colonists persisted in cultivating the outer plantation to the neglect of the inner one, an impulse that clergymen were often helpless to counteract because of their fewness in number and distance from the centers of ecclesiastical authority.

The axiom that a single established church best served the order and stability of the state came under challenge to a greater or lesser degree in all colonies settled during the first half of the seventeenth century. Founders of the post-Restoration colonies, like their predecessors, might have preferred to nurture a close relationship between church and state, but the diverse character of the people most eligible to settle there made religious exclusiveness not only impractical but a contradiction. Thus, except in Pennsylvania and Rhode Island, the increasingly lenient religious atmosphere in the later seventeenth-century colonies was more opportunistic than ideological, more a case of helpless acquiescence than an endorsement of the principle of religious freedom.

It is often assumed that this seventeenth-century tendency toward religious fragmentation and ecclesiastical slackness continued unabated into the eighteenth century, leading to an apathy shaken only briefly by the Great Awakening and finally culminating in the severing of church from state after 1776. Yet this was not quite the way things went. There were always counter-tendencies working to establish cohesion and order in the religious as well as the civil community, and in ways other than the imposition of a simple and primitive conformity. As colonial society matured during the eighteenth century and leadership became concentrated in professional and social elites, religious organizations, like economic and political ones, emerged as significant centers of stability and influence. This period of consolidation led to a revitalization of ecclesiastical authority and restored a degree of tension in American religious life that would have profound consequences in the years ahead.

CHAPTER 3

The Clergymen

Historical thinking about the colonial clergy is at present in some flux, a consequence of two long-term problems of interpretation. First, the clergy has over the years been dealt with in piecemeal fashion, one denomination at a time, and with little attention to the general direction of its professional development or its place in the larger colonial society. True, the social role of the New England clergy has occasionally been examined, but clergymen elsewhere are often treated as a breed apart and left to the church historians. Then there has been a tendency to take at face value the hostile commentary on clerical shortcomings, real or imagined, so characteristic of early American religious discourse. Yet the most striking aspect of colonial religious culture, and its sharpest departure from Old World tradition, was the diversity—and thus the fierce competitiveness—of its beliefs and practices. Conceivably the best way to assess the experience of the many hundreds of ministers who made their way to the colonies from the late-seventeenth century onward would be against a background of Old World expectations as well as certain regional variations in provincial America.

Clergymen immigrating to the American colonies around the turn of the eighteenth century entered a strange and disorienting world.

Confronting them everywhere but in New England was a scene of scattered congregations, competing sects, a chronic shortage of fellow clergymen, and few of the supports that undergirded ministerial authority in the Old World. There were no bishops or consistories to ordain and discipline ministers for the Anglican, Lutheran, and Reformed churches; theological education did not exist outside of New England; livings were unknown, salaries uncertain, and tenure insecure. Even where churches were legally established, their power to collect tithes and exercise moral discipline was resisted by the forces of dissent. Some clergymen found this alien environment so unsettling that they returned home at the first opportunity. But the great majority stayed on, adjusting their professional expectations and remodeling their churches to meet New World realities.

The longest-settled denominations—the Anglican, Congregational, Dutch Reformed, and Quaker—had by the early eighteenth century passed through a time of seasoning into an era of consolidation and growth. This stabilization was part of a larger steadying-down of all seaboard institutions, as economic and political as well as religious power became concentrated in groups whose early arrival gave them preemptive advantages in trade, officeholding, and influence. As the seventeenth-century denominations moved toward stability, a tide of eighteenth-century immigration fostered the rapid growth of the Presbyterian, Lutheran, and German Reformed churches. These second-wave denominations encountered the same problems as had their predecessors: an inadequate supply of ministers, dispersed congregations, and a debilitating fragmentation of authority. Yet they too in time discovered new resources and built ecclesiastical structures that laid down a solid foundation for future growth.

A salient feature of this denominational consolidation was the formation of clerical associations and synods which tended to elevate the ministers' professional self-consciousness and enlarge their power over church affairs at the expense of the laity. An intensifying competition for adherents also led rival denominations to place renewed emphasis on church doctrine. At the same time, increasing

numbers of clergymen labored devotedly to extend worship services
and pastoral oversight to previously unserved areas. When the work
of these dedicated professionals was jeopardized by incompetent
preachers or outright charlatans, the able ministers objected so
loudly as to leave on the record a somewhat skewed impression of
the reputation of the provincial clergy—one that has sometimes
been used to caricature the entire profession. Thus something may
be gained from a fresh look at the professional and personal lives of
American clergymen active from about 1680 to the mid-eighteenth
century. The Anglican, Congregational, and Lutheran and German
Reformed ministers may in their aggregate give us something of a
representative view.

"The precariousness of their Livings": The Colonial Anglican Clergy

The Church of England in America embarked on a period of
consolidation and expansion at about the beginning of the eighteenth century, though the pace of its advance varied from colony to
colony. The bishops of London, within whose jurisdiction the
church in America fell, had been too distracted during the
Anglocentric Restoration years to cultivate their overseas domains,
but after 1680 interest in the provinces rose. Efforts to settle a
bishop in America failed, so the church made plans to strengthen
the ecclesiastical structure by appointing commissaries, or bishop's
agents, in a number of colonies. More important, a missionary
body—the Society for the Propagation of the Gospel in Foreign
Parts—was founded in 1701 with the aim of encouraging a steady
supply of ministers to the provinces.[1]

These efforts did not occur in a vacuum. During the volatile early
years of settlement; power had drifted outward to parish vestries
and lay leaders, who could be expected to resist centralizing
tendencies. Nonetheless, the contest for control of the provincial
Anglican church was more complex than the simple struggle
between vestries and clergymen that has become familiar through

repetition. Since Anglicans were concentrated most heavily in the South, developments in that section reveal much about the character of the eighteenth-century church.

Anglican dominance was never in doubt in Virginia, where until the mid-eighteenth century most inhabitants had no wish but to conform to their comfortably low version of the mother church. Yet when church leaders in England instituted a more assertive policy after 1680, they were met squarely by a colonial elite that had emerged from Bacon's rebellion with new self-assurance and pride of power. Gentry leaders opposed the centralization of church authority in a bishop—even one who stayed in London. In addition, the early vestries asserted their right to hire and dismiss clergymen without approval from the Bishop of London or the governor—a practice that led one outraged English visitor to charge that the typical vestry treated its minister "how they please, paid him what they list, and discarded him whenever they had a mind to it."[2]

Concurrently, the method of choosing vestrymen was undergoing a subtle change. Since vestries set the tax rate for support of the local church and minister, a sum that often exceeded the provincial or county tax,[3] Burgesses had originally provided for the annual election of vestrymen. In 1662 the act was amended to allow vestries to fill their own vacancies. Soon elections were bypassed altogether as the vestries became self-perpetuating bodies. Petitions protesting the long continuance of vestries were circulated at the time of Bacon's Assembly, which passed a bill providing that vestrymen be chosen every three years by the freeholders and freemen of each parish. But with gentry power reaching a peak around the turn of the century, self-selecting vestries became so commonplace that these murmurings were heard no more.[4]

Virginia clergymen attempted to rebalance the scales of power by urging the appointment of a colonial bishop, noting that only he could establish an ecclesiastical order and discipline that would attract qualified ministers to the rural vastness of America.[5] Nor did the founding of the Society for the Propagation of the Gospel relieve the shortage, since the Society concentrated its efforts in colonies where the church was not established or where dissenters were prevalent. Unwilling or unable to press the case for a colonial bishop, Lambeth Palace chose instead to send the first commissary, or bishop's agent, to Virginia. Though the expectation that a commissary would wrest sufficient power from lay and government leaders to effect basic reforms was never met, Virginia's first commissary, the Reverend James Blair, had every hope for success upon assuming his duties in 1690.

A resident of Virginia since 1685 and married to Sarah Harrison, the daughter of a leading planter, Blair possessed a strong will and a determination to occupy a position of eminence in his adopted land. Eminence he doubtless achieved. By the time he died at the age of eighty-eight, Blair had served fifty-three years as commissary, been president of William and Mary College (which he himself founded) for forty-nine years, been a member of the governor's council for half a century, and had acquired wealth and influence beyond that usually associated with, or deemed appropriate to, a clergyman. (Blair's enemies never lost an opportunity to point out that he was a Scot, with proverbial "Scottish" traits.) His long tenure in offices alone would probably have given him a place in Virginia history; his complex character and fiery personality guaranteed it. Testy, arrogant, and with a zest for political intrigue worthy of a Renaissance pope, Blair shunned the contemplative style and plunged headlong into the world of Virginia politics.[6]

His highest priority was to gain permanent tenure for Virginia's ministers, who he felt were being treated like hired hands. He also sought to erect ecclesiastical courts with power to try offenses against public morality. The vestries as a matter of course resisted all his efforts to curtail their choice of ministers, and Blair soon discovered that Virginians had "a great aversion to spiritual courts," viewing them as something akin to the Inquisition. He quickly realized that any effort to strengthen the church required the cooperation of the planter aristocracy. Within a short time the astute commissary had backed off from his advocacy of ecclesiastical courts and had moderated his position on the permanent induction of ministers. This seeming retreat aroused the ire of the Anglican governor and some members of the clergy, who claimed that Blair sought only to be popular.[7]

Blair did manage to improve clerical discipline somewhat by visiting churches and calling ministerial convocations, though his zest for this side of his work languished as the years passed. Perhaps his cherished wish to found a college that would train future ministers for Virginia took precedence over other reforms; certainly the project consumed much of his energy. Nor did his devotion flag when the infant William and Mary College was destroyed by fire in 1705 and had to be entirely rebuilt. Nonetheless, Blair laid the groundwork for the more permanent induction of rectors into Virginia parishes. His proposal that vestries be given a limited time within which to choose a minister, who would then be inducted into his post by the governor, became law in 1748.[8] Though Blair's initial zeal may have waned over time, his long tenure and political sagacity made the office of commissary a center of influence in the church life of Virginia.

Other power centers also challenged the vestries' control over the church. The House of Burgesses and the governor both claimed exclusive jurisdiction over the laying out and dividing of parishes. In 1710 Governor Spotswood sharply admonished the Burgesses to cease the sub-division of parishes "untill her Majesty shall be graciously pleased to yield up That Branch of her Royal Prerogative into Your hands." But when London failed to back the governor, Burgesses continued to set parish boundaries as they had for a century.[9] From the early eighteenth century on, governors, assemblies, and courts of law vied for the power to appoint and depose rectors, the governor, as noted above, finally gaining the right of induction in 1748. The next year, after repeated efforts by a few vestries to remove their ministers, the Burgesses passed a statute granting tenure to rectors formally received by a parish, whether or not they had been inducted by the governor. The rising professionalism and independence of the clergy irritated some leading squires, who believed their benefactions to the church entitled them to some control over its "livings." One of these was Landon Carter, whose efforts to oust the Reverend William Kay from

Lunenburg Parish led to bitter litigation over several years. As a writer in the *Virginia Gazette* observed, some haughty gentlemen would not hesitate to turn an honest parson into a "rotten Pillar of the Church, especially if he should happen to be so *neglectfully* wrapped up in Contemplation, as to forget pulling of[f] his Hat with a . . . how does your Worship do to Day!"[10]

These noisy disputes between certain ministers and a few powerful planters have tended to cloud the reputation of the entire southern Anglican clergy. After mid-century, Presbyterian and Baptist critics added their voices to the clamor. The picture left by these hostile commentators of a slothful and negligent, debauched and drunken Anglican ministry is familiar enough.[11] There are, indeed, well-documented instances of clerical misconduct,[12] including alcoholism (one parson downed all the communion wine as he was carrying it to church), and adultery. Yet, as one southern minister observed, a single slip "seldom misses of being improved into a scandal & prejudice against . . . the church & whole order of the Clergy."[13]

A recent study examining every known accusation of misconduct lodged against Virginia rectors active between 1723 and 1776 concludes that at most 10 percent of the ministers ever had authentic charges brought against them. (In the modern Episcopal Church about 8 percent of the ministers are deposed.) It would appear that the histories of a few notorious misfits who gained their places when ministers were in short supply, or successfully fought ejection after receiving tenure, have served to color the reputation of the faithful 90 percent of Virginia Anglican clergymen.[14]

Another common impression of Virginia's rectors is that of ignorant losers who could find no parish in Britain and barely kept one in America. Yet in 1726 at least twenty-three of the colony's forty-two ministers had attended university, twelve at Oxbridge colleges and others at Scottish universities or Trinity, Dublin. The educational backgrounds of fifty of the seventy-four clergymen active around mid-century have been traced; twenty-three of these had attended Oxford or Cambridge while thirteen had studied at William and Mary. The proportion of native-born ministers, many

educated at William and Mary, rose steadily in the third quarter of
the eighteenth century. The average tenure of rectors in a single
parish was about fifteen years, with many serving in one post until
their deaths.[15] All of which gives weight to Hugh Jones's observation in 1724 that Virginia parsons who "have a mind to do their duty
. . . may live with as much satisfaction, respect, comfort, and love
as most clergymen in England."[16]

Maryland, where the Anglican church was established in 1702, was
the only colony other than Virginia to receive no assistance from the
Society for the Propagation of the Gospel.[17] Its ministers, like
Virginia's, were paid directly out of local taxes that fell on all
tithables in each parish. In other respects the two provinces
differed importantly. Owing to the lateness of Maryland's establishment, its vestries never gained the power that Virginia's had
achieved in the more fluid climate of the seventeenth century.
Maryland vestries were smaller—consisting of six vestrymen and
two churchwardens—and elective, though low turnout at annual
elections meant that many became self-selecting. County courts,
rather than vestries, provided for the poor; vestries, however,
policed moral infractions committed within their parishes.[18] Commissaries were appointed intermittently in Maryland from 1701 to
1734, but none ever acquired the influence, formal or informal, of
Virginia's James Blair.

The provincial governors, whether under royal or proprietary
auspices, held significant ecclesiastical powers. Some high-church
governors used the office to suppress dissent, as when Governor
John Seymour (1703–1709), a strong Anglican, curbed the rights of
Catholics after informing them briskly: "I am an English Protestant
Gentleman and can never equivocate."[19] Most important was the
governor's power both to appoint and to induct rectors. Because
clerical salaries were financed by a public tax, the local vestries
sometimes tried to influence or to obstruct the choice of ministers.
But governors were known to impose clergymen whether wanted
by the vestries or not. This separation of purse from power led to
countless clashes between governors and parishioners. A particularly

dramatic example of this tension occurred in All Saints Parish when the congregation locked an unwanted appointee out of the church, forcing him to climb through a window to claim the pulpit. When the parishioners responded by pelting him with stones, the angry parson pulled out a pistol and threatened to shoot their leader.[20]

The provincial assembly attempted to gain leverage over the clergy by controlling the size of their stipends, which tended to increase rapidly from the 1720s onward. Instead of being paid a set amount of tobacco per annum as in Virginia, Maryland ministers received a forty-pound tobacco poll from each taxable in the parish. The assembly succeeded in reducing the poll to thirty pounds in 1747. Yet owing to rapid population growth and the clergy's ability to resist parish divisions, average salaries rose from about £50 sterling in the early eighteenth century to nearly £200 per annum by the 1760s—roughly double the stipend in Virginia or any other colony.[21]

Marylanders' frustration over their inability to influence church policies or to depose incompetent clergymen rose as competition from dissenting congregations intensified. Rectors of doubtful character were an embarrassment to lay Anglicans and clergy alike, leading both groups to deplore publicly the presence of such persons. Dissenter hyperbole further darkened the picture, as did the aspersions of English clergymen who resented ministers "from the Scotch Universitys, who usually come young, raw, & undisciplin'd, tainted with Presbyterian principles, & no reall friends to our Episcopal Government." Nonetheless, the report of Commissary Christopher Wilkinson to the bishop of London in 1724 suggests that the miscreants were few. "The faults & follies of some Clergymen are too gross to be excus'd or extenuated. But there are not above two that I know of on our [eastern] shore, who deserve the Severe censure the lower house has given 'em." The rest were "free from any Scandalous crimes; & their diligence & industry in the discharge of their office is incredible."[22]

Historians attempting to separate truth from fiction in these accounts have usually settled for ambiguity by allowing that the Maryland ministry contained both saints and sinners.[23] A recent scrutiny of the established clergy throws additional light on this question and on the ministers' backgrounds. Of the approximately two hundred Anglican clergymen serving Maryland parishes between 1692 and 1776, thirty-five—nearly one in six—had some accusation made against their character or professional performance. Some charges were frivolous, the consequence of local factionalism or denominational rivalries. In six cases the accused were found completely innocent. Twenty-nine clergymen may have deserved censure on at least one count, usually drunkenness; six cases involved serious offenses, four of sexual misconduct and two of probable murder. But at most 15 percent of the rectors had authentic charges brought against them.[24]

Maryland ministers, especially in the early years, were frequently drawn from the middle and lower-middle class; many could not afford to attend university in Britain, which in turn made it difficult for them to find livings there. Overall, 53 percent of the Maryland clergy had B.A. degrees and about 25 percent M.A.s, substantially fewer than their counterparts in England.[25] However, the Scottish contingent (about one-quarter of the total) possessed a higher proportion of advanced degrees than did their English brethren in Maryland. The average tenure in a Maryland parish was 12.3 years. Attracted by the high pay, more clergymen applied for openings after mid-century than could be accommodated in the colony,[26] enabling Marylanders to choose among them.

For all this, the cloud of notoriety that has long cast a shadow over the Anglican clergy of Maryland and Virginia must be explained, especially since it darkened no other colony. Charges of misconduct occurred elsewhere, but the reputation of the ministry as a whole was never compromised. Virginia and Maryland seem to represent a special case. The troubles besetting those two provinces stemmed less, it would appear, from the bad or good quality of their clergy than from one prime circumstance: in Virginia and Maryland alone was the clergy exclusively dependent for its support on a direct, colony-wide church tax. Every other province in America relied on the Society for the Propagation of the Gospel for all or part of its clergy's pay, or developed some means other than a parish tax to support its rectors. Only in Virginia and Maryland did clerical salaries and control over the church become perennial issues in local politics, issues that were increasingly caught up in the accelerating debate between provincials and royal authorities. Squabbles between Marylanders and their governors over the salaries, appointment, and removal of ministers heightened as the eighteenth century progressed. Disputes sharpened in Virginia after mid-century when the governors gained the power to induct rectors. Before long the question of church rates became entangled with the provincials' mounting concern about taxation and representation—the Parson's Cause in Virginia being but the most familiar case.

In short, there is ample ground to suppose that Anglican ministers in Virginia and Maryland were no less competent, upright, or dedicated than those in other colonies. But in such circumstances as those just described they offered all-too convenient targets for anyone who wanted to take a shot at the British state or church.

The distinctiveness of the Anglican clergy's situation in Virginia and Maryland becomes evident when contrasted with arrangements for the clergy in other southern colonies, where the prevalence of dissent placed the Church of England in a more tenuous position. Efforts to consolidate church power in the Carolinas and Georgia during the eighteenth century met with at best a partial success. In South Carolina dissenter meetings outnumbered Anglican churches by three to one at the turn of the century. Governor Nathaniel Johnson, a zealous high-churchman, finally managed, with the support of an Anglican council, to push an establishment bill through the assembly in November 1706. But at the insistence of dissenters the provincial treasury assumed responsibility for ministers' salaries and the construction of churches, meaning that in place of parish taxes the burden of support rested largely on import duties and the tax on slaves.[27] Elective parish vestries appointed ministers and made minor repairs to church buildings. By the second decade of the century parishes were becoming key units of local government; dissenters were frequently elected vestrymen and churchwardens, though this ran contrary to the act of establishment. The Society for the Propagation of the Gospel supplied ministers and commissaries, paying all of their salaries until the provincial treasury was able to assume some of the cost. By the 1730s Anglican ministers reported that they were winning many dissenters to the church.[28]

Only in 1758 was an Anglican establishment—albeit a weak one—achieved in Georgia. Parishes and vestries were organized, though dissenters voted for and served on the vestries. Parishes were authorized to collect a rate to pay for communion wine, church repair, and a clerk and sexton's salaries, but apparently only Christ Church Parish in Savannah ever did so. Church buildings and stipends for the clergy were subsidized by several sources—the Society for the Propagation of the Gospel, profits from glebe lands, private subscriptions, direct appropriations from Parliament (a provision peculiar to Georgia), and fees from tavern licenses and liquor duties—but never by a direct parish tax. Not only were dissenters tolerated; Georgia officials sometimes built churches for them and provided glebes for their preachers.[29] North Carolina's establishment was the least effective of any in the colonies. Following a number of abortive attempts in the early eighteenth century, the Anglican governor finally pushed a bill of establishment and a church rate through the provincial assembly in 1764. But with only six ministers to serve twenty-nine parishes and a white population of 100,000, the establishment was little more than nominal. Dissenters openly evaded the act, refused to pay church rates, and by 1765 were loudly declaiming against the twin oppressions of church establishment and the Stamp Act.[30] The endless hand-wringing by colonial Anglicans over the condition of religion in North Carolina indicates that the church never did gain a firm settlement there before the Revolution.

In the North, the Church of England was essentially a voluntary association. With no established religion in Pennsylvania, Delaware, New Jersey, Rhode Island, and most of New York, Anglicans competed on an equal footing with other denominations. Where Congregationalism was established in New England, Anglicans joined with dissenters to agitate for the right to practice their religion freely. The Church of England nonetheless had one advantage the other denominations lacked: it could promote the appointment of staunch Anglican governors who might informally enlarge the church's power. As an Anglican minister in Pennsylvania asserted in 1700, if that province should be converted to a royal government "Quakerism will be rooted out, and the Church will be more than Conquerour."[31]

New York offers an interesting case study of the Anglican church militant. At the end of the seventeenth century dissenters outnumbered churchmen by about forty to one in the conquered colony. But among the governors sent between 1692 and 1708, two zealous sons of the church were determined to improve the position of Anglicanism in New York. One was Benjamin Fletcher, who observed in his opening address to the assembly in 1693, "There are none of you but what are big with the privilege of Englishmen and Magna Charta, which is your right; and the same law doth provide for the religion of the church of England." Fletcher forced a bill through the assembly which called for election of ten vestrymen and two churchwardens in each of the four counties—New York, Westchester, Queens, and Richmond—where Anglicans were most numerous though still a minority. Each county vestry, a secular body entirely separate from the church vestries, was authorized to levy a tax to relieve the poor and to pay the salary of a "good and sufficient Protestant Minister."[32] The governor intended that the vestries should name Anglican ministers, but dissenters both in and out of the assembly chose to interpret the clause to mean any Protestant minister, thereby provoking a controversy that flared intermittently from that time forward.

When the assembly refused with "stubborn ill temper" to grant the governor a veto over the vestries' choice of ministers, Fletcher made his intentions clear: "I have the power of collating or suspending any minister in my government, and I will take care that neither heresy, sedition, schism nor rebellion be preached amongst you."[33] Undeterred, the New York City vestries elected in 1694 and 1695 prepared to appoint dissenting ministers. But in 1696 the Anglicans, having organized themselves sufficiently to capture a seven-to-five majority on the City Vestry, promptly chose the

Reverend William Vesey as minister. A Massachusetts-born, Harvard-educated churchman of moderate principles, Vesey probably allayed dissenter fears. Yet his forty-nine-year tenure as rector of Trinity Parish, as well as the legal incorporation of the parish by the assembly in 1697, established the precedent that Trinity's rector would receive all or a large portion of his salary from taxes raised by the New York City Vestry. Other sources of support for Trinity Parish ministers, assistants, and schoolteachers were the Queen's Farm glebe, granted to the church by royal patent in 1705, private subscriptions, and the Society for the Propagation of the Gospel. Only to the extent, then, that the salary of the senior minister of Trinity Parish was paid from a public rate was the Church of England established in New York County.[34]

Thus, although there exists a general understanding that the Church of England was in some way "established" in the four lower counties of New York province, it would appear on closer examination that such was the case only in the most strained and nominal sense. In the other three counties named in the Vestry Act, the church fared even less well than in New York County. Westchester, Queens, and Richmond were less directly under the eye of the governor and were, at the same time, dominated by dissenters. These places did, to be sure, come under plenty of pressure. With the arrival of Edward Hyde, Lord Cornbury, as governor in 1702, another insistent churchman was on hand determined to do what he could. Cornbury called upon the newly founded Society for the Propagation of the Gospel to supply ministers to New York, and six of the first missionaries sent abroad by the Society were assigned there. Three of them were posted to Westchester County, though the town of Bedford was strongarmed into compliance by the arrest and incarceration of its resident dissenting pastor.[35] When Cornbury dispatched an Anglican missionary in 1703 to take possession of the church in the predominantly Presbyterian town of Jamaica, in Queens County, riots ensued. The missionary left a lively description of what went on there. He had already started the worship service on his first Sabbath at Jamaica when the town's Presbyterian pastor arrived at the church. The latter sent in word that he would preach under a tree, which set off a great whispering through the church as the parishioners tried to decide whether to go or stay. Some who had already exited the church returned for their seats, "and then we had a shamefull disturbance, Hawling and Tugging of Seats; shoving one the other off, carrying them out and returning again for more . . . by which time I had lost about half of the Congregation."[36]

Friction between dissenters and Anglicans was especially aggravated during Cornbury's regime, for the governor had vowed to the S.P.G. that "nothing shall be wanting on my part to promote the Interest of the Church." Cornbury may have been both a tyrant and a fop, but as the historian William Smith, Jr., later observed, "in his zeal for the Church he was surpassed by none." By 1711 at least one leading Anglican was wondering whether such zeal might not be doing the church more harm than good. Lewis Morris feared that tax supported ministers would not make many converts among a people "who think themselves much injured . . . [Moreover,] in the Jersies and in Pensilvania where there is no [ministry] Act there is four times the number of Churchmen than there is in this Province of New York."[37]

But some churchmen would not slacken their efforts to force an establishment on the three counties outside of New York City. When effective missionaries could be placed there the fortunes of the church improved somewhat. But progress of any kind could occur only in the face of obstacles inherent in the very setting. In the early eighteenth century "Poverty Divisions & Differences" caused the Westchester County Vestry to be perpetually in arrears on the Anglican minister's salary, whereas in Queens the tax was as often paid to Presbyterian ministers as to those of the Church of England. When the missionary on Staten Island died in 1739, the Secretary of the S.P.G. was urged to consult the County Vestry about a successor. This "may be a means of bringing in the dissenters to join with the Churchmen in the Call of a Minister of the Established Church," noted one correspondent, "which may very probably prevent those great Animosities which have so often rent the Bowels of this Infant Church."[38]

Efforts to consolidate church power in New York yielded mixed results. Where governors were able to press the issue, as some did in New York City, or where lay gentry happened to be figures of local weight, as in Westchester County, the church gained a foothold that would in time make it an important force. But in most places, including Queens and Richmond Counties, the church made headway only in those pockets where Anglicans formed a numerical majority. Evidence of the slow progress of the church in pluralistic New York is apparent in a 1766 listing of S.P.G. salaries, which shows that after six decades in the colony the Society was still forced to make annual payments of from £30 to £50 each to supplement the salaries of missionaries in Hempstead, Rye, Eastchester, Philipsburg Manor, and Staten Island.[39]

Elsewhere in the North, Anglicanism was either on an equal footing with other denominations, as in Pennsylvania, Delaware, New Jersey, and Rhode Island, or was considered a dissenting religion, as in Connecticut, Massachusetts, and New Hampshire, where Congregationalism was established. The Church of England's ties to British officialdom, as well as support from the S.P.G., contributed significantly to its growth in both North and South. Nevertheless, the ups and downs of an Anglican clergyman's daily existence in the pluralistic vastness of America bore little resemblance to the relatively settled life of a typical English country vicar.

The Rectors' Daily Rounds

Up to the mid-eighteenth century, most colonial Anglican pulpits were occupied by ministers born and educated in Britain. Many of them found the American church "very odd . . . being different to what they have been heretofore accustomed to." If the absence of bishops and supporting ecclesiastical structure was profoundly disorienting, the "oddity" that most rudely jolted professional expectations was the huge size of colonial parishes. Compared to the average English parish of less than five square miles, southern parishes might stretch for 60 to 100 miles; one frontier parish in

South Carolina measured 80 by 130 miles and contained but 700 white inhabitants.[40] This New World circumstance forced all but a few ministers to take up an itinerant life, which involved riding thousands of miles each year through blizzards, floods, and scorching heat to carry the gospel to their scattered flocks. In a typical complaint, a Virginia clergyman wrote that he regularly traveled fifty miles over rivers and swamps to reach his remote congregations, leaving his health "much impaired by being exposed to the excess of the weather (here very hot in the Summer and piercing cold in the Winter and always variable)." The rector of St. James Parish, Goochland, in South Carolina reported that in addition to serving three churches he had seven congregations up in the mountains. Furthermore, he preached twice a year in twelve other places, "which I reckon better than 400 miles backwards and forwards [,] and foard 19 times the South and North Rivers." Even in a tidewater parish such as Virginia's Westover, only twelve miles wide and thirty long, the rector itinerated between three churches.[41]

Churches, chapels of ease, private houses, and barns sheltered worshipers in rural parishes, with the rector usually preaching two Sabbaths a month in the main church and once in three or four weeks at the outlying chapels. Anglican preachers spent many a restless night in small cabins or on the open ground during these itinerations. Adding to their gypsy life was the custom of holding baptisms, weddings, and funerals in parishioners' homes owing to the difficulty of transporting infants, wedding parties, and corpses to a church that might lie ten or more miles distant.[42]

Nor was itinerancy confined to the South. The Reverend William Becket of lower Pennsylvania ministered in the early 1730s to over 1000 people. One year he traveled 1632 miles and another 1156 miles, which obliged him always to keep two horses. Because roads were fairly good in the parish, people came to church "Winter & Summer, some 7 or 8 miles and others 12 or 14," which as Becket noted "is no strange thing, but very common among the Inhabitants of America." Becket reports that his main church—measuring forty by twenty-four feet, with wainscoted walls, glazed windows, pews, and a gallery—had an average of about 150 auditors on the Sabbath. He also served three other churches, including St. John the Baptist, which measured but thirty by twenty feet and was raised in a single day.[43]

John Bartow, a graduate of Cambridge, was the first S.P.G. missionary assigned to Westchester County, New York. Within two years of his arrival in 1702, Bartow was serving at least four places there and making occasional visits to Long Island and New Jersey. He customarily preached twice on the Sabbath in summer and once in winter; he also ministered to the sick and catechized the children, frequently riding ten or twenty miles a day. Bartow often raised special collections for the poor and afflicted of the county, as in 1708 when he collected eleven shillings and sixpence for a distressed widow "who had 9 Children murdered by the Indians." After first preaching in a building that doubled as town hall and prison, Bartow in 1710 persuaded the Town of Westchester to build a church twenty-eight feet square. Because the building was small and topped with a cupola, a subsequent rector thought it resembled a pigeon house in England.[44] Bartow managed to obtain a small glebe from the Town of Westchester, but weary of boarding at private homes he finally bought a house at his own expense. These inconveniences as well as repeated bickering between Anglicans and dissenters made his ministry "very Onerous and difficult." Nonetheless Bartow served faithfully in his mission for twenty-three years until his death in 1725 at age fifty-two.[45]

The S.P.G. missionary Samuel Johnson served Connecticut in the 1720s by itinerating between Stratford, Fairfield, Newtown, and West Haven—a circuit of more than sixty miles.[46] Not every newcomer could adjust to such conditions. The Reverend William Harrison, assigned to New Jersey in 1722, was appalled by what awaited him there. The people were not only too poor to supplement his stipend but behaved as if they should be "rewarded for rideing 20 miles to Church." Harrison found the New Jerseyans' lodgings primitive, their diet strange, and the variable extremes of the region's climate intolerable. Concluding that he could not endure life in the provinces, Harrison begged leave to go home before "the heats return [,] they being very dangerous to one so fatt." Instead the fat Harrison was reassigned in 1723 to Staten Island, New York, where he conducted services in a single church—though one "never finished within, the people being poor." There he bought 330 acres of land with an old ruined house and barn, where he puffed and sweated at part-time farming in order to make ends meet.[47]

Another trying aspect of the provincial clergyman's life was the volatility and unpredictability of local conditions. Some Anglicans spent years building congregations in areas where dissenters prevailed, only to have their followers fall back to Quakerism or some other "heresy" at the rector's illness or death. The energetic John Talbot, having started more congregations in New Jersey than one man could possibly serve, feared they might fall away to dissent "purely for lack of looking after." Jacob Henderson would have left his rural congregations around Newcastle, Pennsylvania in 1713 for a more comfortable position had he not known that a nearby Presbyterian minister would "make great advantage of Such a Vacancy."[48] Two decades later his Anglican colleague at Lewes claimed to be the only clergyman in the area, having outlasted Presbyterian and Quaker preachers. But he could not be very complacent about it: "Our Lord hath sent us forth into America, indeed, as sheep among wolves, and we have great need to be wise as serpents, and harmless as doves." Nor had the region stabilized some thirty years later when the Reverend Charles Inglis, despite his wife's death from a fever which he attributed to the dismal climate, decided to stay at his post in Dover in order to frustrate the proselytizing of dissenters. Even in Virginia, that most Anglican of colonies, dissent was always a latent threat should a parish fall vacant. When the high mortality among ministers vacated 15 Virginia parishes in 1724, Commissary Blair wrote to London that "the Presbyterians taking advantage of the want of Ministers are very busy, fitting up meetings in many places where they had none heretofore."[49]

Fluidity of allegiance seems to have been most pronounced in the early years when ministers were few, or in the countryside where great distances induced provincials to attend the nearest church. The comment in 1711 of a rector in South Carolina sums up the problem. After noting that the people "must have one [religious] leader or another," he observed that "wanting a true and faithfull one [that is, an Anglican], they'd rather follow an Anabaptist, a Presbyterian, or a Quaker than be without one."⁵⁰ This latitudinarian momentum was slowed from about the second quarter of the eighteenth century onward as the number of ministers entering the colonies rose. Now Anglican congregations that had struggled under the direction of lay readers got rectors of their own, or were regularly visited by itinerant clergymen who administered baptism and communion.⁵¹ A renewed emphasis on doctrine followed, and soon catechists were sent out to instruct the youth. True, latitudinarian practice continued in many regions, but in the more settled parts loyalty to a single church was increasingly the custom. City churches especially, benefiting from the presence of full-time ministers, provided a lively program of denominational services. As early as 1724, for example, Christ Church, Philadelphia was renowned for an orthodoxy that produced "2 sermons every Lord's day, Prayers all the week, & Homilies on festivals."⁵²

On the frontier, warfare—whether against the Indians or the French—posed a particular threat to congregation building. The 1715 Yamasee War in South Carolina postponed Anglican efforts to extend the church to newly settled southwestern parishes for nearly a decade. S.P.G. missionaries assigned to those parishes tell of destroyed churches and of settlers forced to flee the frontier to safe haven in Charleston. Even by 1730 some sections had not recovered from the ravages of war. Similarly St. Peter's Church at Albany, New York was compelled to suspend services during King George's War, owing to the depredations of the French.⁵³ Such random and unpredictable events continuously tested the stamina and devotion of the Anglican ministers.

One might suppose that the rhythm of church life in the southern tidewater parishes—where the Church of England is often described as an aristocratic local institution that came to resemble the church at home—should have been a good deal less erratic than the

St. Philip's Church, Charleston, S.C. Erected 1723.
(Picture Collection, The New York Public Library)

above account suggests. And indeed, the Virginia gentry had built such handsome structures as Christ Church in Lancaster County and Bruton Parish Church at Williamsburg, while South Carolina boasted the elegant St. Philips in Charleston. Rectors of these churches no doubt conducted services "with Great Decency and Order" for polite congregations, lived in comfortable houses, and were invited to dine with the great planters.[54] More generous salaries also enabled a number of Anglican clergymen, especially in Maryland, to live as gentlemen. As the tidewater population stabilized and the number of ministers continued to multiply around mid-century, some rectors actually could limit their labors to a single large congregation.[55] Yet most eighteenth-century rectors were not of this sort; they presided over parishes with a primary church and one or more outlying chapels. Church buildings naturally were enlarged and beautified as the population grew, but they displayed a wide range in the degree of their comfort and appointments. The ministers' housing varied equally, as did the level of civility on which they lived.

The most detailed descriptions of the southern clergyman's environment are found in the South Carolina missionaries' reports to the S.P.G. The minister of St. James, Goose Creek, one of the colony's earliest and most stable parishes, declared in 1727 that his main church excelled in beauty all others in South Carolina except St. Philip's. He described with relish the forty-five-by-forty-foot brick structure, with its handsome arched windows, neat and regular pews as well as common benches, and a gallery, its interior adorned with "two rows of round timber pillars, painted marble" and an altarpiece "decently beautified with paintings & guildings grave & commendable." Six miles distant was a new cruciform brick chapel, sixty by twenty-two feet and forty feet wide at the transept. More common at this period was the very small brick church of St. Thomas Parish and its thirty-foot-square wooden chapel with no pews.[56] As for the ministers' housing, Mr. Hunt of St. John's Parish claimed in 1728 to have the best rectory house in Carolina. Built of brick, it had two rooms on each of two floors, a garret, and a cellar. Mr. Guy of St. Andrews, on the other hand, had to be content with "a small boarded house," while clergymen in the most western parishes took lodging in private homes.[57]

Dignified Sabbath rituals apparently prevailed at St. Philip's in Charleston and perhaps at St. James, Goose Creek, both patronized by a few wealthy men. But a scene at St. Bartholomew's Parish in 1746 was more typical of many outlying regions. "The best people used there to go throng and fro' continualy out of chapel, [making] punch in time of sermon or Prayer [or bringing] water in the chapel to give drink to the people," even though the congregation in general seems to have disapproved. The newly arrived minister, Charles Boschi, was shocked to discover that all but a few of the local brides were pregnant before their wedding day. "I was oblige[d] sometimes to call for a chair to make the women to sit down in the time of Marriage because they were fainting away." Nor could Boschi discipline his people since their reluctance to elect him permanently made him "cautious [about] exclaim[ing] against iniquity."[58] On the far frontier, the Reverend Charles Woodmason claimed that after one service his auditors fell to "Revelling Drinking Singing Dancing and Whoring." He also commented on what must have been a significant deprivation of missionary life on the frontier: "How hard the Lot of any Gentleman in this Part of the World! . . . as for Society and Converse—I have not yet met with one literate, or travel'd Person—No ingenious Mind."[59]

Such were the sacrifices made by hundreds of Anglican clergymen in order to plant their church on American soil. Yet despite it all, their efforts bore fruit. From some seventy-five congregations in 1690—all but one (King's Chapel, Boston) located in the South—the number soared to more than three hundred by 1750, over a third of that growth occurring in the North. Another 150 congregations had been added by the time of the Revolution. The Bishop of Oxford, Thomas Secker, was so impressed in 1746 by the vitality of American Anglicanism compared with the "very discouraging" state of the English church that he wrote to Samuel Johnson of Connecticut: "[If God] hath determined our Fall, raise you up in our stead; that his Truth may still have some place of Refuge."[60]

The "clean Air" of New England: Congregational Clergymen

New England Congregationalism also entered a phase of consolidation and reform around the turn of the eighteenth century. Though we can no longer read the seventeenth-century history of Puritanism as a doleful tale of decline and apostasy, Congregational leaders faced a number of challenges by century's end. The original Massachusetts Bay charter was replaced in 1691 with a royal charter that not only gave political rights to non–church members but granted "liberty of Conscience . . . to all Christians (Except Papists)."[61] Religious diversification of the larger New England society was accompanied by the sharpening of theological differ-

ences within Congregationalism itself, especially over how strictly
to enforce the two levels of church membership defined by the
half-way covenant of 1662—that is, baptismal membership and full
communicant membership. The church's interest was so obviously
served by enlarging the baptismal covenant that few clergymen
opposed half-way membership, but controversy continued over how
wide the gateway to full communion should be. Increase and Cotton
Mather guarded the narrow way, giving ground slowly as support
for the principle of exclusivity declined. Solomon Stoddard in the
Connecticut Valley not only widened the gate in the 1670s but did
away with it altogether when he came to view communion itself as
a converting ordinance or avenue to grace. A third body of ministers
was drawn toward a more rational liberalism that appealed to
Boston's merchant community, leading in 1699 to the founding of
the Brattle Street Church, which rejected altogether the ideal of a
covenanted church. A few liberal ministers even began to consider
a rapprochement with Anglicanism, a propensity that by the 1720s
led a number of them—as well as some fifty of their brethren in
England—to return to the mother church.[62]

One consequence of these political and religious changes was the
heightened determination of some Congregational clergymen to
secure a more centralized ecclesiastical structure and to revitalize
church practices. Such reforms were designed to enhance clerical
professionalism and also public support for a strong defense of the
Congregational Way. The movement for consolidation lasted over
thirty years. Although its primary goal of ecclesiastical centralization was defeated in Massachusetts by that most basic of
Congregational impulses—the assertion of local autonomy—it met
with greater success in Connecticut. Moreover, the collateral effort
to keep the church at the center of New England culture by easing
some of its practices and broadening its community role was
strikingly successful.[63]

Periodic gatherings of Congregational ministers and church elders
had taken place in Massachusetts both before and after the adoption
of the half-way covenant, but the revocation of the old charter in 1684
gave new impetus to such conclaves. After 1690 regional associations

of ministers proliferated, while in the eighteenth century the clergy gathered annually in a convention timed to coincide with the meeting of the General Court. As clerical bonds tightened and the role of the laity in church government declined, the ruling elder, who had shared governing power with the minister, became a *"rara Avis . . . like a black swan in the Meadow."*[64] In 1705, consociation, as the movement for ministerial consolidation came to be called, reached a new pitch when delegates from five regional associations adopted a set of proposals aimed at strengthening clerical control over the churches. One proposal noted with concern the unsuitability of some candidates for the ministry and urged that ministers henceforth be screened by the associations before being recommended for vacancies. Another advised that the clerical associations examine charges and recommend action against wayward ministers. The most controversial suggestion urged that regional associations choose delegates to "a standing or stated Council" of clergy and lay leaders whose authority over the churches was to be "final and decisive" unless there existed "weighty Reasons to the contrary." Such proposals were indeed "very strong Presbyterian meat for Congregational palates."[65]

As early as 1700, Solomon Stoddard of Northampton had recommended the formation of a centralized church with regular councils and had organized the Hampshire Association to improve ecclesiastical discipline in his district. A number of eastern ministers also endorsed the plan for standing councils, though division persisted over whether such councils should have binding juridical power over individual churches. The strength of the opposition to consociation is hard to measure, but resistance came from several quarters including Simon Bradstreet of Charlestown and the Reverend John Wise of Ipswich.[66] Wise voiced his opposition in two pamphlets—*The Churches Quarrel Espoused* and *A Vindication of the Government of New-England Churches*—published during a later stage of the controversy. Both would become famous in pre-Revolutionary America owing to Wise's precocious use of natural law to defend local autonomy and his penchant for translating religious values into political principles. At the time of their writing, however, the pamphlets had an essentially conservative objective: to preserve for local churches the same power over their own affairs that they had held since the Cambridge Platform of 1648. Synods and councils simply went against the regional grain, Wise argued, since New Englanders did not like "to be Governed with a Hook in their Nose." "A Democracy in Church or State," he averred, "is a very honourable and regular Government according to the Dictates of Right Reason." Wise rejected as wrongheaded the proposal for church councils since it would "Distribute the Clergy into Inferiour and Superiour Degrees," and he opposed the suggestion that clerical associations be granted sole authority to license ministers. Wise's main point, however, was that power should not be shifted from individual ministers to synods or councils, for such an evasion of individual responsibility would be, in a word, unmanly—a mere "Covering of Figg-Leaves." "If men are plac'd at Helm, to steer in all weather that Blows, they must not be afraid of the Waves, or a wet Coat." The plan for centralized authority was "enough to strangle any Free-born Englishman," he concluded, "and much more these Churches, that have lived in such a clean Air . . . for so long a time."[67]

In the end the proposal for councils with strong central powers was defeated. The issue came to a head in 1725 when Cotton Mather and other ministers, alarmed at Anglican gains in New England and dissension in the Congregational churches, sought permission to hold a synod. But when authorities in England made plain their disapproval, observing that since no "regular Establishment of a National or Provincial Church" existed in Massachusetts a synod would be in "Contempt of His Majesty's Prerogative,"[68] the chance for passage was lost. Still, the consociation movement of the early eighteenth century hardly disappeared without a trace. Annual conventions of ministers (without binding powers) met more regularly from that time forward; a number of regional associations took on central administrative tasks; and some associations won the right to screen ministers before assignment to local congregations.[69] In Massachusetts, moreover, clergymen were not the sole guardians of the Congregational Way.

Provincial and local officeholders—the overwhelming majority of whom were Congregationalists—stubbornly resisted dissenter pressures for implementation of the religious toleration promised in the 1691 charter. Challenges to the established church erupted periodically in the eastern region where noncomformists were concentrated. In Plymouth and Barnstable dissenters balked at paying their rates to the Congregational churches, compelling the General Court to step in with direct appropriations for ministers' salaries and the repair of meetinghouses. County courts also moved to enforce tithing laws when Quakers and Baptists resisted them, more than once arresting and jailing assessors who were themselves dissenters and who refused to levy the church tax.[70] But lobbying in England by the S.P.G. and the London Yearly Meeting of Friends, as well as pressure from Massachusetts governors, gradually wore down the provincials' resistance. Anglicans finally obtained exemption from the tithe in 1727; a more comprehensive bill offered relief to nonconformists in 1731, and the Baptists gained specific exemption in 1734. Even so, Congregational stalwarts threw sand into the machinery of reform whenever they could. Anglicans eventually had to force a court test in 1735 to gain final exemption from church rates, and it was not until 1740 that all dissenters had this right fully guaranteed.[71]

Supporters of ecclesiastical consolidation did not gain all they aimed for in Massachusetts. Yet by the second quarter of the eighteenth century Congregationalism was on such solid footing that it would continue to enjoy a favored position in Massachusetts for the next hundred years.

The consociation movement that met resistance in the stony ground of Massachusetts found more congenial soil in Connecticut. Guerdon Saltonstall, elected governor of the colony in 1708, was himself a Congregational minister. Under his leadership the General Court on May 22, 1708, ordered the Congregational clergy to gather at Saybrook to set rules "for the management of ecclesiastical discipline." The meeting took place in September, producing the Saybrook Platform. In addition to reconfirming general principles of faith, the Platform instituted a presbyterial form of church government. Regional associations of ministers and elders were to meet at least twice a year; these groups in turn were to choose delegates for a General Association that was to meet annually; and locally consociations of ministers in each county were to form standing councils with power to ordain ministers and discipline church members.[72] The Saybrook Platform could not be imposed on local congregations, but in approving the "happy agreement" the General Court urged churches to regard its provisions with reverence. Moreover, pastors and members of churches that subscribed to the Platform could be held in "Scandalous Contempt" if they resisted the decisions of the councils. While some churches, especially those around New Haven, interpreted the articles on church discipline liberally, the Platform was generally regarded after 1708 as the constitution of Connecticut Congregationalism. Five associations and five consociations were formed at once, with others added as the colony grew.[73]

The adoption of the Saybrook Platform clarified lines of authority and so strengthened the establishment in Connecticut that it was long able to resist inroads by nonconformists. Critics of Congregational hegemony characterized Connecticut as "wholly Puritan and withal not a little bigoted and uncharitable."[74] True, the legislature passed a Toleration Act in 1708 and by 1729 had enacted laws exempting Anglicans, Quakers, and Baptists from Congregational church rates. But the magistrates construed these acts so narrowly—requiring resident ministers, public church structures, and a full and active congregation to qualify—that few dissenting congregations could obtain certificates of exemption. So potent was the combined power of church and state in the colony that by 1730 officials had recognized but one Baptist congregation, one Anglican church, and no Quaker meetings.[75] The real growth of religious liberty in Connecticut would have to await the Congregational churches' internal division into New and Old Lights after 1740.

How did these ecclesiastical reforms, as well as shifting social and political currents, affect the professional lives of the Congregational clergy? Though the eighteenth-century ministers remained "faithful shepherds" with strong ties to the Puritan past, they now served a relatively stable society whose religious beliefs were increasingly intertwined with secular and rationalist values. Since Congregationalism generally kept pace with population growth, the established religion was apparently in no immediate danger. But the clergy, ever wary of complacency, were prepared to reform church practices and broaden pastoral activity in ways that would command the continuing allegiance of New Englanders to the Congregational Way.

Congregational church rituals had in many places grown rather forbidding by the late seventeenth century. Sermons frequently lasted almost two hours, psalm singing had lost much of its earlier vigor, and some ministers' exhortations against sin were as likely to put the congregation to sleep as to promote piety.[76] By the early eighteenth century, however, revitalization was under way. Congregations still met twice each Sabbath, with the first service in the morning and another complete service commencing in the afternoon. But meetings were now moved closer together so that parishioners living at a distance could get home before dark. Second and third churches also were being built in many towns during these years to accommodate the expanding population.[77] That churchgoers were not deterred from worship by the icy draughts of winter, felt inside as well as outside the church, is itself mute testimony to their piety. Samuel Sewall tells of one Sunday when it was "so cold that the Sacramental Bread is frozen pretty hard and rattles sadly as broken into the Plates"; at other times the water in the baptismal bowl was known to freeze. Such discomforts were eased slightly by portable foot stoves, but only when Sabbath Day or "Nooning" houses were built in the eighteenth century was relief from the unheated meetinghouse assured. These rough structures contained large stone fireplaces around which families would gather to partake of the meal they had brought from home. Though conscientious pastors tried to make the noon period "serviceable to the Interests of Hol[i]ness," in New England as elsewhere churchgoing had a social dimension, as parents discussed the news of the day and children and youths gave vent to high spirits.[78]

Inside the meetinghouse, men and women often sat together in
pews rather than in the separate sections of earlier times. The
minister opened the service with a prayer and a reading from
Scripture, after which a psalm was sung, though without musical
accompaniment. Attitudes toward musical instruments were changing, however, as hinted in Thomas Brattle's 1713 bequest of an
organ to the Brattle Street Church, an offer eventually refused on
the ground that such an instrument was not mentioned in the Bible.
(Having no such compunctions, the Anglicans of King's Chapel
gladly accepted Brattle's gift later that year.[79]) Psalm singing itself
had sunk to low estate by the late seventeenth century, owing to
"some Indecencies, that by length of Time had begun to grow upon
it." Church deacons were originally responsible for "lining out" the
psalms, or singing out a line which would be returned by the
congregation. But as the original inhabitants died off and psalm
books decayed or were lost, the deacons had settled for a few simple
tunes on which the congregation improvised as the spirit moved
them. The result was an anarchy of song. Individuals adopted their
own tempo and key, leaving every "unskilful throat to chop and
alter, twist and change, according to their infinitely divers . . .
Humors and Fancies." Even Increase Mather allowed that it all
made for an "Odd Noise." The great "singing controversy" began in
1715 when a new psalm book was published with instructions on
how to sing both in unison and on pitch. Many conservatives
resisted the reform, especially the deacons who apparently feared a
loss of authority. But a decade later Cotton Mather could report that
at least a score of tunes were then in use and psalm singing had been
"Reformed, and Refined."[80]

The centerpiece of every worship service was the sermon. In
what amounted to a major reform, the length of sermons had been
reduced to about an hour by the second quarter of the eighteenth
century. And whereas sermons had been delivered from memory in
earlier decades, now preaching from notes was becoming fashionable. New Englanders continued to disdain what Cotton Mather
called "Sudden Sermons"—that is, those not carefully designed and
thought out beforehand—but reading from a full text was frowned

upon. To be sure, written sermons might be more coherent, but as Mather noted, it would require "good Management if they be not the less Affecting."[81] Solomon Stoddard pungently criticized ministers who affected "rhetorical strains of Speech [as if] making an oration in the Schools." "We are not sent into the Pulpit to show our Wit and Eloquence," he declared; "if ministers design to Convert Men, they had need speak peircing words." Not all preachers were as accomplished as Stoddard and Mather, who regularly attracted large congregations. But the once prevalent notion that preaching had grown cold and ineffective in the pre-Awakening years is not supported by contemporary evidence.[82]

Ministers of the early eighteenth century shaped sermons to appeal both to the minds and hearts of their flock. The message was intended to be readily understood and to accord with experience and reason. Frequently sermons were directed toward specific constituencies in the congregation such as women, youths, or servants. At other times they took as themes specific seasonal or current events such as the harvest, epidemics, or war. Preaching was expected to be learned but not ostentatious; neither flowery nor bombastic, but warm enough to stir emotions. Sermons followed a familiar and beloved formula: text, explication of doctrine and proofs from Scripture, and finally application.[83] New Englanders liked nothing better than a vigorous sermon, and they attended upon them in numbers that astounded visitors from less pious societies.

Nor was churchgoing restricted to Sundays, since fast-day services, lectures, catechism classes, and meetings of youth groups and women's societies were held regularly during the week. The eighteenth century, unlike the seventeenth, also saw the solemnity of church life relieved by such social occasions as weddings and funerals. The first wedding performed by a clergyman in Massachusetts took place in 1686; by the early eighteenth century church records contain long lists of marriages presided over by the clergy. Funerals also changed from simple burial rites in which no clergyman participated to elaborate ceremonies involving eulogistic sermons, pallbearers, and a funeral train.[84] In addition to bringing such rites into the church, ministers continued to take the church to the people through election and artillery sermons. All such ecclesiastical and ceremonial occasions were symptomatic of the newly sophisticated ways in which the Congregational establishment was seeking to consolidate its hold over as many aspects of community life as possible.

The Congregationalists enjoyed at least one significant advantage over other denominations: after the first few years, they experienced no shortage of ministers. The early founding of Harvard College assured a steady supply of qualified men, whereas local ordination facilitated their prompt entry into the profession. During the first half of the eighteenth century, the number of ministers graduating from Harvard and Yale kept close pace with the rising number of churches.[85] Since ministers usually served a single congregation, and parishes were small, long itinerations were not a feature of the clergyman's life in eighteenth-century New England, except on the frontier.[86] About ninety-five percent of eighteenth-century Congregational ministers had college degrees and most went on to earn the M.A. Moreover, the level of educational attainment rose between 1700 and 1740, very likely reflecting the clergy's growing professionalism.[87]

Some 987 men trained for the ministry at Harvard and Yale between 1691 and 1760. From 1691 to 1730, over half the graduates from those colleges chose careers in the church; between 1730 and 1760 the proportion dropped to about a third, while the number turning to careers in medicine and law mounted. Even in the later decades, however, graduates entering the ministry outnumbered by more than three to one those choosing careers either as doctors or lawyers.[88] The decreasing proportion may have been somewhat influenced by growing opportunities in business and law; potential ministers seem also to have been deterred by certain problems new to the clergy in the eighteenth century. One was a rising rate of inflation over the first half of the century that lowered ministers' real income by as much as fifty percent. Caught between their dedication to austerity and the need to support their families, the Congregational clergy in the 1720s entered a period of protracted debate with local authorities over the provision of a decent maintenance. Though parsimonious laymen rarely went so far before the Great Awakening as to accuse their ministers of merely seeking "Filthy Lucre," salary squabbles were sufficiently widespread to discourage some young men from contemplating careers in the church.[89]

Another difficulty was that most ministers preferred to locate in eastern New England where the more distinguished pulpits were situated, and where population was denser and salaries higher. Those pulpits, however, were filled by such as Samuel Willard, Benjamin Colman, and the Mathers, whereas openings were most likely to occur in newly settled areas. The age and long tenure of many leading clergymen—Increase Mather and Solomon Stoddard, for example, were both in their seventies by the second decade of the eighteenth century—also limited opportunities for newly ordained men. John Wise made an eloquent plea in 1713 for the place of young men in the ministry. "Every Bird which is pretty well fleg'd must begin to fly," he admonished. Unlike Icarus, "whose Feathers were only glewed on," the abilities of New England youths grew out of their very essence; thus they should be allowed, "with the Lark, now & then to dart Heaven-ward, tho' the shell or down be scarce off their heads."[90]

Whatever the difficulties facing Congregational ministers in the first half of the eighteenth century, these were in the larger sense incidents of professional growth rather than stultification and decline. The ministry continued to attract a solid proportion of the very best college graduates from the same middle- and upper-class families that had always supplied sons to the church. The strength of professional standards is suggested by a study showing that only 3 percent of the four hundred Congregational clergymen active between 1680 and 1740 ever were involved in scandalous episodes. Wrangling over salaries was more vexatious, though many ministers simply kept on doing what they had done all along to make ends meet—farming their own land and taking part of their pay in produce and firewood.[91] Such activities kept them close to their parishioners, as did their endless rounds of catechization, pastoral counseling, visits to the sick, and part-time doctoring and lawyering in areas where professionals were few.[92] The often indispensable part that ministers played in both the secular and spiritual lives of their parishioners seems to have counterbalanced any threatened loss of clerical prestige in the more materialistic eighteenth century.

The clergy's success in accommodating to change and consolidating its position can be measured by the proliferation of Congregational churches. Starting from about 140 churches in New England in 1700, the number more than doubled by 1730, then exceeded 450 by mid-century, an increase that kept pace with population growth. Thus, despite the clergy's fears that the people might "grow weary of their Church-State,"[93] Congregationalism continued in the eighteenth century to hold its place at the heart of New England culture.

Diversity and Renewal: The German Church Clergy

The experiences of a third group, the German Reformed and Lutheran ministers in the Middle Colonies, contrast sharply with those of the southern Anglican and New England Congregational clergy. The Old World clergymen who slowly made their way to the mid-Atlantic region in the eighteenth century found in place of an established church a rich diversity of sects and denominations. If this pluralism was initially unsettling to European sensibilities, far more disturbing was the chronic shortage of ministers, the near-absence of ecclesiastical structures, and the voluntary character of all religious worship. In the face of these seeming handicaps, however, the middle-colony churches made rapid strides over the eighteenth century. All of which raises questions about the conventional interpretation of religious experience in the Middle Colonies.

Religious diversity, according to the standard view, had a pernicious effect on church life in the eighteenth-century Middle Colonies. The sheer variety of sects and denominations competing for adherents, it is claimed, so befuddled the minds of the people that many lay men and women could not decide which to follow. As provincials drifted aimlessly from one denomination to another or turned their backs on all churches, the Middle Colonies supposedly became a region characterized by "religious indifference." Such confusion and drift are thought to have been especially pronounced among immigrant German churchpeople in the 1720s and 1730s, when a shortage of Lutheran and German Reformed ministers left the newcomers almost defenseless against the competing inducements of Anabaptists, Quakers, and other sects. The few ordained clergymen in the region struggled to preserve traditional religion and to assert moral discipline over incoming churchpeople, but with no ecclesiastical structure or state authority to reinforce them, and with their meager salaries dependent on voluntary contributions, ministers were supposedly at the mercy of the people. Only the Great Awakening, according to this view, saved the German churches from imminent collapse.[94]

The evidence does have a certain persuasiveness, inasmuch as both ministers and laymen at the time regularly criticized the condition of the churches. Yet such "evidence" looks different when examined closely within the conventions of eighteenth-century religious discourse, for early religious rhetoric was heavily weighted with sectarian bias and shaped by hidden animosities.[95] Though religious diversity no doubt perplexed many middle-colony inhabitants, very few responded so uncharacteristically for their time as simply to reject all religion. Some adopted a latitudinarian outlook that allowed them to attend whatever house of worship happened to be located in their neighborhood. But many others responded to diversity with a positively sharpened religious self-awareness and an enhanced attachment to the doctrinal uniqueness of their own denomination. Though this second response has not received much attention, there is strong reason to conclude that the devotion of many provincials to their formal, Old World churches, and the competitive impulse this loyalty engendered, fostered a definite surge of congregation building. This less familiar side of middle-colony religious life becomes strikingly evident in the beginnings of the Lutheran and German Reformed churches in the early eighteenth century.

Germans who emigrated to America by the thousands from about the 1720s onward were predominantly churchpeople—that is, Lutherans and German Reformed. Because very few ministers accompanied the early waves of settlers, the German churches usually began as spontaneously gathered congregations. After the stresses of uprooting, transporting, and resettling themselves, these newcomers—like others before and after them—sought the security of familiar ways. The church, offering spiritual succor and cultural reinforcement, became a primary means of reconstituting immigrant communities in the New World. As early as 1710, a number of Dutch and German Reformed laypeople at White Marsh, Pennsylvania "encouraged each other to hold religious services on each Lord's Day, etc., according to the doctrine and Church Order of the Reformed Church, as far as it was known to them."[96] Another group formed similarly at Germantown in 1719. Gathering first in houses, the worshipers read sermons, prayed, and sang together. Having no pastor to administer baptism and communion, they occasionally resorted to neighboring Presbyterian ministers for the sacraments. But by and large such ecumenicism was resisted, since the aim of these congregations was, in the words of an early leader, "without delay to set up a pure religious worship and to maintain it by every agency possible."[97]

A primary stimulus for congregation building was the churchpeople's wish to protect themselves against what they called the "allurements . . . and contamination" of the sects. In this contest the Lutherans and Reformed were at a competitive disadvantage owing to their dependence on an educated, professional clergy. The sects drew their leaders from the laity, which enabled them to create congregations at will and to hold services more regularly. And indeed, some churchpeople did go over to the Dunkers, Seventh-Day Baptists, Mennonites, or Quakers, in order, as one convert explained, to prevent their children from "grow[ing] up like wild sheep," and in view of their urge to "seek pasture and food for their souls wherever they can find it." Most Germans, however, remained "watchful against the sects" by fortifying in various ways their own doctrinal and liturgical identity as Lutherans and German Reformed.[98]

Bereft of ordained clergymen, the early congregations formed voluntarily around schoolmasters and pious laymen. A number of Germans in the Perkiomen Valley appealed in 1720 to a newly arrived schoolmaster, John Philip Boehm, to serve as reader at their Reformed devotions. Still without a minister in 1725, the settlers implored Boehm to continue in that office, promising to support him to the best of their ability with voluntary contributions. Not an ordained clergyman, Boehm at first declined. But when the people "pressed upon my conscience whether . . . I should leave them thus without help" among the ravenous sects, Boehm consented to take on the expanded role being urged upon him. Dividing the settlers into three groups, he drew up a constitution subscribed to by each, after which the congregations thus formed issued individual calls for Boehm's services.[99] He rode a circuit of over sixty miles in ministering to the three churches in his immediate charge, sharing authority with the founding elders and deacons in each congregation.

Other Reformed congregations were coalescing similarly in the Conestoga Valley under the leadership of a pious tailor and lay reader from Heidelberg named John Conrad Tempelman. There, as elsewhere, each congregation elected elders who "exercised a strict and careful supervision" over the members. Though the faithful initially "gathered in houses here and there," before long they were raising log churches throughout the region. Pennsylvania would see no ordained Reformed minister until 1727, but the voluntary gathering of congregations in the preceding decade confirms that these people in substantial numbers would rather "be edified by an unordained teacher than remain entirely desolate of spiritual nourishment."[100]

Over two thousand Palatine Germans emigrated to New York in 1710 to work in Governor Robert Hunter's naval stores program. Accompanied by two clergymen, the Palatines' religious needs were met at least partially as long as they lived together in concentrated settlements. One minister reported that he had at Germantown "70 men and 69 women communicants." But when the naval stores scheme failed in 1712, the Palatines dispersed throughout the upper

Hudson, Mohawk, and Schoharie Valleys.[101] John Frederick Hager,
the Reformed minister, and his successor, John Jacob Oehl, strove
mightily to serve their now scattered congregations. But inevitably,
in New York as in Pennsylvania, the early Reformed church relied
heavily on lay readers and whatever tracts or prayer books could be
sent from home.[102]

The history of the Lutheran Church in the Middle Colonies
began as early as 1649 when a group of laymen, including Germans,
Scandinavians, and Frisians brought to New Netherland by the
Dutch West India Company, organized the first congregation.
Persecuted by Peter Stuyvesant, and then attended intermittently
by pastors from 1669 onward, the few congregations in New York by
the end of the seventeenth century depended heavily on the
leadership of devout lay elders. In 1703 Justus Falckner initiated his
ministry to the middle-colony Lutherans, and was joined in 1710 by
the Reverend Joshua Kocherthal, pastor to the Palatine Lutherans.
By now there were some fourteen congregations stretching from
Albany to the Raritan Valley of New Jersey, all falling to Falckner's
charge when Kocherthal died in 1719. The Reverend William
Berkenmeyer, sent over by the Amsterdam Consistory in 1725,
spent the next twenty-six years organizing the New York and New
Jersey churches into a kind of presbyterial system. Control over
local finances and congregational affairs remained in the hands of
deacons and overseers, however, as did much of the work of
organizing and collecting the pastor's salary. With congregations
scattered over hundreds of miles and ministers few, Lutherans in
the region had no choice during the first century of church life but
to place much of their spiritual welfare in the hands of laymen.[103]

As the swelling tide of Germans turned toward Pennsylvania in
the 1720s, Lutherans once again confronted a leadership crisis, the
congregation at Tulpehocken's being a typical history. The band of
largely Lutheran Palatines that moved from New York to settle on
Tulpehocken Creek in 1723 was without a minister for several years.
Intensely religious, the Palatines held services in their houses or in
a fort built for protection against the Indians, receiving occasional
visits from itinerant Lutheran and German Reformed preachers. In

1727 all able-bodied members of the community—young and old, men and women—built a church and a schoolhouse of hewn logs and rough boards. Because the people were poor, support for the church was "gathered in pennies, so that one contributed to it six pence, another eight pence, and another a shilling." A Lutheran schoolmaster arrived from Germany that same year, and in addition to operating a school for the congregation he probably served as lay reader on the Sabbath. The congregation, according to a contemporary account, "gathered themselves on a Sunday under a *Vorleser* out of their own midst, until they at times called a minister who distributed the Lord's Supper to them."[104]

These early congregations often went for years without a resident pastor. Yet so eager were the provincials to hear sermons and to partake of church sacraments that any self-proclaimed preacher who came within range might be called into service. With no Lutheran or Reformed synods to authenticate ordination papers or regulate the acceptance of calls, false claims and forged documents were a commonplace. (Actually this was a problem that beset all professions in the colonies.) Thus a number of notorious charlatans wandered through the colonies preaching sermons patched together out of books and offering communion "for cash in hand." One such mountebank, touting himself as the Prince of Württemberg turned Lutheran preacher, was driven out of Georgia only to turn up in Pennsylvania, where he was reported roving "about the whole country, whoring, stealing, gluttonizing, and swilling."[105] The eighteen-year-old boy preacher Henry Goetschi administered communion and performed marriages for several congregations. A number of German schoolmasters and tailors also passed themselves off as preachers. Such versatility could arouse suspicion, as when one vagabond wandered into a German settlement claiming to be a minister but let it be known that in a pinch he could also serve as a bloodletter or dentist.[106] These stories are sometimes used to show the disarray of middle-colony religious life or the low caliber of the colonial "clergy." But they show other things as well: the settlers' craving for religious leadership and denominational legitimacy, at almost any price, in that highly competitive environment.

One consequence of this early religious instability was that pious and strong-minded lay elders became the focus of continuity and leadership in the middle-colony Lutheran and Reformed churches. When ordained clergymen finally began arriving in numbers in the second quarter of the eighteenth century, they often had trouble wresting control from lay leaders. Most congregations were understandably reluctant to deliver themselves over to untested preachers, at least not without a conclusive trial period. Those few churches already fortunate enough to have found devout and Godly preachers—ordained or not—resisted all efforts by newcomers to dislodge them. One such case was that of the aforementioned John Philip Boehm. Boehm had been a Reformed schoolmaster in Lambsheim, Germany, before coming to Pennsylvania in 1720. A man of blamless conduct, and more knowledgeable about Reformed doctrine and liturgy than any of his neighbors, Boehm had been the obvious choice to lead the Perkiomen congregations. But when the first ordained minister reached the valley in 1727, he denounced Boehm as an incompetent preacher unfit to administer the sacraments, and attempted to displace him in the three congregations. Boehm's followers balked, and then sent him to the Dutch Reformed ministers in New York armed with a petition praying that he be ordained. Pointing out that since the Germans lived among all sort of "errorists," the petitioners had the choice either of abandoning themselves to "the constant attacks of ravening wolves in sheep's clothing" or of turning to Boehm, "who was known among us as a man of more than ordinary knowledge in the sound doctrine of truth, of praiseworthy life and of exemplary zeal." After lengthy correspondence with the classis in Amsterdam, the New York ministers took an unprecedented step. They ordained Boehm to the Reformed ministry.[107]

A similar elevation was realized by the tailor, John Bernhard Van Dieren, a native of Königsberg who became a Lutheran deacon in New York. Van Dieren had a pious nature, though no formal theological training, when he took up schoolteaching in his spare time and acquired the ambition to become a preacher. Referring vaguely to a prior ordination, he began in the 1720s to preach with considerable success throughout parts of Pennsylvania, New Jersey, and New York. The incoming professional clergy scorned Van Dieren as a "preaching vagabond," but he was vigorously defended by his congregations, which he continued to serve throughout an apparently irreproachable life. In later years the Lutheran leader Henry Muhlenberg, who had a shrewder appreciation of Van Dieren's ministry than did most of his brethren, enumerated the principal factors in its success: "the man's awakened condition, his edifying speech . . . the lack of preachers, the free American air, and the man's inner desire and aspiration."[108]

Muhlenberg had himself learned first hand about the "free American air" in 1742, when he arrived in Pennsylvania to find pretenders occupying each of the three pulpits to which he had been assigned by the consistory in Germany. The most irritating intruder was an old Lutheran preacher, Valentin Kraft, who had been dismissed from his church in Germany but claimed that at any moment letters would arrive from Darmstadt authorizing his call to Pennsylvania. When Muhlenberg appeared with his letters testimonial, one congregation responded wearily that "they had already been taken in so often, and who knew whether I had not written the letters myself?" The elders could not force the congregation to accept a preacher since, as Muhlenberg put it, "everything depends on the vote of the majority"; nor would "the government . . . concern itself with such matters." Lacking any coercive sanctions, the newcomer saw that "a preacher must fight his way through with the sword of the Spirit alone." Muhlenberg proved up to the challenge. Making no attempt to oust Kraft forcibly, he took turns with him preaching to the congregations, meanwhile engaging the elders in quiet discussion. The coarse and cantankerous Kraft made a bad showing against Muhlenberg's superior learning and dignity. But not all at once. It took Henry Muhlenberg more than six weeks to get possession of his Pennsylvania pulpits.[109]

Establishing the validity of his call was only the minister's first step toward gaining authority. Since many congregations had been operating for years under fairly open and democratic forms, their sense of collective proprietorship over church affairs constituted a formidable barrier to any clerical gestures toward control. Pastors had to strike a delicate balance between their sacerdotal responsibilities and the opinions of a congregation upon whose affections and financial support they were dependent. The clergyman's mettle was most severely tested when he attempted to discipline parishioners for moral offenses. Henry Muhlenberg once barely escaped a caning when he spoke privately to a member about his wife's unchaste life. "If we come too close to their consciences," he observed, "they let loose and cry out, 'What right has the parson over me?'" Disgruntled members sometimes refused to contribute to the minister's salary. If denied communion, they threatened to go over to the sects.[110]

Nor did the sects let pass any opportunity to defame the church clergy. They accused the ministers of materialism for insisting on fixed salaries and seized with glee on any lapse in clerical behavior. Thus the Reverend Michael Schlatter, the German Reformed pioneer, thought his mother church would best be advised to send only young men "inured to toil [and of] correct deportment," who were capable of "long suffering and sympathy toward those who oppose them . . . that they may win such and bring them into the right way."[111]

Some clergymen simply could not adjust to these rude conditions. One such was the Lutheran minister Tobias Wagner, an irascible man and a stiff, unpopular preacher. Wagner had been seeking a permanent post for a year when he was sent to the church at Tulpehocken. Angered by the congregation's refusal to offer him more than one year's tenure, but unable to do better elsewhere, Wagner finally returned to Germany in disgust. As Henry Muhlenberg observed, Wagner "had no insight into the circumstances of Pennsylvania. He imagined that one could bend and force the people here . . . as in Germany with the secular or consistorial arm of the law. But . . . experience proves something different."[112]

Against such a background, what generalizations can be drawn about the character of religious life in the Middle Colonies during the first half of the eighteenth century? That it was diverse, competitive, and volatile is beyond question. No established church dominated the landscape in New York, New Jersey, and Pennsylvania, as in New England and the South. The result was a kind of free market for theistic beliefs and practices that reflected almost every color in the spectrum of western Christendom. Many orthodox ministers from the Old World churches found such diversity confusing; some felt mightily afflicted in this "soul destroying whirlpool of apostasy," as one of them called it. But such rhetoric obscures the ways in which diversity and competition may have affected the actual development of religious life and institutions.[113]

This is a subject about which numbers may tell us more than words, since the incidence of formed congregations is the best single measure we have of that most elusive phenomenon, religious commitment. The Middle Colonies had more congregations per capita than either New England or the South by the middle of the eighteenth century.[114] Moreover, the Great Awakening was not responsible for this surge, since it started in the two or three decades preceding the revival when Germans and Ulster Scots began entering the region in considerable numbers. And there is testimony that some provincials recognized the contribution made to church vitality by religious liberty and competition. Lewis Morris, among other New York Anglicans, noted how much faster his church grew in Pennsylvania and New Jersey, where people freely joined the communion of their choice "upon Principle." William Smith, Jr. linked the religious diversity of New York with the thriving condition of its churches at mid-century. Thomas Jefferson observed in 1781 that "difference of opinion is advantageous in religion." Pointing to the then regularized competition among denominations in Pennsylvania and New York, he noted with approval that "they flourish infinitely."[115] These and similar comments suggest that vigorous religious competition in the Middle Colonies stimulated rather than discouraged church growth. Religious chauvinism may have been especially pronounced among the German immigrants, reflecting their sense of isolation and disorientation in an English culture. But, for whatever reason, most Germans remained within the Lutheran and Reformed denominations, fostering their rapid expansion from the early decades of the eighteenth century onward.[116]

Another factor shaping German church life was the short supply of ministers, which shifted responsibility for religious leadership to the laity. With the initial gathering of congregations, building of churches, and conducting of services being largely in the hands of devoted laymen, the German churches very early took on some of the characteristics of voluntary associations. Voluntarism is a rich theme in American life, especially in the nineteenth century, but it was in the religious life of the eighteenth century that groups formed from below through voluntary association first emerged as significant instruments for change. True, such groups could be unruly and factious; they were subject to manipulation; and, as we have seen with the German congregations, they could sometimes be worked upon by charlatans. But voluntary associations by their very nature have a way of reflecting popular attitudes and aspirations more accurately than do institutions whose order has been imposed upon them by inheritance and customary acquiescence. Thus voluntary associations frequently achieve a kind of stability— despite surface appearances—that makes them real centers of influence.[117] That the German congregations sustained themselves for years without permanent clergymen or ecclesiastical apparatus testifies to an inner strength possibly lacking in some of the more structured established churches.

For the German churchpeople, to be sure, voluntarism was not an end in itself. The element that most clearly distinguished their churches from the sects was the office of minister, and the Lutheran and Reformed congregations—even as they found remarkable resources in themselves while making do—constantly sent emissaries to Germany pleading for qualified clergymen. When ordained ministers at last arrived in substantial numbers in the 1740s and 1750s, they were welcomed, after some initial testing, not only for their priestly authority but because they enhanced the churches' distinctive identity in a pluralistic society. Nevertheless, the early history of voluntarism was not easily overcome. The elders' insistence on hiring ministers for limited terms was one effective means

Inside the old Evangelical Lutheran Church, York, Pennsylvania. Sketched by the Pennsylvania folk artist Lewis Miller in 1800. The church was built about 1760 and measured sixty-seven by forty feet. Note the sexton chasing a dog, the wall paintings of Martin Luther and the Apostles, the children seated by the pulpit railing, and the men's choir in the gallery.

The Historical Society of York County, Pennsylvania.

of preserving some control over them; another was the laity's desire for close involvement in every aspect of church affairs.

Some ministers, as we have seen, would not compromise what

they saw as professional standards, and returned to Germany. But the majority stayed on, discovering perhaps that the ultimate test of a minister's power was his ability to gain and hold a voluntary following. For as Henry Muhlenberg observed: "It means something more here in this land . . . than it does in Germany, for a person to adhere to the church . . . People here cannot be attracted to services by honor, respectability, material advantages, gain, expensively decorated church buildings, and high and manifold gifts or offices."[118]

A new kind of religious institution emerged from this formative era of German church founding. Both the Lutheran and Reformed denominations, after a difficult beginning in which much energy was expended resisting the encroachments of the sects, had by 1750 achieved an extraordinary growth. Lay leaders gradually gave way as ordained ministers arrived in America,[119] but lay involvement would continue strong throughout the colonial era. Moreover the German churches, owing to their voluntary character and broad base, had acquired a new and unanticipated aid to both vitality and stability. That religion had flourished in the diverse society of the Middle Colonies through the voluntary participation of its inhabitants may have fortified Americans of the Revolutionary generation as they embarked on a still newer experiment that rested heavily on the uncoerced virtue of its citizens.

At the end of the seventeenth century, the metaphor most commonly used to portray religious conditions in the middle and southern colonies was that of scattered sheep without a shepherd. An early governor of North Carolina feared that if help did not arrive soon, "the very footsteps of religion will, in a short time, be worne out."[120] Shepherds were more numerous in Congregational New England of course, yet even there church leaders sought a more stable footing for the Congregational Way as a hedge against complacency in changing times. By the mid-eighteenth century conditions had distinctly improved. Ministers were visibly present in every section except the far frontier, and ecclesiastical consolidation was well under way in all denominations. Churches were being built or enlarged everywhere, as one of the basic institutions of a stabilizing society took its place in the hierarchy of power. There is little in this changed landscape that accords with the notion of declension. Nor did the churches fail to attract a wide following among the people of provincial America.

CHAPTER 4

The Churchgoers

Churchgoing, which was strong in most parts of provincial America, must be seen as one gauge of religious feeling and belief. In the colonial era, however, churchgoing was subject to a number of variables, such as community cohesion, family tradition, geography, and various others already referred to. Such variables were in turn affected by the kinds and classes of people involved; whether male or female, young or old, rich or poor. Thus a closer look at who went to church in colonial America may be of some help in discovering why they did so.

A Word about Numbers

Recent estimates suggest that a majority of adults in the eighteenth-century colonies were regular church attenders. Though the worship of God was no doubt the primary motive for churchgoing, eighteenth-century worshipers, like those of today, found that church attendance served a number of non-spiritual needs. The quest for community, long recognized as an incentive for churchgoing, must have operated with particular force among inhabitants of the dispersed farming society of early America. Churches in both country and town were vital centers of community life, as government proclamations were broadcast from the pulpit and news of prices and politics was exchanged in the churchyard. In a society formed from the uprooted communities of the Old World, moreover, the church congregation served as a primary agency by which immigrants recovered something of what they had left behind.[1] Family tradition was another strong stimulus to churchgoing. Pious colonial parents promoted the religious education of their children and instilled in them habits of regular church attendance. In some congregations the founding elders and their offspring gained such firm control over the church that newcomers or persons not descended from "Godly parents" were made to feel unwelcome. Such "tribalism" apparently characterized the early Puritan churches, and a similar turning inward has been detected among the Quakers of Pennsylvania.[2]

Inhabitants living on the geographic periphery of colonial parishes found their churchgoing practices being shaped by circumstances over which they had little control. As towns expanded, owing to natural increase and in-migration, a rising proportion of the outlivers lost touch with the central church. Distance and bad weather made travel to Sabbath services so hazardous that outlying hamlets frequently were granted "winter privileges," or the right to conduct their own services under lay direction. As peripheral districts gained population additional parishes were formed, and soon the former outlivers emerged as pillars of newly gathered churches.[3]

The factors just noted also were significant determinants of the degree of church adherence, that is, of whether individuals became communicants, half-way members, regular attenders, pew holders, irregular attenders, or in a very few cases "scoffers."[4] In all eighteenth-century churches a minority of the adherents were communicants. Self-imposed scrupulosity accounts for some of this, especially in the Congregational churches, where admission standards remained high, and the Anglican church, where the absence of an American bishop meant that only those confirmed in England were canonically qualified to take communion. The Anglican rector at Lancaster, Pennsylvania, thus reported that "the dreadful Apprehension which some People conceive about *receiving unworthily,* frighten many a religious well-meaning Person from the Lord's Table." Farther south, Devereux Jarratt found that many Virginians considered communion "a dangerous thing to meddle with."[5] Since all groups but the Congregationalists suffered a shortage of both ministers and catechists, the preparation of colonists for communicant membership was never easy in America. Another deterrent was that churchgoers bereft of a minister for their own denomination often attended some other nearby church, where they would have been less likely to join as formal communicants.

The conventional ratio of one communicant for every three or four non-communicating church attenders is probably too low for most colonial churches, at least until the late eighteenth century.[6] However that may be, many non-communicants participated vigorously in church life, serving as deacons or vestrymen and supporting their churches financially through the purchase of pews and contributions to the minister's salary.[7] This probably explains why most ministers habitually referred to churchgoers interchangeably as *parishioners, members, auditors,* and *adherents.* In any case, we cannot restrict our consideration of "churched" Americans to communicants alone, since this not only contradicts eighteenth-century usage but excludes from consideration the majority of colonial churchgoers.

The clergymen have left a good deal of information about local churchgoing practice, the best of it for many denominations coming from the S.P.G. correspondence. In describing the religious complexion of their territory, the missionaries had little difficulty identifying most inhabitants with a specific denomination or sect. One writes that of several hundred white people inhabiting a North Carolina parish in 1710, only "five or six [were] of no professed religion"; among 1750 whites in Sussex County, Pennsylvania, a minister reported that 1075 were Anglicans, 600 Presbyterians, and 75 Quakers. An early eighteenth-century notice from the rector of St. Philip's, Charleston, provides typical details: the parish con-

tained 150 white families, or "300 Souls (besides young children)."
Of the 300 adults, 80 professed the Church of England whereas the
remaining 220 were "Dissenters of all Sorts"—including 150 Pres-
byterians, 8 Independents [Congregationalists], 40 Anabaptists, 10
Quakers, and "above 12" he could not assign. Yet these last were not
"Infidels because they say they believe in Christ . . . [though they]
Deny the necessity of ordinances, & Publick worship."[8]

New England was universally regarded as the best churched
section. Visitors marveled at the regularity of religious practice in a
land where "every five Miles, or perhaps less, you have a Meeting-
House." Boston, a city of 15,000 inhabitants, had eighteen churches
by 1750—ten of them representing the Congregational establishment. Large church buildings were needed to accommodate city
congregations that ranged up to 1500 persons and more by mid-
century. Indeed, as early as the 1720s Cotton Mather of Second
Church scorned a congregation of a thousand as "Thinner . . . than
Ordinary."[9]

Middle-colony church life, though reflecting the rapid changes
overtaking that section in the eighteenth century, was anything but
moribund. New York, New Jersey, Pennsylvania, and Delaware
were collectively subject to a 530-percent white population growth
between 1710 and 1760 (nearly double the rate in either New
England or the South), which added disproportionately large communities of Germans and Scots to the initial Swedish, Dutch, and
English populations. Churches, like other middle-colony institutions, experienced strain as new congregations and sects proliferated in the hothouse environment generated by the fierce competition for adherents. By 1750, the middle region had more
congregations per capita than any other section, though with the
shortage of clergymen many of them were served by itinerant
preachers.[10] Philadelphia had twenty principal churches by the
1760s, and New York City eighteen. Churches were often the
largest public buildings in eighteenth-century cities, though none
could match New York's magnificent Trinity Church. After its
enlargement in 1737, Trinity measured "about 148 feet long,
including the tower and chancel, and 72 feet in breadth." Nor by the

Wineglass pulpit, St. Peter's Church, Philadelphia. Erected 1761
From *Old Philadelphia Houses* © 1966 by Elizabeth McCall. Courtesy Architectural Book Publishing Company.

later years were such churches confined to the cities. The beautiful Dutch Reformed church at Claverack, New York, built in 1767, could accommodate over a thousand worshipers, as could a number of Quaker meetinghouses in Pennsylvania.[11]

The Anglican church in the Chesapeake was settled on a sufficiently solid foundation by 1701 that the newly organized S.P.G. could direct its resources to the needier Carolinas and later

Georgia, where dissenters abounded. Religious competition once again stimulated growth in all denominations; by 1750 South Carolina, for example, had almost twice as many churches per capita as did either Virginia or Maryland. Charleston, the South's only city—with a population of around 12,000—boasted a number of fine churches including Anglican St. Philip's, described by one admirer as "the most elegant Religious Edifice in British America." Though one hundred feet long and sixty wide, its congregation was so numerous that a second large church, St. Michael's, was built in 1761. Nonetheless, by mid-century the South as a whole lagged behind the North in congregation formation, opening opportunities for the evangelical Presbyterian and Baptist preachers who appeared in increasing numbers from that time forward.[12]

The number of congregations and size of church buildings certainly tell us something about early American religious life, as do ministers' reports on the provincials' attitudes toward the sacraments. A further sense of popular religious practices can be gained from a look at the social, political, and cultural, as well as the religious, values associated with provincial churchgoing.

Churchgoing and Social Rank

With the majority of adults worshiping regularly, church life was not the exclusive domain of any single class. The Church of England has most often been portrayed as the shrine of the wealthy, and many southern vestries were dominated by "the most substantial and intelligent Persons in each Parish." Yet the main body of Anglican worshipers was composed of smaller landholders and their families. Responses to the bishop of London's 1724 questionnaire from rectors of sixty parishes in Virginia, Maryland, and South Carolina reveal the wide embrace of the church at that time. The ministers stated repeatedly that "all" or "most" inhabitants attended the parish church or one of the many chapels of ease raised in remote sections to accommodate the scattered population. At Christ Church in Lancaster County, Virginia, "almost all white persons in the parish . . . attend[ed] divine Service"; elsewhere ministers noted that their parishioners were drawn from the lesser as well as the better sort.[13]

Northern Anglicans also sought leading men for their vestries, though in rural New York small farmers served alongside great landowners, and in Marblehead, Massachusetts, the number of middle-class ship captains serving as vestrymen reflected the seafaring character of that town. Even at King's Chapel, Boston, one of the wealthier Anglican churches in New England, an occasional rope maker or baker found a place among the merchants, public officials, and attorneys on the vestry.[14] A few northern Anglican congregations may have equaled the gentility of the dominant Congregational, Dutch Reformed, and Quaker meetings, but most were far from affluent. Christ Church in Boston's North End ministered to tradesmen, artisans, and mariners; parishioners of St. Michael's in Marblehead were described as "poor"; at St. Peter's, Salem, twenty-nine of forty-six male members were of the "lower class." Connecticut rectors frequently complained about their inability to attract people of rank to the church in a region where the Congregationalists monopolized political and social power. Though the Church of England was growing rapidly throughout the colony in the 1720s and 1730s, its adherents were small tradesmen, farmers, and "the poorer sort of people."[15] In the Middle Colonies the picture was more varied. New York City's Trinity Church benefited from the patronage of Anglican officials and the addition of Anglicizing Dutch and Huguenot leaders to its communion; St. Peter's in Philadelphia gained from the defection of some leading Quaker merchants and, after 1732, from the sympathy (and eventual membership) of Governor Thomas Penn.[16] In the countryside, however, early eighteenth-century congregations were composed of families engaged in "Agriculture and handy Craft Employments" whose "general Condition [was] low in the World."[17]

New England Congregational meetings necessarily embraced every economic level in a society where church and town were often synonymous. True, Boston's Brattle Street Church attracted the most affluent congregation in town, whereas New North, founded in

1714, contained many lower-middle-class families. The Mather's heavily attended Second Church was perhaps the most representative of Boston's several Congregational churches in that it attracted a cross-section of the town's inhabitants.[18] Detailed information about the economic status of congregations outside of Boston is harder to obtain. We do know that at the end of the seventeenth century Salem Village church members were drawn largely from the middle income group. Moreover, since the pre-Awakening conversion age of New Englanders was the middle twenties and older, an age that correlated with marriage and householding, it seems likely that members in full communion were from a stable, propertied segment of the community.[19] In Northampton, nearly all young men identified as members of the community between 1727 and 1746 joined the church. Connecticut congregations frequently chose to incorporate all baptized members "in the watch and care of the church."[20] In short, Congregationalism was sufficiently inclusive in the early eighteenth century to have gathered in all social ranks. Those few inhabitants who remained outside the churches' embrace were most likely newcomers, bachelors, or transients who had not yet developed strong attachments to the town and its institutions.

If the established Anglican and Congregational churches cannot be identified with a specific social level, did not the Baptists, Quakers, and other dissenting denominations attract a disproportionate number of the poor? The Baptists certainly made an issue of scorning displays of wealth and "fashionable vices." When ridiculed as a contemptible people of low degree, they responded that God "had chosen the poor of this world to be rich in faith." Yet historians have generally declined to depict the membership as poor, especially in the North where Baptists usually split off from the Congregational churches.[21] In Virginia the Baptists in general may have occupied a lower economic rung than the Anglicans. Yet there is more than a little truth in one Virginia Baptist's assertion that "the greater part of every denomination, are as poor, and as unlearned as we."[22]

Quakers in the Middle Colonies seem to have done very well.

Quakers Riding to Meeting
(New-York Historical Society)

Their early arrival in Pennsylvania and New Jersey, combined with a doctrine of hard work and mutual assistance, brought the Quakers—as well as other sects like the Mennonites—substantial economic prosperity. Sectarians usually headed the tax lists in rural Pennsylvania counties during the eighteenth century. Friends also prospered in northern cities, the Quaker grandees of Philadelphia and Newport being compared with the aristocratic planters of the South and the merchant princes of Boston. Quakers may have enjoyed less secure circumstances in the South and parts of New England, where they were vilified initially as pariahs and troublemakers. Yet even there most Quakers seem to have been solidly middle-class, and some were quite well off.[23] A similar pattern holds for the rural New York Dutch Reformed; in New York City and Albany the prosperity of Dutch church members equaled or surpassed that of the Anglicans.[24]

The Presbyterian and German churches began their rise only in the second decade of the eighteenth century as immigrants from Ulster and Germany poured into Pennsylvania and the backcountry. The economic standing of their adherents reflected this late start, though Presbyterians in Pennsylvania's Chester and Lancaster counties had moved into the upper tax brackets in proportion to their numbers by 1782. The German churchpeople ascended the ladder more slowly, the Reverend Michael Schlatter reporting in 1746 that "some of these Congregations were so poor, that it was utterly impossible" for them to furnish even half the salary for a minister.[25]

This scattered evidence illustrates the hopelessness of assigning a precise social or economic character to any of the eighteenth-century denominations. It also suggests a perspective, drawing on the principle of hegemony, from which to consider their relative status and power. With a regional rather than a colonies-wide approach, it is evident that three churches and one sect achieved political and social preeminence in the seventeenth century because they were the officially established or dominant religious institutions in specific areas: the Anglican church in the South, the Congregational churches in New England, the Dutch Reformed Church in New York, and the Society of Friends in Pennsylvania. Even when the Dutch Reformed Church was forced to share its privileged position with the Anglicans after 1664, it retained many leading merchants and professionals as parishioners and thus much of its influence.[26] The Society of Friends, though not established, gained an equivalent preeminence in Pennsylvania and West Jersey, where the initial proprietors were of that faith. The hegemony enjoyed by these denominations because of close links with the founding generation and preemptive economic advantages meant that persons of wealth or those seeking proximity to patronage and power were attached to their worship. Thus Anglican ministers in lower Pennsylvania complained that their parishioners were "awed by the Quaker party. . . . [and] will truckle to power, who otherwise would be faithfull Church men." Similarly in Connecticut those "looking towards the Church are commonly the poorer Sort of People" since the Congregationalists held most positions of authority.[27] In the South, on the other hand, the Church of England was the religion of fashion and influence.

That the Quakers are found among the hegemonic four suggests that the church-sect dichotomy emphasized by Weber and Troeltsch—who theorized that sects recruited their adherents from the economically deprived segment of the community[28]—has little explanatory force for colonial America. Denominations that rose subsequent to and in competition with the leading four—such as the Baptists in Virginia, the Presbyterians in Pennsylvania, and, indeed, the Anglicans in New England—might be expected to attract the meaner sort to their communion, though pending fuller study of the economic condition of dissident congregations we can hardly claim that their adherents were characterized by material deprivation. Nor would the evidence presented here support such a correlation. But should deprivation be defined more broadly to encompass exclusion from a community's system of rewards and alienation from its governing values (a by-product of which might be economic deprivation),[29] we arrive at a description that fits rather closely with much that we know about colonial America's religious dissidents. This form of deprivation, which will be examined in subsequent chapters, may tell us considerably more about the attitudes and aspirations of the dissenting denominations than a straight economic analysis could do.

A Gentleman's Religion

The white, male gentry occupied a prominent, if frequently unappreciated, place in provincial religious life. Philip Fithian's sketch of Virginia Sabbath gatherings, which featured gentlemen planters exchanging news about tobacco prices and horseflesh before and after Anglican services, has often been cited to show the shallowness, or even hypocrisy, of southern gentry religion. Because a number of prominent later-eighteenth-century Virginians were acknowledged deists and advocates of the separation of church from state, modern writers tend to dismiss most southern gentlemen as no more than "nominal Anglicans." Yet the personal beliefs and practices of the gentry belie such loose characterization. True, the

Anglican church represented the pinnacle of rational religion in eighteenth-century America. The scientific revolution, Enlightenment humanism, Locke, and the Scottish common sense writers—all much admired by the southern gentry—had shifted the emphasis from an interventionist God to one whose greatest gift to humankind was natural reason. But if God became more remote, the moral system of Jesus, widely studied and appreciated for its simplicity and rationality, continued central to the Anglican code. For southern gentlemen the meaning of earthly life, the doing of good to one's fellow sojourners, and expectations about the hereafter were shaped in a matrix of New Testament moderation and enlightened rationalism.[30] The most vocal critics of this system were northern Calvinists like Fithian who clung longer to an active, omnipotent God.

The religious attitudes of southern Anglican gentlemen appear in various of their writings. William Byrd II, whose diaries meticulously record the details of his religious thought and practice between 1709 and 1741, is a representative figure of that era. Byrd usually attended the parish church at Westover, located one quarter mile from his house. In a pattern typical for that region Byrd went to church about half the time, concentrating his attendance in the mild spring and fall seasons and on Sundays when the rector preached the sermon. When harsh weather, domestic responsibilities, or, occasionally, lassitude kept him from church, Byrd always read a sermon in his study, usually one of Tillotson's.[31] In 1728 he was appalled to discover that some North Carolinians did not "know Sunday from any other day, any more than Robinson Crusoe did"; and he noted with disapproval in 1739 that John Carter of Shirley had not been to church in six months.[32] Nor did Byrd restrict his religious observance to the Sabbath. He began and ended most days with prayer and usually read a sacred selection in Greek or Hebrew after his morning devotions.

As for Byrd's inner beliefs, we find his creed, recorded on the flyleaf of his diary in 1710, emphasizing man's God-given reason and also the law of nature as sources of guidance. "I believe that God made man . . . [and] insp[ire]d him with a reasonable soul to distinguish betwe[en] Good and Evil. That the Law of nature taught him to [embrace?] the Good and avoid the Evil because the good tends manifestly to his happiness and preservation; but the Evil to his [misery] and destruction." Byrd believed in Adam's fall, the virgin birth, and Jesus' sacrifice to "redeem Mankind from the punishment of their sins." He also believed in a day of judgment, an afterlife of "unspeakable happiness" for those who had led good lives, and a state of "Sorrow & misery" for those who were obstinately impenitent. Yet his was a merciful God who allowed for human frailties and would help man to conquer his depraved nature. Nor did Byrd completely reject the mystical side of religion. He saw signs from God in the weather and in dreams, and he believed that an epidemic which killed some of his slaves was a punishment for his own sins. Byrd's demeanor at church was devout (he frequently says so himself), and on at least one occasion he shed "tears of repentance" while reading a sermon by Tillotson.[33]

Other gentlemen of Byrd's generation were equally devoted to the Church of England both as institution and as source of solace. Robert "King" Carter is an example. In 1720 Carter instructed an English friend to see that "the principles of our holy religion" were instilled in his sons, then attending school in the mother country. "I am of the Church of England way, so I desire they should be. But the high-flown up top notions and the great stress that is laid upon ceremonies, any farther than decency and conformity, are what I cannot come into the reason of. Practical godliness is the substance—these are but the shell." Thus when a fever epidemic brought illness and death to his parish in 1721 Carter's "practical godliness" told him that "Afflictions are very proper for us in our way to heaven," and, at the death of a friend, that "God's will must be submitted to." William Fitzhugh, a generation earlier, had displayed a resignation toward death that was even more submissive. When his cousin's "two sweet Babes" died in 1687, Fitzhugh had counseled that such a loss could be "easily and cheerfully born," if the parents would consider that a "troublesome . . . terrestial being [had been exchanged for] a certain & happy Celestial habitation."[34] Southerners, like northerners, appear to have viewed immoderate grief as an actual defiance of the Creator.[35]

That some gentlemen of the later Revolutionary generation had moved a good deal further toward deism than, say, William Byrd is well known. Thomas Jefferson is the classic case, for by some time in his twenties Jefferson had rejected both the Trinity and the Bible's miraculous explanations for physical phenomena. He also came to believe that a self-serving priesthood, starting with Paul, had so encrusted Christianity with creed and dogma as to distort the simple teachings of Jesus—all commonplaces of Enlightenment secularism.[36] Nonetheless Jefferson considered himself a "real" Christian, described the moral system of Jesus as the most "sublime ever preached to man," and believed in a future state of rewards and punishments. His anticlericalism, moreover, was usually directed against the early church fathers, or pointed at the New England Calvinists on whose "formidable sway" he blamed both New England religion and politics.[37] But if he wanted nothing to do with "pious young monks from Harvard and Yale," Jefferson had many friends among the Anglican clergy whom he regarded as enlightened and moderate. He sponsored young men for training and ordination in England; following disestablishment of the Virginia Anglican church, it was Jefferson who organized a voluntary subscription to pay the salaries of his parish minister and clerk. His personal religious practices included assiduous reading of the Bible and theology, regular churchgoing, and baptism, marriage, and burial within the Church of England for himself and family. Jefferson may well have participated in the ceremonial aspects of his church—while declining to stand godfather for a friend and, so far as we know, to take communion—because he believed that religious observance promoted public virtue and social harmony.[38]

George Washington's active membership in the Anglican church also reflected in part his sense of community and public leadership. No member of the Truro Parish Vestry attended meetings more faithfully than did Washington during the years he was at home. Moreover, Washington's minister at Pohick Church reportedly stated that he "never knew so constant an attendant on church as Washington." Because Washington believed that the church fostered morality and social stability, he no doubt considered it his duty to set a good example.[39] James Madison also was respectful toward religion, attending church and regularly conducting family worship. Henry Laurens of South Carolina was a "strict and exemplary" son of the Church of England who attended services regularly and took monthly communion.[40]

Robert Carter of Nomini Hall was Philip Fithian's employer and surely one of the characters in his famous sketch of the planter gentry at church. Carter was a churchwarden and vestryman of Cople Parish and a regular churchgoer. During this phase of his life, Carter's faith seems to have been more or less in line with that recommended in Edward Synge's *A Gentleman's Religion*, a work found in many southern libraries, including Carter's.[41] A gentleman would find, according to Synge, that nothing in Christian religion "contradicts the clear and evident Principles of Natural Reason." Worship of Synge's reasonable God would be rewarded with future happiness; neglect and contempt of religion would be punished with future misery; and if evil men sometimes seemed to prosper, all would get their just return in the afterlife.[42]

This moderate and non-insistent faith, so outside the Calvinist understanding of Philip Fithian, typified the religious attitudes of Robert Carter and many of his gentry friends up to the era of the American Revolution. Still, "moderation" may itself be deceptive. One wonders how Fithian might have reacted to Carter's astounding conversion to the Baptist faith in 1778, his subsequent freeing of 500 slaves, and his attraction late in life to a Swedish mystic.[43]

As the religious beliefs of three generations of southern Anglican gentlemen took a rationalist direction, the outer forms of religious practice were adjusted accordingly. Sermons of about twenty minutes length emphasizing "sound morality, or deep studied Metaphysicks" apparently were fairly common by the late colonial years. The appropriate demeanor in church was respectful attention to the sermon and knowledgeable participation in the prayers and responses, but not outward displays of "enthusiasm."[44] Auditors might congratulate the rector on a well-constructed sermon, but speculations on how it might apply to their own moral growth were reserved for personal diaries or family discussion. Religion thus became increasingly private and compartmentalized; it did not flow so easily into every corner of daily life as it had in William Byrd's time. When church services drew to a close in those rural parishes the people, having performed a basic communal and spiritual rite, then saw themselves free to mingle and gossip. Northerners may have found these practices offensive, but criticism of religious style did not run in one direction only. Many a southern gentleman would probably have agreed with Thomas Jefferson that the New Englanders' Calvinist God was "a daemon of malignant spirit."[45]

Though northern Sabbaths were more austere, religious rationalism was making headway there as well. The external forms of piety continued to be most closely observed in New England, which had according to Cotton Mather "the Best Sabbaths of any Countrey under the Cope of Heaven." Even during the Revolution—often depicted as a time of religious decline—Abbé Robin, a French army chaplain, found Boston to be "a mere desert" on the Sabbath, with church services and Bible reading the sole occupations of the day. When a French companion of Robin's shocked the locals by daring to play his flute on a Sunday, the townspeople, "greatly enraged, collected in crowds round the house . . . and forced him to desist."[46] Leading northern gentlemen, like their counterparts in the South, were highly visible members of this churchgoing society. Selectmen in towns across New England were active churchmen, forty to fifty percent of them electing to become members in full communion during the eighteenth century when the average male was tending toward halfway membership. Merchants and lawyers joined public officials as elders, deacons, and vestrymen in all northern colonies. That the church afforded not only religious but political and social opportunities in the North as well as the South can hardly be doubted.[47] Religious practice in New England and the Middle Colonies may have been conducted with greater solemnity, but the increasingly rationalist beliefs of gentlemen leaders in all sections seem to have been quite similar.

John Adams complained at age nineteen about devoting Sunday to "the Frigid performances . . . [of] Frigid John Calvin." Six years later he explicitly rejected the doctrine of predestination as capricious and arbitrary. Adams's belief in the "efficacy of human endeavours" marks him as an Arminian rationalist at the age of twenty-six, and his religious reading was strikingly similar to that of the southern deists. Adams was in his own phrase a "churchgoing animal for seventy-six years." He believed in an afterlife where "the Joys of heaven [or] the Horrors of Hell" would reward or punish earthly behavior. His main deviation from the positions of the southern rationalists was that he retained some belief in the miracles of the Bible; moreover, though he advocated toleration of all religions Adams never encouraged abolition of the Congregational establishment, fearing the consequences of a drop in support for the clergy.[48]

By the mid-eighteenth century rationalism was a rising strain in the religious thought of New England gentlemen of every political hue. Thomas Hutchinson belied his descent from Great-Great-Grandmother Anne Hutchinson by developing a tolerant urbanity. Though he remained a Congregationalist, Hutchinson noted in 1771 that the moderation of the Anglican church suited his personal beliefs better than did the doctrinaire side of his native denomination. A member of Boston's New Brick Church, Hutchinson was a frequent auditor at Anglican King's Chapel; as a loyalist exile in London, he faithfully attended the Church of England.[49]

Many middle-colony gentlemen also cultivated a genteel rationalism. New Yorker William Livingston's polemics against Anglican "priestcraft" represented the extreme of anticlericalism: "I Believe, that there is more Iniquity committed under the Robe, than is repented of under the Gallows." Yet he described himself as "a sincere professor of the religion of Jesus" as expounded in the Bible and believed in the divine redemption of man. Breaking off from the Dutch Reformed Church in 1752 because of its reluctance to conduct services in English, Livingston became a communicating member and trustee of the First Presbyterian Church.[50] Benjamin Franklin, historically cast as the consummate rationalist, also believed in "one God, Creator of the Universe," and the immortality of the soul. He expected reward or punishment in the next world commensurate with his conduct in this. As a young man Franklin had attended the Presbyterian Church when there were prospects for a sermon relating Christian morality to the practice of virtue. Finding instead dry doctrine, Franklin stopped going and bought a pew for his family at Anglican Christ Church, where two of his children were baptized and he himself was eventually interred. Though he rarely if ever, so far as we know, attended services, Franklin gave regular financial support to the Church of England and a number of other denominations. He also prayed privately, recommended the efficacy of public worship, and during King George's War proposed the first public fast in Pennsylvania. What Franklin liked least was dogma of any kind, including the dogma of deism. His youthful view that "vital Religion has always suffer'd, when Orthodoxy is more regarded than Virtue" changed little over a long life.[51]

The similarity of belief among the educated gentry in all colonies is notable. True, there are exceptions like the Baptist convert Robert Carter, or "the last of the Puritans" Samuel Adams. But there does seem to be evidence that some form of rationalism—unitarian, deist, or otherwise—was often present in the religion of gentleman leaders by the late colonial years.

Samuel Adams may better exemplify the middling rank than the gentry, having been a man modest in estate if rich in fame. Originally destined for the ministry, Adams was always a devout Congregationalist. The intensity of his political passion has been attributed to his stern Puritan moralism. It may be that piety sits better on the brows of less aristocratic types. In Virginia many Baptists openly professed their lack of learning and wealth, even to the point of extravagence, and adopted an austere demeanor that made an arresting contrast to the Anglican style.[52] The Presbyterian planter James Gordon of Lancaster, Virginia, occasionally attended Anglican services in the years before a Presbyterian meetinghouse was erected in his district. But Gordon did not think the Anglicans really practiced "vital religion," and he often stayed home on the Sabbath studying the Bible or reading a sermon to his slaves. When by the 1750s Presbyterian itinerants began to preach in the region, as many as 800 to 900 people—Gordon prominent in their number—turned out to hear them.[53]

Two of the fullest religious accounts from men of middle rank are those of Nathan Cole and Hermon Husband. Cole, a Connecticut farmer and Congregationalist, turned fervent New Light after hearing the English evangelist George Whitefield preach in 1741. After a prolonged period of painful thought, Cole quit the Congregational church altogether in protest against the continuing acceptance of unregenerate members, becoming a Separatist, a lay exhorter, and eventually a Baptist. Hermon Husband, the son of a Maryland planter who raised his family in the Church of England, was at the age of fifteen also stirred by Whitefield's preaching. In 1750, when he was twenty-six years old, Husband wrote his *Remarks on Religion*, a vivid description of his movement from Anglicanism to Presbyterianism to Quakerism in a course of earnest and anxious searching. Henry Muhlenberg made extensive notes on the religious questings of many Pennsylvania and New York men of middling rank, faithful churchgoers of "humble and hungry heart." He also thought that simple people were usually more devout than educated ones.[54]

Somewhere between the simple and the educated, the evangelicals and the rationalists, lay a broad, more or less undifferentiated ground of orthodoxy. And for the men in particular, churchgoing was coming increasingly to serve more than one function. There were the spiritual functions, to be sure; there were social and political ones as well. The balance among them naturally varied, but the mounting importance of the secular side in general seems to have been accompanied by a tendency on the men's part to transfer more and more of their families' devotional responsibilities to the women.

"Daughters of Zion"

By the second half of the eighteenth century mothers were becoming the primary custodians of the family's religious heritage, and in genteel households they took significant responsibility for the children's religious education, often in conjunction with a private tutor. A number of wealthy women also left substantial legacies to their churches.[55] Some have left us glimpses of their religious views as well.

Few women of the mid-eighteenth-century South were of higher social rank than Eliza Lucas Pinckney of South Carolina. Yet in Mrs. Pinckney's religion there was not the faintest tinge of aristocratic frivolity. She was certainly a reasonable woman, and her upbringing as well as her reading—which included Milton, Locke, and Robert Boyle—had persuaded her that it would "dishonour our religion [to] affirm there is anything in it contrary to reason."[56] Still, it was faith as well as reason that mediated all her closest attachments, even when tested by sorrow and death. The Lord's wisdom was infinite, and the "most dutiful step we can take [is] patiently to submit." Though only twenty when her young brother fell mortally ill in Antigua, the anguished Eliza told herself to "hush, 'tis the almighty's will," and in bidding him adieu she resignedly urged upon him fortitude and a "relish for immortal joys." In later life as a wife and mother, she prayed each morning "next to my God, to make it my Study" both to please Mr. Pinckney and to guard their children against the "budings of vice, and to instill piety, Virtue and true religion into them."[57]

Elizabeth Colden DeLancey of New York admitted her children to the breakfast table only after they presented in writing a comment on "some moral sentence," her aim being to raise them "as shall most conduce to his glory their good & my own happyness." A devout Anglican, Mrs. DeLancey prayed to her "kind Benefactor" to protect her family's health, to guide her sons in their choice of career, and for assistance in a variety of similar matters.[58] Among the Dutch of Albany, "it was on the females that the task of religious instruction generally devolved," noted Anne Grant, one consequence being the absence among them of "that monster in nature, an impious woman." Maria Van Rensselaer actively supported religion at Rensselaerswyck and urged that the area be assigned a resident minister. As she observed during one especially trying period of her life, if the Lord "had not been my joy and strength, I should long ago have perished in my sorrow."[59]

When Esther Edwards Burr left Northampton, Massachusetts for New Jersey—where her husband, Aaron Burr, Sr., was a Presbyterian minister and president of the college at Princeton—she and Sarah Prince of Boston sustained their close friendship by exchanging private diaries that monitored their religious growth. Only Esther Burr's side of this correspondence remains. It offers an intimate look into the world of pious women of upper rank, whose reference point for events both spiritual and mundane was the salvation of their souls. Esther Burr's journal also records a variety of encounters with women of rank in the Middle Colonies. As a daughter of Jonathan Edwards, Esther's standard for piety was high, and although she sometimes found middle-colony females wanting, she met many women "of good sense and piety" with whom she spent sweet hours in religious conversation. That some middle-colony women involved themselves in church politics is revealed in a journal entry about the "four *Popes* of Newyork, *women popes*," who turned out to be leading parishioners of New York City's First Presbyterian Church with considerable influence over the choice of a new minister.[60]

Besides spiritual refreshment, religion offered women of energy and intellect an outlet to the wider world, as well as opportunities for self-expression, personal growth, and even leadership. Many women spoke with authority about complex theological issues. William Byrd II recorded that his wife and sister-in-law spent one evening at Westover in "fierce dispute about the infallibility of the Bible." Frances Carter of Nomini Hall discussed with her daughter the question of whether women had souls, and she conversed "with great propriety" about religion to tutor Philip Fithian, demonstrating "a very extensive knowledge." Devereux Jarratt was instructed in vital religion by the New Light wife of the planter whose children he tutored.[61] In New England the religious writings of such pious matrons as Elizabeth Cotton and Jerusha Mather Oliver were incorporated into sermons or published for the enlightenment of a wider audience.[62]

Women of middle and lower status also found that religious activity offered them a wider stage. The Society of Friends in America defined women and men as equal in the sight of God, opening to females a prominent role in their public ministry. Though Mary Dyer's martyrdom on a Boston scaffold was a unique case, a good many other Quaker women were made to suffer, physically and mentally, for their public preaching. A number of them gained approval from their meetings to leave home and family for extended periods in the eighteenth century to spread the Quaker message. For those at home the Women's Meeting in each congregation exercised significant powers, disciplining female members, regulating marriages, and overseeing church attendance by both men and women.[63] No other denomination matched the Friends in opening opportunities to women, though New Light and especially Baptist meetings sometimes allowed them a voice in church government and a vote on new members.[64]

Occasionally a woman appeared with sufficient self-confidence to test the boundaries of women's religious sphere. Besides Anne Hutchinson and Mary Dyer in the seventeenth century, such a one was an elderly parishioner of Henry Muhlenberg in mid-eighteenth-century Pennsylvania. This unnamed woman did not shrink from challenging Muhlenberg on such theological points as original sin and conversion, and was much distressed at his seeming to teach that the Jews were under sentence of damnation. Muhlenberg clearly found her conversation edifying, and used her as a "bellwether" of the congregation.[65] Another was the Congregationalist Sarah Haggar Osborne of Newport, Rhode Island. Mrs. Osborne started conventionally enough as leader of a young women's prayer society, following the scriptural rule that older women might instruct the younger. But for some reason this modest venture began to take on the most gratifying momentum. Slaves, male and female, took to attending the Sunday evening prayer meetings; on other evenings came "Little white Lads" and girls from the neighborhood; and during the revival of 1766–1767 between 300 and 500 persons were crowding into the Osborne house every week. For Sarah Osborne it was all wonderfully inspiriting. Languor and sick spells faded away; she now slept well, had a good appetite, and knew "nothing about weariness." The meetings in due course came under criticism from a clergyman who questioned the appropriateness of Mrs. Osborne's leadership. But Sarah Osborne, with all respect, would have none of it. Souls everywhere had been awakened, including her own, and she was not going "to shut up my Mouth and doors and creep into obscurity."[66]

The relief that religion brought to the ordinary colonial woman's life of toil, especially on the frontier, is frequently noted in Henry Muhlenberg's record of his pastoral encounters. Muhlenberg tells of aged and ill women who found their only solace in God, of widows with large families rising above adversity through Christian faith, and of women afflicted with melancholia who found surcease from it in religion. One Pennsylvania frontierswoman gave her husband some concern from the frequency with which she would go off to sit in the woods by herself, and he spoke to the pastor about it. But the reason should have been obvious. She was "somewhat weak physically and always had a flock of children around her"; she was not really "melancholy," just worn out—and when things got too much, the best restorative she could think of was a session of solitary prayer.[67]

The sisterhood of the Ephrata cloister at Lancaster, Pennsylvania offers the most striking case of an institutional haven for women who believed themselves, from whatever causes, to have reached the end of their earthly tether. This Seventh Day Baptist community— which had male as well as female houses—was headed by Conrad Beissel, who believed in a life of celibacy and regarded marriage as the penitentiary of carnal man.[68] A number of women joined the Ephrata cloister when they were quite young. Life in the Saron, or sisterhouse, took many of its features from the nunneries of Europe, a circumstance that provided a satiric foil for Ephrata's critics. The sisters' habit consisted of a vest and long skirt, belted at the waist and covered with a large apron that resembled a monk's scapulary. Their heads were covered by a rounded hood.[69] The sisters' dedication to a "modest, quiet, tranquil and retired" life was

An Ephrata Sister, from a sketch on the fly-leaf of a manuscript hymnal, dated 1745.

regulated by a hierarchy of overseers, sub-prioress, and prioress. Whereas some young women found the regimen too harsh or finally rejected the celibate life, a number of others remained in the Saron, some for forty or fifty years.[70]

A few women left their husbands and families to join the sisterhood, the most notable being Maria Christiana, wife of the German printer Christopher Sauer. Mrs. Sauer was for many years under-prioress of the Saron, until a son finally persuaded her to return to her family.[71] Other women entered the Ephrata community when they were widowed and remained for the rest of their lives.

The Ephrata experience represents an extreme of female piety in colonial America. Most women followed the more orthodox path of participation with their families in local religious institutions. Yet the rising proportion of women associated with a number of churches and sects suggests that religion offered them satisfactions that nothing else in their existence could provide. Starting from their customary if circumscribed role as guardians of family piety and teachers of the young, many women sought and found in religious life a larger scope for their energy and talents.

More Godly Women Than Men

Recent writings on the feminization of colonial religion have pointed to the disproportionate number of female members in some denominations. A study of seventeenth-century Massachusetts Congregational meetings concludes that "women consistently became a numerical majority of the church within the first five years of its foundation." A sampling of twenty-eight congregations in Connecticut and Massachusetts finds female adherence rising from 46 percent in the 1630s to 70 percent by 1759.[72] Cotton Mather, observing congregations of three or four hundred communicants of which only one quarter might be men, concluded that there were "far more *godly Women*" than men in the world. Where churches differentiated between full and half-way membership, the ratio among members in full communion favored women by about two to one. Members owning the half-way covenant were more equally divided, with men in a number of instances forming the majority.[73]

Several reasons have been advanced for the preponderance of women in the Congregational churches. Cotton Mather, and later the Reverend Benjamin Colman, ascribed women's superior religious understanding to their experiences in childbirth. Since each delivery put a woman at risk, her spirit was repeatedly tempered and enlarged by encounters with death. Another explanation emphasizes the less rigorous admission procedure available to women. In the Congregational, Baptist, and other churches that required new members to discuss their conversion experiences publicly, women, who were prohibited from speaking in church by biblical injunction, might write out their narratives or relate them privately to the minister. A fair number of the men, without such an option and not finding a public confession to their liking, may thus have settled for half-way membership.[74] The closer balance of males to females among half-way covenanters lends substance to this view.

Feminization of the Congregational churches has also been linked to changing power relationships in the later seventeenth century. As the ministers' rising professionalism led them to reduce the laity's power in church government, laymen proved less amenable to a more passive role than did laywomen. Moreover, men increasingly absorbed in secular pursuits may have been just as glad to let religion move into the female sphere; New Englanders, as in other societies confronting value conflicts, may simply have dealt with them "by assigning one set of goals to men, and another to women."[75]

Whether females outnumbered males in other than the Congregational churches is less clear, though if value conflicts or a professionalizing ministry were leading causes of feminization all denominations would presumably be affected. Quaker meetings seem to have been quite evenly balanced between men and women since Friends were admonished to marry "in unity," that is, within the Society. Those "marrying out" were frequently disowned. In some meetings more men than women married out, but in others the reverse was true.[76] Ezra Stiles listed Rhode Island churchgoers of all denominations by family group, which implies a roughly equal proportion of males and females. When occasionally Stiles drew up separate lists of men and women in Congregational churches alone, the balance often, though not always, favored women. The large number of widows residing in port towns was another factor that could sharply tip the scale toward feminization.[77]

Between 1762 and 1790, female members usually outnumbered male in Virginia Baptist meetings, and a few women even gained prominence as preachers. Sometimes wives were converted first and then enrolled their husbands. Community studies of the German and Swedish Lutheran churches in Pennsylvania during the second half of the eighteenth century suggest that there too women may have outnumbered men as confirmands and communicants.[78] Muhlenberg's diary, on the other hand, offers no evidence of feminization among his Lutheran parishioners, since male and female confirmands over the decades joined the church in approximately equal proportions.[79] And neither Anglican records nor churchgoer's diaries indicate that more females than males worshiped in the Church of England. Ministers always reported attendance in terms of families, often denoting "men and women," which suggests a rough balance. Indeed, Samuel Johnson of Connecticut specifically stated that he had "as many men as women" among his communicating members.[80] Thus the evidence for a secularizing male population that consigned religion to the women's sphere becomes somewhat indeterminate.

If, on the other hand, the assertion of ministerial authority over congregations explains any disproportion of female over male church members, the tendency toward feminization should be most evident among denominations with a strong professional clergy. The Congregational churches certainly meet this test, since feminization started around the same time that Puritan divines entered New England in numbers. A sampling of other denominations yields further supporting evidence. In the New York City Dutch Reformed Church, whose long-settled domines were among the most professional-minded clergymen in the colonies, some 65 percent of communicants in the early decades of the eighteenth century were female.[81] But in the Philipse Manor Dutch church, which had no permanent minister until 1785 and thus depended on the leadership of male elders and deacons, the balance of men and women members remained about even.[82] Particularly telling is evidence from Trinity Lutheran Church in New York City for the years 1704 to 1723, when the congregation must have been led primarily by laymen since its minister itinerated among twenty-seven churches in New York and New Jersey. Of the total 168 members in the New

Old Dutch Church of Philipse Manor, New York. Erected 1697.
(Courtesy of Sleepy Hollow Restorations, Tarrytown, New York)

York City church, 52 percent were male and 48 percent female. In contrast, at the Round Top Lutheran Church in Dutchess County, New York, during the 1760s and 1770s, when a minister was permanently resident in the area, about 60 percent of the communicant members were women. A similar pattern can be discerned in scattered Presbyterian records for New York and New Jersey.[84]

In the Anglican South, where male vestries had appropriated much of the authority normally reserved to ecclesiastics in England, the church seems to have retained a masculine tone. Whether this changed as governors gained greater power over the Anglican church after mid-century, or whether other denominations were feminized as clergymen grew in numbers and in professional self-consciousness, remains to be explored. But from the evidence surveyed here, feminization—though kept at bay as long as elders and deacons exercised real power in the early churches—followed with striking regularity upon the assumption of congregational control by a full-time resident minister. Thus feminization appears to be linked less to the secularization of the masculine sphere than to the loss of power by lay males to a professionalizing clergy.

Young and Old

Churchgoing was largely an adult activity in colonial America, especially where homesteads were widely scattered. Parents simply would not expose small children to the long journeys and extreme temperatures that churchgoing entailed in rural areas. Anglican parish reports indicate that older youths concentrated their attendance in the Lenten period when rectors gave instruction in the catechism, though schoolmasters regularly catechized young people and parents also were encouraged to do so. Devereux Jarratt recalled that his parents taught their children short prayers and "made us very perfect in repeating the Church Catechism."[85] With no bishop resident in the colonies confirmation in accordance with church canons was impossible, but ministers apparently examined youths at about age sixteen or older and, when satisfied with their level of understanding, admitted them to communion.[86] The sons of Robert Carter III, eighteen-year-old Ben and sixteen-year-old Bob, often "begged" Philip Fithian to let them go to church despite poor weather, and occasionally the boys attended even when their parents would not venture forth. This along with similar evidence from William Byrd's diaries suggests that Sunday was an important day on the social calendar of Virginia's young people.[87]

Middle-colony Lutherans and German Reformed often traveled ten or fifteen miles to worship, which generally restricted church-going to adults. The Presbytery of Hanover County, Virginia, noted as late as 1775 that its boundaries were so extensive that "women, children, and servants" often could not attend church. One consequence was that baptism of colonial children was often delayed, less through parental neglect—though that was sometimes a factor—than the inaccessibility of churches and ministers. When clergymen traveled out to such areas, children were brought to them by the score, even by the hundreds, to be baptized. "Baptized Children till was weary" was a familiar comment from frontier itinerants.[88]

In the towns and cities youths participated more regularly in church life. The Anglican rector at Philadelphia, for example, organized a society of young men which met on Sunday evenings to hear sermons, read Scripture, and sing psalms.[89] Henry Muhlenberg provides an unusually full picture of the religious training given children at the Philadelphia Lutheran church. Sunday morning catechism classes, or *Kinderlehre*, were held in the schoolhouse adjacent to the church. (Muhlenberg's notation on a three-year-old child who got lost on her way to *Kinderlehre* suggests that instruction began at an early age.)[90] Muhlenberg often undertook that catechizing himself, leaving morning church service to an assistant pastor. He advocated that children be confirmed by age fourteen, observing that some German and English sects were "sharply critical of us because they consider that we take them too young."[91] Though a few Lutheran children were confirmed at fourteen, or even thirteen in a case or two, admission was more commonly delayed until age sixteen or seventeen and many persons were confirmed only after marriage.[92] Owing to the paucity of Lutheran clergy in the early eighteenth century, Muhlenberg frequently found himself instructing both young and old. During a 1752 sojourn in New York City—where the Lutheran church was often bereft of a regular minister and many adults never had received instruction—Muhlenberg reported that "a number of young people and at least as many adults, some sixty, seventy, and more years of age, came to *Kinderlehre.*"[93]

New England children below the age of seven or eight rarely attended the Congregational churches, though religious education certainly went on at home. Churchgoing boys in the mischievous pre-adolescent years were herded into "boys pews" or ranged along the gallery stairs where appointed monitors watched over them, dealing out "raps and blows" to those making "Indecent Gestures and Wry Faces" during service.[94] The more decorous girls sat on little stools in the pews or aisles. Judging from the diary of eleven-year-old Anna Green Winslow, the religious training of young females was well advanced by eleven or twelve. Anna solemnly recorded the biblical texts and applications of the Reverend Mr. Beacon's sermons at Boston's Old South Church, especially those directed to "the young people." She also read daily from the Bible and regularly attended Thursday lecture and catechism.[95]

Young men's as well as young women's societies were encouraged by some Congregational ministers as "Nurseries of Early Piety."[96] The Reverend John Barnard of Andover preached to such a group in 1727; Jonathan Edwards formed a number of youth groups in his Northampton church. Cotton Mather describes a society of young men that met for two hours on Sunday evenings. Members studied the day's sermon, took turns leading prayers, and subscribed their names to a pledge "to walk orderly." If any member failed to live up to the pledge, the others would "Blot him out of the List."[97]

Congregationalists became formal church members at a later age than did Anglicans, Lutherans, and most others, perhaps because of stricter admission standards. In the early eighteenth century, Andover females and males joined as half-way members around ages twenty and twenty-four, respectively. Before 1730, Andover women delayed entry into full communion until ages twenty-six to twenty-eight, while men did not become full members until their middle to late 30s.[98] At Norton and Middleborough, and in the Connecticut town of Milford, males admitted to full communion before 1740 averaged between twenty-eight and thirty-nine years of age. At Woodbury, Connecticut, where admission policies were quite lenient, women joined the church in their early to middle twentys whereas men were about five years older.[99]

Thus in most denominations prior to the Great Awakening maximum involvement in the church's life was delayed until late adolescence or young adulthood, when religious matters might, presumably, be approached with greater maturity.

If churches were not the terrain of the very young they were certainly familiar ground to the aged. Sermons were regularly directed to elderly churchgoers, and ministers spent a large part of their time visiting aged parishioners who were too feeble to travel to church. In both North and South piety was expected to intensify as men and women moved into old age. Being closer to the eternal resolution, the elderly were presumed to possess a sharpened religious sensibility.[100] Some grandparents took upon themselves the religious instruction of the young. And many, like Mary Fish Silliman of Connecticut, wrote out and circulated their spiritual meditations among family members in an effort to enhance the religious understanding and observance of children and grandchildren.[101]

In New England Congregational meetings, age was often the equivalent of wealth or generosity to the church as a consideration in assigning pews. "Age, estate, and places of trust," or "Age, Honor, [and] Usefulness" were the standard formulas applied by seating committees until the middle of the eighteenth century. Many churches also set aside a section near the pulpit for the hard of hearing, which was known as the "Deaf Pew."[102] So far as can be gleaned from scattered records, age was subordinate to public distinction and wealth as a factor in Anglican church seating, whether in the North or South.[103] Nor did age seem to figure in the seating plans of Henry Muhlenberg's Lutheran churches, though Muhlenberg personally demonstrated a high regard for the religious opinions of his elderly parishioners.[104] The aged appear to have been disproportionately represented in the congregations of colonial America—a fact of religious sociology that is evident in all faiths and times.

Blacks, Indians, and Indentured Servants

Blacks, Indians, and white servants could also be found at church, though their involvement, subject to some regional and denominational variation, was for the most part quite restricted. The Church of England encouraged its ministers throughout the eighteenth century to convert the "infidels"—the term commonly applied to Negroes and Indians—and many took the charge seriously. The Reverend Anthony Gavin, who believed that slavery was "unlawfull for any Christian," baptized almost as many blacks as whites on his first tour of the South Carolina backcountry in 1738. Slaveowners often resisted missionary efforts out of fear that Christianity would make their slaves prideful and rebellious, even though many clergymen took care to preach up humility and obedience to their black converts. What conversion to Christianity actually did for them under such circumstances is difficult to judge. Nevertheless when slaves ran away or were suspected of plotting rebellion, local authorities were quick to accuse Christian missionaries of fomenting disorder.[105]

White resistance to slave conversion appears to have fluctuated according to the proportion of blacks in the population. Thus early support for S.P.G. missionaries' work in baptizing and catechizing slaves in South Carolina declined as blacks came to outnumber whites in the colony after about 1708. Virginia rectors reported occasional success in Christianizing slaves, but as blacks rose from less than 10 percent of the population in 1680 to around one-third by 1740 white resistance stiffened. Maryland's population was only 12 to 18 percent black in the first third of the century, which may account for the greater willingness of white masters there to allow slaves to be baptized and catechized.[106]

This shading of attitudes is apparent in the responses of southern rectors to the bishop of London's 1724 questionnaire on the state of the colonial church. All nine respondents from South Carolina reported little or no success in converting Negroes, typically because "their Masters will not consent to Have them Instructed."[107] About half of the twenty-eight Virginia respondents had managed to baptize "several," and in rarer cases "many," Negroes, though only three or four noted that some blacks actually came to church. But in Maryland nearly a third of the rectors had baptized "many" slaves, some of whom attended church and took communion. Though a number of ministers had to "press" masters to instruct their slaves, the tone of the Maryland responses is more sanguine, and one rector stated that slaves in his parish had "free liberty from their masters to attend divine service & other means of instruction.[108] Yet if black conversions were more numerous in Maryland, there is no reason to question the conventional view that the overwhelming majority of southern blacks remained unchurched. As one writer summed it up in 1705: "Talk to a *Planter* of the *Soul* of a *Negro* . . . [and he will respond that whereas the body is worth £20] the souls of an hundred of them would not yield him one farthing."[109]

Masters were undoubtedly the primary obstacle to slave conversions, but language was a further barrier among first-generation Afro-Americans. Moreover, since Sunday was the slaves' only day off, many spent it cultivating their own garden plots and a few "work[ed] for themselves on hire."[110] Thus, as a rule, southern blacks figured no more than marginally in church life during the first half of the eighteenth century. Even fewer Indians were converted to the white people's religion in the South, most likely because the tribes had a strong religion of their own. Southern ministers, already overtaxed by the demands of their white parishioners reported uniformly that Indians were averse to the Christian religion.[111]

The lower number of blacks in the North suggests that the white population there should have been more receptive to missionary efforts. And, indeed, only New York and New Jersey, which along with Rhode Island contained the largest proportion of blacks, passed laws stipulating that baptism did not alter the slaves' condition of servitude.[112] Conversion did little to ease the burden of slavery in any northern colony, but it appears that more slaves became church adherents there than in the South. S.P.G. schoolmasters like Elias Neau in New York gave much time to instructing northern blacks in the principles of the Christian faith. When Neau died in 1722, his successor in New York City found "Swarms of Negroes comeing about my door & asking if I would be pleased to teach them." If passivity and submission were again the dominant themes of such instruction, a few blacks gained an education and some personal advancement through their involvement with the church.[113]

As was the case in the South, Indians proved more resistant than blacks to the S.P.G.'s attempts to convert them, though one missionary successfully formed a congregation of them at Albany. Farther west at the Mohawk Castle mission the Reverend William Andrews had a sorrier tale to tell. Most of the Indians who looked in at the church door during services in his little chapel would "go away Laughing." Others beat a drum to disrupt worship or said they would attend only if given a dram of rum. Of the twenty-four who did come to chapel, "all [are] women excepting two men." But not even all these could be admitted to communion, owing to their drunkenness and scandalous living. Andrews finally concluded that it was not really possible to convert Indians to Christianity.[114]

In Boston, Cotton Mather organized a Society of Negroes which met on Sunday evenings for religious instruction. That blacks attended Mather's church is evident from the remarks he addressed to them in his printed sermons. Mather's deepest concern for blacks, as for whites, was to get them to Christ. "Oh! That more pains were taken, to show the *Ethiopians*, their *Sin*, which renders them so much *Blacker* than their *Skin*!" exhorted Mather. Would that he could "lead them unto the Saviour, who will bestow upon them a *Change* of *Soul*, which is much better than a *Change* of *Skin*!" Participation of blacks at other Congregational churches was probably quite limited, though some church records of the pre-Awakening years indicate that a few slaves, and even an occasional Indian "servant," owned the covenant.[115] Still, these converts were barred from most church activities; they sat in the rear of meetinghouses, and their burial plots were segregated from those of white parishioners.[116]

Though the public attitude of the Society of Friends toward both blacks and Indians was remarkably enlightened for the eighteenth century, the number of either group embraced by Quaker meetings was very small. Nor are Negroes often mentioned in Presbyterian, Lutheran, or Reformed records.[117] Thus even in the North only a few Negroes, and even fewer Indians, were brought within the fold of the early eighteenth-century Christian churches.

White servants too were less likely to partake of religious instruction and Sabbath activities, especially in rural sections. As Dr. Thomas Bray noted of Maryland, since the distance to church was often ten or fifteen miles, "Servants & Children, God help them, must remain at Home." And this in a colony where the number of bonded servants was already large and growing. John Harrower, an indentured servant and tutor in Virginia, went to church only about seven times a year. Most Sundays he remained at home with his young charge; on occasion he spent Sunday catechizing the slaves.[118] In South Carolina, Commissary Alexander Garden expressed the hope in 1740 that catechized slaves might achieve a level of understanding equal to "the lower Sort of White People, Servants and Day Labourers (Specially in the Country)"[119]—suggesting that these classes of whites, while not entirely ignorant, were those least involved in southern church life.

In Congregational New England white servants were catechized along with children during family worship, and they went to church with the family unless the care of small children kept them at home. In the Middle Colonies, where many indentured servants settled after 1720, the picture is more blurred. Lutheran and Reformed ministers expressed much concern about the souls of German servants in the region, especially those placed in English families where their native religion was neglected. Still, servants regularly appear on Henry Muhlenberg's lists of confirmands.[120] A Quaker family in Pennsylvania encouraged a devout young woman in its employ to pursue the role of "speaker" in the Society of Friends. And Quakers were expected to include their servants as part of the family when attending meeting.[121] Nonetheless, it seems likely that in America, as in England at this time,[122] servants and the poor made up a disproportionately high percentage of those outside the embrace of some religious community

The Great Awakening and Church Membership

The Great Awakening of 1739–1745 temporarily altered the pattern of church adherence described above. Indeed this foremost revival, as well as periodic and more localized quickenings, can be defined in part not only by surging church admissions but by heavier concentrations than usual from two constituencies: men and young people. A typical report came from the Reverend Peter Thacher of Middleborough, Massachusetts: "the Grace of God has surprisingly seized and subdued the hardiest men, and more Males have been added here than the tenderer sex." In addition, many youths were "crying and wringing their hands, and bewailing their Frolicking and Dancing." At Woodbury, Connecticut between 1740 and 1742, First Church added fifty-nine male to forty-six female members. The awakened flocked to their minister in Wrentham, Massachusetts, "especially young People, under Soul Distress." From Natick came word that "Indians and English, Young and Old, Male and Female" had been called to Christ.[123] In New England those who joined the churches during the revival were on average six years younger than members affiliating before the Awakening, a pattern that pertained also in the Middle Colonies. Considering the ministers' perennial concern for the rising generation, this melting of young hearts was especially gratifying. The addition of larger numbers of men also tended, at least temporarily, to slow the feminization of churches.[124]

Women nonetheless continued to be drawn into the churches during the Great Awakening, where they spoke up more confidently than ever before. Boston's anti-revivalist minister Charles Chauncy, alarmed when "FEMALE EXHORTERS" began to appear, declared that "encouraging WOMEN, yea, GIRLS to speak in the assemblies for religious worship" was a clear breach of the Lord's commandment. One Old Light explained the peculiar susceptibility of women and youths to the emotionalism of the revival as follows: "The aptness of Children and Women to weep . . . in greater Abundance than grown Persons and Men is a plain proof . . . that their Fluids are more numerous in Proportion to their Solids, and their Nerves are weak."[125]

The revival's emphasis on the spoken rather than the written word, and its concern for reaching out to new constituencies, gave it a broad social base. Blacks and Indians, groups with an oral tradition, frequently attended revival meetings in the North. George Whitefield, finding that Negroes could be "effectually wrought upon, and in an uncommon manner," developed "a most winning way of addressing them."[126] In New England, blacks and Indians drawn to the Awakening were sometimes brought directly into the body of the church. Plymouth New Lights had among their members at least "a Negro or two who were directed to invite others to come to Christ," and at Gloucester, where a number of blacks joined the church, there was "a society of negroes, who in their meetings behave very seriously and decently." When the New Light preacher Eleazer Wheelock visited Taunton, Massachusetts, in 1741, he left "almost all the negroes in town wounded: three or four converted."[127] And Wheelock's work among the Indians led, of course, to the founding of a school that later became Dartmouth College. David Brainerd gained a number of converts to Christianity among the Indians of New Jersey. James Davenport was responsible for the conversion of Samson Occum, an eighteen-year-old Mohegan from Connecticut. Occum attended Wheelock's school at Lebanon, Connecticut for four years, was ordained by the Presbyterian Church in 1759, and carried the message of the revival to many of his brethren in Connecticut and New York.[128] Scattered evidence suggests that the Awakening may have had a more significant and long-range impact on blacks than on any other northern group. Ezra Stiles, for example, reported in the mid-1760s that his Newport congregation was composed of 500 whites and 70 blacks, with 55 blacks being communicants. One hundred blacks "constantly" attended Anglican services at Newport, Rhode Island, in 1743.[129] S.P.G. reports elsewhere in New England and the Middle Colonies also show a rise in the number of blacks being baptized and catechized.

Nor can it be doubted that the revival reached out to servants and laborers among the white population. As Dr. Alexander Hamilton commented with typical astringency during a 1744 trip throughout the North, even "the lower class of people here. . . . talk . . . about justification, sanctification, adoption, regeneration, repentance, free grace, reprobation, original sin, and a thousand other such pritty, chimerical knick knacks as if they had done nothing but studied divinity all their life time."[130] Still, the lowly origins of the awakened can easily be overstated. It is quite possible that the likeliest prospects for conversion came, after all, from the growing and varied ranks of the middle class, people who counted just a bit less than they felt they should in church and town, and for whom the revival opened up new possibilities and uncertainties— great hopes, great fears, great expectations.[131]

Religious awakening came later to the colonial South, starting in the mid-1740s with Presbyterian itinerants and reaching full pitch in the 1760s and 1770s with the Baptist and Methodist revivals. How churchgoing was affected by these revivals remains to be explored, though long-standing regional characteristics probably shaped the southerners' response. Men and women may have continued to participate in church life in relatively equal numbers, whereas young people and Indians, pending new evidence, appear to have been only marginally affected by the revival.[132] Negroes were another matter, however, for all evangelical denominations reported growing numbers of blacks among their adherents. Presbyterian Samuel Davies counted several hundred Negroes in his New Side congregations in Virginia. The added dimension that religion gave to black lives is implicit in Davies's comment about the slaves' delight in psalmody: "Whenever they could get an hour's leisure from their masters, [they] would hurry away to my house. . . . to gratify their peculiar taste for Psalmody. Sundry of them have lodged all night in my kitchen; and, sometimes, when I have awaked about two or three a-clock in the morning, a torrent of sacred harmony poured into my chamber, and carried my mind away to Heaven. In this seraphic exercise, some of them spend almost the whole night." Another glimpse of slave piety comes from the pen of Philip Fithian. Dadda Gumby, the oldest slave on Robert Carter's plantation, asked Fithian one hot July Sabbath if he was going to church, to which Fithian replied, "No Dadda it is too hot." "Too hot, Good God, too hot!" exclaimed the old slave. "I shall affront you, Master—Too hot to serve the Lord! Why I that am so old & worn out go on Foot."[133]

To be sure, only a tiny proportion of blacks were active Christians before the Revolution. Yet great changes were in the making. In religion the implied promise of some small measure of fulfillment, in a life that otherwise had little of it, was considerable, and a foundation was being laid upon which future generations would construct the central institution of Afro-American culture.

The Great Awakening caused a visible warp in the configuration of colonial church adherence. True, for most groups the change was no more than temporary, as pre-Awakening patterns reemerged once the revival subsided. One continuing legacy of the Awakening, however, was that it stimulated a rise in the number of preachers, especially lay preachers, thereby facilitating the extension of religion to the frontier and other underserved sections. Individuals who had been beyond the reach of ministers and churches—owing more to circumstances than choice—were now brought within the purview of a structured religious community. That this previously isolated constituency tended to have a higher proportion of young people, immigrants, and economically marginal persons than were located in the longer settled towns and cities goes far to explain the popular overtones of the revival. The growth of religious institutions was not dependent, of course, on the Great Awakening or any other revival. Far from reviving a languishing church life, the Awakening bespoke the vitality and widening reach of an expanding religious culture. Nor was the revival confined to matters of the spirit. Quickening social and political currents also would find expression through the medium of religion, especially evangelical religion—a matter which bears looking into.

PART II

RELIGION AND POLITICS

CHAPTER 5

"The Hosannas
of the Multitude":
The Great Awakening
in America

The Great Awakening—that intense period of revivalist tumult from about 1739 to 1745—is one of the most arresting subjects of American history. The eighteenth century, and the latter part of the seventeenth, were of course punctuated with religious episodes that seemed to erupt without warning and draw entire communities into a vortex of religious conversions and agitations of soul. Yet those episodes tended not to spread beyond the individual churches or towns in which they originated.[1] By the third decade of the eighteenth century, however, a number of currents were converging to prepare the way for an unprecedented burst of religious fervor and controversy.

The two major streams of thought shaping western religious belief in the eighteenth century—Enlightenment rationalism and Continental pietism—were by the 1720s reaching increasing numbers of Americans through the world of print, transatlantic learned societies, and such recently arrived spokesmen as the Anglican moderate George Berkeley, on the one side, and the Dutch Reformed pietist Theodore Frelinghuysen, on the other.[2] By the 1730s, American clergymen influenced by the spiritual intensity and emotional warmth of Reformed pietism were vigorously asserting that religion was being corrupted by secular forces; in their view a conversion experience that touched the heart was the only road to salvation. The rationalists demurred, preferring a faith tempered by "an enlightened Mind . . . not raised Affections." This contest between reason and innate grace was in one sense as old as Christianity itself. In New England, where it was often cast as a competition between Arminians and Antinomians, only the Calvinists' ability to hold the two elements in exquisite balance had averted a schism.[3] Rationalist attitudes, as noted earlier, were sufficiently prevalent in the eighteenth-century South to obstruct the development of heart religion there until the later colonial years. In the Middle Colonies, every point of view was heard, though by the 1730s tension was rising between the entrenched ministers of more orthodox opinion and incoming clergymen who insisted on conversion as the *sine qua non* of vital religion.

Adding to currents of religious unease in the early eighteenth century were a number of other developments: an accelerating pace of commercial growth; land shortages as well as land opportunities; the unprecedented diversity of eighteenth-century immigration; and a rapid climb in total population. Population growth now created dense settlements in some rural as well as urban areas, facilitating mass public gatherings. Moreover, the proliferation of churches and sects, intensifying denominational rivalries, and smallpox and earthquake alarms that filled meeting-houses to overflowing all contributed to a sense of quickening in church life.

Into this volatile and expectant environment came some of the most charismatic and combative personalities of the age. And as the electricity of a Tennent crackled, and the thunder of a Whitefield rolled, a storm broke that, in the opinion of many, would forever alter American society. The Great Awakening created conditions uniquely favorable to social and political, as well as religious, reform by piercing the facade of civility and deference that governed provincial life to usher in a new age of contentiousness. By promoting church separations and urging their followers to make choices that had political as well as religious implications, the

Awakeners wrought permanent changes in public practices and attitudes. Before it subsided, the revival had unsettled the lives of more Americans and disrupted more institutions than any other single event in colonial experience to that time. To see how a religious movement could overspill its boundaries to reshape cultural understanding and political expectations, we must take a closer look at some of the churches and people caught up in the revival.

Presbyterian Beginnings

The Great Awakening began not as a popular uprising but as a contest between clerical factions. Thus only those churches with a "professional" clergy and organized governing structure—the Presbyterian, Congregational, Dutch Reformed, and eventually the Anglican—were split apart by the revival. The newer German churches and the sects, having little structure to overturn, remained largely outside the conflict.[4] These events have usually been viewed from the perspective of New England Congregationalism, though the first denomination to be involved in the Awakening was the Presbyterian Church in the Middle Colonies. All of the strains and adjustments experienced by other colonial denominations over a longer time span were compressed, in the Presbyterian case, into the fifty years from the beginning of Ulster immigration around 1725 to the Revolution. Thus the Presbyterian example serves as a kind of paradigm of the experience of all churches from their initial formation through the Great Awakening and its aftermath.[5] It reveals too how a dispute between ministers rapidly widened into a controversy that tested the limits of order and introduced new forms of popular leadership that challenged deferential traditions.

Presbyterians looked to the future with reasonably high hopes by the third decade of the eighteenth century. To all appearances they possessed a more stable and orderly church structure than any of their middle-colony competitors. Unlike the Anglicans, they required no bishop to perform the essential rites of ordination and confirmation; nor did they suffer quite the same shortage of ministers as the German churches. The supply of Presbyterian clergy, if never adequate, had at least been sufficient to support the formation of a rudimentary governing structure. Three presbyteries and the Synod of Philadelphia were in place before the first wave of immigration from Ulster reached the Delaware basin, enabling the twenty-five to thirty ministers active in the Middle Colonies to direct growth and protect professional standards in the period of expansion after 1725. Congregations were under the care of laymen ordained to the office of "elder" and, when available, ministers. Supervising presbyteries in each region maintained oversight of local congregations and ordained and disciplined the clergy. At the top was the synod, which provided a forum where clerical disputes over church doctrine and governing authority could be resolved *in camera*.[6]

Yet the controls imposed by the Presbyterian hierarchy were hardly all that they appeared to be. Beneath orderly processes were tensions which had been expanding steadily before finally bursting forth in fratricidal strife and schism after 1739. Any reading of eighteenth-century Presbyterian records discloses at least three kinds of strains beneath the surface: between parishioners, between people and minister, and within the professional clergy itself.

The Presbyterian Church was the focal point and mediator of Scotch-Irish community life from the late 1720s on, when thousands of Ulster Scots began entering the colonies annually. As the westward-migrating settlers moved beyond the reach of government and law, the Presbyterian Church was the only institution that kept pace with settlement. By stretching resources to the limit, the synod, and especially the presbyteries, kept in touch with their scattered brethren through itinerant preachers and presbyterial visitations. Ministers, invariably the best educated persons on the early frontier, were looked to for leadership in both religious and community affairs, and they often took up multiple roles as doctors, teachers, and even lawyers. So closely did the Scotch-Irish identify with the Kirk that it was often said they "could not live without it."[7]

But if the church was a vital center it was also an agency of control. Presbyterian ministers—whom some regarded as a "stiff-necked . . . [and] pedantick crew"[8]—expected to guide their parishioners' spiritual growth and moral safety in America as they had done in the Old Country, and at first, by and large, they succeeded. Congregations gathered spontaneously in Scotch-Irish settlements, much as they did in immigrant German communities. A major difference between the two societies was that from an early stage lay Presbyterians submitted themselves to clerical authority. As soon as a Presbyterian congregation was formed, it requested recognition and the supply of a minister from the local presbytery. Often the presbytery could provide only a probationer or itinerant preacher for the Sabbath, and many settlements were fortunate to hear a sermon one or two Sundays a month. The congregations nonetheless proceeded to elect elders, deacons to care for the poor and sick, and trustees to oversee the collection of tithes for the minister's salary. The governing "session," comprised of elders and minister, functioned as a kind of court, hearing charges and ruling on a variety of matters, including disputes between parishioners over land or debt, domestic difficulties, and church doctrine. The main responsibility of the session was to enforce moral discipline. Its rulings could be appealed to the supervising presbytery. The presbytery minutes consequently have much to tell us about the quality of clerical authority. But they also disclose the growing undercurrent of resistance that such authority aroused among the freer spirits in the Scotch-Irish settlements.[9]

The minutes of the westernmost Presbytery of Donegal, Pennsylvania, with their unceasing concern for communal harmony and moral order, recall the social ethos of early New England communities, where religion also was a source of both cohesion and strain. Donegal Presbytery met seventeen times between October 1732 and November 1735 at nine different locations, an itinerary that enabled it to assert direct authority over widely dispersed congregations. During these "visitations," members of the presbytery dealt with administrative problems, questioned parishioners and ministers on points of doctrine, and presided over hearings in cases of moral discipline on appeal from the sessions. In the early years appeals were handled with dispatch, as when one parishioner requested reconsideration of the session's refusal to baptize his child, which had been born "before the time in reference to his marriage." After investigating the marriage and finding it sound, the presbytery granted his request.[10] Cases of fornication and adultery were so common in one church that the elders requested guidance from the presbytery about granting membership to persons "guilty of uncleanness." The presbytery admonished all sessions "not to be hasty or precipitant in admitting of persons guilty of fornication," but to wait until evidence was obtained in private discussion "of their true & sincere sense of sorrow for their sin," after which a "publick profession" was required. The same rule applied in cases of adultery, whether "single or double" (by one or both parties). One couple was forced to appear on the Sabbath in public confession "twice from the woman & three times from the man (it being Adultery in him)." Other cases involved disputes over false swearing, drunkenness, an alleged breach of contract regarding a £5 loan, an argument between two neighbors about timber rights, and the barring of parishioners from church privileges for failure to pay their share of the minister's salary.[11]

The case of Elizabeth Ross, heard by the presbytery on October 16, 1734, illustrates both the judicial and the consensual character of these proceedings. Mrs. Ross had been accused by Thomas Wilkie, a fellow parishioner, of appearing in public drunk, and the local session had heard witnesses and taken depositions in the case. The accused's husband, John Ross, had charged Wilkie with giving false evidence and had demanded that he "publickly own that he had wronged Elizabeth Ross," pending which Ross refused to accept the session's jurisdiction and appealed the case to the presbytery. This appeal over his head offended Ross's minister, who made a public display of his anger. At the presbytery hearing, two witnesses testified that they had not seen any symptoms of drunkenness in Mrs. Ross. The decision handed down by the presbytery is a masterpiece of nicely balanced justice. John Ross was declared "very culpable" for abusing the witnesses against his wife and was admonished for refusing to accept the authority of the session. The presbytery also concluded that Thomas Wilkie did not have just grounds to charge Mrs. Ross with drunkenness, but because Wilkie did not lie intentionally he was declared not guilty of perjury. Further, the minister was censured for wrangling publicly with John Ross "inasmuch as his Character & Station require that he should be Examplary in meekness & patience." The final scene before the presbytery was heavy with the symbolism of consensus. The clerk records that the decision was greeted with "great Joy and Satisfaction," after which "all Parties did in a vary Christian manner Submit to and acquiesce in the above determination . . . by Joining of hands & agreeable words declaring their mutual reconciliation to Each other."[12]

The conciliatory efficacy of such proceedings, and the clergy's warrant to preside over them, persisted as long as the church fathers spoke with one voice. The clergy's power to withhold membership, baptism, and communion, to say nothing of the influence they exerted for community approval or non-approval, gave ministers a strong hold over their parishioners. But should unity within the clergy loosen, other tensions below the surface of provincial society might be difficult to suppress.

The first portent of trouble for Donegal Presbytery came as early as 1735. The Nottingham church in Lancaster County had become embroiled over points of doctrine, and the minister, William Orr (a conservative sort), had aroused lively opposition from a portion of his congregation. One parishioner, a Mrs. Robinson, went so far as to accuse him of "unchast behaviour with Mary Barns." When the furor of denials and counter-denials so widened the breach in the congregation that Orr asked for a separation from the Nottingham Church, the entire affair was referred to the presbytery. In a long and vividly detailed hearing, Orr's witnesses testified that Mrs. Robinson was a notorious woman whose word was not to be trusted. One said that Mrs. Robinson's shipmates on the voyage from Ireland had suspected her of witchcraft, and had wanted to make her recite the Lord's Prayer as a test. She was further accused of drunkenness, of

"Cursing & swearing profanely," and of having a stormy domestic life.

But if Mrs. Robinson was to some a person of bad repute, she was clearly useful to the disaffected and apparently evangelical-tending faction of Nottingham church.[13] Orr, protesting that the opposition "first attacked My principles & now has Entered upon my Character," found himself repelling charges of drunkenness, of neglecting family worship, and of misconduct with "Married women & young women too." Most of the witnesses seem to have vouched for Orr's sobriety and morals, so that after arbitration by "two indifferent persons" appointed by the presbytery, the charges against him were finally withdrawn. Nevertheless, difficulties continued, and shortly thereafter Orr once again asked for, and this time obtained, his release. When the presbytery was slow to grant him a certificate of good standing (perhaps in the hope of persuading him to stay, though one wonders), Orr refused to preach any longer at Nottingham. Denouncing the presbytery as "a company of damn'd Hypocrites," he departed the district in the spring of 1736 without a certificate, for which he was subsequently censured.[14]

Here was a new and ominous note. The presbytery had now moved from arbitrating the petty disputes of disgruntled parishioners to engaging in semipublic debate with a fellow minister. By the late 1730s, moreover, the procedures developed by the synod and presbyteries to regulate clerical conduct and standards were under steady assault from an evangelical* faction in the church. When several members of that faction formed the New Brunswick Presbytery in 1738 to facilitate the ordination of evangelical preachers,[15] the stage was set for a showdown that would shatter ministerial unity, elevate discontent within congregations, and usher in the Great Awakening.

*As Winthrop S. Hudson has suggested, evangelicalism was more "a mood and an emphasis" than a systematic theology. Its major characteristics in the colonies were a resistance to formalism, a stress on individual religious introspection, and an ecumenical spirit. *Religion in America: An Historical Account of the Development of American Religious Life* (New York, 1965; second ed. 1973), p. 78.

New Sides vs. Old Sides

The Great Awakening split the Presbyterian Church apart, and through the cracks long-suppressed steam hissed forth in clouds of acrimony and vituperation that would change the face of authority in Pennsylvania and elsewhere. As the passions of the Awakening reached their height in the early 1740s, evangelical "New Side" Presbyterians turned on the more orthodox "Old Sides" with the ferocity peculiar to zealots, charging them with extravagant doctrinal and moral enormities. The internecine spectacle that ensued, the loss of proportion and professional decorum, contributed to the demystification of the clergy, forced parishioners to choose between competing factions, and overset traditional attitudes about deference and leadership in colonial America.

The division that surfaced in 1740–1741 had been developing for more than a decade. Presbyterian ministers had no sooner organized their central association, the Synod of Philadelphia, in 1715 than the first lines of stress appeared, though it was not until a cohesive evangelical faction emerged in the 1730s that an open split was threatened. Most members of the synod hoped to model American Presbyterianism along orderly lines, and in 1729 an act requiring all ministers and ministerial candidates to subscribe publicly to the Westminster Confession had been approved.[16] In 1738 the synod had further ruled that no minister would be licensed unless he could display a degree from a British or European university, or from one of the New England colleges (Harvard or Yale). New candidates were to submit to an examination by a commission of the synod on the soundness of their theological training and spiritual condition. The emergent evangelical faction rightly saw these restrictions as an effort to control their own activities. They had reluctantly accepted subscription to the Westminster Confession, but synodical screening of new candidates struck them as an intolerable invasion of the local presbyteries' right of ordination.[17]

The insurgents were led by the Scotsman William Tennent, Sr., and his sons, William, Jr., Charles, John, and Gilbert. William, Sr.

had been educated at the University of Edinburgh, receiving a bachelor's degree in 1693 and an M.A. in 1695. He may have been exposed to European pietism at Edinburgh, where new ideas of every sort were brewing in the last quarter of the seventeenth century.[18] Though ordained a minister of the Anglican church in 1706, Tennent did not gain a parish of his own, and in 1718 he departed the Old World for the New. When he applied for a license from the Synod of Philadelphia in 1718, Tennent was asked his reasons for leaving the Church of England. He responded that he had come to view government by bishops as anti-scriptural, that he opposed ecclesiastical courts and plural benefices, that the church was leaning toward Arminianism, and that he disapproved of "their ceremonial way of worship." All this seemed sound enough to the Presbyterians, and Tennent was licensed forthwith.[19] Having a strong interest in scholarship and pedagogy,[20] Tennent built a one-room schoolhouse in about 1730 in Neshaminy, Bucks County—the Log College, as it was later derisively called—where he set about training young men for the ministry. Exactly when Tennent began to pull away from the regular synod leadership is unclear, but by 1736 his church at Neshaminy was split down the middle and the anti-evangelical members were attempting to expel him as minister.[21]

In 1739 the synod was confronted with a question on professional standards that brought the two factions closer to a complete break. When the previous year's synod had erected commissions to examine the education of all ministerial candidates not holding degrees from approved universities, Gilbert Tennent had charged that the qualification was designed "to prevent his father's school from training gracious men for the Ministry." Overriding the synod's rule in 1739, the radical New Brunswick Presbytery licensed one John Rowland without reference to any committee, though Rowland had received "a private education"—the synod's euphemism for the Log College. Sharply criticizing the presbytery for its disorderly and divisive action, the synod refused to approve Rowland until he agreed to submit himself for examination, which he in turn refused to do.[22]

Since education was central to the dispute, it is unfortunate that no Log College records have survived to describe the training given the remarkable group of men that came under William Tennent, Sr.'s tutelage. We do know that they emerged to become leaders of the revivalist movement, and would in turn prepare other religious and educational leaders of the middle and southern colonies. The little existing evidence casts doubt on the synod's charge that Tennent and his followers were "destroyers of good learning" who persisted in foisting unlettered Log College students upon an undiscriminating public. As Gilbert Tennent insisted, the insurgents "desired and designed a well-qualified Ministry as much as our Brethren." To be sure, their theological emphasis was at variance with that of the Old Side clergy, and there may have been parts of the traditional curriculum they did not value as highly, as had been true with the innovative dissenting academies in Britain. But as competition between the two factions intensified, restrained criticism gave way to enmity. Thus when the synod charged that Gilbert Tennent had called "Physicks, Ethicks, Metophysicks and Pnuematicks [the rubric under which Aristotelian philosophy was taught in medieval universities] meer Criticks, and consequently useless," its members could not resist adding that he did so "because his Father cannot or doth not teach them."[23]

Yet there is much that attests to both William Tennent, Sr.'s learning and his pedagogical talents. That he was a polished scholar of the classics, spoke Latin and English with equal fluency, and was a master of Greek was confirmed by many who knew him. He also "had some acquaintance with the . . . Sciences." A hint of the training Tennent offered comes from the licensing examination given his youngest son Charles in 1736 by the Philadelphia Presbytery, among whose members were several who would later emerge as chief critics of the Tennents. Young Charles was tested on his "ability in prayer [and] in the Languages," in the delivery of a sermon and exegesis, and on his answers to "various suitable questions on the arts and sciences, especially Theology and out of Scripture." He was also examined on the state of his soul. Charles Tennent was apparently approved without question.[24]

The strongest evidence of the quality of a Log College education comes, however, from the subsequent careers and accomplishments of its eighteen to twenty-one "alumni." Their deep commitment to formal education is demonstrated by the number of academies they themselves founded, including Samuel Blair's "classical school" at Faggs Manor in Pennsylvania, Samuel Finley's academy at Nottingham, and several others.[25] Two early presidents of the College of New Jersey (Princeton) were Samuel Finley and Samuel Davies (the latter having been educated by Blair at Faggs Manor).[26] Moreover, the published sermons and essays of Samuel Finley, Samuel Blair, and Gilbert Tennent not only pulse with evangelical passion but also display wide learning. In the opinion of a leading Presbyterian historian the intellectual accomplishments of the Log College revivalists far outshone those of the Old Side opposers, among whom only the scholarly Francis Alison produced significant writings. As George Whitefield observed when he visited Neshaminy in 1739 and saw the rough structure of logs that housed the school: "All that we can say of most universities is, that they are glorious without."[27]

But the distinction that the Log College men would achieve was still unknown in 1739, when the New Brunswick Presbytery defied the synod by licensing John Rowland. It was at this juncture, moreover, that the twenty-six-year-old English evangelist, George Whitefield, made his sensational appearance. Whitefield's visits to New Jersey and Pennsylvania in the winter of 1739–1740 provided tremendous support for the Presbyterian insurgents, as thousands of provincials flocked to hear him and realized, perhaps for the first time, something of what the American evangelists had been up to. The public support that now flowed to Tennent and the New Side exhilarated its members, inciting them to ever bolder assaults on the synod.

The revivalists had to this point preached only in their own churches or in temporarily vacant pulpits, but that winter they began to invade the territory of the regular clergy. This action raised the issue of itinerant preaching, perhaps the thorniest of the entire

The Reverend Gilbert Tennent, 1703–1764
New-York Historical Society

conflict, for it brought the parties face to face on the question of who was better qualified to interpret the word of God. It was in this setting that Gilbert Tennent was moved on March 8, 1740 to deliver his celebrated sermon, *The Danger of an Unconverted Ministry*, to a Nottingham congregation engaged in choosing a new preacher.[28] It was an audacious, not to say reckless, attack on the Old Side clergy, and Tennent would later qualify some of his strongest language. But the sermon starkly reveals the gulf that separated the two factions by 1740. It also demonstrates the revivalists' supreme disregard for the traditional limits on public discussion of what amounted to professional questions.

Tennent began by drawing an analogy between the opposers in the Philadelphia Synod who rejected experiential religion, and the legalistic Pharisees of old who had rejected the radical teachings of Jesus. The Pharisees, he declared, were bloated with intellectual conceit, letter-learned but blind to the truths of the Saviour. They "loved the uppermost Seats in the Synagogues, and to be called Rabbi, Rabbi." They were masterly and positive in their sayings, "as if forsooth Knowledge must die with them." Worst of all, they "had their Eyes, with Judas, fixed upon the Bag. Why, they came into the Priest's Office for a Piece of Bread; they took it up as a Trade . . . O Shame!"[29] For all these worldly conceits Jesus had denounced them as hypocrites and a generation of vipers. Tennent went on to pronounce a similar judgment on the Pharisees of his own time— "unconverted [and] wicked Men" who as nearly resembled the old Pharisees "as one Crow's Egg does another." If men are not called to the ministry by a "New Birth. . . . their Discourses are cold and sapless, and as it were freeze between their lips."[30]

Tennent's solution to the problem of unconverted ministers, in addition to prayer for their "dear fainting Souls," was "to encourage private Schools, or Seminaries of Learning, which are under the Care of skilful and experienced Christians." As for itinerant preachers, Tennent assured his Nottingham auditors that it was no sin but a right well within their Christian liberty to desert their parish minister for a converted preacher. "Birds of the Air fly to warmer Climates in order to shun the Winter-cold, and also doubtless to get better Food"; should humankind do less? In the only light moment of the sermon, Tennent exclaimed: "*Faith* is said to come by *Hearing* . . . But the Apostle doesn't add, *Your Parish-Minister*." Thus Tennent concluded: "Let those who live under the Ministry of dead Men . . . repair to the Living, where they may be edified."[31]

In this influential and widely disseminated sermon[32] Tennent set forth the three principal issues over which Presbyterians would divide: the conversion experience, education of the clergy, and itinerant preaching. While his tone may have owed something to Whitefield's recent influence—humility was never a strong point with the evangelists—it also reflected the growing self-confidence of the insurgents, as a wave of public support lifted them to popular heights. During the synod of 1740 the anti-revivalist clergy, in a demonstration of their reasonableness, agreed to certain compromises on the issues of itinerancy and licensing,[33] but when the revivalists continued to denounce them publicly as carnal and unconverted, their patience came to an end.

The break between Old Side and New Side Presbyterians came during the synod of 1741 when a protest signed by twelve ministers and eight elders demanded that the revivalists be expelled from the synod. In a preemptive move, the New Side clergy voluntarily withdrew from the Philadelphia Synod to their presbyteries, where their work continued with great zeal and met with success that would outshine that of their rivals. In 1745 the evangelical party, joined by other friends of the revival from the Middle Colonies, formed the Synod of New York, which would sustain a lively existence until 1758 when the Presbyterian schism was finally repaired.

Disagreements over theological emphasis, professional standards, and centralized authority were the most immediate causes of the Presbyterian schism, but other differences between Old and New Sides had the effect of making the conflict sharper. Disparities in education, age (and therefore career expectations), and cultural bias are of special interest.

The twelve Old Sides who moved to expel the revivalist radicals in 1741 have sometimes been labeled the "Scotch-Irish" party for good reason.[34] Nine were born in Northern Ireland, and two in Scotland (the birthplace of the twelfth is unknown). All were educated abroad, mainly in Scotland, and especially at the University of Glasgow. Most came to the colonies between the ages of twenty-eight and thirty-two, after having completed their education.[35] The typical Old Side clergyman was about forty-two at the time of the schism. The New Side ministers who formed the Synod of New York in 1745 numbered twenty-two. Of the twenty-one whose places of birth can be ascertained, ten were born in New England or on eastern Long Island, one in Newark, New Jersey, eight in Northern Ireland (including Gilbert, William, Jr., and Charles Tennent), one in Scotland, and one in England. Most of those born abroad emigrated to the colonies during their middle teens; Charles Tennent was but seven, and the oldest was William

Robinson, the son of an English Quaker doctor, who emigrated at about twenty-eight after an ill-spent youth.[36] The educational profile of the New Side preachers is in striking contrast to that of the Old. Of the twenty-two, nine received degrees from Yale College, two were Harvard men, and ten were educated at the Log College. One had probably gone to a Scottish university. The typical New Side minister was about thirty-two at the time of the schism, or a decade younger than his Old Side counterpart.[37]

Several tendencies suggest themselves. The Old Sides, more mature than their adversaries, were also more settled in their professional careers; further, their Scottish education and early professional experiences in Ulster may have instilled a respect for discipline and ecclesiastical order that could not easily be cast aside.[38] They knew it was difficult to keep up standards in provincial societies, especially the heterodox Middle Colonies where competition in religion, as in everything else, was a constant challenge to good order. Still, it was irritating to be treated as intruders by the resident notables, or by such as the Anglicans, who pretended to look down on the Presbyterians as "men of small talents and mean education."[39] There was security in knowing that the first generation of Presbyterian leaders had been educated and licensed in accordance with the most exacting Old World criteria. But the tradition must be continued, for succeeding generations would gain respect only if the ministry were settled on a firm professional base. Though Harvard and Yale were not Edinburgh and Glasgow, they did pattern their curricula after the British universities and to that extent could serve until the Presbyterian Church was able to establish a college of its own. And only if Presbyterian leaders could control the education and admission of candidates to the ministry might they hold their heads high among rival religious groups.[40] A professional ministry was thus crucial to the "Scotch-Irish" party's pride and sense of place.

The New Side party, on the other hand, cared less about professional niceties than about converting sinners. Its members were at the beginning of their careers, and most, being native-born or coming to the colonies in their youth, were not so likely to be imbued with an Old World sense of prerogative and order. They never doubted that an educated clergy was essential, but education had to be of the right sort. By the 1730s Harvard and Yale were being guided, in their view, by men of rationalist leanings who simply did not provide the type of training wanted by the revivalists.[41] Thus the New Sides chafed against the controls favored by their more conservative elders, controls that restricted their freedom of action, slowed their careers, and were in their opinion out of touch with New World ways.

The anti-institutionalism of the revivalists caused some critics to portray them as social levellers, though there were no significant distinctions in social outlook or family background between Old and New Sides.[42] But as with any insurgent group that relies in part on public support for its momentum, the New Sides tended to clothe their appeals in popular dress. At every opportunity they pictured the opposers as "the Noble & Mighty" elders of the church, and identified themselves with the poor and "common People"—images reinforced by the Old Sides' references to the evangelists' followers as an ignorant and "wild Rabble."[43]

The revivalists may not have been deliberate social levellers, but their words and actions had the effect of emphasizing individual values over hierarchical ones. Everything they did, from disrupting orderly processes and encouraging greater lay participation in church government, to promoting mass assemblies and the physical closeness that went with them, raised popular emotions. Most important, they insisted that there were choices, and that the individual himself was free to make them.

The people, it might be suspected, had been waiting for this. The long years of imposed consensus and oversight by the Kirk had taken their toll, and undercurrents of restlessness had strengthened as communities stabilized and Old World values receded. Still, the habit of deferring to the clergy was deeply rooted in Presbyterian culture, making inertia an accomplice of church authority. By 1740, however, with the clergy themselves, or a part of them, openly promoting rebellion, many Presbyterians "in imitation of their example," as it was said, joined the fray. The result was turbulence, shattered and divided congregations, and a rash of slanderous reports against Old Side clergymen. Most such charges were either proved false or are deeply suspect, owing to their connection with the factional conflict.[44] But aspersions against the ministerial character had now become a subject of public debate, suggesting that the schisms of the Awakening were effectively challenging the old structures of authority.

Examples of competition between clerical factions leading to popular tumults are too numerous to describe here, but the case of Middle Octerara Church in western Pennsylvania and its pastor, the Reverend Alexander Craighead, is representative. Craighead was tending toward evangelical attitudes by the later 1730s, as shown by his refusal to baptize the children of couples who had not experienced conversion. By the end of the decade his church had divided into pro- and anti-Craighead factions, and in December 1740 the controversy was referred to Donegal Presbytery, where a trial was held to determine whether Craighead was fit to continue at his post. Since the presbytery was dominated by Old Sides, the embattled minister denied that its "carnal" and graceless members had any authority over him. He then cut loose publicly, accusing them of "whoredom, drunkenness, Sabbath breaking, Lying etc."

With such charges resonating through the parish, Craighead's supporters were emboldened to add their voices to the clamor, and the presbytery's proceedings were now "interrupted by the people rising into a tumult, and railing at the Members in the most Scurrilous & opprobrious terms." The scandalized presbytery charged Craighead with slander and with offering "harrangues to amuse the populace." He had invited "the whole Congregation, which was very great, to the tent, where they were entertained with the reading of a paper he calls his defence," and in which he denounced the Old Sides "by name." All of this had heaped such reproach and contempt on the presbytery that they had no choice but to suspend Craighead from his pastorate.[45] Clearly undeterred by the presbytery's action, laypersons loyal to the New Sides appeared at the presbytery's spring meetings in 1741 to bring charges against four sitting members for drunkenness, blasphemy, and other wickedness. New and Old Sides meanwhile continued to belabor each other publicly as "dead Drones," "blackguard Ruffians," "Quacks or Montebanks," liars, and heretics.[46]

So volatile had the revival become that it could no longer be contained within a single region. Thus when George Whitefield carried the crusade northward, the tumults and divisions that had seized the Presbyterian Church spread to the Congregational meetinghouses of New England

The "divine fire" Kindled in New England

Whitefield's initial visit to Boston in September 1740 was greeted with tremendous interest, for the "Grand Itinerant" was the first figure of international renown to tour the colonies. During an eleven-day period he preached at least nineteen times at a number of different churches and outdoor sites, including New South Church where the huge crowd was thrown into such a panic that five were killed and many more injured. Fifteen thousand persons supposedly heard Whitefield preach on Boston Common. Even allowing for an inflated count, these were surely the largest crowds ever assembled in Boston or any other colonial city. As Samuel Johnson once said, Whitefield would have been adored if he wore a nightcap and preached from a tree. Whitefield's tours outside of Boston, and then into western Massachusetts and Connecticut, were attended by similar public outpourings. No one, it seems, wanted to miss the show. In December Gilbert Tennent arrived in Boston, having been urged by Whitefield to add more fuel to the divine fires he had kindled there. Tennent's preaching, which lacked Whitefield's sweetness but none of his power, aroused a popular fervor that matched or exceeded that inspired by the Englishman.[47]

Most Congregational ministers, including those at Boston, had welcomed Whitefield's tour as an opportunity to stimulate religious piety. Tennent's torrid preaching may have discomfited some, but it was not until 1742 that three events led to a polarization of the clergy into "New Light" supporters and "Old Light" opposers of the Great Awakening. First came the publication in Boston of Tennent's sermon, *The Danger of an Unconverted Ministry*, which one Old Light would later blame for having "sown the Seeds of all that Discord, Intrusion, Confusion, Separation, Hatred, Variance, Emulations, Wrath, Strife, Seditions, Heresies, &c. that have been springing up in so many of the Towns and Churches thro' the Province. . . . " Another was the publication of Whitefield's 1740 *Journal*, in which he criticized "most" New England preachers for insufficient piety and observed of Harvard and Yale that "their Light is become Darkness."[48] The final provocation was the arrival in Boston on June 25, 1742 of the Reverend James Davenport, a newly fledged evangelist who already had Connecticut in an uproar and would soon have all Boston by the ears.

Davenport had been expelled from Connecticut on June 3 after being adjudged "disturbed in the rational Faculties of his Mind."[49] Now the twenty-six-year-old evangelist was determined to share his special insights with the people of Boston. Forewarned about Davenport's odd behavior, the ministers of Boston and Charlestown (the majority of whom favored the Awakening) requested that the intruder restrain his "assuming Behavior . . . especially in judging the spiritual State of Pastors and People," and decided not to offer him their pulpits. Davenport was undeterred. He preached on the Common and in the rain on Copp's Hill; he proclaimed first three and then nine more of Boston's ministers "by name" to be unconverted; and he announced that he was "ready to drop down dead for the salvation of but one soul." Davenport was followed, according to one critic, by a "giddy Audience . . . chiefly made up of idle or ignorant Persons" of low rank. To some of Boston's soberer citizens the crowd appeared "menacing," and one newspaper essayist found Davenport's followers "so red hot, that I verily believe they would make nothing to kill Opposers."[50] Such was the anarchy threatened by religious enthusiasm.

Clearly something had to be done. When the Congregational clergy of Massachusetts held their annual convention on May 25,

1743, the now vocal critics of the Awakening seized the occasion to publish a manifesto which inveighed against "disorderly tumults and indecent behaviour," condemned itinerant preachers, and deplored the spirit and practice of church separation. Though signed by the convention moderator only, the declaration purported to speak for all Massachusetts pastors.[51] Supporters of the revival promptly denied that they had been fully consulted, and on July 7, 1743, a second convention was called. Soon there appeared another manifesto which took a decidedly more positive view of the revival. Though critical of lay exhorters and "unscriptural" church separations, its primary message was that many persons had been "awakened to a solemn Concern about Salvation." It closed, moreover, with a millenarian flourish that belied its otherwise moderate tone, praying that "the present Appearances may be an Earnest of the glorious Things promis'd to the Church. . . . AMEN! *Even so come LORD JESUS; Come quickly!*" The second declaration was signed by sixty-eight ministers from Massachusetts and New Hampshire, and was later subscribed to by at least forty-five others from Maine to Connecticut.[52] Thus did the division between New and Old Light Congregational ministers break into public print.

In the months that followed, New Englanders, like middle-colony Presbyterians before them, would witness and then be drawn into a fierce struggle between the two factions, as their once-decorous ministers impugned the intelligence and integrity of their rivals in public sermons and essays. The Old Light writers were especially bellicose, losing no opportunity to rebuke the "enthusiastic, factious, censorious Spirit" of the revivalists.[53] Schisms were threatened everywhere, and as early as 1742 some congregations had "divided into Parties, and openly and scandalously separated from one another." As the Connecticut Old Light, Isaac Stiles, warned, the subversion of all order was threatened when "Contempt is cast upon Authority both Civil and Ecclesiastical."[54] Most distressing to those who believed that "Good Order is the Strength and Beauty of the World," was the Awakening's tendency to splinter New England society. "Formerly the People could bear with each other in Charity when they differ'd in Opinion," recalled one writer, "but they now break Fellowship and Communion with one another on that Account."[55]

Indeed, awakened parishioners were repeatedly urged to withdraw from a "corrupt ministry." "O that the precious Seed might be preserved and *separated* from all gross Mixtures!" prayed the Connecticut New Light Jonathan Parsons.[56] And spurred on by Parsons and other New Lights, withdraw they did. In Plymouth and Ipswich, from Maine to the Connecticut River Valley, the New England separatist movement gained momentum from 1743 onward.

Minority Rights and Divided Sovereignty: The Great Awakening as a Radical Model

Religion has always been considered a likely agent of radicalism. Nor is there reason to doubt that the tremendous stir of the Great Awakening altered the social and political equilibrium of colonial life. Just as the revival marked a significant divide in popular thought and practice, so too it would supply the most pertinent and usable model for radical activists in the years that lay ahead. Many features of the Awakening foreshadowed what was to come.

Since the Awakeners began as an insurgent minority in every church, they could advance their religious ideology only by overturning the orthodox majority, or, when that failed, by withdrawing from or bringing down the institutional structures that sheltered orthodoxy and fortified its authority. For such work they required allies, and owing to the importance of the laity in colonial church life, as well as shifting values in eighteenth-century provincial society at large, the revivalists found their allies among the people. Together they launched a mass movement that made bold assaults on established forms of church government and traditional assumptions about deference and social order. Evangelical preachers constantly exhorted their followers not to shrink from painful choices between alternative religious doctrines, and urged them to act on those decisions by separating from unregenerate churches.

The separatists constructed parallel—in the eyes of some, "extra-legal"—organizations to compete with those from which they had seceded. Impelled to justify their opposition, the revivalists developed novel arguments defending the rights of minorities, and they increasingly characterized the authority against which they were rebelling as illegitimate, even tyrannical.

In all these actions the dissidents and their followers cut through the still powerful proscriptions against opposition to settled authority, and they did so not only in theory but in practice. The institutional disruptions and church separations of the Great Awakening thus provided a kind of "practice model" which enabled the provincials to "rehearse"—though unwittingly—a number of the situations, and the arguments appropriate to them, that would reappear with the political crisis of the 1760s and 1770s.

A central issue separating supporters of the revival from its opponents concerned the divisibility, or as some argued the indivisibility, of ecclesiastical authority. The question was warmly debated at the time of the Presbyterian schism. Old Side Presbyterians shared a corporate view of church government; that is, once decisions had been approved by the central synod, all members were expected to abide by its rulings. Did any "Society . . . [ever] incorporate themselves under any Form of Government," asked one Old Side, without submitting to its authority "whether they approved of these Rules or not?" The minority must always accede to the decisions agreed upon by the majority. Yet the revivalists claimed the liberty "to question and judge all, and refuse[d] Subjection to every proper Judicature."[57] Worse yet, the New Sides encouraged contentions and divisions within congregations, though it was "the Duty of Ministers to crush such Factions." Rather than promoting schisms, the Old Sides admonished, preachers should teach their flocks to "love God, love your Neighbour, [and] obey them that have Rule over you." Where divisions were threatened in New England, ministers and elders accused the insurgents of "disorderly Walking, Contrary to the Gospel" and church covenant.[58]

But the Awakeners were not listening. Their heated brains had

raced beyond the old clichés about corporate solidarity that tradi-
tionally governed institutional and social relationships. No longer
was conscience to be sacrificed for outward appearances of unity.
"Pray must we leave off every Duty, that is the Occasion of
Contention or Division?" asked Gilbert Tennent. "Surely, it cannot
be reasonably suppos'd, that we are exhorted, to a Unity in any
Thing that is wicked, or inconsistent with the . . . greater Good of
our poor Souls." The Reverend Samuel Finley was even more
direct—and certainly more modern—in exhorting his followers to
"make a Party for Jesus Christ. . . . [though the] Commotion rends
the Church; divides Congregations and Families; [and] sets People
at Variance."[59] New England separatists were fond of quoting 2
Corinthians 6:14–17—"Be ye not unequally yoked together with
Unbelievers. . . . Wherefore come out from among them, and be ye
separate."[60]

As evangelical factions formed in congregations throughout the
Middle Colonies and New England, leaders of the revival were
pressed ever harder to justify their divisive behavior. In an age
when factionalism was widely denounced as destructive of the larger
common good, the revivalists were on slippery ground. Their
primary experience—and everyone else's—was with political factions, but these always carried a taint of impropriety, if not of
positive corruption, and strictures against them were so strong that
no systematic theory of parties emerged during the eighteenth
century. In the religious sphere, on the other hand, the situation
was not so clear. Religious factions had a long and almost respectable history in the eighteenth-century mind, making it easier to
justify divisions over questions of eternal truth. Thus, beginning in
the 1740s and continuing into the next decade, Presbyterian and
Congregational separatists constructed a defense that stressed the
rights of minorities against majorities, and of individuals against the
whole, in matters of conscience.

Their arguments drew on such Latitudinarian writers as William
Chillingworth and John Tillotson, and they displayed a familiarity
with Locke's *Letter Concerning Toleration*. Chillingworth and the
Latitudinarians made a clear distinction between the essentials of

religious doctrine, readily discoverable from Scripture, and the nonessentials, imposed by men. The nonessentials usually led to church divisions, they believed, and anyone who separated from a church where nonessentials were insisted upon should not be judged a schismatic.[61] As the debate on these questions advanced in America, and the opposers probed for every weakness in the revivalists' argument, the defenders of separatism found themselves moving beyond the standard phrases of the English tolerationists. Particularly striking was the Americans' propensity to cast their defense of religious rights in an increasingly political idiom.

The Presbyterian New Sides wrote a number of tracts in vindication of their withdrawal from the Philadelphia Synod. Samuel Blair rejected outright the synod's power to lay down "obligatory" rules in all cases or to claim, in his words, a "Legislative, or Law-Making Authority." Ministers were required to follow ecclesiastical regulations based on Scripture, but if a "Minority" found a rule to be contrary to God's word it was "sinful for them to obey it." To be sure, "on any other Score than that of Conscience . . . the minor Part [must] be subject to . . . the Major." But "is there no Authority besides absolute and unlimited?" asked Blair. To insist, as the Presbyterian Old Sides did, that "church Judicatures have . . . Authority to enjoin whatsoever they think proper . . . on pain of Exclusion" was "a Tyrannical and Church-dividing Principle." Blair explores minority rights at length in this essay.[62] He is aware that followers of private conscience could potentially split the church along every different line of interpretation, yet even this danger pales beside the greater peril that absolute power in the hands of a majority of "fallible imperfect Creatures" might lead to corruption of the whole. Gilbert Tennent concurred. The minority "ought freely to submit to the Conclusions of the Majority, in Matters relating to [church] Government" or there would be no government. But "the Major Party may be mistaken as well as the Minor, and consequently abuse their Power." Should the majority err by imposing mere "circumstantials" as terms of communion, true Christians had no choice but to "obey God rather than Man," and "withdraw."[63]

The New England separatists also wrote treatises justifying their
rising opposition. According to Solomon Paine of Connecticut, God
"hath given to Evry Man an unalianable Right, in matters of the
worship of God, to Judge for himself as his Conciance receives the
Rule from God, who alone hath Right to Chalenge this Sovraignty
over and propriety in them." Elisha Williams applied the principle
of minority rights to the selection of ministers. "Where a minor Part
cannot in Judgment acquiesce in the Choice made by the major Part
of the worshipping Assembly, they have [a] *Right to withdraw* and
choose a Minister for themselves" or to attend another church.
Furthermore, each person in the congregation was "equally vested
in the same Right, and hold it independent one of another, and each
one independent of the whole, or of all the rest." Here was a
stunning statement of the atomized character of the voluntary
church.[64]

Williams was not yet prepared to extend minority rights to the
civil community, "where the Right of each Individual is subjected to
the Body . . . [and] the Act of the Majority is legally to be considered
as the Act of the whole." But that the right of private judgment
might have applications in the political as well as the religious
sphere is hinted in the pamphlet's closing paragraph. Shifting
suddenly from a discussion of the Toleration Act and the "unalien-
able Rights" of private conscience to the subject of civil privileges,
Williams declared: "The Rights of Magna Charter depend not on
the Will of a Prince, or the Will of the Legislature; but they are the
inherent natural Rights of *Englishmen.* . . . Christian *Liberty,* as
well as Civil, has been lost by little and little." Williams's familiarity
with Locke's two *Treatises on Government,* and his fusing of
religious to political themes resulted, according to one historian of
political theory, in a doctrine of "startling originality" which could
have been conceived only in the eighteenth-century American
colonies.[65]

The division of Congregational churches was often acrimonious,
as for example in Easton, Massachusetts, where the Reverend
Solomon Prentice threatened to "breake . . . [the] Heads" of anyone
who interfered with his newly separated congregation.[66] The debate

was not everywhere this shrill. At Ipswich, the New Lights constructed an elaborate contractual argument to justify their separation from the Chebacco Church. Church covenants, like contracts, they argued, bound the participants to mutual obligations. The individual parishioner owed obedience to the church, whereas the church owed to the parishioner "the Word, Sacraments, Discipline etc. agreeable to the Gospel." But should the church fail in its responsibilities, the covenant was "vertually dissolved, and the Party injured . . . [was] at Liberty from his Obligation." If blocked by the pastor or a majority of the church members from withdrawing, the injured member could "seek Relief in a Way Extra-judicial," that is, by breaking off without permission. Such an extraordinary act of defiance was "lawful, [or] at least excusable," for the sole reason that, "To promote the Interest of true and vital Religion" was the noblest, the most "just Cause," and to this end "all Forms however useful must give Way."[67]

From the 1740s on, the separating brethren grew in number until thousands of Congregationalists throughout the North joined Presbyterian thousands in the Middle Colonies in open rebellion against the "spiritual Tyranny" of traditional church authority.[68]

"Who is upon GOD's Side?"

As the Great Awakening broke down social cohesion in America, it simultaneously elevated the individual. During the more communal seventeenth century, colonists had rarely conceived of themselves apart from a larger collectivity—the family, the congregation, or the town. But the eighteenth-century revival penetrated and shattered that unitary cosmos by directing its message to the individual. In exhorting their followers to make personal decisions for God, and then to act on those decisions regardless of their effect on the larger society, the revivalists gave sanction to a new dynamic in human relationships.

Gilbert Tennent's "terrible and searching" sermons made it difficult for any person to submerge his or her identity in the group.

"Awake then, *you sluggish Souls* . . . *Wretched Sinners*! isn't there one Soul among you that will be perswaded to awake this day? . . . Not one Lidia open her Heart to hear the Word of Christ?" Once awakened, moreover, the individual had to face wrenching decisions. Was his minister in a state of grace? Should he seek greater edification elsewhere? A person was not like a stone, "without Choice, Sense, and Taste." So Tennent thundered: "Let all the Followers of the Lamb stand up and act for GOD against all opposers: Who is upon GOD's Side? who?"[69] Samuel Finley was no less explicit: "I look upon all Neutres, as Enemies, in Affairs of Religion. Away with your carnal Prudence! And either follow *God* or *Baal*. *He that is not actually with us, is against us.* . . . " Thus were parishioners exhorted to act in support of their decisions, though "your Neighbours growl against you, and reproach you."[70]

This last notion captures vividly the new spirit of defiant individualism that was one of the most radical manifestations of the Awakening. No longer were consensual values to prevail over individual ones, at least in matters concerning the soul. Now private judgment and intuitive understanding had equal if not superior claim on the conscience. In a word, decision making had been internalized.

In New England the shift from collective to individual accountability was equally pronounced. Jonathan Edwards warned in 1741 that persons who stood at a distance from the Awakening, "doubting [and] wondering . . . silent and inactive," might bring upon themselves the Curse of Meroz.[71] Symbolic of the transference of religious authority from the community to the individual were changes in church practice regarding admission to membership. In early New England, the elaborate scrutiny of an applicant's life and state of grace had been a kind of community rite. It involved an initial examination of the candidate by the church elders and minister, followed by a narration of the individual's conversion experience before the entire congregation. Next came an investigation of the candidate's life and moral conduct, during which church members might question the townspeople at large about his character and reputation. Finally, the candidate was subjected to a close scrutiny of his spiritual development by the body of church members. Only if approved after these various tests was the candidate received into the covenant, at which time he solemnly promised to cleave forever to his fellow members "in brotherly love and holy watchfulnesse."[72]

Contrasted with this consensual mode, religious conversions of the revivalist era were individualistic and egocentric. Some clergymen even warned potential converts that it was a "dangerous Sin" to place explicit faith in the judgment of others, "neglecting Self-Examination."[73] Upon feeling the requisite stirrings and warmings, one often struggled alone toward grace, or gained assurance in a rapturous moment of soul-flooding light. In many churches, including Jonathan Edwards's Congregational meeting at Northampton, it was by 1735 no longer "the Custom . . . [for new members] to make a credible Relation of their inward Experience the Ground of Admission." Instead, the converted went about "*themselves* publishing their own experiences from time to time and from place to place, on all occasions and before all companies . . . [in] common *conversation*."[74] As thousands of provincials experienced conversions at the height of the Awakening, even the ministers found it impossible to examine each case, and the burden of decision fell ever more directly on the lay men and women. The most radical New Lights denied all sense of commonalty, asserting the "absolute Necessity for every Person to act singly . . . as if there was not another human Creature upon Earth."[75]

Jonathan Edwards, of course, finally rejected the "promiscuous admission" of new members and sought to restore the covenant bonds that sweetly knit members together in a visible church, precipitating a crisis with his Northampton congregation that ended in his dismissal in 1750. By the late 1740s, Edwards had concluded that the conversion experience should be "under the direction of *skilful guides* [and proceed] with great seriousness, preparation and prayer . . . in [God's] house, and in the presence of his people." But by mid-century such a step seemed regressive to many provincials, who for a decade now had been told from pulpits across the land that the individual, standing alone in the sight of God, was the primary vessel of salvation. Did not the law of Christ specifically forbid people "to judge one another?" asked Edwards's New Light critic, Solomon Williams of Connecticut. And might not Edwards's "skilful Guides direct every Man, Woman and Child, what Experiences to relate, and what to omit, what are fit to be published, and what not?" Only God could see into the heart, and neither ministers nor congregations should interpose themselves between the individual and his Creator.[76]

To be sure, separatist Presbyterians and Congregationalists formed new societies of believers that in a number of cases reproduced the covenanted communities of old. But from the viewpoint of radicalism the essential thing is that they did so only after breaking sharply from a tradition of fraternity and consensus that had governed church life for generations. If such a departure seemed bold in the 1740s it would shortly come to lose its novelty. Once having taken part in the dismantling of old institutions and the shaping of new ones, Americans at every social level would find themselves less hesitant to do it again.

The Great Awakening, as Richard Hofstadter put it, was "the first major intercolonial crisis of the mind and spirit" in eighteenth-century America.[77] No previous occurrence in colonial history compared with it in scale or consequences. True, the floodtide of evangelical fervor soon subsided, but nothing could quite restore the old cultural landscape. The unitary ideal of the seventeenth century continued to be eroded in the post-Awakening years by further church separations. Moreover, as the Reverend William Shurtleff noted in 1745, the "dividing Spirit is not confin'd to those that are Friends" of the revival.[78] Nor was it confined to the religious sphere. That "dividing Spirit" would be manifested every-where after mid-century in the proliferation of religious and political factions.

CHAPTER 6

The Political Awakening

The relationship between the Great Awakening and the American Revolution has long been one of the nicer perplexities of early American History. That the Awakening fostered a shift in political as well as religious consciousness is frequently asserted. Yet there has been little agreement about how the revival helped to prepare the provincial mind for revolution. A recent attempt to link the retrograde Calvinism of the Awakeners to the Revolutionary impulse—rather than the more "obvious" coupling of rationalist liberals and Revolutionaries—has struck some critics as improbable.[1] For such an argument implies not only that most revivalist clergymen became supporters of the Revolution—which they did—but also that the rationalist opposers of the revival became reluctant revolutionaries or outright loyalists—which they frequently did not. Should we move beyond theological differences, however, to consider the revival's impress on patterns of leadership and on popular participation in organized opposition to authority, we might discover a more pivotal linkage between the Awakening and the Revolution.

Eighteenth-century Americans found it far easier to break through the classic taboos against schism and public contention in the religious rather than the political sphere, especially after 1720 when Anglo-American political thought entered a quiet phase that celebrated stability and unity, public virtue and the common good. True, radical whigs regularly jogged the collective memory about the evils of power and its tendency to encroach on liberty, but the prevailing political atmosphere was moderate, even complacent.[2] Religious strife, on the other hand, was endemic throughout America by the mid-eighteenth century. And within religion's zealous precincts the provincials would discover a less ambiguous, a more propulsive, source of political radicalism.

Clergymen, along with other community leaders, were expected to set the tone of eighteenth-century public discourse and to indicate by their own example the limits of acceptable behavior. Thus when the people saw their ministers locked in public combat, in the course of which they openly heaped verbal and printed abuse on each other and vigorously contested for popular support, it seemed increasingly apparent that something was changing—that a kind of license was being granted for a more broadly based and contentious style of public life. Through it all impressions were accumulating and expectations were being aroused that would alter the way Americans responded to issues of every sort.

Though new political attitudes and a heightened partisanship were manifested to some degree in every colony, for our purposes a look at three of them—Connecticut, Pennsylvania, and Virginia— will illustrate the changing tone of public life.

From Religion to Politics in Connecticut

The proverbial land of steady habits, Connecticut in the post-Awakening years became a colony where a "dividing, party-Spirit . . . threat[ened] like a Bear, to rend us in Pieces."[3] Connecticut's vaunted harmony had been subjected to increasing strains since the late seventeenth century as an expanding economy, land disputes, and dissent from the Congregational Way occasionally gave rise to discord. Yet the public face of unity remained more or less intact until the Great Awakening, when first the Congregational establishment and then the political establishment were riven into New Light and Old Light parties. The majority of Connecticut ministers initially had welcomed the revival, but when evangelical excesses and separatist rumblings began to threaten both religious and civil peace, orthodox ministers joined an alarmed magistracy to uphold order. By aligning itself squarely with the orthodox churches, the Connecticut government not only exacerbated the religious split but gave it the added dimension of a political contest between "ins" and "outs."

At the urging of Old Light ministers, the Connecticut legislature in 1742 and 1743 passed a remarkable series of laws designed to suppress revivalist, or New Light, activity. A May 1742 "Act for regulating Abuses and correcting Disorders in Ecclesiastical Affairs" forbade uninvited ministers—from Connecticut and elsewhere, ordained and lay—to preach or exhort in neighboring parishes under pain of fines, loss of salary, or expulsion from the colony. This law was then invoked to deprive New Light ministers in West Haven, Lyme, and elsewhere of their pulpits, and to expel from the colony such itinerants as Samuel Finley and James Davenport. In May 1743, the legislature moved to prevent separatist New Light congregations from seeking the protection of a 1708 law granting limited toleration by specifically prohibiting all persons worshiping as Presbyterians or Congregationalists from claiming legal exemption as dissenters. Other laws passed in these years required legislative approval for any new seminary of learning (thereby suppressing the evangelical Shepherd's Tent at New London), instituted an oath of religious orthodoxy for students and faculty at Yale, and barred the hiring of any minister who did not possess a college degree. In addition, marriages and baptisms performed by separatist preachers were disallowed, with some New Light ministers being jailed for officiating at weddings of their own church members.[4]

It was a dazzling display of raw power by the establishment. So dazzling, indeed, that it offended not only revivalists but moderates—many of whom had for years resisted the centralizing impulse of the Saybrook Platform—and aroused the ever latent localism of Connecticut's towns and congregations. Yet the authorities, wrapped in self-righteous oblivion, proceeded to enforce the new laws with such overweening harshness that the colony erupted from the mid-1740s on in a rash of church separations and political schisms.

At Canterbury the reborn lawyer, Elisha Paine, led a group of evangelical separatists out of the town church. Arrested in 1744 as an exhorter and imprisoned for a month at Windham jail, Paine continued to preach from his cell, attracting such large crowds that his supporters built a stand of bleachers. In a single year at Norwich forty separatists who refused to pay church rates to an Old Light minister were confined in jail. So many persons were imprisoned for nonpayment of rates in Windham County—a hotbed of separatism—that another story had to be added to the jailhouse. The ailing mother of Isaac Backus was carried off to a dank cell, a preacher from Mansfield was incarcerated for six months, and innumerable separatists had their personal property seized for nonpayment of church taxes. Throughout the 1740s evangelical ministers and their sympathizers were haled before the General Assembly to be publicly humiliated. Meanwhile the ministerial consociations denied ordination or salaries to New Light preachers and secured the expulsion from Yale of the sons of leading separatists.[5]

Warming to the task, the legislature—urged by such as the Old Light preacher Isaac Stiles to deny public office to men who "breaketh any of the wholesome Laws of the Government" or of God—set about weeding New Lights out of the government. Justices of the peace who failed to prosecute separatists in Branford and Hartford with sufficient vigor were removed from office. A former rector of Yale and moderate opponent of the law against itinerancy, Elisha Williams, was dropped as judge of the supreme court in 1743; nor was he supported for justice of the peace at Hartford two years later. New Light sympathizers elected from Canterbury, Plainfield, and Lyme were denied their seats in the General Assembly.[6] At the local level Old Lights made alliances with Anglicans in order to block the election of New Lights to the assembly. In the mid–1740s several Anglicans were elected to the legislature with the support of Old Lights. Apparently even a Church of England man was preferable to a New Light enthusiast.[7]

Richard Bushman has observed that the revival "broke the seal on political controversy" in Connecticut.[8] The Old Lights were responsible for the initial politicization of the religious split, but with matters of conscience at stake the New Lights rapidly developed a political response of their own. A typical power struggle occurred in the town of Branford, where the Reverend Philemon Robbins was a dedicated New Light with a large following in his own and neighboring churches. In 1742 Robbins had preached to a Baptist congregation at Wallingford, for which he was suspended from the New Haven consociation. Robbins's efforts to compose his differences with the consociation failed, but his popularity with the people was unimpaired. In 1745 the ecclesiastical society at Branford voted fifty-two to fifteen to continue him as minister, and on November 4, 1745 the church specifically renounced the Saybrook Platform. A few months later the New Haven consociation found Mr. Robbins guilty of promoting "schismatic contentions, separations and divisions," and demanded that he confess the same before that body. Robbins resisted and the Branford society again supported him, noting that since the church had renounced the Saybrook Platform the consociation was assuming "a pretended government and jurisdiction over this church and society" which had no force. The consociation thereupon deposed Robbins and stopped his salary. The people—at first fearfully and then more boldly— continued to attend Robbins's sermons and to support him with voluntary contributions.[9]

When the Branford Old Lights petitioned the assembly for assistance, the separatist majority in the town appointed agents to present their case at Hartford. Another effort at compromise failed, and the assembly thereupon ejected Branford's two New Light representatives, replacing them with the town's leading Old Light. Justices of the peace favoring the revival also were dismissed. As the rift widened New Lights continued to gain political strength in Branford, and soon the "gentlemen who had been kept out of the assembly because they had been friends to the religious awakening, were now chosen again by the freemen." The displaced justices also were returned to office as the Old Lights lost credit with the people.[10]

Over the several years of this controversy at Branford countless meetings were held by both sides, votes were taken, petitions circulated, agents appointed, and pamphlets printed.[11] A similar politicization of the religious dispute was taking place in other churches and ecclesiastical societies throughout the colony. From Hebron, Canterbury, and Stonington came petitions signed by hundreds of New Lights. In 1754, over one thousand names were gathered for a petition to the king alleging denial of the Toleration Act in Connecticut. Sermons and pamphlets thundered against the "corrupt Constitution" of the colony's ecclesiastical establishment. One unanticipated consequence of this campaign was the loosening of ties between church and state, as New Lights came to favor voluntary support of minister's salaries, a position that developed less from principle than from their circumstances as outsiders.[12]

Though religious strife declined in Connecticut after about 1748 owing to the balm of time and compromise, concurrent tensions of a secular character were increasingly being subsumed under the New and Old Light party labels. Currency disputes and land controversies fed readily into the division because they, like the religious question, involved challenges by outsiders to those in authority. The struggle was now for power and the right to set the direction of government, especially as imperial measures moved to the fore in the 1760s.[13] William Samuel Johnson noted that the New Lights, though initially formed around the religious issue, had by 1763 gained a majority in the government "owing to their superior Attention to Civil Affairs and close union among themselves in Politicks." True, New Lights controlled the General Assembly, but it took something more to dislodge Old Lights from the council and the governor's chair. The Stamp Act provided the occasion. When one of the most prominent Old Lights in the colony, Jared Ingersoll, agreed to serve as stamp distributor, the complete rout of the orthodox party was assured. As if heeding New Light Jonathan Lee's

1766 election sermon, which recommended that the governor and council members should be "cordial friends to Christ and his church, and patriots to the republick, " the deputies replaced the Old Light governor and four councillors with resolute New Lights. [14]

Thus was a religious dispute transmuted into a political one from 1742 onward. Still, Connecticut's experience shows clearly that the divisions of the Great Awakening did not translate directly into the divisions of the American Revolution. In the more than thirty years between those two events, many new issues—to say nothing of an entire generation of citizens—were added to the New and Old Light party configurations. As the *New London Gazette* declared in 1767, "Calvinism and Arminianism have for several years lost their theological meaning and have been used mostly in their political sense." [15] True, theological issues were reactivated from time to time, perhaps inevitably in a colony where religious values formed a common touchstone of the culture. But just as some early New Lights had been attracted to the party's daring antiauthoritarianism, others were by mid-century attracted to its growing power. Thomas Clap, the rector of Yale College, shifted from Old to New Light after 1740 partly to assure the independence of the college and the continuation of its government subsidy. The politically ambitious Roger Sherman, an outspoken Old Light when he lived in western Connecticut, joined a New Light church and adjusted his politics accordingly when he moved east to New Haven. And more than one political commentator accused paper money advocates, Susquehanna land speculators, and other secular interests of hypocritically joining the New Light party "under the Paint of Religion." [16] Such opportunists were nothing more than "Political New Lights [who hoped] . . . to advance some worldly Interest by this Means, tho' they were not from Principle, and Conscience on that side the Question." [17]

Nor was the brash contentiousness of the new politics confined to New Lights alone. The "outs" of every political or religious hue tended in the later colonial years to employ a more bluntly assertive style. In 1775 even Benjamin Gale, the outspoken Old Light activist turned patriot, while professing a distaste for radical methods allowed that "different sentiments of the *mode* of opposition must not divide us in making opposition."[18] Such was the legacy of the Great Awakening in Connecticut. New forms of political behavior, leaders who did not shrink from appeals to the populace at large, and new ways of thinking about authority were now familiar and available to any individual or group that believed its cause was just.

Denominational Politics in Pennsylvania

Religion and politics were perhaps more closely intertwined in Pennsylvania than in any other colony. The temptation is strong to portray Pennsylvania's eighteenth-century partisan broils as a kind of forerunner of modern ethnic politics. To be sure, Philadelphia saw the formation around mid-century of such fraternal societies as the Hibernian Club and the Deutschen Gesellschaft von Pennsylvanien, which would later take on a political dimension. Throughout the colonial years, however, these were philanthropic societies which concentrated almost exclusively on providing material assistance to needy immigrants from the old country.[19] But if ethnic consciousness had not yet assumed a political form, the same cannot be said of religious consciousness. Indeed, as often as not the two converged. With the post-1740 growth of denominationalism, churches and sects offered ready-made institutional structures and a corps of articulate leaders for whatever cause or grievance their congregations believed needed attention or remedy. Though not every clergyman or elder sought a public role,[20] those with a taste for political action soon discovered that church networks could be used to promote both the religious and civil rights of their adherents.

The Society of Friends had no choice but to augment its influence in Pennsylvania by political means since Quakers were reduced to a minority within two decades of the colony's founding. By 1740, with the great German and Ulster migrations at floodtide, Quakers probably accounted for no more than a quarter of the inhabitants. Yet the Friends managed to retain political power by weighting representation in the assembly toward Philadelphia, Chester, and Bucks counties where Quakers were most heavily concentrated, and by cultivating alliances with the German pietists and churchpeople. By 1750, the expansion of western settlement, mounting tension between the British and French empires, and a revitalization of the Society of Friends' peace doctrine gave new urgency to the perennial issue of Quaker pacifism and frontier defense. The question was further complicated by the ethnosectional character of the dispute, since the Germans and Scotch-Irish were predominantly settled in the western region.[21] Another threat to Quaker hegemony was the proprietary party, a political faction that by 1740 had formed around the authority of the now-Anglican governor as a counterweight to the Quaker-dominated assembly. Despite these challenges and the continuing flow of non-Quakers into the colony, Quakers retained considerable power in the assembly up to the eve of the Revolution, largely because of their remarkable ability to combine religion and politics.

The Anglican minister, William Smith, charged that the Quakers turned their Philadelphia Yearly Meeting into a political cabal. "Convened just before the Election, and being composed of Deputies from all the monthly Meetings in the Province, [it] is the finest Scheme that could possibly be projected for conducting political Intrigues, under the Mask of Religion." Smith's own partisan disposition led him to overstate the case, but it is clear from the record that the Quakers discussed political issues, among other subjects, at their annual conclave. The Pennsylvania Society of Friends was organized on several levels—local monthly meetings, regional quarterly meetings, and the colony-wide Philadelphia Yearly Meeting, the last convening shortly before election day. This web of meetings facilitated rapid communication among the Friends and could readily be mobilized to promote political goals.[22]

As the paradox of Quaker membership in an assembly responsible for the military defense of the colony became distressingly evident after mid-century, the Yearly Meeting devoted ever more time to the issue. In 1755, following a prolonged debate that John Woolman described as "the most weighty that ever I was at," *An Epistle of*

Tender Love and Caution to Friends in Pennsylvania urging
Quakers not to pay taxes for military supplies was distributed among
the membership.[23] At the same time the Yearly Meeting appointed
a special standing committee whose function was to take immediate
action when Quaker interests were threatened, as well as to alert
the influential London Yearly Meeting at home. This special
committee was expanded into the permanent Philadelphia Meeting
for Sufferings in 1756, which included four members from each
Quarterly Meeting. Convening at least once a month, it undertook
to disseminate literature vindicating the Society's position on
defense and to engage in a kind of "preventive lobbying" with the
assembly and executive. Or, as an order of the Yearly Meeting put
it, representatives from the Meeting for Sufferings were to "appear
in all Cases, where the Reputation & Interest of Truth and our
Religious Society are concerned."[24]

When the governor of Pennsylvania formally declared war on the
Indians in the spring of 1756, six "conscience Quakers" withdrew
from the assembly in accordance with the Philadelphia Yearly
Meeting's advice that Friends not accept civil office if its duties were
repugnant to Quaker doctrine. Other Quakers in the assembly
thought it unwise to abandon the political arena. Noting the rise of
proprietary party strength and the weakening of their traditional
alliance with the Germans, a number of the more worldly Friends
chose to remain in office throughout the war years. During the
1760s, moreover, several conscience Quakers were drawn back into
the assembly. As the devout James Pemberton reasoned, "the
Interest of our Society has Suffered in Some cases either through
inattention or thro absence of [assembly] members acquainted with
our circumstances." Thus Pemberton agreed in 1765 to stand for the
assembly as the best way "to preserve unanimity[,] to keep out an
Envious Presbyterian & to [protect] our rights & Liberties."[25] As
the Quaker "politiques" continued to participate in government the
Society of Friends' influence over them lost some of its force. But
proprietary party leaders, recalling the historic connection between
Quaker religion and politics, held fast to their belief that the sect
had "prov'd their very Religion to be a political Engine, to which

they themselves pay no conscientious Regard, but as it suits their crafty Purposes."[26]

Presbyterians formed a second group in Pennsylvania's denominational politics. As early as 1729 James Logan feared that the Presbyterians would "make themselves Proprietors of the Province," and as Ulster immigration swelled, Quaker apprehension mounted. But with many Scotch-Irish settling in the frontier counties, which sent only one or two representatives each to the assembly in contrast with eight representatives from each eastern county, the Quakers managed to retain control over the legislature. By 1760 the longer settled southeastern counties of Philadelphia, Bucks, and Chester contained 16,221 taxables, whereas the western counties of Lancaster, York, Berks, Northampton, and Cumberland had drawn nearly equal with 15,443 taxables. Representation continued as before, however, with the three eastern counties sending more than twice the number of delegates to the assembly as did the five western counties.[27] As a consequence of this obvious inequity, western concerns received short shrift in the provincial assembly.

In the 1760s western grievances that had been accumulating for years finally burst forth with explosive fury. Proprietary land policies and underrepresentation were significant irritants, but the catalyzing event was Pontiac's War, together with the assembly's continuing failure to provide adequate frontier defenses. Enraged at the assembly's seeming disregard for their plight, a number of Scotch-Irish from the western Lancaster County town of Paxton finally took matters into their own hands. First they killed twenty Conestoga Indians in two raids in December 1763. Then in February 1764 they and other westerners marched over 200 strong to the outskirts of Philadelphia, where they finally dispersed after the government promised a speedy consideration of their grievances.[28]

Whether the assembly was actually prepared to redress frontier grievances when it met later in February may never be known, for just as debate began two pamphlets challenging the Quakers' fitness to govern Pennsylvania made their appearance. Because it was immediately evident that the pamphlets had been written by Presbyterians, their publication signaled the start of Pennsylvania's denominational wars. *A Declaration Of the distressed and bleeding Frontier Inhabitants*, proclaimed the westerners' indignation at seeing their Indian enemies "cherished and caressed as dearest Friends. . . . [by] a certain Faction that have got the political Reigns in their Hand." On the heels of this came *The Quaker Unmask'd*, charging that Friends showed "more real Affection for Enemy Savages than for their fellow Subjects, of certain Denominations." Because some Friends had taken up arms against the Paxton Boys, the entire Society was accused of hypocrisy. The time had come, concluded the author, for Pennsylvanians to ask themselves "whether Quakers are fit to be their Representatives, or not."[29]

Now the Quaker politiques were ignited.[30] They and their allies in the assembly responded with a virulent anti-Presbyterian campaign, which destroyed all chance for compromise and spurred members of that denomination to unite in a colony-wide "Presbyterian Party." By fusing politics to religion, the bitter aftermath of the Paxtonian winter of 1763–1764 raised denominational consciousness in Pennsylvania to unprecedented levels, drew lay leaders and ministers alike into politics, and gave shape to group loyalties that in many cases would carry over to the Revolutionary era.

Drawing on stereotypes dating from the seventeenth century, Quaker party propagandists from 1764 onward reviled the Presbyterians as a coarse and lawless rabble, the very antithesis of the peace-loving Friends. The Paxton marchers "were of the same Spirit with the . . . blood-thirsty Presbyterians, who cut off King Charles . . . Head."[31] One author gleefully seized on a 1641 episode when, he charged, "the Scotch Presbyterians . . . without the least Remorse . . . murder'd four thousand of the Native Irish, Men, Women and Children, in the Isle Mc'Gee much in the same Manner their Offspring murder'd the Indians at Lancaster." Building on memories of the English Civil War, Quaker party writers laced their pamphlets with allusions to the Presbyterians' "Oliverian Spirit" and seditious proclivities. Retracing the history of Scottish resistance to the British crown from the Civil War to the Jacobite uprising of 1745, the Quaker polemicists charged that wild-eyed Presbyterians were incapable of "a firm Attachment to the KING, and the laws of our Country." In both church and state their governments were fashioned "after the Model of a Geneva Republic." "Whoever heard," one writer asked, "of a Presbyterian Sermen upon the Duty of Submission to the present Establishment?"[32]

That Presbyterians throughout the province would close ranks in response to this ferocious attack might have been foreseen. And as the potential for a powerful alliance between the Presbyterians and the proprietary party grew, Quaker party leaders concluded that the best way to curb both groups was to press for Pennsylvania's conversion to a royal colony. The campaign for a royal charter thus became the focal point of the assembly elections of 1764 and 1765. In 1764, leadership of the anti-charter or proprietary group fell disproportionately to the Presbyterians—both lay and clerical— owing to the political diffidence of Governor John Penn and the travels to England of such proprietary party activists as William Allen and the Reverend William Smith. Moreover, the zest with which Presbyterian leaders threw themselves into the fray, their skillful use of church networks, and their shrewd manipulation of religious sensibilities demonstrated that the Sons of the Kirk would henceforth rival the Quakers in the art of denominational politics.[33]

On March 30, 1764, three leading Philadelphia Presbyterians, the Reverends Gilbert Tennent, Francis Alison, and John Ewing, wrote a pastoral letter to their fellow ministers in Pennsylvania urging that everyone under their influence be advised not to sign any petition for a royal charter.[34] One week earlier, on the very day that the assembly voted to seek a royal charter, the ministers and elders of the Philadelphia Presbytery had sent a circular letter to all congregations in Pennsylvania containing "proposed articles of union." The letter observed that while Presbyterians were now very numerous in the province, "we are considered as *Nobody*, or a body of very little weight and consequence." Indeed, having little to fear "from any opposition that can be made to their measures by us . . . , some denominations openly insult us." What was needed, declared the Philadelphia leaders, was a means "to unite us more closely together; so that when there may be a necessity to *act as a body*, we may be able to do it . . . [especially] to defend our civil or religious liberties." In order to promote Presbyterian unity and welfare, it was proposed that each congregation and district set up committees to correspond regularly with each other, and further that each church send representatives to a yearly or half-yearly general meeting of the denomination. In pursuance of these goals, a twenty-eight-member Philadelphia committee of correspondence was named whose members—including John Allen, son of the Presbyterian Chief Justice William Allen, and the proprietary party activist Samuel Purviance, Jr.—were to keep in touch with Presbyterians in the counties. In addition, a general meeting was called for the last Tuesday in August.[35]

The Presbyterian unification meeting, duly held at Lancaster on August 28, 1764, was promptly labeled by Quaker party propagandists as a "Synod . . . to settle Election-Tickets, for the Province."[36] The Quakers, after all, knew something about the wider purposes to which such meetings could be put. Nor did the Presbyterians deny that their pre-election conclaves were used to organize political support. What little we know about this first meeting at Lancaster comes from satirical writings about it by the Presbyterians' opponents. One reported scornfully that after the Reverend John Ewing was chosen moderator, the convention of "good Republicans" discussed how to take the election from "these cursed Quakers" and establish Presbyterianism in Pennsylvania. An impudent elder supposedly questioned whether ministers should "trot about the Country after Politicks" or engage in "Writing Lampoons, Satires and Libels." Rejecting the notion of Presbyterian unanimity, the elder then declared that he would be " a free Agent and think for myself." But, the satirist concludes, the conclave overrode his objections and voted out a series of resolutions, one opposing all kings except those of the Presbyterian faith and another recommending that Presbyterians voting contrary to their ministers' instructions be excommunicated.[37]

A "Scribbler" also noted disdainfully that Presbyterian "Haberdashers in Politics" had met at a Lancaster tavern "to chuse Legislators for the whole Province." In this piece the ministers were unanimously accused of corruptly infecting their parishioners with an itch for politics. "Even the Pulpit is turn'd to a Drum Politic to enlist Party-Voluntiers. . . . In short so high does this kind of Enthusiasm swell among the Sons of the Kirk, that Opposition Sentiments are almost become a Criterion of Orthodoxy!" Another pamphlet charged that ministers had become "the Minions of arbitrary Power" by urging Presbyterians to "read political Papers, and sign Petitions thereupon, as a Sabbath-Day's Exercise."[38]

Presbyterian preachers, to be sure, employed the institutional structure of their church to good advantage in preparing for the election of 1764. But their parishioners were hardly being led by the nose. Presbyterian activists included such politically astute laymen as Colonel John Armstrong of Cumberland County, James Burd and the Edward Shippens, Sr. and Jr., of Lancaster, and above all Samuel Purviance, Jr. of Philadelphia. These men carried on a lively correspondence about their political forays among Lutherans, Baptists, and German Reformed, as well as Presbyterians in Chester, Bucks, Lancaster, and the western counties.[39] In building a coalition against the royal charter, they tried to construct assembly tickets that would attract the broadest support. Samuel Purviance, Jr., for example, proposed that German candidates be added to the Philadelphia ticket. "The design is by putting in two Germans to draw such a Party of them as will turn the scale in our favour," he informed Colonel James Burd. Denominational partisanship had reached such a pitch in Pennsylvania by 1764 that William Allen, describing the results of the Philadelphia election to Thomas Penn, automatically reached for religious labels to identify the contesting factions. "We had great help from the Lutherans, and Calvinist among the Dutch[;] from the other Sects we had great opposition: we had about half of the Church of England, and the Presbyterians to a man."[40]

That the Presbyterians made their votes count in the 1764 election was widely acknowledged. The election was the "warmest & most close ever known here," commented one observer, "the

Presbyterian party having made use of every artifice in their power." Though the anti-charter coalition was not strong enough to capture the assembly, they did manage narrowly to defeat the Quaker party luminaries Benjamin Franklin and Joseph Galloway in Philadelphia County.[41] Certainly the Presbyterian vote contributed significantly to this outcome. Yet, according to contemporary witnesses, it was the German churchpeople, more than any other single group, who tipped the scales in the Philadelphia election.

Pennsylvania's Germans had from the early eighteenth century aligned themselves politically with the Quaker party. Whereas the German quietist sects shared the Friends' pacifist principles, the later-arriving Lutherans and German Reformed initially trusted the Quaker assembly to protect their liberties against both proprietary and royal authorities. As the peace issue came to dominate politics in the 1750s and 1760s, such German sectaries as the Mennonites, Schwenkfelders, and Moravians tightened their ties with the Quakers. But the churchpeople, many of whom had settled closer to the frontier, expressed growing concern about the assembly's failure to formulate a strong defense policy. The March of the Paxton Boys and its aftermath created a crisis for the Lutherans and German Reformed that would be resolved by a decisive shift in their political allegiance.

When word reached Philadelphia in early February 1764 that the marchers were heading for the city, Quaker party leaders urged the Germans to take up arms against them. As the Reverend Henry Muhlenberg noted in his journal, however, the Philadelphia Germans preferred neutrality to "Wag[ing] war against their own suffering fellow citizens for the sake of the Quakers and Herrnhuters and their creatures . . . the double-dealing Indians." Muhlenberg, his colleague the Reverend Paul Brycelius, and the Swedish Lutheran minister Charles Wrangel actively prepared their congregations for a restrained response to the Paxton Boys. On February 6, Brycelius went out to warn the Germantown congregation to remain calm and there ran into an advance contingent of Paxtonians. Taking advantage of this unexpected opportunity, he told the men that an armed advance into Philadelphia "would cause a great and horrible blood-bath . . . [which] appeared to give them pause and to make an impression on them."[42]

The provincial government was obviously aware of the clergy's potential influence over the Paxton marchers, for they had dispatched other Philadelphia ministers to act as the initial peacemakers. The Presbyterian Gilbert Tennent and two Anglican clergymen met with the Paxton men at Germantown on the night of February 6, having been asked by the governor "to see what they could do among these people." On the following day Benjamin Franklin and other provincial officials, including the Reverend Dr. Wrangle, rode to Germantown where, after a lengthy meeting in a tavern, the westerners agreed to return home on the assurance that their grievances would be taken up by the assembly and governor.[43]

Henry Muhlenberg had reluctantly been drawn into the politics of the Paxtonian affair, since he thought it inappropriate for ministers to take an active part in such matters: "Our office rather required us to pray to God . . . for protection and mercy and to admonish our fellow German citizens to fear God, honor our king, and love our neighbor."[44] Thus Muhlenberg's journey from noninvolvement to cautious involvement to full participation in political affairs says much about both the secularization of the church in America and the powerful influence that a respected minister could exert among his people.

The royal charter campaign of 1764 was the catalyst that finally pushed Muhlenberg into partisan politics. Unlike his Swedish colleague Dr. Wrangel, who industriously circulated petitions supporting proprietary government among his parishioners, Muhlenberg at first abjured such activity. When a frontier resident pleaded with him in March of 1764 to send a circular letter to all German Lutheran congregations urging them not to sign petitions for royal government, Muhlenberg responded that "we preachers could not permit ourselves to interfere in such critical, political affairs." Moreover, he initially urged his own elders not to involve themselves in the controversy. In July, however, Muhlenberg noted that "conditions in the province look[ed] very dark and dangerous." At the urging of William Smith, the Anglican provost at the College of Philadelphia, and of Dr. Wrangel, Muhlenberg translated some political materials from English into German and allowed his elders to circulate petitions favoring retention of the proprietary charter.[45] His interest no doubt escalated when two Germans, Henry Keppel, an elder in Muhlenberg's church, and Frederick Antis, of the prominent German Reformed family, were added to the proprietary party assembly slate for Philadelphia County. By election time in early October, Muhlenberg was fully committed, and his church became the gathering point for Lutheran voters from Philadelphia and the surrounding countryside. At one o'clock on the first afternoon of the election, Muhlenberg went to the schoolhouse "where all the citizens who are members of our Lutheran congregation assembled to discuss the election and then proceeded to the courthouse in an orderly group." Benjamin Franklin was sure that the German vote had cost him the election: "They [the proprietary party] carried (would you think it!) above 1000 Dutch from me."[46]

Muhlenberg meanwhile summed up the Philadelphia results in a paragraph that shows how fully he had adopted the language of denominational partisanship:

> There was great rejoicing and great bitterness in the political circles of the city, since it was reported that the German church people had gained a victory in the election by putting our trustee, Mr. Henry Keple, into the assembly—a thing which greatly pleased the friends of the Proprietors, but greatly exasperated the Quakers and German Moravians. Never before in the history of Pennsylvania, they say, have so many people assembled for an election. The English and German Quakers, the Herrnhuters, Mennonites, and Schwenckfelders formed one party, and the English of the High Church and the Presbyterian Church, the German Lutheran, and German Reformed joined the other party and gained the upper hand—a thing heretofore unheard of.[47]

The proprietary group, having won significant ground in 1764, decided to make a spirited push for an assembly majority in the 1765 election, especially after the Stamp Act created confusion in Quaker party ranks. Samuel Purviance, Jr. was again active in "concert[ing] some measures for dividing the Qu——r Interest." In Bucks County he organized a "considerable meeting of the German, Baptist and Presbyterians . . . to attempt a general confederacy of the three Societies in opposition to the ruling party."[48] In Lancaster County he recommended that the proprietor's friends "run" (Purviance's word)[49] some "popular Lutheran or Calvinist." Moreover, he proposed that word be spread through the country that the proprietary party "intend to come well armed to the Election & . . . if there's the least partiality . . . that you will thrash the Sheriff every Inspector Quakers & Menonist to Jelly." Such a bellicose report, "industriously spread before the Election . . . will certainly keep great Numbers of the [pacifist] Menonists at home," schemed Purviance.[50]

The political strength displayed by the German churchpeople in 1764 made Muhlenberg the object of persistent overtures from the Quaker party prior to the election of 1765. Two party leaders, John Hughes and Henry Pawling, visited him as early as February 1765 attempting to gain his support for a royal charter. According to Muhlenberg's detailed journal notes, he told them that he preferred to stay out of politics, though he had been asked from time to time to "prepare the members of the German congregation for the coming election day on behalf of one or another interested party." This he had been reluctant to do until 1764, when Pennsylvanians had reason to fear that the priceless religious and civil privileges granted by Charles II in the proprietary charter might be given away. Hughes observed that by not supporting the movement for a royal charter the Germans, who should cherish their king the more because of his Hanoverian origins, "openly declared that they are enemies of our king!" To this Muhlenberg replied tartly that according to the rights granted by Charles II every inhabitant could vote as he wished at election time. And, Muhlenberg added, when in 1764 the Lutherans had unanimously decided to support several Germans for election to the assembly, "I approved it because we German citizens are not bastards but His Majesty's loyal subjects and naturalized children. . . . therefore we have the right and liberty to have one or more German citizens in the Assembly and to learn through them what is going on."[51]

Soon, however, Muhlenberg had drawn back again from the political precipice, finding it "scandalous that the two parties . . . [should] descend to personalities and carry their bitter enmity to such lengths in anonymous writings and engravings." He had been deeply offended by blasphemous cartoons, using representations of Satan and abusing the Scriptures, which had been hawked about the city by a harlequin on horseback. To Muhlenberg, now chastened, "religion and politics are thereby mortally poisoned and wounded." Yet no one with Muhlenberg's weight and influence among such a large bloc of voters as the Lutherans now constituted could avoid involvement in the fevered campaign of 1765. That Muhlenberg was still somewhat naive about politics is shown in his reaction to Governor John Penn's granting of charters of incorporation to the Lutheran, Reformed, and Swedish churches shortly before election time. To Muhlenberg's innocent eye, "this has been done by the finger of God!" But that a less exalted hand was at work is revealed in Governor Penn's private statement that he had granted the charters at the instigation of proprietary party leaders "with a view to engage these people to vote against the Quaker faction."[52]

As it turned out, the charters and other party inducements brought the desired result, for at nine o'clock on the morning of the election Muhlenberg once again rang his schoolhouse bell "& within a few hours about six hundred German citizens assembled in and before the schoolhouse and marched in procession to the courthouse to cast their votes. They conducted themselves very soberly and honorably and acted in a body [that is, voted unanimously] to the delight and also the dismay of the English nationality, depending upon which of the two parties the people belonged to." But at this election the other side, still smarting from the close call of the previous year, had worked harder to bring out its vote. Muhlenberg therefore had to record that the Quaker party won the election "*per fas et nefas*, and . . . are jubilant over it."[53] Thus closed the first phase of the political education of the Reverend Henry Muhlenberg.

Though Quakers were the first to practice denominational politics in Pennsylvania, by the mid-1760s all denominations and sects in the colony knew how to mobilize political opinion through the manipulation of ethno-religious sensibilities and networks. Few practitioners of the new politics were as skilled or open in its use as Samuel Purviance, Jr., yet virtually all the denominations of Pennsylvania had had their political consciousness raised, and would put it to good use in the decade ahead.

Dissenters vs. Anglicans in Virginia

Religious partisanship came late to Virginia, where a homogeneous population and the Church of England sustained establishment stability throughout the early years of the Great Awakening. Even a brief visit from George Whitefield in December of 1739 barely ruffled the surface calm.[54] Several Log College firebrands visited Hanover County in the mid-1740s, but it was not until the Presbyterian New Side minister, Samuel Davies, settled there permanently in 1749 that dissent became an issue of consequence in Virginia.

Davies's success, which owed much to his political skill, illustrates the close involvement with politics that characterized the ministerial office in the later colonial years. Davies's first object in Virginia was to secure the legal right to itinerate, or move freely about, among several congregations, he being the only Presbyterian preacher resident in the colony. The effort involved him directly with every branch of the Virginia government. Gambling that Lieutenant Governor William Gooch, originally a Church of Scotland man though officially pledged to support the established Anglican church, might respond favorably to a proper show of deference and moderation, Davies—who by his own description was "free from enthusiastic freaks"—stopped at Williamsburg for an interview with the governor before proceeding to Hanover County. Gooch, finding the young parson "dignified and courteous in manner," granted Davies a license to preach at four separate

meetinghouses erected by the rapidly expanding Presbyterians in
northwestern Virginia.[55]

Less hospitable to the newcomer were members of the Council
and House of Burgesses, most of them Anglicans, who shared the
church's alarm about "schism spreading itself through a colony
which has been famous for uniformity of religion." When Attorney
General Peyton Randolph in 1750 asserted that enforcement of the
Toleration Act would only sow confusion in Virginia, Davies argued
the dissenters' case before the Council with such ingenuity and
knowledge of law that it was soon whispered about that the attorney
general had met his match.[56] Even after Davies won the legal
argument, Randolph and others in government sought to delay or
circumvent the act's application on the flimsy ground that Davies
was in violation of the rule against itinerancy. But as Davies pointed
out in a letter to the bishop of London, "the extremes of my
congregation lie eighty or ninety miles apart, and the dissenters
under my care are scattered through six or seven different counties." As was well known, Anglican ministers traveled between
several chapels of ease in large parishes, and yet none of them
incurred "the odious epithet of an itinerant preacher." If dissenters
were denied the right to itinerate, "can [they] be said to be tolerated
at all?" wondered Davies. Unable to stop Davies's ministry by
appeals to the law, some Virginia Anglicans resorted to ridicule,
charging that Davies preached to "great numbers of poor people,
who, generally, are his only followers." Davies brushed off such
taunts as the lame grumblings of worldly Anglicans who "discard
serious religion as the badge of the vulgar."[57]

Samuel Davies was in many ways the ideal apostle of dissent to
the decorous Virginians. A man of considerable charm and obvious
intellect, Davies disarmed his critics by rejecting religious extremes. "I have no ambition to Presbyterianize the colony," he told
the Virginia commissary. He also denounced personal revelation
and sudden spiritual impulses as presumptuous and enthusiastical.
Moreover, he found Virginia's Anglican ministers to be "gentlemen
of learning, parts and morality," though he would have given much
to see them "inflamed with Zeal."[58]

Yet even with the diplomatic Davies as its chief spokesman Presbyterianism did not secure a firm base in Virginia until the outbreak of the French and Indian War, when the interests of Presbyterians—settled in greatest numbers in the exposed western section—and those of the royal government converged. Since frontier defense was a major concern of all Presbyterian congregations, both Old and New Side preachers worked to stiffen their parishioners' resolve to defend their homes—and thus the colony— against Indian and French attacks. John Craig, an Old Side minister in frontier Augusta County, was one of the staunchest advocates of strong defenses, berating those who would flee the frontier as cowards and "a lasting blot to our posterity." Craig urged that a series of small forts be built and saw to it that his own church was well fortified. Samuel Davies, too, put all his eloquence and personal influence behind the movement for a strongly defended frontier. Asserting that it was not only lawful but a Christian duty to take up arms, Davies urged his people cheerfully to pay taxes for the Fort Duquesne expedition and to "use our influence to diffuse a military spirit around us." He was, he told them, "particularly solicitous that you, my brethren of the dissenters, should act with honour and spirit . . . as it becomes loyal subjects, lovers of your country, and corageous Christians."[59]

In giving form and resolution to the combined political and material interests of his parishioners Davies also served their religious interests, for his growing reputation as the best recruiting officer in the province gave the Presbyterians added leverage in agitating for their rights. When Governor Fauquier arrived in 1758 he developed cordial relations with the Presbyterians, promising to exert himself to secure for them all the immunities of the Toleration Act. When the House of Burgesses proved less forward in supporting religious liberty, the Presbyterians began circulating petitions in the backcountry and dispatched a minister and leading elder to assert direct pressure on the legislature at Williamsburg. Moreover, as early as 1758 the denomination signaled its rising importance in elections by extracting from candidates promises to protect the Presbyterians' religious and civil privileges "before they would agree to vote them Burgesses."[60] But if Presbyterians were becoming adept at denominational partisanship, the Baptists were not far behind.

To the genteel leaders of the Anglican community the Baptists constituted both a religious and a cultural oddity. Almost everything they believed and did, especially the more extreme Separate Baptists, made the gentlefolk of Virginia uneasy. Baptist religious practices were egalitarian, ardent, and peculiar. They included such collective intimacies as the laying on of hands, kisses of charity, and the washing of feet. Worse even than the Calvinists of New England, who at least included educated gentlemen within their ranks, the Baptists required no formal religious training of their preachers. Moreover, the Baptists' worldly face was equally strange; relentlessly solemn, they seemed to disapprove of all conviviality and merriment. By opposing gambling, horse racing, dancing and other customary pleasures, the Baptists represented a standing rebuke to the prevailing social style of the Virginia tidewater.[61] In short, they reminded the genteel Anglicans of nothing so much as the levellers of seventeenth-century England. And, indeed, some Baptist men even "cut off their hair, like Cromwell's round-headed chaplains."[62]

To be sure, the repugnance felt by Virginia Anglicans toward the Baptists can easily be overstated. And as James Madison pointed out in 1774, exaggerated accounts of Baptist behavior also served a political purpose: "incredible and extravagent stories . . . told in the House [of Burgesses] of the monstrous effects of the enthusiasm prevalent among the sectaries . . . [were] greedily swallowed by their enemies."[63] Nonetheless, it does not take much digging in the records of late colonial Virginia to find that the Baptists were seen as rather a disagreeable presence. The Baptists themselves cared little how they appeared to men and women of fashion. Being almost complete outsiders, they had nothing to lose by confronting authority—a circumstance that seems to have infused them with a great deal of energy and perseverance.

Beginning in 1770, the Baptists initiated petition campaigns to the Virginia legislature asking for full religious freedom under the provisions of the Toleration Act. These petitions were circulated with great industry. "Vast numbers readily, and indeed eagerly, subscribed to them." So vigorous did the petitioning become that during one four-week period in 1772 five separate petitions were addressed by Baptists to the legislature. The concerted character of this campaign is evident from the identical wording of the petitions from Lunenburg, Mecklenburg, Sussex, and Caroline counties. Such activity continued to the Revolution and beyond, with one famous 1776 petition, circulated by the Baptists but receiving support from other dissenters as well, garnering 10,000 signatures.[64] Whether the Baptists attempted to sway the outcome of elections this early, as they would a few years later by endorsing specific candidates in local contests, is not clear. But that they were acquiring the numbers and concentrated strength for such political action was evident from the crowds of up to two thousand attracted to their camp meetings. Such numbers soon enabled the Baptists to give "a cast to the [political] scale, by which means many a worthy and useful member was lodged in the house of assembly, and answered a valuable purpose there."[65]

The American Revolution provided the Baptists with the ultimate political leverage, and they used it boldly to gain religious equality. A Baptist petition of May 19, 1776, stated their case forthrightly. If the Baptists were granted full religious rights and the Church of England disestablished, "we will gladly unite with our Brethren of other denominations, and to the utmost of our ability promote the common cause of *Freedom*."[66] May 1776 was a critical time for the Revolutionary movement in Virginia. By bartering their support of the Patriot cause for religious liberty, the Baptists and other Virginia dissenters who made similar demands knew they were dealing from a position of strength. Years of experience contesting for their religious rights, as well as a growing recognition that organized numbers meant power, prepared Virginia's dissenters for full political citizenship. Thus Baptists and Anglicans, backcountry Presbyterian farmers and tidewater gentleman planters, struck bargains and surmounted their differences, at least temporarily, in 1776. Facilitating that convergence was the realization that each group's long-term goals, in the one case political, in the other religious, could best by achieved by severing ties with England.[67]

Denominational politics forms the bridge between the Great Awakening and the American Revolution. From 1740 to 1776, thousands of provincials from every rank and section—Old Lights as well as New—became embroiled in political activity as a consequence of their religious loyalties. Denominations organized committees of correspondence, wrote circular letters, adjusted election tickets for religious balance, voted *en bloc*, and signed political petitions "as a Sabbath-Day's Exercise."[68] Many ministers actively encouraged the use of ecclesiastical structures to communicate party views to their parishioners. Lay members, and in a number of cases clergymen themselves, provided the leadership for movements whose initially religious aims rapidly became indistinguishable from political ones.

In the long run it struck the provincials as more or less logical that the congregation should become a basic unit or cell of politics, and regional associations and synods the interconnecting tissue. As the number of congregations rose rapidly in the eighteenth century, denominational bodies often achieved a closer and more vital relationship with the people than did governmental institutions. The "federal" character and representative practices of most church governments made them efficient agencies for both religious and political activity, as colonial politicians never tired of observing. Indeed, all that has been said and written about the New England town as the "school of democracy" can be applied with equal or greater force to the church congregation. The congregation, moreover, unlike New England town government, was ubiquitous. It existed all over the colonies; and it reached out to rich and poor, men and women, the schooled and the unschooled.

CHAPTER 7

Religion and
the American Revolution

On March 22, 1775, Edmund Burke addressed Parliament on the subject of the American rebellion. The "fierce spirit of liberty is stronger in the English Colonies probably than in any other people of the earth," declared Burke, ascribing this feature of the American character to the colonists' English origins, their popular assemblies, and their heritage of religious dissent. Expanding on the last point, Burke continued: "Religion, always a principle of energy, in this new people is no way worn out or impaired. . . . The people are Protestants; and of that kind which is most adverse to all implicit submission of mind and opinion." Indeed, religion in "our Northern Colonies is a refinement on the principle of resistance."[1]

Joseph Galloway made the same point, though in less temperate language, five years later in his *Historical and Political Reflections on the Rise and Progress of the American Rebellion*. The Revolution was started by "republican sectaries," charged Galloway, specifically a seditious combination of Congregationalists and Presbyterians "whose principles of religion and polity were equally averse to those of the established Church and Government."[2]

Burke and Galloway were describing a tradition of popular

resistance that was rooted in sixteenth-century religious dissent and in the religious politics of Stuart England.[3] This ideology of dissent—as improved by Enlightenment whigs and eighteenth-century radical publicists—was amplified in America, where dissenters formed a majority of the inhabitants. By the 1760s it had also taken on certain features from evangelical religion, such as a concern for individual accountability and the rights of minorities in matters of conscience. Nonetheless, the American ideology of dissent was firmly grounded in reason as well as emotion, which gave it special force among provincial leaders—including many Anglicans—who prided themselves on taking a rational approach to Revolution issues. No doubt millennial expectations and evangelical preaching helped to move a good many Americans into the patriot camp. But by 1775–1776 the emotionalism of the Great Awakening had subsided or been diluted by a widening current of Enlightenment rationalism. Thus evangelical Calvinism and religious rationalism did not carve separate channels but flowed as one stream toward the crisis of 1776.

When Burke observed that "an Englishman is the unfittest person on earth to argue another Englishman into slavery," he implicitly pointed to the body of belief upon which many Americans would base their justification for revolution. Though the secular side of that ideology has been exhibited in various scholarly writings over the past two decades, the religious side of opposition thought has received somewhat less attention.[4] Yet the least ambiguous justification for opposition to Britain in the 1770s, the line of argument least weighted with qualifications and requiring the least remodeling to fit American circumstances, drew on the religious politics of the seventeenth and early eighteenth centuries—specifically the radical resistance in England to the doctrine of divine right and passive obedience. The linking of patriot opposition to this cherished tradition of resistance fortified Americans who otherwise might have lost their way in the ambiguities clouding such largely secular issues as representation, social compact, and divided sovereignty.[5] A brief look back at the history of resistance to divine right absolutism in England may suggest why that tradition retained a powerful hold on the eighteenth-century American imagination.

The Ideology of Dissent

Stuart assertions of divine right during the first half of the seventeenth century prompted English libertarians to fashion a coherent theory of opposition to absolute authority. Drawing on Reformation thought, the Christian Platonism of the Florentine humanists, and emergent notions of republicanism and religious toleration, English radicals shaped an ideology that challenged the cramped views of divine right political theorists and high-church conservatives alike.[6]

John Milton's political writings opposing the absolutist claims of Charles I were seminal to the development of this religious-political canon in England. Milton not only denied that a king's right to rule came from God, but argued that kings were "indebted and obliged for their authority to the people only, and consequently are accountable to them for it." Rejecting the notion that Scripture forbade opposition to a corrupt and tyrannical king, Milton recapitulated the basic argument against passive obedience and nonresistance. When a king defied the higher law the duty of a true Christian was clear, since there was "much more of God in the people whenever they depose an unjust king than in the king that oppresses an innocent people."[7]

A companion theme sounded repeatedly by Milton pointed to the danger posed to both state and church by "Episcopacie." The number and power of bishops, he declared, had risen sharply under the first two Stuart kings. By extending their influence into government, these church tyrants—like the bishops of imperial Rome—might gradually aggrandize more and more power until they destroyed the balance of the constitution. In one pamphlet Milton compared the bishops to a monstrous wen on the head of the state, which gradually swelled up until it nearly equaled the size of the head itself. Being of no use, this foul disfigurement should be cut off at once. "As wise and famous men have suspected and fear'd the Protestant *Episcopacie* in *England*," he warned, "as those that have fear'd the Papall."[8] In his political pamphlets, as well as in the better known essays on freedom of the press and education, Milton popularized much of the language and imagery with which subsequent writers would carry on the seventeenth-century radical heritage.

The religious content of not only the Civil War but the Exclusion Crisis and the Glorious Revolution led to the firm joining of civil and religious rights in English liberal thought. The terms "Whig" and "Tory" first entered the English political lexicon during the Exclusion Crisis of 1679–81, establishing direct associations in the public mind between those two parties and specific religious attitudes. From that time forward tories were generally believed to favor an established church whose privileges were protected by the state, and a state whose authority was sufficiently sanctified to command the obedience of all subjects. Whigs, on the other hand, were more liberal in both politics and religion, and in 1688 they firmly repudiated the high-church doctrines of divine right and passive obedience.[9]

Following the Glorious Revolution many Anglican clergymen, preferring the *via media* to the extremes of church doctrine, had no difficulty taking the oath of allegiance to the new constitutional monarchs, William and Mary. But a number of high-Anglican priests could not bring themselves to swear fidelity to the Calvinist William, or to surrender the divine right and nonresistance doctrines that in their minds formed the indissoluble links between church and state. These "nonjurors" constituted a small but vocal wing of the Anglican establishment after 1688, providing over the years a philosophical redoubt for Jacobites, divine right dogmatists, and disgruntled conservative clergymen.

Because the decades following 1688 were a testing time for Revolution principles, divine right and passive obedience continued to be debated, though with declining intensity, by political writers. William Molesworth, for example, devoted a full chapter and more of his 1694 pamphlet, *An Account of Denmark*, to warning against the pernicious connections between "Popery" and political slavery, asserting that blind obedience to religious absolutism was soon followed by the destruction of a nation's liberty.[10] The term "popery," it might be noted, had taken on new meaning in England by the end of the seventeenth century, referring not only to the Jacobite threat but even more pointedly to the nonjuring or Anglo-Catholic "high flyers" of the Church of England. When the post-Revolution consensus began to disintegrate, as inevitably it did, the high-church nonjurors and their tory allies in Parliament formed the vanguard of an emergent political opposition that reached its apogee in the near hysteria of the Sacheverell affair of 1709–1710.

The impeachment trial of the Reverend Doctor Henry Sacheverell contributed significantly to the development of eighteenth-century radicalism by dramatically recalling to robust life the passions of the previous century's religious-political contests. At the same time it transmitted them with vivid immediacy to a new generation of Anglo-Americans. Henry Sacheverell was but the most famous of a number of conservative clergymen sounding the "Church in Danger" alarm by the turn of the eighteenth century as the whig government made concessions to the forces of dissent and religious toleration. When a resurgent Tory Party exploited the "Church in Danger" theme to turn out a host of Anglican clergymen for its side in the elections of 1698 and after, the phrase "high-church tory" clearly had become more than a shibboleth.[11]

Benjamin Hoadly, rector of St. Peter Poor, London, was perhaps the most incisive polemicist among the radical Anglican churchmen who took up their pens to do battle against the "Priestcraft" of the high flyers. Could the tory clergy be interpreting the Pauline scriptures aright, Hoadly wondered, when they claimed that since the power to govern came from God "the governed Part of Mankind [lost] the Right of Self-Defence . . . against all possible Attempts of their Governours"? Just as a child must resist "a Parent who should in a Fit of Madness command his Child to cut his Brother's Throat," so too the people should reject the notion of "Absolute passive Obedience . . . [when] a Governour turned Publick Enemy." High-church doctrine would not only deny that the people had acted rightly in deposing James II in 1688, but would allow the gospel to "patronize the most abject, the most universal Slavery."[12] When Henry Sacheverell was invited by the tory Lord Mayor of London to preach the annual Fifth of November sermon at St. Paul's in 1709,[13] for which he subsequently was impeached and tried for sedition, the controversy turned into a cause célèbre. Sacheverell's sermon, *The Perils of False Brethren, both in Church, and State*, lashed at deists, Socinians, Arians, skeptics, and "whosoever presumes to Recede the least Tittle from the express Word of God, or to explain the Great Credenda of Our Faith in Newfangl'd Terms of Modern Philosophy." He denounced the "execrable" practice of Occasional Conformity to the church as being like occasional loyalty to the state. The climax of the sermon, and the part seized on in the impeachment proceedings, came when Sacheverell endorsed with all the passion at his command the political theory of high Anglicanism. He affirmed the citizen's obligation to offer "Absolute, and Unconditional Obedience" to lawful government and asserted the "utter Illegality of Resistance upon any Pretence whatsoever." In short, "the English Government can never be Secure on any other Principles, but strictly Those of the Church of England." Dissenters, moreover, "must Betray That Government They are Enemies to upon Principle."[14]

To leading whigs the sermon called into question the settlement of 1688–89, and they promptly moved a bill of impeachment. During the three and a half weeks of Sacheverell's trial before the House of Lords, the best legal minds in England explored the subtleties of the doctrines of resistance and obedience as well as the meaning of limited monarchy. It could hardly be said that the prosecution was fully agreed on the issue of when resistance to authority was appropriate, but all rejected the position taken by Sacheverell. Defense counsel tried to soften the doctor's words by granting the legitimacy of the Revolution of 1688, and attempting to reshape the nonresistance doctrine to apply to the Crown-in-Parliament rather than to the Crown alone.

Sacheverell was convicted by a division of sixty-nine to fifty-two. Yet instead of being banished from his pulpit, fined, and imprisoned as many whigs had expected, he received the far milder rebuke of a three-year suspension and the public burning of his sermons. When the moderate sentence was announced on March 21, 1710, high churchmen and tories celebrated it as a vindication, lighting bonfires and ringing church bells throughout the kingdom. More ominously, dissenters' houses were attacked, Sacheverell cocks fought Hoadly cocks, Hoadly was burned in effigy, and his church was threatened with destruction. The tories managed to force an election in the fall of 1710 following a tour by Sacheverell through nine counties—"the most extraordinary Progress ever made by a private individual in Britain," according to one historian—during which prospective tory candidates made themselves conspicuous at the side of the new hero. The "Church Party," as it was now called, won handily.[15]

The tory ascendancy would last only until 1714. Henry Sacheverell quickly fell from public view as it became evident that his meteoric career did not portend a new age of absolutism. But if the Sacheverell affair flared but briefly in the long history of English politics, the name of Henry Sacheverell looms much larger in the history of Anglo-American radicalism. For by vigorously defending the high-church doctrines of nonresistance and passive obedience, and then tying them to the Tory Party, the Sacheverell episode made a permanent contribution to popular political imagery. From 1710 on, Sacheverell's name became a negative symbol to radical dissenters who equated civil with religious liberty and opposed the doctrines of high-church absolutism. Such imagery is omnipresent in the works of writers who transmitted the English opposition heritage to the American colonies, where the debate over obedience and resistance to authority was waxing rather than waning.[16]

In 1720 Thomas Gordon, a young Scotsman, and John Trenchard, a seasoned pamphleteer of earlier liberal causes, began a collaboration in radical polemics with the publication of *The Independent Whig.* Gordon had come to Trenchard's attention during the Bangorian Controversy when the Scot had defended Benjamin Hoadly's liberal theology in a series of keenly satirical pamphlets, one of which was entitled *An Apology for the danger of the Church,*

proving that the Church is and ought to be always in danger, and
that it would be dangerous for her to be out of danger. . . . (1719).
Designed as the scourge of the high-church party, *The Independent*
Whig was subtitled "a Defence of Primitive Christianity, and of Our
Ecclesiastical Establishment, Against the Exorbitant Claims and
Encroachments of Fanatical and Disaffected Clergymen." Its fifty-
three essays fulminated against the evils of "Popery" and
"Priestcraft" but did not oppose an appropriately circumscribed
Anglican establishment. Indeed, the authors' stated purpose was "to
illustrate the Beauty of Christianity, by exposing the Deformity of
Priestcraft; to distinguish the good Clergy from the bad, by giving to
each his Share of Praise or Infamy."[17]

A central proposition of *The Independent Whig*, and of Trenchard
and Gordon's subsequent collaborative effort, *Cato's Letters*—
subtitled "Essays on Liberty, Civil and Religious, And other
important Subjects"—was that all public authority was subject to
restraint and scrutiny by the people. Attempts by the high clergy to
smuggle modified versions of divine right and passive obedience
into the eighteenth century deeply alarmed the *Independent Whig*.
From its introductory philippic against priestcraft and blind obedience to either king or bishop, the *Whig* never strayed far from this
dominant theme. The notorious Sacheverell was invoked frequently
to remind the reader of what happened when priests acquired
political ambitions. In vivid prose the *Whig* pointed to "the
High-Church Jacobite Clergy of England" as the greatest threat to
liberty.[18] They were responsible for such "Corruptions and Fop-
peries . . . [as] the ungainly Brats of Passive Obedience [and] the
Divine Right of Kings and Bishops." Yet a true Englishman
understood that since 1688 the clergy had no power except that
granted to it by Parliament. No threat was posed to the present
constitutional monarchy, declared the *Whig*, by consigning the old
Stuart adage "No Bishop, No King" to the ash heap. "This stupid
Saying has formerly filled our Prisons with Dissenters, and chased
many of them to *America*."[19]

Cato, using a slightly more secular voice, continued the warnings
against the combined powers of church and state. "When Religion

is taught to speak Court-Language, and none are suffered to preach it, but such as speak the same Dialect," both civil and religious liberty were imperiled. In his farewell Cato noted the great popularity of his writings, which had no other view "but the Good of my Country and of Mankind; by shewing them the Advantage and the Beauty of Civil and Ecclesiastical Liberty, and the odious Deformity of Priestcraft and Tyranny."[20]

Religious politics ebbed rapidly in England after about 1720. With the Lutheran George I, himself an Occasional Conformist, on the throne, and with Robert Walpole directing national energy into more secular channels, a moderate Anglicanism came into fashion. Even religious dissent lost some of its attraction, with only about seven percent of the population falling into that category between 1715 and 1740.[21] On the periphery of the British Empire, however, religious issues continued to be debated long after they had subsided in England itself. In the American colonies, a number of which had been settled at least in part by refugees from the religious politics of the Old World, two-thirds or more of the people fell under the designation of dissenters. This created a receptive environment for a literature that denounced ecclesiastical tyranny and promoted freedom of conscience. Even Americans who had not directly experienced the conflicts of the Stuart years found their religious and political attitudes being shaped by English writers who had.[22] Moreover, the most resonant strain of that literature, especially in colonies where the Anglican church was expanding rapidly, was the writing by such as Milton and Trenchard and Gordon that attacked ecclesiastical tyranny, divine right, and nonresistance. For out of all the religious and political writings by the English reformers, only *The Independent Whig*, with its single-minded concentration on the dangers of church and state combined, and a pamphlet by Milton condemning the "hireling" clergy were republished in American editions before the Revolution.[23]

The appetite with which the colonials devoured the radical whig polemics is evident in their newspapers and pamphlets from the 1720s onward. The Morris-Cosby conflict in New York during the mid-1730s, for example, yielded a series of essays on the people's right to resist tyrannical government, "especially in an Age of Liberty in which *the slavish Doctrine of passive Obedience* is out of Fashion."[24] Similar references occur throughout the colonies. The most direct and ingenuous borrowing of opposition rhetoric prior to the 1760s is found, of course, in the Reverend Jonathan Mayhew's sermon, *A Discourse Concerning Unlimited Submission*, preached in Boston on January 30, 1750 to mark the anniversary of the execution of Charles I.

Eager to embellish his already considerable reputation among English radicals, and irritated by the rising power and self-assurance of Boston's Anglican clergy, Mayhew called up the ghost of Charles I in order to bury it again in obloquy. He began by noting that around the January 30 anniversary "the slavish doctrine of passive obedience and nonresistance is often warmly asserted"; at the same time dissenters were frequently castigated as schismatics and traitors. Such "Tyranny, PRIESTCRAFT, and Nonesense" merely demonstrated that "a spirit of domination is always to be guarded against, both in church and state." After reviewing the scriptural passages enjoining Christians to obey civil rulers who exercised their authority with probity, Mayhew posed the central question. Were there any circumstances where instead of "absolute submission to our prince . . . disobedience and resistance may not be justifiable"? Drawing a distinction between good rulers and bad, Mayhew concluded that Scripture does not require submission "to such rulers as act in contradiction to the public good." In the time of Charles I, such resistance was "absolutely necessary. . . . And who so proper to make this resistance as the Lords and Commons"?[25]

In an extended footnote Mayhew carried the argument a step further. To disobey rulers who governed in a manner "inconsistent with the commands of God" was not only lawful but "glorious." Such disobedience was "a duty, not a crime." Moreover, the people themselves were the "proper judges" of a prince who exalts himself into a tyrant.[26] Mayhew balanced this highly individualistic right of resistance with a more conventional view in the text, noting that a people may "arise unanimously" only after long suffering to overthrow their prince. He also praised the reigning king, George II, for ruling in accordance with law.[27]

That the provincials savored this debate over obedience and resistance, especially to the extent that it pointed the finger at Anglican pretensions to prerogative power, is evident in their response to the publication of Mayhew's sermon. John Adams claimed that the *Discourse* was "read by everybody," and it touched off a six-month newspaper war in Boston over questions of obedience to authority. A reprinting followed within a few months, and the sermon was soon regarded as "a classic formulation of the necessity and virtue of resistance to oppression."[28]

The issue cropped up periodically thereafter. In 1753, William Livingston of New York wrote two essays on "Passive Obedience and Non-Resistance" for *The Independent Reflector*, a publication deliberately styled on *The Independent Whig*. Intended primarily as a vehicle to oppose Anglican control of King's College, *The Independent Reflector* railed against the "politico-theological Jargon" of churchmen who denied the people's right to resist an unjust prince. In one passage Livingston charged a local churchman with contending "as strenuously for Non-Resistance, as if he had been animated with the very Soul of SACHEVEREL."[29] In Virginia's debates over the Two-Penny Acts and the Parsons' Cause the theme appeared again when Landon Carter and Richard Bland accused the Reverend John Camm of advocating "principles of passive obedience." Even "God himself," declared Carter, "knowing the Imperfection of Man, and the World he lives in, did not intend that every Command of *his* should be invariably observed, in all Cases." John Adams's 1765 *Dissertation on the Canon and Feudal Law* took direct aim at a priesthood that supported the divine origins of government along with "the most mischievous of all doctrines, that of passive obedience and nonresistance."[30]

That Americans should return so often to these timeworn themes in a land where divine right had never gained much of a toehold seems odd. Nor is there any evidence that provincial Anglicans seriously promoted the doctrine of passive obedience to either bishop or king.[31] Nonetheless, "country" politicians constantly worked on the old fears of absolutism by hinting that sinister combinations of high flyers in church and state threatened colonial liberties. The explanation of this unwonted emphasis may lie not only in the colonists' susceptibility to the ideology of dissent but also in the meagerness of alternative grounds upon which they could base a political opposition.

With whig politicians retreating toward the moderate middle by the second quarter of the eighteenth century, political writings that stressed stability and reconciliation in public life came to enjoy a kind of vogue in ruling circles. Montesquieu's glorification of the self-balancing mechanisms of the English constitution, as well as a reading of Locke that highlighted the passages advising restraint, soon cut away much of the ground for opposition to government. Parties were everywhere disdained as "the madness of many, for the gain of the few."[32] Even the radical whigs thought it preferable to bear with some injustice than to rise precipitantly against it. Trenchard and Gordon praised the liberality of the British system of government and counseled obedience to it as long as the constitution was "preserved entire." Following Locke, this meant that Parliament continued to meet, courts remained open, and force was not used against the people. Such a formula left little room for a legitimate opposition. To be sure, the radical whigs distrusted power and warned about its tendency to corrupt those who long held it. Yet they, like other political writers of the time, balanced the scales between obedience and resistance so evenly as to discourage a formal opposition, much less the overthrow of government by force.[33]

That many provincials were drawn into this moderate political consensus is evident from copious writings urging that faction and self-interest be subordinated to the common good. Yet as concern rose after mid-century over imperial reforms that seemed to be altering their constitutional relationship with England, the Americans cast about for a way to resist these vexing changes. Secular political theory, with its many restrictions and qualifications, offered ambiguous guidance at best. But should their religious as well as civil liberties come under attack, a new element would be added that might outweigh conventional inhibitions about resistance—

even in an era of moderation. For if the people's religious rights were invaded, all of the old injunctions against blind obedience to sinful magistrates would instantly come into play. Did not the Bible admonish Christians "to obey God rather than men"? And had not Locke himself written that "obedience is due first of all to God, and afterwards to the laws"?[34] Should the provincials ever be persuaded that a conspiracy was brewing in England to attack not only their civil but their religious liberties, a potent justification for resistance would become available to them.

The "infernal confederacy": Controversy over an American Bishop

Only against this background of seventeenth- and eighteenth-century ecclesiastical politics can we comprehend the colossal uproar touched off by the Anglican bishop controversy of 1767–1770. Historians disagree about whether the threat to settle a resident bishop of the Church of England in America was real or imagined. Those who believe it was real point to a coterie of northern Anglicans eager to complete the structure of their colonial church who combined with sympathetic prelates in England to press the cause at Whitehall.[35] Other historians assert that most American Anglicans did not want a resident bishop, and that in any case the Stamp Act riots foreclosed the possibility that England might have imposed one. Nor is there much evidence that Whitehall—or even the diocese of London—considered such a course.[36] Still, the pervasiveness of American anxiety regarding a bishop cannot be denied. The question was hotly discussed in correspondence, and it was perhaps the pivotal issue in the New York assembly election of 1769.[37] Provincial presses worked over-time in the later 1760s turning out pamphlets, broadsides, and newspaper essays on the subject. Indeed, the controversy easily consumed as much paper as the Stamp Act dispute, and probably exceeded it over the long run since the question of episcopacy was debated periodically from at least 1702 onward.[38]

John Adams would later claim that "the apprehension of Episcopacy" contributed as much as any other cause to the American
Revolution, capturing the attention "not only of the inquiring mind,
but of the common people. . . . The objection was not merely to the
office of a bishop, though even that was dreaded, but to the
authority of parliament, on which it must be founded." That politics
rather than religion lay at the heart of the controversy was noted by
many Americans. The Presbyterian leader, Francis Alison, declared
in 1766 that he did not care if the Anglicans had "fifty Bishops in
America. . . . What we dread is their political power, and their
courts." Similarly William Livingston was not "prejudiced against
any episcopalian for his religion. . . . It is the politics of the church
. . . its thirst of domination" that dissenters feared. Southern
opponents felt the same, one exclaiming: "Never was a Controversy
carried on where Religion had so little Concern."[39] That the threat
of episcopacy alarmed provincials of every rank and section demonstrates how widespread was the fear of a combined church and
state in colonial America. One need not have read Milton and
Hoadly, or even be literate, to believe that bishops endangered civil
as well as religious liberty. Such a view of episcopacy was regularly
transmitted from dissenting pulpits, and in colonial homes everywhere it was imbibed from childhood.

Adding to the colonists' anxieties, especially in cities and larger
towns, was the noticeably Anglican orientation of officeholders
recently arrived from England. A number of them seemed bent on
making the colonies as much like the mother country as possible.
Governor Francis Bernard of Massachusetts, charged by Jonathan
Mayhew with being deep in the plot for an Anglican bishop, had
actually broached the idea of an American peerage as a way of
reorganizing power to support imperial government. Leading Anglicans wanted Rhode Island and Connecticut brought under royal
charters, a move that would both have Anglicized their governments and strengthened the Church of England. The royal governor
of North Carolina showed in his 1764 program to fortify the Church
of England what a committed Anglican could do to overcome
decades of resistance to establishment.[40] In Pennsylvania many who

fought against proposals to royalize that colony did so out of concern
that the Church of England might thereby gain preferential status.
New York's Anglican leaders were forever trying to bolster the
church. In 1763 they unsuccessfully attempted to extend the
Ministry Act to the Manor of Philipsburgh; and the Provincial
Council—all of whose members but one were Anglicans—repeatedly refused to charter dissenting churches.[41] So noticeable had
become the appointment of Anglicans to provincial councils and
judicial offices that Ezra Stiles feared patronage positions at every
level might soon be used to "subserve the proselyting to the Mother
Church." And, to be sure, in 1768 the Reverend Samuel Cooper of
Boston reported that an Anglican postmaster in that city was
refusing to distribute anti-episcopal writings through the mails.
Such "insolence of office," concluded Cooper, "[is] what our poor
America is likely more and more to feel."[42]

Dissenters feared Anglican expansion in part because churches
and ministers were carriers of a national as well as a religious
culture. That is, the Church of England, like its German, Scottish,
and Dutch counterparts, not only preserved transatlantic patterns of
language and custom but inculcated attitudes toward government
and authority—by no means always congenial—through the agency
of worship rituals, ecclesiastical forms, and church schools. Thus the
Anglicization of American society, in the face of a reverse process
that had been in silent motion for a very long time, was closely
connected with the expanding presence and vigor of the Church of
England. William Smith of Philadelphia made this connection
explicit in a 1762 report to the Bishop of London on the state of
Anglicanism in the colonies. "The Church is the firmest Basis of
Monarchy and the English Constitution," he declared. But if
dissenters of "more Republican . . . Principles [with] little affinity
to the established Religion and manners" of England ever gained
the upper hand, the colonists might begin to think of "Indepen-
dency and separate Government." Thus "in a *Political as well as
religious* view," Smith stated emphatically, the church should be
strengthened by an American bishop and the appointment of
"prudent Governors who are friends of our Establishment."[43]

The politically astute Smith, nurtured in the denominational politics of Pennsylvania, chose not to make a public issue of episcopacy at a time when tension between colonies and mother country was on the rise. But churchmen less attuned to political and religious sensibilities committed a number of blunders that played into the hands of the dissenter majority. In Massachusetts, for example, Anglicans at Cambridge unwisely elected to construct a church within sight of that nursery of Congregationalism, Harvard College. The young rector, the Reverend East Apthorp, then built an adjacent mansion of such magnificence that Jonathan Mayhew was widely believed when he hinted that its true purpose was to serve as the palace for an American bishop. When in 1763 Apthorp wrote a defense of the S.P.G. that included gratuitous comments about the fanaticism of the Congregationalists' Puritan forbears, Mayhew responded with such cutting invective that he was answered in turn by none other than the Archbishop of Canterbury. Mayhew's response to the archbishop, the final sally in this exchange, explained that Americans felt compelled to stop episcopacy at its inception, since—drawing here on a familiar whig axiom— "people are not usually deprived of their liberties all at once, but gradually; by one encroachment after another, as it is found they are disposed to bear them."[44]

The episcopacy issue declined in 1765 as attention became riveted on the Stamp Act. Nonetheless such works as John Adams's *Dissertation on the Canon and Feudal Law*, written that same year, continued to remind Americans about the "infernal confederacy [of] ecclesiastical and civil tyranny." And Adams's allusion in the *Dissertation* to the Mayhew-Apthorp controversy was no doubt meant to alert his readers to the proximity of the danger. Anglican clergymen in New England were more subdued after 1765, apparently chastened by Lambeth's coolness to an American bishopric and by the Stamp Act violence. But middle-colony priests seized on the stamp riots as a reason to press even harder for a bishop. "We firmly believe," they declared, "that [the government's] best Security in the Colonies does, and must always arise, from the Principles of Submission and Loyalty taught by the Church"—principles that the Anglican clergy were "constantly instilling . . . into the People."[45] As late as 1780 middle-colony churchmen continued to argue that had the dissenters' "Republican; levelling Principles" been offset by the appointment of an American bishop, and a consequent rise in the number of Anglicans, the Revolution might never have occurred.[46]

Following repeal of the Stamp Act, leading Anglican ministers determined to approach their fellow colonists directly to explain the church's need for a bishop. The Reverend Dr. Thomas Bradbury Chandler was chosen to write a moderate statement designed to reassure Americans that a bishop would have none but ecclesiastical authority. Chandler's *Appeal to the Public in Behalf of the Church of England in America* pointed out that a bishop was needed to confirm new church members and to ordain and discipline the clergy, but that he would have no civil authority, establish no ecclesiastical courts, and institute no tithes. Chandler immediately weakened his case, however, by referring to the Church of England as the "true Religion" and by noting that even if an American bishop should accept of civil office—perhaps as justice of a provincial court—no harm would be done since bishops were persons of known ability and integrity. In order to show how frivolous were dissenter fears of a tithe, Chandler added that even if three bishops came to America they could be supported by a tax of only four pence in £100.[47] The good doctor seemed to have no idea how unreassuring these arguments, well intended though they were, must have sounded to colonials who believed that bishops represented the entering wedge of tyranny.

The *Appeal* by itself might have caused no more than a minor tempest (even William Livingston considered Chandler to be an upright man, though he detested the doctor's "high-flying Notions"), but it was not the only provocation. In the same year, 1767, John Ewer, Bishop of Llandaff, preached the annual sermon in London to the S.P.G., using the occasion for a slashing attack on the colonists' religion. Their Puritan ancestors, Ewer alleged, had abandoned England and its church to live "without remembrance or knowledge of God . . . in dissolute wickedness, and . . . brutal

This engraving of a half soldier–half bishop landing in Boston is a satire
on the militancy of the English church and state combined. Note the
bishop's mitre, the "Thirty Nine Articles" shield, and the cannon
inscribed "Alliance between Church & State." (n.d., circa 1770s)
British Museum

profligacy." Subsequent generations of Americans were no better,
and at this day religion was to them "but an impediment in the way
of avarice." No word or act from London could have been better

calculated to enrage the provincials. News of the bishop's tirade, reaching the colonies at about the same time that Chandler's *Appeal* made its appearance, touched off a full-scale assault on the Church of England that continued well into 1770.[48]

Charles Chauncy, one of the first Americans to read Ewer's sermon, claimed that the colonists had never before been alerted in such bald terms to the church's intent to episcopize them. Associations of New England ministers voted to condemn the sermon, and even the usually cautious Reverend Andrew Eliot of Boston labeled it an abusive calumny.[49] In New York, William Livingston shot off *A letter to the Right Reverend Father in God, John, Lord Bishop of Llandaff: Occasioned by Some Passages in His Lordship's Sermon . . . in which the American Colonies are Loaded with Great and Undeserved Reproach*, which was promptly reprinted in Boston. Then writing as "The American Whig," Livingston with the occasional assistance of fellow dissenters, launched a series of sixty-four weekly newspaper essays that from mid-March 1768 to late July 1769 descanted on the Anglicans' uncontrollable urge to encroach on the liberty of dissenters. Livingston's characterization of the campaign for a bishop as "this ecclesiastical stamp-act" and similar thrusts provoked Chandler, the Reverend Charles Inglis, and other Anglicans to respond with a series of newspaper essays that also ran for sixty-four weeks. The dissenters thereupon abandoned any semblance of reasoned debate in favor of biting satire in an additional sixty-eight essays that continued until January 29, 1770. In Philadelphia, dissenters and Anglicans did weekly battle in the newspapers from March through the end of December 1768, under the pseudonyms "Centinel," "Anti-Centinel," "The Anatomist," and "The Remonstrant." A number of the dissenter essays were picked up by other provincial newspapers, and one New York printer gathered the writings on both sides of the question into an 837-page collection that he reprinted and sold in two-volume sets.[50]

That the actual settlement of a bishop in America was ever seriously contemplated during these trying times is, as noted earlier, extremely unlikely. Yet the provincials could hardly be sure of this. They knew only that a number of Anglicans had worked for decades to obtain a bishop, and that the man elevated as Archbishop

of Canterbury in 1758 had expressed support for the cause. They
also knew that land for a bishop's glebe had actually been offered to
the church by Sir William Johnson of New York. By the later 1760s,
moreover, efforts to bind the colonies more closely to the mother
country in other ways were ominously evident. Against the background of the Stamp Act, the visible presence of British troops, and
rumors about the creation of an American peerage, the provincials
had little reason to doubt that the Church of England was about to
be strengthened at the expense of dissenting denominations.[51]

As early as 1760, Ezra Stiles had called for a defensive coalition of
dissenters against "a formal attempt on the chastity and order of our
churches," and in 1766 such a "confederacy" came into being. By
that year, Pennsylvania Presbyterians like Francis Alison and the
activist layman Samuel Purviance, Jr., had joined with their brethren in New York to promote an alliance with the Connecticut
Congregationalists. Stiles invited the cooperation of Massachusetts
ministers when he attended the Harvard commencement in July,
and by late summer had crafted a constitution for the union of
dissenters. The plan was progressing well enough that a general
meeting at Elizabeth Town, New Jersey, was called for November,
1766.[52] Convening from November 5 through November 7, thirty-
one clergymen from Presbyterian and Congregational churches in
Pennsylvania, New York, New Jersey, and Connecticut formed a
loose confederation. Its strictly political character is evident in the
convention's assurances that it would exercise no ecclesiastical
authority over ministers or congregations, but concern itself exclusively with safeguarding dissenters' rights against Anglican encroachments, especially those of "a few high flyers" in the Middle
Colonies. The convention aimed to extend the union throughout the
colonies, and laid plans to correspond with their own brethren in
Massachusetts, New Hampshire, Connecticut, and Rhode Island, as
well as with Reformed ministers in New York, New Jersey, and
Pennsylvania. The convention agreed to meet annually, each
presbytery or association being entitled to send two ministers as
delegates.[53]

Thereafter, meetings were held every year to 1775—convening

alternately in New Jersey and Connecticut—with delegates attending regularly from Connecticut, New York, New Jersey, Pennsylvania, Delaware, and Maryland, occasionally from the Carolinas, and once from the "Presbytery of Boston." The Massachusetts clergy generally declined to attend, however, fearing that the Church of England might "look upon so extensive a Confederacy as now proposed" as a move toward independence.[54] Ezra Stiles also drew back in the late 1760s. Moreover, his Old Light correspondent from Connecticut, the Reverend William Hart, in 1768 foresaw dangerous "changes in all respects, in America and in Brittain. I suspect things are ripening for some great revolution."[55] Elsewhere the union movement gained adherents. In 1769 the convention added South Carolina as a regular correspondent, and by 1770 committees of correspondence also had been set up in Maryland, Virginia, North Carolina, and Georgia.[56]

This "Congress," as its members sometimes called it, thus constituted a colonies-wide organization of Congregational and Presbyterian churches whose objective was to protect the religious and political liberties of American dissenters. It established not only provincial committees of correspondence but a central committee to correspond with the Dissenting Deputies in England. It was to the London Deputies the convention wrote in 1771 warning that the consequence of sending a bishop to America would be to "break that strong connection which now happily subsists between Great Britain and her colonies, who are never like to shake off their dependence on the mother country until they have Bishops established among them."[57] Considering the patriotic activities of the convention itself, as well as the political leadership provided in 1775–1776 by such of its members as John Witherspoon, Francis Alison, and William Tennent, Jr., it is perhaps understandable that Joseph Galloway and others pointed to a combination of Presbyterians and Congregationalists as primary instigators of the American Revolution.

Even during the so-called lull of the early 1770s, when dissenters might have been expected to relax their vigil, Anglican provocations kept them on guard. In 1770 it was a petition to London from Maryland rectors praying for a bishop; in 1771 it was Thomas

Bradbury Chandler's address to the Virginia clergy urging them to the same course. In 1773 word may have leaked out about plans for a 24,000-acre tract of land to be conveyed to St. Peter's Church in Albany "For the Sole Use and Benefit of An American Bishop."[58] The next year New York's government refused to grant incorporation to the Dutch Reformed Church at Albany, though that denomination had been treated tenderly by royal authorities since the seventeenth century. No wonder the loyalist rector, Jonathan Boucher of St. Barnabas Church in Maryland, armed himself with a pistol when in July 1775 he delivered his sermon "On Civil Liberty, Passive Obedience, and Nonresistance."[59]

Attacks on episcopacy and on blind obedience to government came most often from rational-minded liberals of the educated elite. They knew well the history of Stuart England, had studied the chronicles of their own forbears in America, and were avid readers of such radical tracts as *The Independent Whig*. Regularly involved in the life of their communities, these politically active liberals were keenly responsive to writings that helped make sense of their own civil and religious universe.

New Light Congregationalists, Baptists, and other evangelicals also opposed episcopacy, of course, bishops being the ultimate symbol of the very establishment restraints they had fought against, and separated from, since at least the 1740s. They too had some acquaintance with the history of seventeenth-century England, and had long scorned the Church of England "as a traditional opponent of the revival and as a haven for the excommunicate and unregenerate of other churches."[60] Thus an ideology of dissent that linked religious with civil tyranny created a common ground upon which rationalists and evangelicals alike could join to justify their opposition to England. And so it was that the Reverend William Emerson, a Massachusetts New Light, sounded much the same as any liberal clergyman when he noted "the near connection there is between our civil and religious privileges. . . . After taking away the liberty of taxing ourselves, and breaking in upon our charters . . . [Great

Britain now threatens to tax] us to support the pride and vanity of diocesan Bishops."⁶¹

Each time the boundary between religion and politics was thus crossed and blurred, the more readily were Americans of all denominations drawn to the opposition party.

The Clergy, the People, and the Patriot Cause

When in December 1775 the Continental Congress sought to persuade the alienated Carolina Regulators to join the patriot cause, it turned to the Presbyterian clergy for help. "The education of most of these men [the Regulators] have been religious," observed the North Carolina delegation. Since they "look to their Spiritual pastors with great respect . . . truths from their mouths come with redoubled influence" upon the Regulators' minds. Clearly it was not only in New England that clergymen molded political opinion by discussing public issues from the sacred desk. In all parts of America preachers declaimed against absolutism and episcopacy until the people "fancied they saw civil and religious Tyranny advancing with hasty Strides." As Ambrose Serle informed the Earl of Dartmouth from New York City in 1777, "your Lordship can scarcely conceive what Fury the Discourses of some mad Preachers have created in this Country."⁶²

Patriots never doubted the influence of the clergy in forming public opinion, generally agreeing with John Adams that instilling high principles in civil as well as religious conduct was fully compatible with spiritual leadership.⁶³ New Englanders, of course, were accustomed to hearing election sermons, artillery-day sermons, and solemn orations from the pulpit during fast and thanksgiving days, many remarkably political in tone.⁶⁴ Preachers in colonies outside New England, as we have seen, also used their pulpits as drums for politics. John Adams was delighted to discover in 1775 that the Philadelphia ministers "thunder and lighten every sabbath" against British oppression. When the House of Burgesses appointed a day of fasting and prayer in 1774 to rouse Virginians against the closing of Boston's port, Thomas Jefferson recorded that the pulpit oratory ran "like a shock of electricity" through the whole colony. Landon Carter's minister "did very Pathetically exhort the people in his sermon to support their Liberties . . . and in the room of God save the king he cried out God Preserve all the Just rights and Liberties of America."[65]

Nor was the ministers' influence limited to sermons. The Reverend John Elder of Paxton, Pennsylvania—still politically active at the age of sixty-eight—sat on his county's committee of correspondence, as did many middle-colony preachers. The Synod of New York and Philadelphia sent a pastoral letter to be read from all Presbyterian pulpits on June 29, 1775. It urged elders to maintain discipline over their congregations, parishioners to repent of their sins in order to deserve God's mercy in the coming conflict, and unity, fasting, and prayer. The letter's influence extended at least as far as Virginia, where it was reprinted in the *Virginia Gazette* (Dixon and Hunter) on September 9, 1775.[66] Anglican clergymen in the southern colonies were far more likely to take the patriot side than were their northern colleagues. Many of them served actively on committees of safety and as chaplains, officers, and even common soldiers in the army. South Carolina was distinguished for the number of ardent patriots among its Anglican clergy, three-quarters of whom supported the Revolution. A similar proportion of the Anglican rectors resident in Virginia in 1776 favored the American cause.[67]

The New England clergy's opposition to British measures is well documented. The quiet efforts of Dr. Samuel Cooper of Brattle Street Church and the more public patriotism of Charles Chauncy added significantly to resistance activity in Boston. The Reverend Jonas Clark of Lexington was the Revolutionary scribe of his town, writing up petitions and instructions on political subjects throughout the era and making his house a center for political gatherings. Two fiery young Congregational ministers converted entire towns in western Massachusetts from tory to whig by haranguing the people in town meeting and Sabbath convocation alike. Many New England parsons served on committees of correspondence and safety, and it was alleged that some threatened to withhold communion from loyalists. The Reverend John Cleaveland of Ipswich is said to have preached all the young men of his congregation into the army and then, accompanied by four of his sons, marched off himself to war.[68]

Along the frontier preachers played an especially critical role as missionaries for the Revolution, carrying the whig gospel to hamlets and homesteads beyond the reach of newspapers and committees of correspondence. The Continental Congress subsidized a four-month tour by two Presbyterian ministers to the North Carolina backcountry in an effort to woo settlers to the patriot side.[69] John Witherspoon addressed a special plea to recently arrived Scots, many of whom were settled on the frontier, to support the Revolution. The Congress also asked other ministers in western regions to "use their pastoral Influence to work a change in the disposition of the people. . . . [who were] not accustomed to speculate politically." They were especially gratified when the Pennsylvania Lutheran and Reformed ministers agreed to write pastoral letters "to set their Brethren in North Carolina right."[70]

The Reverend William Tennent and William Henry Drayton of the provincial congress were dispatched by the South Carolina Committee of Safety in 1775 to persuade that colony's backsettlers to sign the Association. Tennent enlisted the aid of Presbyterian and German preachers in the region and frequently preached two- or even three-hour sermons to their assembled congregations. Sometimes he succeeded spectacularly, as at Congaree where he converted the people from loyalism to the Association and then saw them form into volunteer companies. Philip Fithian toured the Virginia–Pennsylvania frontier in 1775 with considerable success. He preached mainly to New Light Presbyterians, noting that they "thronged" into the church at Sunbury, Pennsylvania on the continental fast day.[71]

Thus did the colonial clergy during the Revolutionary years perform functions of a sort they had already been exercising for some time. It was still the case some fifty years later, according to Alexis de Tocqueville, that in the American West you would "meet a politician where you expected to find a priest."[72]

For all their involvement in secular politics, the patriot clergy influenced public opinion primarily through preaching. The sermon literature of the 1770s—north and south, evangelical and rational-ist—shows a striking uniformity of language and belief. Nearly every sermon addressed the political crisis, and did so in the idiom of the radical whigs.[73] Preachers in all sections agreed that Great Britain was falling prey to vice and corruption. A power hungry ministry and venal Parliament, declared the Massachusetts New Light Samuel Langdon, had promulgated "new invented maxims of policy" that threatened to reduce the colonists to slavery. The most wicked maxim, commented on with remarkable consistency every-where, was Parliament's assertion that it could bind the colonies "in all cases whatsoever." Such a claim, according to the Baptist preacher Samuel Stillman, denied that government was a compact based on the consent of the people as explained by the "justly celebrated Mr. Locke." The Virginia Anglican rector, David Grif-fith, thought the notion that Americans were represented in Parliament to be as absurd as the doctrine of transubstantiation.[74]

A few preachers apologized for the excessive political content of their sermons, but most simply pointed to the widely accepted belief that human liberty was of divine origin.[75] Since "liberty, traced to her true source, is of heavenly extraction," declared the Anglican Jacob Duché of Philadelphia, "we are bound to stand fast in our civil as well as our spiritual freedom." The New England Calvinist Nathaniel Whitaker, citing Richard Price on civil liberty and Locke on natural law, concluded that "liberty is the cause of God and truth"; thus submission to British claims "to bind us in all cases whatsoever" would be sinful in the eyes of God. Griffith of Virginia proclaimed in almost identical words that "the cause of truth and justice is the cause of God." Could Americans faced with British oppression "conform to the once exploded, but again courtly, doctrines of passive obedience and non-resistance"? asked the Massachusetts Congregationalist William Gordon.[76]

Another theme was that "self-preservation is an instinct by God implanted in our nature." The Reverend John Carmichael, Presby-terian of Pennsylvania, noted that God provided plants and animals with natural defenses against their enemies. Humankind's special gift was reason, which enabled men and women to study God's word as a guide to earthly behavior. Scripture, always in harmony with "the great law of nature," taught that when rulers "lust for absolute dominion" and break covenants the people must resist in the interest of self-preservation. The Reverend Simeon Howard of Massachusetts sought in an Artillery Day sermon to demonstrate that "Self-preservation is one of the strongest, and a universal principle of the human mind."[77]

Most preachers also invoked some form of the jeremiad. The Anglican Duché exhorted his auditors to "Banish the Syren LUXURY. . . . Call upon honest industry, sober frugality, [and] simplicity of manners" with the same emotion that the New Light Samuel Langdon worked up against "profaneness, intemperance, unchastity, the love of pleasure, fraud, avarice, and other vices." The Charleston Baptist Oliver Hart and the Boston rationalist Charles Chauncy, with equal passion, warned the colonists to renounce sin if they would gain God's favor in the war against England.[78]

The Revolutionary crisis thus gave a kind of license to preachers of moderate temper to experiment with a more emotional style. The Anglican William Smith advised his congregation to resist attempts on their liberties with "a holy fervor, a divine enthusiasm." And he further invoked the language of the Great Awakening in urging Americans to unite by bearing with each other "in things not essential to the main point." Similarly the intellectual Presbyterian, John Witherspoon, looked upon the opportunity to form a new government on just and equal principles "with a kind of enthusiastic satisfaction."[79]

Above all, however, the familiar injunctions against passive obedience to wicked rulers supplied a common language of opposition. In a sermon to the provincial congress of Georgia the Reverend John Zubly hoped that the colonies and mother country could be reconciled, but never under the "odious doctrines [of] unlimited passive obedience and non-resistance." Rector David Griffith's sermon, *Passive Obedience Considered*, proved so acceptable to the General Convention of Virginia that it was ordered to be printed. Comparing the colonies to ancient Israel, Griffith asserted that God did not expect the Israelites in Egypt "to pay a blind obedience" to all of Pharaoh's ordinances. Nor did Paul teach absolute and unlimited submission. There were times when a corrupt government made resistance not only justifiable but "a necessary duty." A Pennsylvania Presbyterian noted that "the antiquated doctrine of passive-obedience and non-resistance . . . has been sufficiently exploded by many eminent writers, both ancient and modern," and he summoned up the dark images of Charles I and James II to remind his audience that religious and civil liberty stood or fell together.[80]

At Princeton, John Witherspoon's May 1776 sermon also harked back to the religious persecutions of the Civil War. The moderate Witherspoon refused to attack the king and ministers directly, though he left no doubt about the justice of the American cause in view of British demands for "absolute submission." When Samuel Langdon denounced those who "cry up the divine right of kings" in his 1775 Massachusetts election sermon, he merely repeated—though with ever closer application—a formula that by the 1770s had become a standard feature of the patriot sermon.[81] In such phrases, then, clergymen throughout the colonies nurtured their parishioners' disinclination to submit mutely and unthinkingly to political authority.

Once blood had actually been shed, the patriot sermon took on additional features, as the familiar lessons and allegories from Scripture—especially the Old Testament—supplied a common idiom and interpretation to events. Ministers everywhere compared America's break from Britain with the division of the Jewish tribes under the tyrant Rehoboam, or with the misunderstanding between Canaanites and Gileadites. The slavery from which the colonists were being delivered was of course like that of the Israelites under Pharaoh, and as early as 1776 George Washington was cast as Moses. In sermons to militia units preachers recalled how Jonathan and his armor bearer put the mighty Philistine host to flight. And perhaps the most attractive analogy of all was that of David and Goliath.[82]

Since the colonials could see themselves as simply responding to British aggression, especially after Lexington and Concord, the

(*top*) "An Appeal to Heaven" was a popular motto, used on standards of the Third Connecticut Regiment and a number of naval batteries. (*bottom*) "Resistance to Tyrants is Obedience to God" was the motto of the Gostelowe Standard No. 10.

Pennsylvania Society of Sons of the Revolution

morality of a defensive war was widely emphasized as a justification
for taking up arms. As a Presbyterian preacher told his congregation
at Chester County, Pennsylvania, "a defensive war in a just cause
[was] sinless."[83] And meanwhile, the "appeal to heaven" for God's
assistance in a righteous cause sounded from pulpits throughout the
land. He might interpose with miracles, as with the drowning of
Pharaoh's army in the Red Sea. Or he might strike armies with
panic, so that "a thousand shall put ten thousand to flight." In any
case, as John Locke put it, in a conflict which no earthly judge could
settle "the appeal lies only to Heaven." Trenchard and Gordon's
Cato had similarly declared that "when there is no stated Judge
upon Earth, we must have Recourse to Heaven."[84] So prevalent was
the belief that God would award victory to a people fighting for
justice in his name that a number of colonial regiments marched into
battle bearing flags inscribed with "AN APPEAL TO HEAVEN."[85]

And at last when it was all over, the Revolution could be
recognized as a "principal Link . . . [in the] grand chain of
Providence" ushering in the golden age of the church. Evidence of
God's special care was everywhere, most notably in the sublime
person of George Washington—"a general destined by Heaven for
just such a period, country, and cause as ours!" Washington was a
Moses; he was also "the Joshua of the day and admiration of the
age"; he had been called by the Most High to "save his country from
the chains of slavery."[86]

Religious doctrine and rhetoric, then, contributed in a fundamental
way to the coming of the American Revolution and to its final
success. In an age of political moderation, when many colonials
hesitated at the brink of civil war, patriotic clergymen told their
congregations that failure to oppose British tyranny would be an
offense in the sight of Heaven. Where political theory advised
caution, religious doctrine demanded action. By turning colonial
resistance into a righteous cause, and by crying the message to all
ranks in all parts of the colonies, ministers did the work of secular
radicalism and did it better: they resolved doubts, overcame inertia,
fired the heart, and exalted the soul.

CHAPTER 8

The Formation of
American Religious Culture

Whatever may have been the fluctuating fortunes of religion over the past two hundred years, religion to this day seems, somehow, to occupy a larger place in American culture than it does in the life of most western societies. If elsewhere religion is seen mostly at the surface of things, in ecclesiastical ceremonies and feast-day rituals, in the United States it breaks through the confines of church and congregation to influence civil, social, and other aspects of the national life. This blurring of religion's normative boundaries began with the earliest settlements. Indeed, it was in the seventeenth and eighteenth centuries that the mold was set in which American religious institutions have developed ever since. Religion permeated early American life in part because religious institutions had to be built anew in the colonies, a task that incorporated the laity into the very fabric of the churches at the same time that it built the churches into the structure of civil society. Over the years, commentators, especially foreign ones, have been repeatedly struck by two aspects in particular of American religion, one being the social dimension of American religious practice, and the other, the latitudinarianism that resulted from the voluntary character of American church life.

Newcomers to the United States are often taken aback by the number and variety of functions and services that have somehow got themselves attached, logically or not, to churches: everything from hayrides, fish fries, and singles retreats to addict rehabilitation, soup kitchens, and shelter programs. At the same time, religion itself has seeped out to the community in almost imperceptible ways, probably reaching its high point in the mid–nineteenth century. As Tocqueville wrote of the 1830s, the "religious aspect of the country was the first thing that struck my attention." Frances Trollope noted how religion crept into the most ordinary conversations, and the Englishman Thomas Hamilton was surprised to find that even "grog parties" began and ended with prayer.[1]

The beginnings of this "social religion," as one might call it, were evident in the seventeenth and early eighteenth centuries, when the churches had little choice but to be "of the world." In many settlements churches were social and political as well as religious centers, with the elders and clergy providing not only basic services but leadership in community formation. As society stabilized in the eighteenth century and secular institutions took over some of these tasks, it was only natural for the churches to seek other ways of securing their constituencies. Thus the scope of church life broadened to include functions previously not there— weddings and funerals in New England, educational services in the South and Middle Colonies, political functions everywhere, and even military leadership along the frontier. In the cities and large towns, where religious leaders competed with newspapers, politicians, and incipient cultural institutions for authority in the public sphere, churches also expanded such services as schools, aid to the poor, and societies for women and youths. It was this activism and closeness to the grain of their communities, I have suggested, that made the early congregations as potent a local force as the town meeting or any other secular institution.

The latitudinarian tendency of American religion is another of its most frequently noted characteristics. An Anglican minister wrote from South Carolina in the 1720s that his parishioners were

"Latitudinarian in Protestantism . . . and do not imagine much real difference in Principle 'twixt Churchmen & Dissenters of all Denominations." In the 1780s Crèvecoeur noted that not only was national identity soon lost in the pluralism of America but "the strict modes of Christianity as practiced in Europe are lost also." Owing both to interfaith marriages and to the inconvenience of traveling to the right church if a "wrong" one were closer by, many Americans, according to Crèvecoeur, simply attended the church in their neighborhood. Two other important, if often contradictory, forces in American religious culture—rationalism and revivalism—also encouraged latitudinarianism by pointing up the broad areas of agreement in Protestant belief while decrying the "non-essentials" stressed by some religious formalists. Contributing further to a latitudinarian direction was the emergent denominationalism, or free church autonomy, of American Protestantism, a tendency that accelerated as church was separated from state in the aftermath of the Revolution. As a growing number of denominations competed for adherents in the free air of religious voluntarism, points of theology proved less attractive to potential adherents than did a church's social program, the popular appeal of its preachers, or its geographical proximity.[2]

This latitudinarian direction was already surfacing in some parts of the eighteenth-century colonies, especially the Middle Colonies and other provinces where a diverse population and religious rivalry had fostered a clerical style that was often aggressively promotional. Nonetheless, tension always existed between the colonists' latitudinarian proclivities and the periodic efforts by some churches, such as the German Lutheran and the northern Anglican, to identify themselves with a distinctive doctrine and liturgy—a tension that continues to the present day. One manifestation of it has been the periodic appearance throughout American history of evangelical awakenings, during which preachers deplore the laxity of religious practice while exhorting the seekers to cast aside worldly things for the penitent and gracious heart. Yet even these calls for a return to piety tend to shun intricate theological reasoning, emphasizing instead a fundamentalist biblicism of broad popular appeal. It might perhaps be added that these same movements of renewal, occurring from time to time even in the oldest and most sophisticated of the denominations, continue to serve as a major reinfusive force in American church life.

Certain other features of American religious practice have also been noted with some regularity. Both Tocqueville and Michel Chevalier were struck in the 1830s by the extraordinary diligence with which Americans observed the "outward duties" of religion. Harriet Martineau also reported that the "eagerness for religious instruction and the means of social worship are so great that funds and buildings are provided wherever society exists." James Bryce observed in the 1880s that Americans were "assiduous church-goers."[3] We have noted in the preceding chapters that in the eighteenth century too, churchgoing and church building were seen as matters of prime importance, and I have attempted to show why this was so.

Nonetheless, for many years church historians asserted that no more than 5 to 20 percent of colonial Americans were churchgoers, and though that figure was based on little but rough impressions it has gained a wide circulation. Recent estimates, on the other hand, based on ministers' reports and on the ratio of congregations to inhabitants, indicate that no less than some 60 percent of the adult white population attended church regularly between 1700 and 1776.[4] The number of congregations offers an especially good gauge of colonial religious commitment since the forming of congregations was never imposed by magistrate or clergyman but occurred through voluntary action of the people. Moreover, the organizing of a congregation involved gathering the faithful, designating elders and deacons, engaging a minister and collecting tithes for his salary, building the church, hiring a sexton for its maintenance, and so on. Considering the vigorous pace of congregation building, the notion of an eighteenth–century–long hiatus, or trough, in American religious observance has little historical logic. An eighteenth century of "Enlightenment" skepticism coming between a "Puritan" seventeenth century and an "evangelical" nineteenth century simply does not add up. Indeed, it has recently been suggested that although the Enlightenment facilitated a range of responses to religious belief, atheism cannot be seen as one of them, and the latest community studies leave little doubt as to the vigor of religion in eighteenth-century American culture.[5]

Rather than hurrying Americans into secular modernity at the turn of the eighteenth century, as Parrington did, we would do better, I believe, to depict the seventeenth century as an era of transplantation (accompanied by both disorder and creative innovation), the eighteenth as one of stabilization (with the elaboration of basic institutions, and with the Revolution and Federal Constitution as major steps in that process), and, if "modernization" is the term we want, saving it for the nineteenth century. By putting off the advent of modernization, and thus of secularization, we can write the history of colonial America—especially its religious history—more nearly on its own terms. Nor need this reclassification obscure the changes that were gathering strength in American society from at least the mid–eighteenth century onward, as the spread of Enlightenment rationalism, the rise of free trade ideas, and a growing insistence upon individual worth sharpened demands for political accountability and economic latitude that would eventually carry Americans into the modern age.

What, then, was the role of religion in that process? In Europe and Britain the churches frequently have been associated with traditional values, but in America religion has always borne a more ambiguous relationship to modernism. As often as not it has served as an agent of change and a stimulus to radical individualism. Such nineteenth-century reform movements as abolitionism, temperance, and female suffrage drew regularly on religious principles and the leadership of churchwomen and churchmen. And in colonial America, owing largely to the continuous replenishment and reinvigoration of the dissenting tradition, religion must be counted as having been more often an ally of the future than of the past. As settlement spread, traditional doctrines and practices either proved their utility or were refashioned to fit the new environment. The more liberal denominations promoted improvement in this world as well as the next, thereby supplying an ethical foundation upon which a modern state and economy could be constructed. Pietistic and evangelical congregations too—despite their craving for soul glory and suspicion of worldly things—pushed into the future by vehemently defending freedom of conscience and by shearing off from institutions that obstructed their vision. It was in religious debate that the colonists refined their understanding of natural rights, which served them so well politically, and sharpened their defense of self-interest, a concept that would underpin the new economic liberalism.

And finally, the absence of anticlericalism in the American Revolution, especially when contrasted with the French, Russian, and other modern revolutions, is yet a further indication of how compatible early American religion was with the processes of change. Because the colonies possessed no single established church that was perceived as being in league with the government, the American revolutionaries did not have to overthrow a church along with the state. Indeed, clergymen appear again and again as prime leaders of the rebellion, especially in newly settled sections or among Americans who found it impossible to oppose an earthly king except in the name of the King of Heaven. And if a minority of Anglican ministers chose to support the old regime, the specter they raised in doing so only threw the contrasting position of the patriot clergy into bolder relief. The threat of an Anglican bishop was thus one more windfall for the revolutionaries, uniting as it did the religious and political opposition in a single set of grievances: hierarchy, taxation without representation, repression of dissent, and corruption. With the great body of American clergy and the great aggregate of provincial churches untainted in any way by association with the imperial regime, there was no impediment to religion's assuming the unique and respected position it would shortly occupy in the life of the new republic. Had it been otherwise, Tocqueville could almost certainly not have declared that "There is no country in the world where the Christian religion retains a greater influence over the souls of men than in America."[6]

Notes

CHAPTER 1

1. See, for example, *The Journal of Rev. Michael Schlatter*, in Henry Harbaugh, *The Life of Rev. Michael Schlatter* (Philadelphia, 1857), 154–55; Richard J. Hooker, ed., *The Carolina Backcountry on the Eve of the Revolution: The Journal and Other Writings of Charles Woodmason, Anglican Itinerant* (Chapel Hill, N.C., 1853), 14. On execution sermons, see *The Diary of Samuel Sewall, 1674–1729*, ed. M. Halsey Thomas (New York, 1973), I, 509, and *The Diary of Cotton Mather, 1681–1708*, ed. Worthington C. Ford, Massachusetts Historical Society, *Collections*, 7th Ser., VII (1911), 279.

2. David Lundberg and Henry F. May, "The Enlightened Reader in America," *American Quarterly*, 28 (1976), 262–71; David D. Hall, "The Uses of Literacy in New England, 1600–1850," in *Printing and Society in Early America*, ed. William L. Joyce *et al.* (Worcester, Mass., 1983), 31–33. George L. McKay, *American Book Auction Catalogues, 1713–1934* (New York, 1966). In Connecticut and Massachusetts alone over 1800 sermons were published between 1740 and 1800; Nathan O. Hatch, *The Sacred Cause of Liberty: Republican Thought and the Millennium in Revolutionary New England* (New Haven, Conn., 1977), 176.

3. G. Thomas Tanselle, "Some Statistics on American Printing, 1764–1783," in *The Press and the American Revolution*, eds. Bernard Bailyn and John B. Hench (Boston, 1981), 327–30.

4. Daniel J. Boorstin, *The Americans: The Colonial Experience* (New York, 1958), 125; Louis B. Wright, *First Gentlemen of Virginia: Intellectual Qualities of the Early Colonial Ruling Class* (San Marino, Calif., 1940), 134–35; Frederick B. Tolles, *Meeting House and Counting House: The Quaker Merchants of Colonial Philadelphia, 1682–1763* (1948; reprint ed. New York, 1963), 163; Samuel Eliot Morison, *The Oxford History of the American People* (New York, 1965), 212; Hall, "Uses of Literacy," 1, 21–24.

5. *The Diary of Colonel Landon Carter of Sabine Hall, 1752–1778*, ed. Jack P. Greene (Charlottesville, Va., 1965), II, 616, 744; *Journal & Letters of Philip Vickers Fithian, 1773–1774: A Plantation Tutor of the Old Dominion*, ed. Hunter Dickinson Farish (Williamsburg, Va., 1945), 133,

137; Julia Cherry Spruill, *Women's Life & Work in the Southern Colonies* (1938; reprint ed., New York, 1972), chap. 6.

6. Hooker, ed., *Carolina Backcountry*, 61, 56.

7. From "Recollections" of William Senhouse [typescript]; manuscript deposited in the Cumbria Record Office, Carlisle, England. I wish to thank James Brandow for bringing this memoir to my attention.

8. Winton U. Solberg, *Redeem the Time: The Puritan Sabbath in Early America* (Cambridge, Mass., 1977), *passim; The Journal of Madam Knight* [Sarah Kemble Knight] (New York, 1935), 54; Elias Neau to the Secretary, Sept. 26, 1712, Journals of the Society for the Propagation of the Gospel in Foreign Parts, II, 6 (Micro Methods, Ltd.); Douglas Greenberg, *Crime and Law Enforcement in the Colony of New York, 1691–1776* (Ithaca, N.Y., 1974), 112.

9. Robert G. Pope, *The Half-Way Covenant: Church Membership in Puritan New England* (Princeton, N.J., 1969); Edwin Scott Gaustad, *Historical Atlas of Religion in America*, rev. ed. (New York, 1976); Patricia U. Bonomi and Peter R. Eisenstadt, "Church Adherence in the Eighteenth-Century British American Colonies," *William and Mary Quarterly*, 3d Ser., XXXIX (1982), 245–86.

10. Hooker, ed., *Carolina Backcountry*, *passim; Life and Letters of the Rev. John Philip Boehm, . . . 1683–1749*, ed. William J. Hinke (Philadelphia, 1916); *Journal of Rev. Michael Schlatter*.

11. Bonomi and Eisenstadt, "Church Adherence," 247.

12. The folk religion that was in variant degrees mixed with formal Christian practice among all ranks, including the clergy, in 17th-century America lost respectability over the 18th, especially where scientific and Enlightenment thought made its influence felt. For a discussion of 17th-century popular religion, see David D. Hall, "A World of Wonders: The Mentality of the Supernatural in Seventeenth-Century New England," in David D. Hall and David Grayson Allen, eds., *Seventeenth-Century New England* (Boston, 1984), 239–74.

13. The quotation is from Clarendon's *History of the Rebellion*; see Roland N. Stromberg, *Religious Liberalism in Eighteenth-Century England* (London, 1954), 124.

14. Vernon L. Parrington, *Main Currents in American Thought* (1927; New York, 1930), vii.

CHAPTER 2

1. Henry P. Van Dusen *et al.*, *Church and State in the Modern World* (New York, 1937), 1–42; Evarts B. Greene, *Religion and the State: The Making and Testing of an American Tradition* (New York, 1941), chap. 1.

2. Darrett Rutman, *Winthrop's Boston: A Portrait of a Puritan Town*, 1630–1649 (1965; reprint, New York, 1972); Philip F. Gura, *A Glimpse of Sion's Glory: Puritan Radicalism in New England*, 1620–1660 (Middletown, Conn., 1984); David D. Hall, "A World of Wonders: The Mentality of the Supernatural in Seventeenth-Century New England," in David D. Hall and David Grayson Allen, eds., *Seventeenth-Century New England* (Boston, 1984), 239–74; Jon Butler, "Magic, Astrology, and the Early American Religious Heritage, 1600–1760," *American Historical Review*, 84 (1979), 317–46; Keith Thomas, *Religion and the Decline of Magic* (New York, 1971).

3. Charter of James I (1606) in W. W. Hening, ed., *The Statutes at Large: Being a Collection of All the Laws of Virginia* (1619–1792) (Richmond, Va. 1809), I, 68–69.

4. Perry Miller, *Errand into the Wilderness* (Cambridge, Mass. 1956), chap. 4; Babette M. Levy, *Early Puritanism in the Southern and Island Colonies*, in *Proceedings* of the American Antiquarian Society, 70 (1960), 96; Jack P. Greene, ed., *Settlements to Society, 1607–1763: A Documentary History of Colonial America* (New York, 1966), 40; George MacLaren Brydon, *Virginia's Mother Church and the Political Conditions Under Which It Grew* (Richmond, Va. 1947), I, 12, 40.

5. Miller, *Errand into the Wilderness*, 125; Edmund S. Morgan, *American Slavery, American Freedom: The Ordeal of Colonial Virginia* (New York, 1975), 111 n16, 36; Darrett B. Rutman, *American Puritanism: Faith and Practice* (New York, 1970), 51; William H. Seiler, "The Anglican Parish in Virginia," in James Morton Smith, ed., *17th-Century America: Essays in Colonial History* (Chapel Hill, N.C. 1959), 129.

6. Brydon, *Virginia's Mother Church*, I, 43–47, chaps. 10 and 13.

7. *Virginia's Cure: or, An Advisive Narrative Concerning Virginia* (London, 1662), in Peter Force, coll., *Tracts and Other Papers* (New York, Peter Smith reprint, 1947), III, no. 15, p. 16; see also Bernard Bailyn, "Politics and Social Structure in Virginia," in Smith, ed., *17th-Century America*, 90–115.

8. William Bradford, *History of Plimoth Plantation* in Perry Miller and Thomas H. Johnson, eds., *The Puritans: A Sourcebook of Their Writings* (New York, rev. ed., 1963), I, 97; Greene, ed., *Settlements to Society*, 111.

9. Winton U. Solberg, *Redeem the Time: The Puritan Sabbath in Early America* (Cambridge, Mass. 1977), 117; Edward Howes to John Winthrop, Jr., *Winthrop Papers*, 3: 100–101, as quoted in *ibid*, 129.

10. The most detailed discussion of Puritan radicalism is in Gura, *A Glimpse of Sion's Glory*. Ronald D. Cohen, "Church and State in Seventeenth-Century Massachusetts: Another Look at the Antinomian

Controversy," in Alden T. Vaughan and Francis J. Bremer, eds., *Puritan New England: Essays on Religion, Society, and Culture* (New York, 1977), 178–79; Edmund S. Morgan, *The Puritan Dilemma: The Story of John Winthrop* (Boston, 1958), 143, 147.

11. Miller, *Errand*, 29; Nathaniel Ward, *The Simple Cobbler of Aggawam*, in Miller and Johnson, eds., *The Puritans*, 227, 230; William G. McLoughlin, *New England Dissent, 1630–1833: The Baptists and the Separation of Church and State* (Cambridge, Mass. 1971), I, chap. 1.

12. Samuel Eliot Morison, *Builders of the Bay Colony* (Boston, 1930; rev. ed., 1958), 117.

13. Edmund S. Morgan, *Visible Saints: The History of a Puritan Idea* (New York, 1963); Rutman, *American Puritanism*, 31; David D. Hall, *The Faithful Shepherd: A History of the New England Ministry in the Seventeenth Century* (Chapel Hill, N. C. 1972), 185–86ff; Stephen Innes, *Labor in a New Land: Economy and Society in Seventeenth-Century Springfield* (Princeton, N.J., 1983), 147–48.

14. Johannes Megapolensis and Samuel Drisius to the Classis at Amsterdam, August 14, 1657, *Ecclesiastical Records of the State of New York*, ed. E. T. Corwin (Albany, N.Y., 1901), I, 400.

15. Sydney V. James, *Colonial Rhode Island* (New York, 1975), chaps. 2 and 3; *Records of Rhode Island*, I, 234, cited in Theodore Dwight Bozeman, "Religious Liberty and the Problem of Order in Early Rhode Island," *New England Quarterly*, 45 (1972), 51.

16. Philip F. Gura, "The Radical Ideology of Samuel Gorton: New Light on the Relation of English to American Puritanism," *William and Mary Quarterly*, (hereafter *WMQ*) 3d Ser. XXXVI (1979), 78–100; James, *Colonial Rhode Island*, 29; Roger Williams to Governor John Winthrop, Providence, March 8, 1641, *The Complete Writings of Roger Williams* (New York, 1963), VI, 141–42.

17. John Tracy Ellis, ed., *Documents of American Catholic History* (Milwaukee, 1962), 95; Clayton Colman Hall, ed., *Narratives of Early Maryland, 1633–1684* (New York, 1910), 16–17, 20–23; Russell R. Menard and Lois Green Carr, "The Lords Baltimore and the Colonization of Maryland," in David B. Quinn, ed., *Early Maryland in a Wider World* (Detroit, 1982), 178, 183–85.

18. Hall, ed., *Narratives of Early Maryland*, 23; John Tracy Ellis, *Catholics in Colonial America* (Baltimore, 1965), 334; Levy, *Early Puritanism*, 133, 204–5.

19. Ellis, *Catholics in Colonial America*, 335–36; Russell R. Menard, "Maryland's 'Time of Troubles': Sources of Political Disorder in Early St. Mary's," *Maryland Historical Magazine*, 76 (1981), 124–40.

20. A number of Protestant legislators who were not members of the

anti-Catholic party also supported the bill. George Petrie, "Church and State in Early Maryland," *Johns Hopkins University Studies in Historical and Political Science*, Ser. 10, no. IV (1892), 29–30. J. Thomas Scharf says that Catholics outnumbered Protestants by 10 to 7; *History of Maryland* (Hatsboro, Pa., 1879), I, 178. The fullest older account is Bradley T. Johnson, *The Foundation of Maryland, and the Origin of the Act Concerning Religion of April* 21, 1649 (Baltimore, 1883); the best recent account is John D. Krugler, "'With promise of Liberty in Religion': The Catholic Lords Baltimore and Toleration in Seventeenth-Century Maryland, 1634–1692," *Maryland Historical Magazine*, 79 (1984), 21–43.

21. William Hand Browne, ed., *Archives of Maryland, Proceedings and Acts of the General Assembly of Maryland, January* 1637/8–1664 (Baltimore, 1883), I, 246; Scharf, *History of Maryland*, I, 148, 177–78.

22. *Archives of Maryland*, I, 244–45. Though Jews were clearly excluded from Maryland's toleration act, it is nonetheless true that the few Jews resident in the colony during the Catholic period were not molested. The exception was one Jacob Lumbrozo, arrested for blasphemy in 1659 but never brought to trial. Jacob R. Marcus, *The Colonial American Jew*, 1492–1776 (Detroit, 1970), I, 449–50; see also 335–39, 450–53.

23. Lois Green Carr and David William Jordan, *Maryland's Revolution of Government*, 1689–1692 (Ithaca, N. Y., 1974), 33; Sydney E. Ahlstrom, *A Religious History of the American People (New Haven, Conn.* 1972), 194; Kenneth L. Carroll, "Persecution of Quakers in Early Maryland (1658–1661)," *Quaker History*, 53 (1964), 67–80; Petrie, "Church and State in Maryland," 35–36.

24. Carr and Jordan, *Maryland's Revolution*, 37–40, and *passim*.

25. Ellis, *Catholics in Colonial America*, 344–48.

26. Henry H. Kessler and Eugene Rachlis, *Peter Stuyvesant and His New York* (New York, 1959), 66, 77; Frederick J. Zwierlein, *Religion in New Netherland* (Rochester, N.Y. 1910); George L. Smith, *Religion and Trade in New Netherland* (Ithaca, N.Y., 1973), chap. 10.

27. Johannes Megapolensis and Samuel Drisius to the Classis, August 5, 1657, in Corwin, ed., *Ecclesiastical Records*, I 396; Smith, *Religion and Trade*, chap. 12.

28. Megapolensis to Classis of Amsterdam, March 18, 1655, *Ecclesiastical Records*, I, 335; Director in Holland to Stuyvesant: Jews, April 26, 1655, *ibid*, I, 338; Zwierlein, *Religion in New Netherland*, 255, chap. 8; Marcus, *Colonial Jew*, I, chap. 9. Because of the Jews' destitute condition the Dutch Reformed Church "had to spend several hundred guilders for their support"; Megapolensis to Classis, March 18, 1655, *Ecclesiastical Records*, I, 335.

29. Megapolensis and Drisius to Classis, August 14, 1657, *Ecclesiastical*

Records, I, 400; Smith, *Religion and Trade,* 221–23; Extact from a Letter of the Directors to Stuyvesant, April 16, 1663, *Ecclesiastical Records,* I, 530.

30. Albert Bushnell Hart, ed., *American History Told by Contemporaries* (New York, 1896), I, 455–56.

31. According to the Puritan minister John Higginson, the Quakers were an insufferable people whose so-called inner light was nothing but "a stinking vapour from hell"; George Bishop, *New-England Judged* (London, 1703), 242.

32. Hart, ed., *American History Told by Contemporaries,* I, 456; Richard P. Hallowell, *The Quaker Invasion of Massachusetts* (Boston, 1887), 138. Hallowell's appendix provides a convenient collection of eyewitness reports, anti-Quaker laws, and trial records. For a useful discussion of Puritan views of these early Quakers, see Carla Gardina Pestana, "The City upon a Hill under Siege: The Puritan Perception of the Quaker Threat to Massachusetts Bay, 1656–1661," *New England Quarterly,* LVI (1983), 323–53.

33. Humphrey Norton, *New-England's Ensigne* (London, 1657), 40, 72, 81. These reports came mostly from Quaker sources, but the closeness of the Massachusetts deputies' votes on penalties for Quakers suggests that the colony was far from unanimous about prosecuting them; Hall, *Faithful Shepherd,* 229–30.

34. A fourth Quaker, William Leddra, was hanged later in 1660; again it was apparent that Leddra's "meek and cheerful suffering . . . took much hold on the people and wrought tenderness in many." William Sewel, *The History of the Rise, Increase, and Progress of the Christian People Called Quakers* (Philadelphia, 1811), I, 395–97, 401; Bishop, *New-England Judged,* 125, 201.

35. Daniel Neal reprints the magistrates' defense in *The History of New-England, Containing an Impartial Account of the Civil and Ecclesiastical Affairs of the Country to . . .* 1700 (London, 1720), I, 310–312; Hart, ed., *American History Told by Contemporaries,* I, 456.

36. Rufus M. Jones, *The Quakers in the American Colonies* (New York, 1911, 1966), 58. Philip Gura argues that the early radical sects of Massachusetts Bay had prepared the soil for the Quakers; *A Glimpse of Sion's Glory,* chap. 5.

37. Nathaniel B. Shurtleff, ed., *Records of the Governor and Company of the Massachusetts Bay in New England* (Boston, 1854), IV, Part 2, 2–4, 59, 69, 88. In 1675 the General Court was still making sporadic efforts to contain the Quakers' "damnable heresies" and "abominable idolatries," and in 1677 constables were ordered to break down the doors of Quaker meetinghouses and arrest the congregants. If they refused to do so the

constables were to be fined 40 shillings. *Ibid*, V, 60, 134. In some communities, however, Puritan-Quaker relationships were more cooperative; see Jonathan M. Chu, "The Social and Political Contexts of Heterodoxy: Quakerism in Seventeenth-Century Kittery," *New England Quarterly*, 54 (1981), 365–84.

38. Shurtleff, ed., *Records of Massachusetts Bay*, October 2, 1678, V, 199.

39. William G. McLoughlin, *New England Dissent*, I, 49, 76, 83, 120–22. Compared with Quaker punishments, those meted out to the Baptists were "mild." *Ibid*, 59.

40. Norman Sykes, *From Sheldon to Secker: Aspects of English Church History*, 1660–1768 (Cambridge, 1959), esp. chap. 3.

41. Philip S. Haffenden, "The Anglican Church in Restoration Colonial Policy," in Smith, ed., *17th-Century America*, 178, 180–85.

42. Another blow to the church would be the accession of the Catholic King James II in 1685, for the Church of England could expect little encouragement from a monarch "whose ultimate if rather confused aim had become the Catholicization of the empire." Haffenden, "Anglican Church," 190.

43. S. Charles Bolton, *Southern Anglicanism: The Church of England in Colonial South Carolina* (Westport, Conn., 1982), 19.

44. *Ibid*, 8; Marcus, *Colonial Jew*, I, 344, 459–60; Ellis, *Catholics in Colonial America*, 286; Paul Conkin, "The Church Establishment in North Carolina, 1765–1776," *North Carolina Historical Review*, 32 (1955), 1–30.

45. Reba Carolyn Strickland, *Religion and the State in Georgia in the Eighteenth Century* (New York, 1939), 183–84; *Ibid.*, 77–82.

46. Marcus, *Colonial Jew*, I, 353–54, 357; Strickland, *Religion and State in Georgia*, 120, 183–84.

47. *Records of Rhode Island*, I, 288; Bozeman, "Religious Liberty in Rhode Island," 57–58; "Laws of Rhode Island, 1647," Rhode-Island Historical Society *Collections*, IV (1838), 230. In 1641 the first civil compact among Rhode Islanders had provided "that no one be accounted a delinquent for DOCTRINE." *Ibid*, 213. See also Greene, *Religion and the State*, 49.

48. Roger Williams, *The Bloudy Tenent of Persecution, for cause of Conscience, discussed, in A Conference between Truth and Peace* (1644), *Publications of the Narragansett Club* (Providence, Rhode Island), 1st Ser., III (1867), 3–4; Williams, "To the Town of Providence, January 1654/55, *Writings*, VI, 278–279.

49. Williams to Major Mason, Providence, June 22, 1670, *Writings*, VI, 344–347; Williams, *George Fox Digg'd out of his Burrowes* (Boston 1676), *Publications of the Narragansett Club*, 1st Ser., V (1872), 11. Edmund

Burroughs was, along with George Fox, a leader of the Society of Friends in England.

50. From the charter granted by Charles II, July 8, 1663, in Rhode Island Historical Society *Collections*, IV (1838), 242–43.

51. Samuel Smith, *The History of the Colony of Nova-Caesaria, or New-Jersey* (Burlington, N.J., 1765), Appendix, 529; John E. Pomfret notes the large contribution made also by the Quaker Edward Byllynge; *The Province of West Jersey*, 1609–1702 (Princeton, N.J., 1956), 93–94; William W. Sweet, *Religion in Colonial America* (New York, 1942), 159.

52. Quoted in Edward C. O. Beatty, *William Penn as Social Philosopher* (New York, 1939), 122.

53. The grant of religious freedom is in Article 35 of the Frame of Government.

54. Marcus, *Colonial Jew*, I, 442. Looking beyond legal statutes to practice, it might be noted that many Catholics driven out of Maryland after 1692 sought and found refuge in Pennsylvania. Moreover, both Catholics and Jews openly practiced their faiths in Pennsylvania during the 18th century, the Jews from at least 1761 onward, and Catholics perhaps as early as 1708 and certainly by 1733 when a small chapel and priests' residence were constructed on Walnut Street. Marcus, *Colonial Jew*, I, 323–24; Ellis, *Catholics in Colonial America*, 370–76.

CHAPTER 3

1. Philip S. Haffenden, "The Anglican Church in Restoration Colonial Policy," in James Morton Smith, ed., *17th-Century America: Essays in Colonial History* (Chapel Hill, N.C., 1959), 166–91.

2. Bernard Bailyn, "Politics and Social Structure in Virginia," *ibid.*, 90–115; Philip Alexander Bruce, *Institutional History of Virginia in the Seventeenth Century* (New York, 1910), I, 135–36; William H. Seiler, "The Anglican Parish in Virginia," in Smith, ed., *17th-Century America*, 119–25; George MacLaren Brydon, *Virginia's Mother Church and the Political Conditions Under Which It Grew* (Richmond, Va., 1947), vol. I.

3. Seiler, "Anglican Parish," 137.

4. "An Act for Chooseing of Vestries," *The Statutes at Large: Being a Collection of All the Laws of Virginia* (1619–1792), ed. W. W. Hening (Richmond, Va. 1809), II, 356; Bruce, *Institutional History*, I, 66–67; Seiler, "Anglican Parish," 127. When population growth led to the subdividing of parishes, vestry elections were frequently held in both the new and parent parishes; Joan Rezner Gundersen, "The Myth of the Independent Virginia Vestry," *Historical Magazine of the Protestant Episcopal Church*, XLIV (1975), 134–37.

5. In the early 1670s no more than half of Virginia's parishes had rectors; by the end of the century the ratio had improved to about two-thirds, though several parishes shared a minister. Haffenden, "Anglican Church in Restoration Policy," 185; Brydon, *Virginia's Mother Church,* I, 241: Joan R. Gundersen, "The Search for Good Men: Recruiting Ministers in Colonial Virginia," *Historical Magazine of the Protestant Episcopal Church,* XLVIII (1979), 453–64. Not until the mid-18th century would Virginia have a sufficient supply of rectors for its growing Anglican population; after 1758 there was actually a surplus; *ibid.,* 454.

6. Parke Rouse, Jr., *James Blair of Virginia* (Chapel Hill, N.C., 1971) offers an interesting account of Blair's long life in Virginia. See also Seiler, "Anglican Parish," 280–89; Brydon, *Virginia's Mother Church,* 230, 286–87, 351–53.

7. A Memorial. . . . by Dr. Blair, 1697, in *Historical Collections Relating to the American Colonial Church,* ed. William S. Perry (Hartford, Conn., 1870, AMS reprint, 1969), I, 15; Rouse, *James Blair,* 39–42; Col. [Robert] Quarry to the Lord Bishop of London, Oct. 15, 1703, in Perry, ed., *Historical Collections,* I, 82–87.

8. Rouse, *James Blair,* 179–83; Gundersen, "Myth of the Independent Vestry," 137–38.

9. *Journals of the House of Burgesses of Virginia,* 1702–1712 (Richmond, Va., 1912), ed. Henry R. McIlwaine, 281; Brydon, *Virginia's Mother Church,* 334.

10. *Virginia Gazette,* (Hunter) April 3, 1752; Rhys Isaac, *The Transformation of Virginia,* 1740–1790 (Chapel Hill, N.C., 1982), 143–45.

11. Isaac, *Transformation of Virginia,* chap. 7. For a discussion of this problem, see Arthur Pierce Middleton, "The Colonial Virginia Parson," *William and Mary Quarterly,* 3d Ser., XXVI (1969), 425–40.

12. See, for example, Mr. Blair to the Bishop of London, Williamsburg, May 13, 1724, Fulham Papers, XII, 5–6, Lambeth Palace Library, London (World Microfilm Publications).

13. Vestry and Churchwardens of St. Anne's, Albemarle, to the Council and President Blair, n.d., Fulham Papers, XIV, 300 (micro.); Clergy of South Carolina to the Secretary, Jan. 2, 1728, SPG Records, Letterbooks Series A, XX, 104, London (Micro Methods, Ltd.).

14. Joan Gundersen, "The Anglican Ministry in Virginia: A Study of a Social Class" (unpublished Ph.D. diss., University of Notre Dame, 1972), chap. 6 and p. 163. It is worth noting that the early histories of Virginia Anglicanism were written by New Light ministers predisposed to believe the worst of the orthodox clergy; Hugh Jones, *The Present State of Virginia* (1724), ed. Richard L. Morton (Chapel Hill, N.C., 1956), 231 n36, 254 n272.

15. Gundersen, "Search for Good Men," 458–63; Brydon, *Virginia's Mother Church*, I, 353; Edward L. Goodwin, *The Colonial Church in Virginia* (Milwaukee, 1927), Appx.

16. Jones, *Present State of Virginia*, 101.

17. In the very earliest years of the 18th century a few clergymen briefly received stipends from the SPG; Carol Lee van Voorst, "The Anglican Clergy in Maryland, 1692–1776" (unpublished Ph.D. diss., Princeton University, 1978), 223.

18. *Ibid.*, 174–76; Gerald E. Hartdagen, "The Vestries and Morals in Colonial Maryland," *Maryland Historical Magazine*, 63 (1968), 360–78.

19. Quoted in Aubrey C. Land, *Colonial Maryland: A History* (Millwood, N.Y., 1981), 105–6.

20. Nelson W. Rightmyer, *Maryland's Established Church* (Baltimore, 1950), 97–104; van Voorst, "Anglican Clergy in Maryland," 77. For a similar incident see *Maryland Archives* (Baltimore, 1895), XIV, 368. Both occurred in the years immediately following the Stamp Act and probably reflect the colonists' heightened sensitivity to taxation without representation.

21. Hugh Jones to the Bishop of London, Cecil County, Md., Oct. 19, 1741, Fulham Papers, III, 191–92 (micro.); van Voorst, "Anglican Clergy in Maryland," 50–54, 223–50.

22. Christopher Wilkinson to the Bishop of London, Queen Anne County, Md., May 26, 1718, Fulham Papers, II, 250–51 (micro.); Wilkinson to the Bishop, Queen Anne County, Nov. 20, 1724, Fulham Papers, III, 45 (micro.).

23. David C. Skaggs and Gerald E. Hartdagen, "Sinners and Saints: Anglican Clerical Conduct in Colonial Maryland," *Historical Magazine of the Protestant Episcopal Church*, XLVII (1978), 187. The article includes a review of the literature on this controversy.

24. van Voorst, "Anglican Clergy in Maryland," 204–18. Appx. C lists all cases with their disposition.

25. Another 15 percent had matriculated but did not obtain degrees. *Ibid.*, 130–44.

26. *Ibid.*, 125, 198, 100.

27. S. Charles Bolton, *Southern Anglicanism: The Church of England in Colonial South Carolina* (Westport, Conn., 1982), 147; M. Eugene Sirmans, *Colonial South Carolina: A Political History, 1663–1763* (Chapel Hill, N.C., 1966), 94–99, 244.

28. *Ibid.*, 97–98; Frederick Dalcho, *An Historical Account of the Protestant Episcopal Church in South-Carolina* (Charleston, S.C., 1820).

29. Reba Carolyn Strickland, *Religion and the State in Georgia in the Eighteenth Century* (New York, 1939; AMS reprint, 1967), 102–13, 70–71.

30. Sarah M. Lemmon, "The Genesis of the Protestant Episcopal

Diocese in North Carolina, 1701–1823," *North Carolina Historical Review,* 28 (1951), 426–62; Paul Conkin, "The Church Establishment in North Carolina, 1765–1776," *N.C. Hist. Rev.,* 32 (1955), 1–30.

31. Mr. Edward Portlock to the Archbishop of Canterbury, Philadelphia, July 12, 1700, Fulham Papers, VII, 28 (micro.).

32. Governor Fletcher's Opening Address, April 10, 1693, in Edward T. Corwin, ed., *Ecclesiastical Records of the State of New York* (Albany, N.Y., 1901–1916), II, 1054; The Ministry Act, 1693, *ibid.,* II, 1077.

33. Fletcher to the Assembly, Sept. 22, 1693, *ibid.,* 1075–76.

34. Minutes of the Meetings of the Justices, Church Wardens, and Vestrymen of the City of New York, 1694–1747, transcript by George H. Moore, New York Public Library, Manuscript Room; Morgan Dix, *A History of the Parish of Trinity Church in the City of New York* (New York, 1898), I, chaps. 5, 6, 11, and esp. pp. 90–91, 184, 484. See also Jean Paul Jordan, "The Anglican Establishment in Colonial New York, 1693–1783 (Columbia University Ph.D. diss., 1971). The Vestry Minutes show that from £100 (presumably New York money) in 1704, Vesey's salary rose to £160 by 1712. When Vesey died in 1746, his successor was paid only £100 by the Vestry. I wish to thank Irmgard Carras for help in researching these points.

35. For the fullest account of these events see Dix, *History of Trinity Parish.*

36. John Bartow to the Secretary, Westchester, N.Y., Dec. 1, 1708, SPG Records, Letterbooks Series A, III, 524–34 (micro.).

37. Cornbury to the Secretary, New York, Sept. 22, 1705, SPG Records, Letterbooks Series A, II (micro.); William Smith, Jr., *The History of the Province of New-York from the First Discovery to the Year 1732,* ed. Michael Kammen (Cambridge, Mass., 1972), I, 117; Lewis Morris to the Secretary, New York, Feb. 20, 1712, SPG Records, Letterbooks Series A, VII, 168 (micro.).

38. Justices, Church Wardens, & Vestry of the Parish of Westchester to the Society, [n.d.], American Papers of the SPG, Lambeth Palace, XIV, 307 (World Microfilm Publications); Edward Vaughan to the Secretary, Dec. 4, 1710, Mr. Poyer to the Secretary, May 3, 1711, Mr. Bartow to the Secretary, April 31 [sic], 1711, SPG Records, Letterbooks Series A, VI, 2, 72–73 (micro.); Minutes of Meeting [London], Dec. 21, 1739, American Papers of the SPG, Lambeth Palace, III, 272–74 (micro.).

Officials also tried to strengthen Anglicanism by paying the salaries of French and German Reformed ministers in the hope that they would come over to the Church of England; Corwin, ed., *Ecclesiastical Records,* III, 1817 and *passim.*

39. Appendix to *A Sermon Preached before the Incorporated Society*

for the Propagation of the Gospel in Foreign Parts . . . On Friday, Feb. 20, 1767, *by John Lord Bishop of Llandaff* (London, 1767).

40. Jones, *Present State of Virginia*, 100; van Voorst, "Anglican Clergy in Maryland," 152; Thomas Morritt to the Secretary, Winyaw, S.C., Sept. 1, 1729, SPG Records, Letterbooks Series B, IV, Part 3, 234, United SPG Archives, London.

41. Mr. Forbes's Account of the State of the Church in Virginia, Upper Parish, Isle of Wight County, July 21, 1724, Fulham Papers, XII, 63 (micro.); Anthony Gavin to the Bishop of London, Aug. 5, 1738, Fulham Papers, XII, 273–74 (micro.); Answer to the Bishop of London's Queries, Westover Parish, 1724, Fulham Papers, XII, 59 (micro.).

42. Jones, *Present State of Virginia*, 97.

43. Mr. Becket to the Secretary, Lewes County, April 15, 1732, from Reverend William Becket's Notices and Letters concerning incidents at Lewes Town, 1727–1742, Historical Society of Pennsylvania, Philadelphia; Becket, History of His Church, Oct. 11, 1728, *ibid.*

44. Bartow to the Secretary, Westchester, May 11, 1709, SPG Records, Letterbooks Series A, IV, 496–98 (micro.); Mr. Stannard to the Secretary, Nov. 5, 1729, SPG Records, Letterbooks Series A, XXII, 363 (micro).

45. Mr. Bartow to the Secretary, Westchester, Dec. 1, 1708, SPG Records, Letterbooks Series A, III, 524–34 (micro.); Robert Bolton, *History of the Protestant Episcopal Church in the County of Westchester* (New York, 1855).

46. Answer to the Bishop of London's Queries, Stratford, 1724, Fulham Papers, I, 209 (micro.).

47. William Harrison to the Secretary, Hopewell, N.J., Nov. 3, 1722, SPG Records, Letterbooks Series A, XVI, 217–18 (micro.); Answer to the Bishop of London's Queries, 1724, Fulham Papers, XLI (micro.).

48. Talbot to the Secretary, Rhode Island, Dec. 13, 1707, SPG Records, Letterbooks Series A, III, 158 (micro.); Mr. Henderson to the Secretary, Newcastle, July 26, 1713, SPG Records, Letterbooks Series A, VIII, 479–80 (micro.).

49. William Becket to the Secretary, April 15, 1732, Dec. 1, 1732, in Reverend William Becket's Notices and Letters concerning incidents at Lewes Town, 1724–1742, Historical Society of Pennsylvania; Inglis to the Secretary, Dover, July 2, 1765, Dec. 1, 1766, SPG Records, Letterbooks Series B, XXI, 147, 150 (micro.); Mr. Commissary Blair to the Bishop of London, Williamsburg, July 17, 1724, Fulham Papers, XII, 21 (micro.).

50. James de Gignillat to the Secretary, Goose Creek, S.C., July 15, 1711, SPG Records, Letterbooks Series A, VI (micro.).

51. Mr. Gavin to the Bishop of London, Aug. 5, 1738, Fulham Papers,

XII, 273–74 (micro.); Mr. Becket to the Secretary, Lewes Town, April 14, 1722, SPG Records, Letterbooks Series A, XVI, 156 (micro.).

52. Mr. Urmston to the Secretary, Cecil County, Md., June, 1724, Perry, ed., *Historical Collections*, IV, 237; see also Answers to the Bishop of London's Queries from St. Philip's, Charleston, S.C., and Trinity Church, New York City, 1724, Fulham Papers, IX, LXI (micro.).

53. Mr. Hunt to the Secretary, May 6, 1728, and Mr. Varnod to the Secretary, April 3, 1728, SPG Records, Letterbooks Series A, XXI, 97–104 (micro.); David Humphreys, *An Historical Account of the Incorporated Society for the Propagation of the Gospel in Foreign Parts . . .* (London, 1730), 94; Sirmans, *Colonial South Carolina*, 111–15; Joseph Hooper, *A History of Saint Peter's Church in the City of Albany* (Albany, N.Y., 1900), especially chaps. 3–6.

54. Isaac, *Transformation of Virginia*, 58–65, 143–44; for a detailed description of services at St. Philip's, see Richard J. Hooker, ed., *The Carolina Backcountry on the Eve of the Revolution: The Journal and Other Writings of Charles Woodmason, Anglican Itinerant* (Chapel Hill, N.C., 1953), 70.

55. van Voorst, "Anglican Clergy in Maryland," 66; Gundersen, "Search For Good Men," 454.

56. Richard Ludlam to the Secretary, St. James, Goose Creek, S.C., December 12, 1727, SPG Records, Letterbooks Series A, XX, 98–104 (micro.); Mr. Hasell to the Secretary, June 4, 1728, SPG Records, Letterbooks Series A, XXI, 108–16 (micro.). For the enlargement of this and other South Carolina churches around mid-century, see *ibid.*, Letterbooks Series B, XVI, p. 143, XVII, p. 176, and *passim*.

57. Mr. Hunt to the Secretary, May 6, 1728, SPG Records, Letterbooks Series A, XXI, 97–104 (micro.); Mr. Guy, History of His Church, 1728, SPG Records, Letterbooks Series A, XX, 110–15 (micro.).

58. Charles Boschi to the Secretary, St. Bartholomew's Parish, S.C., April 7, 1746, SPG Records, Letterbooks Series B, XII, 110–12 (micro.). Rural churches in Virginia, such as the one at Lickinghole in Goochland Parish, which used a quart-sized pewter tankard and delft plate for communion, faced similar problems; see *The Douglas Register . . . kept by the Rev. William Douglas from 1750 to 1797*, ed., W. Mac. Jones (Baltimore, 1966), p. 7 and *passim*.

59. Hooker, ed., *Carolina Backcountry*, 56, 61, 38.

60. Edwin Scott Gaustad, *Historical Atlas of Religion in America*, rev. ed. (New York, 1976), 9, Appx. B (Gaustad's count may actually be somewhat low; see Bonomi and Eisenstadt, "Church Adherence," 273, Table II); Bishop [Thomas] Secker to Dr. Samuel Johnson, Papers Relating to the American Colonies, I, 36, Lambeth Palace Library, London.

61. Charter of the Province of Massachusetts Bay, 1691, in *Publications of The Colonial Society of Massachusetts*, II (Boston, 1913), 22.

62. David D. Hall, *The Faithful Shepherd: A History of the New England Ministry in the Seventeenth Century* (Chapel Hill, N.C., 1972), 200–7; chap. 9, 272–75; M. Louise Greene, *The Development of Religious Liberty in Connecticut* (Boston, 1905), 195–96.

63. These developments can be followed in J. William T. Youngs, Jr., *God's Messengers: Religious Leadership in Colonial New England, 1700–1750* (Baltimore, 1976); Susan M. Reed, *Church and State in Massachusetts, 1691–1740* (Urbana, Ill., 1914); Greene, *Religious Liberty in Connecticut.*

64. Hall, *Faithful Shepherd*, 218–20; Williston Walker, A History of the Congregational Churches in the United States (New York, 1894), 185, 201; Youngs, *God's Messengers*, 73, 155 n30.

The quotation is from John Wise, *The Churches Quarrel Espoused* (Boston, 1713, 2nd ed. 1715), 15. A decline in the number of church elders is particularly noticeable after the mid-1660s, whereas church deacons— who had a strictly fiscal and administrative rather than a governing role— continued to be chosen by all churches; Harold Field Worthley, *An Inventory of the Records of the Particular (Congregational) Churches of Massachusetts, Gathered 1620–1805*, Harvard Theological Studies, XXV (Cambridge, Mass., 1970); also see Walker, *History*, 229–30. Christine Heyrman tells me that the 1730s saw a return to the appointment of elders in many Congregational churches, especially in northern New England; personal communication, Sept. 12, 1985.

65. Youngs, *God's Messengers*, 69–72; Walker, *History*, 202–4; Henry Martyn Dexter, *The Congregationalism of the Last Three Hundred Years as Seen in Its Literature* (New York, 1880), 493. The Proposals will be found in Williston Walker, ed., *The Creeds and Platforms of Congregationalism* (New York, 1893), 465–95.

66. Stoddard's recommendations are in *The Doctrine of Instituted Churches* (1700), as discussed in Perry Miller, *The New England Mind: From Colony to Province* (Cambridge, Mass., 1953), 257–65. See also Increase Mather, *A Disquisition Concerning Ecclesiastical Councils* (Boston, 1716); and Dexter, *Congregationalism*, 510, 531–33.

67. Wise, *The Churches Quarrel Espoused*, 9; John Wise, *A Vindication of the Government of New-England Churches* (Boston, 1717), 67; *Churches Quarrel*, 54, 53, 94, 108.

68. Mr. Delafay, Secretary to the Lords Justices, to the Governor of Massachusetts, Whitehall, Oct. 7, 1725, Papers Relating to the American Colonies, I, 13, Lambeth Palace Library, London. Other letters expressing the concern of the Bishop of London and Archbishop of Canterbury, as well

as that of Massachusetts Anglican ministers, are contained in the same volume of manuscripts in the Lambeth Palace Library.

69. Youngs, *God's Messengers*, 73–76; Miller, *Colony to Province*, chap. 28.

70. Reed, *Church and State*, 68–70. For an extensive discussion of resistance to and enforcement of these laws, see chaps. 4 and 5.

71. *Ibid.*, 103–41, 164, 185; William G. McLoughlin, *New England Dissent, 1630–1833: The Baptists and the Separation of Church and State* (Cambridge, Mass., 1971), I, part 3. It was well after the Revolution, in 1833, that the last vestiges of the church-state connection were eradicated; *ibid.*, II, chap. 63.

72. Greene, *Religious Liberty in Connecticut*, 135. The Saybrook Platform is reproduced in Walker, ed., *Creeds and Platforms*, 495–516.

73. Benjamin Trumbull, *A Complete History of Connecticut, Civil and Ecclesiastical . . . 1630 . . . 1764* (New Haven, Conn., 1818), I, 486; Walker, ed., *Creeds and Platforms*, 504; Greene, *Religious Liberty in Connecticut*, 135–46.

74. The speaker was the Anglican, Caleb Heathcote, of New York; quoted in Greene, *ibid.*, 178.

75. McLoughlin, *New England Dissent*, I, chaps. 14, 15.

76. Increase Mather commented in 1682 on the evils of sleeping at sermons: "Some woeful Creatures, have been so wicked as to profess they have gone to hear Sermons on purpose, that so they might sleep, finding themselves at such times much disposed that way." *The Puritans: A Sourcebook of Their Writings*, eds., Perry Miller and Thomas H. Johnson (New York, 1963), I, 348. See also Ola Elizabeth Winslow, *Meetinghouse Hill, 1630–1783* (New York, 1952), chap. 9.

77. Cotton Mather, *Ratio Disciplinae Fratrum Nov Angelorum* (Boston, 1726), 43; Walker, *History*, 242; Bruce C. Daniels, *The Connecticut Town: Growth and Development, 1635–1790* (Middletown, Conn., 1979), 96–97.

78. M. Halsey Thomas, ed., *The Diary of Samuel Sewall, 1674–1729* (New York, 1973), I, 94; Winslow, *Meetinghouse Hill*, 57; Mather, *Ratio Disciplinae*, 45; Alice Morse Earle, *The Sabbath in Puritan New England* (New York, 1900), 109–10.

79. Mather, *Ratio Disciplinae*, 52; Walker, *History*, 239; Henry Wilder Foote, *Annals of King's Chapel* (Boston, 1896), I, 208–11. The liberal Brattle no doubt saw little difference between his own Brattle Street Church—described by one contemporary as "midway between the Church of England and Dissenters"—and King's Chapel; Kenneth Silverman, *The Life and Times of Cotton Mather* (New York, 1984), 148, 216.

80. Mather, *Ratio Disciplinae*, 55; Thomas Walter, *The Ground Rules*

of Musick Explained (Boston, 1721; 3rd ed., 1740). 4; Winslow, *Meeting-house Hill*, chap. 10. See also Laura L. Becker, "Ministers vs Laymen: The Singing Controversy in Puritan New England, 1720–1740," *New England Quarterly*, LV (1982), 79–96.

81. Mather, *Ratio Disciplinae*, 61, 59.

82. Solomon Stoddard, *The Presence of Christ with the Ministers of the Gospel* (Boston, 1718), 27–28. The notion developed from revivalist preachers' depictions of orthodox ministers as "dead drones" and such; see chap. 5. For an intimate look at a vital Congregational church, see Christine Leigh Heyrman, *Commerce and Culture: the Maritime Communities of Colonial Massachusetts, 1690–1750* (New York, 1984), 284–93 and *passim*.

83. An excellent recent discussion is in Charles E. Hambrick-Stowe, *The Practice of Piety: Puritan Devotional Disciplines in Seventeenth-Century New England* (Chapel Hill, N.C., 1982), 117ff.

84. David E. Stannard, *The Puritan Way of Death: A Study in Religion, Culture, and Social Change* (New York, 1977), 109–22.

85. James W. Schmotter, "The Irony of Clerical Professionalism: New England's Congregational Ministers and the Great Awakening," *American Quarterly*, 31 (1979), 162 fig. 1.

86. Some pulpits were briefly filled by neighboring preachers when a vacancy occurred, but such vacancies were of short duration; *ibid.*, 158.

87. Youngs, *God's Messengers*, 11–12. In Schmotter's analysis about 12 percent of clergymen active in 1700 had not graduated from college; by 1740 this figure had dropped to 3 percent. "Irony of Clerical Professionalism," 157.

88. James W. Schmotter, "Ministerial Careers in Eighteenth-Century New England: The Social Context, 1700–1760," *Journal of Social History*, 9 (1975–76), 250, Table 1.

89. Cotton Mather, *A Monitory Letter About the Maintenance of an Able and Faithful Ministry* (Boston, 1700), 8; Stephen Botein, "Income and Ideology: Harvard-Trained Clergymen in Eighteenth-Century New England," *Eighteenth-Century Studies*, 13 (Summer 1980), 396–413; Schmotter, "Ministerial Careers," 253–55.

90. *Ibid.*, 255–57; Wise, *Churches Quarrel*, 66.

91. Schmotter, "Ministerial Careers," 254 fig. 2, 251; Youngs, *God's Messengers*, 12; Clifford K. Shipton, "The New England Clergy of the 'Glacial Age,'" *Colonial Society of Massachusetts, Transactions*, 32 (1933–37), 50. Only 5 percent of the 400 left the ministry because of money problems; *ibid.*

92. Youngs, *God's Messengers*, 42–46. For insight into the life of a typical 18th-century New England clergyman, see Francis G. Walett, ed., *The Diary of Ebenezer Parkman, 1703–1782* (Worcester, Mass., 1974).

93. Gaustad, *Atlas*, 15 fig. 13, Appx. B; U.S. Bureau of the Census, *Historical Statistics of the United States, Colonial Times to 1970* (Washington D.C., 1975), Pt. 2, 1168; Mather, *Ratio Disciplinae*, 196.

94. Martin E. Lodge, "The Crisis of the Churches in the Middle Colonies, 1720–1750," *Pennsylvania Magazine of History and Biography*, 95 (1971), 195–200; Charles H. Maxson, *The Great Awakening in the Middle Colonies* (Chicago, 1920).

95. Rhys Isaac, *The Transformation of Virginia, 1740–1790* (Chapel Hill, N.C., 1982), chaps. 7–11; Bonomi and Eisenstadt, "Church Adherence," 245–86.

96. William J. Hinke, ed., *Life and Letters of the Rev. John Philip Boehm. . . . 1683–1749* (Philadelphia, 1916), 23, 157; Joseph Henry Dubbs, *The Reformed Church in Pennsylvania* (Lancaster, Pa., 1902), 65.

97. Hinke, ed., *Life and Letters of Boehm*, 162.

98. Ibid; *The Journal of Reverend Michael Schlatter*, in Henry Harbaugh, *The Life of Reverend Michael Schlatter* (Philadelphia, 1857), 202; *Boehm's Life and Letters*, 162.

99. *Ibid.*, 29, 159.

100. *Ibid.*, 62–63; Dubbs, *Reformed Church*, chaps. 5–7; *Schlatter's Journal*, 137.

101. Walter Allen Knittle, *The Early Eighteenth-Century Palatine Emigration* (Philadelphia, 1936), chaps. 6–8. The quotation is in Corwin, ed., *Ecclesiastical Records*, III, 1968.

102. The SPG actually paid part of Hager's salary and sent him printed matter, presumably in German, in an unsuccessful effort to attach the Germans to the Church of England; *ibid.*, 2003–6 and *passim*.

103. Sydney E. Ahlstrom, *A Religious History of the American People* (New Haven, Conn., 1972), 252–53; *The Albany Protocol: Wilhelm Christoph Berkenmeyer's Chronicle of Lutheran Affairs in New York Colony, 1731–1750*, ed. John P. Dern (Ann Arbor, Mich., 1971), 36, 66–70.

104. Theodore E. Schmauk, *A History of The Lutheran Church in Pennsylvania (1638–1820) from the Original Sources* (Philadelphia, 1903), 435–45, 446, 462–68.

105. *The Journals of Henry Melchior Muhlenberg*, trans. Theodore G. Tappert and John W. Doberstein (Philadelphia, 1942), I, 85, 154.

106. *Minutes and Letters of the Coetus of the German Reformed Congregations in Pennsylvania, 1742–1792, Together with Three Preliminary Reports of Reverend John Philip Boehm, 1734–1744* (Philadelphia, 1903), 9; Dieter Cunz, *The Maryland Germans, A History* (Princeton, N.J., 1948), 66. The church at Tulpehocken had 12 different preachers between 1728 and 1743, a few of them ordained but most not. Schmauk, *Lutheran Church in Pennsylvania*, 468–522.

107. *Boehm's Life and Letters*, 162; *ibid.*, 27–39.
108. Schmauk, *Lutheran Church in Pennsylvania*, 457–58; Muhlenberg, *Journals*, I, 237.
109. *Ibid.*, I, 65–75; quotations on 67. Muhlenberg also had to thwart the efforts of the Moravian Count Zinzendorf to usurp his Philadelphia pulpit; *ibid.*, 76–82.
110. *Ibid.*, 100. Boehm reported that, if refused communion, his people denied "that anyone has a right to speak to them about their wicked life, and want to play the master"; *Boehm's Life and Letters*, 267.
111. *Ibid.*, 162; Muhlenberg, *Journals*, I, 249; *Schlatter's Journal*, 211.
112. Schmauk, *Lutheran Church in Pennsylvania*, 521–42; quotation on 534.
113. *Boehm's Life and Letters*, 162. For a recent essay that questions many of the old assumptions, see J. William Frost, "Sect, Church, and Secularization: Religion in Colonial Pennsylvania," paper presented to the Philadelphia Center for Early American Studies, December, 1981.
114. Gaustad, *Historical Atlas of Religion in America*, Appx. B; Frederick Lewis Weis, *The Colonial Clergy of the Middle Colonies: New York, New Jersey, and Pennsylvania*, 1628–1776 (1957; reprint ed., Baltimore, 1978); Bonomi and Eisenstadt, "Church Adherence," 273, Table II.
115. Lewis Morris to the Secretary, New York, Feb. 20, 1712, SPG Records, Letterbooks Series A, VII, 168 (micro.); Smith, *The History of the Province of New-York*, ed., Michael Kammen (Cambridge, Mass., 1972), I, 203–8, 244; Jefferson, *Notes on the State of Virginia* (New York, 1964), 154. The Middle Colonies were frequently pointed to as the region where diversity and liberty thrived; see, for example, James Madison to Edward Livingston, July 10, 1822, in Adrienne Koch, ed., *The American Enlightenment* (New York, 1965), 465–66.
116. Gaustad, *Atlas*, 18, 28. To trace this growth, consult *Minutes and Letters of the Coetus of the German Reformed Congregations in Pennsylvania*, 1742–1792, and *Reports of the United German Evangelical Lutheran Congregations in North America, Especially in Pennsylvania*, trans. Jonathan Oswald (Philadelphia, 1880–1881), 2 vols.
117. Oscar and Mary Handlin, *The Dimensions of Liberty* (Cambridge, Mass., 1961); for the colonial churches as voluntary associations, see esp. pp. 93–94; Arthur M. Schlesinger, "Biography of a Nation of Joiners," *American Historical Review*, 50 (1944), 1–25.
118. Muhlenberg, *Journals*, I, 381.
119. For a good example of how lay elders declined in importance as the clergy professionalized, see *Documentary History of the Evangelical Lutheran Ministerium of Pennsylvania and Adjacent States: Proceedings of*

the Annual Conventions, 1748–1821 (Philadelphia, 1898). For the German Reformed, see Dubbs, *Reformed Church in Pennsylvania,* chap. 11.
120. C. F. Pascoe, *Two Hundred Years of the S.P.G.* (London, 1901), 123.

CHAPTER 4

1. Robert C. Pope, *The Half-Way Covenant: Church Membership in Puritan New England* (Princeton, N.J., 1969), especially 256–73; Patricia U. Bonomi and Peter R. Eisenstadt, "Church Adherence in the Eighteenth-Century British American Colonies," *William and Mary Quarterly,* 3d Ser., XXXIX (1982), 245–86; Timothy L. Smith, "Congregation, State, and Denomination; The Forming of the American Religious Structure," *WMQ,* 3d Ser., XXV (1968), 155–76.
2. Gerald F. Moran and Maris A. Vinovskis, "The Puritan Family and Religion: A Critical Appraisal," *WMQ,* 3d Ser., XXXIX (1982), 31–37; Susan S. Forbes, "Quaker Tribalism," in *Friends and Neighbors: Group Life in America's First Plural Society,* ed. Michael Zuckerman (Philadelphia, 1982), 145–73.
3. James Walsh, "The Great Awakening in the First Congregational Church of Woodbury, Connecticut." *WMQ,* 3d Ser., XXVIII (1971), 543–62: Joan Gundersen, "Family Ties: Ethnicity and Family in Viginia's Great Awakening" (unpublished paper, 1984); Bruce C. Daniels, *The Connecticut Town: Growth and Development, 1635–1790* (Middletown, Conn., 1979), 96–98.
4. The terms "scoffer" and "atheist" were sometimes used by religious zealots to denounce members of rival sects, whose only sin was that they held beliefs opposed to those of the name-callers.
5. Mr. [Thomas] Barton to the Society, Lancaster, Pa., Nov. 16, 1764, Records of the Society for the Propagation of the Gospel in Foreign Parts, Letterbooks Series B, XXI, 14 (Micro Methods, Ltd.); *The Life of the Reverend Devereux Jarratt* (Baltimore, 1806; reprint ed., New York, 1969), 102.
6. See *The Journal of Reverend Michael Schlatter,* in Henry Harbaugh, *The Life of Reverend Michael Schlatter* (Philadelphia, 1857), 154–55; for northern Anglicans, American Papers of the SPC, vol. 4, Lambeth Palace Library, London (World Microfilm Publications). In a typical early comment, Mr. Bartow of Westchester County, New York, noted in 1717 that he had but 26 actual communicants out of 179 parishioners who professed adherence to the Church of England; Bartow to the Secretary, Westchester, N.Y., Sept. 12, 1717, SPG Records, Letterbook A, XII, 415 (micro.).
7. See, for example, *First Record Book of the "Old Dutch Church of*

Sleepy Hollow," Organized in 1697 . . . to 1791 (Yonkers, N.Y., 1901), 193: M. Eugene Sirmans, *Colonial South Carolina: A Political History,* 1663–1763 (Chapel Hill, N.C., 1966), 98; and *infra* n81.

8. James Adams to the Secretary, Caratauk, N.C., March 27, 1710. SPC Records, Letterbook A, V, 137 (micro.); Mr. William Becket, History of His Church, Oct. 11, 1728, in "Rev. William Becket's Notices & Letters concerning incidents at Lewes Town, 1727–1742," Historical Society of Pennsylvania, Philadelphia; William Dunn to John Chamberlayne, Charlestown, S.C., July 20, 1708, American Papers of the SPG, Lambeth Palace Library, XVI, 226 (micro.).

9. Edwin Scott Gaustad, *The Great Awakening in New England* (New York, 1957), 30; *Bowen's Picture of Boston* (Boston, Mass.; 3rd ed., 1838), 108–29; Franklin Bowditch Dexter, ed., *Extracts from the Itineraries and Other Miscellanies of Ezra Stiles* . . . (New Haven, Conn., 1916), 25–26; *Paterna: The Autobiography of Cotton Mather,* ed. Ronald A. Bosco (Delmar, N.Y., 1976), 72.

10. U.S. Bureau of the Census, *Historical Statistics of the United States, Colonial Times to* 1970 (Washington, D.C., 1975), Pt. 2, 1168; Bonomi and Eisenstadt, "Church Adherence," 273 Table II; Frederick Lewis Weis, *The Colonial Clergy of the Middle Colonies* (1957; reprint ed., Baltimore, 1978).

11. Lawrence A. Cremin, *American Education: The Colonial Experience,* 1607–1783 (New York, 1970), 536; Rufus Jones, *The Quakers in the American Colonies* (1911; reprint ed., New York, 1966), 523. The description of Trinity Church is from William Smith, Jr., *The History of the Province of New-York,* ed. Michael Kammen, I (Cambridge, Mass., 1972), 203; for the Claverack church see Franklin Ellis, *History of Columbia County, New York* (Philadelphia, 1878), 243–47.

12. Bureau of the Census, *Historical Statistics,* II, 1168; Edwin Scott Gaustad, *Historical Atlas of Religion in America,* rev. ed. (New York, 1976), Appx. B; Bonomi and Eisenstadt, "Church Adherence," 273. For the description of St. Philip's, see Richard J. Hooker, ed., *The Carolina Backcountry on the Eve of the Revolution: The Journal and Other Writings of Charles Woodmason, Anglican Itinerant* (Chapel Hill, N.C., 1953), 70.

13. Hugh Jones, *The Present State of Virginia,* 96; "Answers to the Bishop of London's Queries, 1724, Fulham Papers, Lambeth Palace Library (World Microfilm Publications, London), III, 48–71 (Md.); IX, 160–71 (S.C.); XII. 41–84 (Va.).

14. *Ibid.,* IV, 151; Bruce E. Steiner, "New England Anglicanism: A Genteel Faith?" *WMQ,* 3d Ser., XXVII (1970), 122–35; Robert Bolton,

History of the Protestant Episcopal Church in the County of Westchester (New York, 1855); Henry W. Foote, *Annals of King's Chapel* (Boston, 1896), II, 605–10. For a recent analysis of the Marblehead church leadership, see Christine Leigh Heyrman, *Commerce and Culture: The Maritime Communities of Colonial Massachusetts, 1690–1750* (New York, 1984), 266–67.

15. Sir Harry Franklands on the State of Religion at Boston, London, Dec. 13, 1748, Papers Relating to the American Colonies, I, 39, Lambeth Palace Library, London; Steiner, "New England Anglicanism," 125–26; Francis L. Hawks and William S. Perry, eds., *Documentary History of the Protestant Episcopal Church. . . . Connecticut* (New York, 1863), I, 105, 119, 161, 166, and *passim.*

16. Adrian Howe, "Accommodation and Retreat; Politics in Anglo-Dutch New York City, 1700–1760," (Ph.D. diss., Melbourne University, 1983), 412–13; Jon Butler, *The Huguenots in America: A Refugee People in New World Society* (Cambridge, Mass., 1983), 193–94; Frederick B. Tolles, *Meeting House and Counting House* (Chapel Hill, N. C., 1948), 1911, 141–42.

17. Mr. Robert Weyman to the Society, London, Aug. 3, 1728, Fulham Papers, Lambeth Palace Library, VII, 1 (micro.); Morgan Dix, *A History of the Parish of Trinity Church in the City of New York* (New York, 1898), I, chaps. 9–14.

18. Charles W. Akers, "Religion and the American Revolution: Samuel Cooper and the Brattle Street Church," *WMQ*, 3d Ser., XXXV (1978), 482; David Levin, *Cotton Mather: The Young Life of the Lord's Remembrancer, 1663–1703* (Cambridge, Mass., 1978), 178, 271–73.

19. Paul Boyer and Stephen Nissenbaum, *Salem Possessed* (Cambridge, Mass., 1974), 99; Philip J. Greven, Jr., "Youth, Maturity, and Religious Conversion: A Note on the Ages of Converts in Andover, Massachusetts, 1711–1749," *Essex Institute Historical Collections,* CVIII (1972), 119–34; Walsh, "The Great Awakening in the First Congregational Church of Woodbury, Connecticut," 546.

20. Patricia J. Tracy, *Jonathan Edwards, Pastor: Religion and Society in Eighteenth-Century Northampton* (New York, 1980), 94; Richard L. Bushman, *From Puritan to Yankee: Character and the Social Order in Connecticut, 1690–1765* (Cambridge, Mass., 1967), 159.

21. William Fristoe, *A Concise History of the Ketocton Baptist Association* (Staunton, Va., 1808), 72; Robert Baylor Semple, *A History of the Rise and Progress of The Baptists in Virginia,* ed, G. W. Beale (Philadelphia, 1894 [orig. publ. 1810]), 38; C. C. Goen, *Revivalism and Separatism in New England, 1740–1800* (New Haven, Conn., 1962), 189–91; William G. McLoughlin, *New England Dissent, 1630–1833: The Baptists and the*

Separation of Church and State (Cambridge, Mass., 1971), I, 347–48 and chap. 16.

22. Richard R. Beeman and Rhys Isaac, "Cultural Conflict and Social Change in the Revolutionary South: Lunenburg County, Virginia," *Journal of Southern History*, XLVI (1980), 545–47; David Thomas, *The Virginian Baptist* (Balitmore, 1774), 55.

23. James T. Lemon, *The Best Poor Man's Country: A Geographical Study of Early Southeastern Pennsylvania* (Baltimore, 1972), 20–22, 188–90; Gary B. Nash, *Class and Society in Early America* (Englewood Cliffs, N.J., 1970), 185–86; Tolles, *Meeting House and Counting House*, chap. 6; Rufus M. Jones, *The Quakers in the American Colonies*, chap. 3; Arthur J. Worrall, *Quakers in the Colonial Northeast* (Hanover, N.H., 1980).

24. E. T. Corwin, ed., *Ecclesiastical Records of the State of New York* (Albany, N.Y., 1901), I; Howe, "Accommodation and Retreat."

25. Lemon, *Best Poor Man's Country*, 20–21, 189; Abstract of Two Letters . . . [to] His Majesty's Dutch Chapel at St. James, and the Dutch Ministers of London [1746?], Papers Relating to the American Colonies, I, 37, Lambeth Palace Library, London.

26. Howe, "Accommodation and Retreat." See also Gerald F. DeJong, *The Dutch Reformed Church in the American Colonies* (Grand Rapids, Mich., 1978). The Reformed Church is still the largest and most influential denomination in many towns along the Hudson River initially settled by the Dutch.

27. The Inhabitants of St. John's Parish, in Kent County, to Mr. Archibald Cummings, Pennsylvania, April 15, 1732, SPG Records, Letterbook A, XXIV, 359 (micro.); Barry Levy, "The Birth of the 'Modern Family' in Early America: Quaker and Anglican Families in the Delaware Valley, Pennsylvania, 1681–1750," in *Friends and Neighbors*, ed. Michael W. Zuckerman, 26–64; Mr. Arnold to the Secretary, West Haven, Conn., Sept. 22, 1736, SPG Records, Letterbook A, XXVI, 255 (micro.).

28. Charles Y. Glock, "The Role of Deprivation in the Origin and Evolution of Religious Groups," in *Religion and Social Conflict*, eds. Robert Lee and Martin E. Marty (New York, 1964), 24–26.

29. *Ibid.*, 27–29ff.

30. Hunter Dickinson Farish, ed., *Journal & Letters of Philip Vickers Fithian, 1773–1774: A Plantation Tutor of the Old Dominion* (Williamsburg, Va., 1943, 1945), 220 and *passim*; Henry F. May, *The Enlightenment in America* (New York, 1976), 66–87; Richard Beale Davis, *Intellectual Life in the Colonial South, 1585–1763* (Knoxville, Tenn., 1978). vol. II.

31. *The Secret Diary of William Byrd of Westover, 1709–1712*, ed.

Louis B. Wright and Marion Tinling (Richmond, Va., 1941); *William Byrd of Virginia: The London Diary (1717–1721) and Other Writings*, ed. Louis B. Wright and Marion Tinling (New York, 1958); *Another Secret Diary of William Byrd of Westover, 1739–1741, with Letters and Literary Exercises 1696–1726*, ed. Maude H. Woodfin, trans. and collated by Marion Tinling (Richmond, Va., 1942).

32. William Byrd, *History of the Dividing Line betwixt Virginia and North Carolina Run in the Year of Our Lord 1728*, in Louis B. Wright, ed., *The Prose Works of William Byrd of Westover* (Cambridge, Mass., 1966), 195; Woodfin, ed., *Another Secret Diary*, 6.

33. Wright and Tinling, eds., *Byrd's Secret Diary, 1709–1712*, xxviii n12, 278–79, 175. I wish to thank Peter Eisenstadt for his insightful reading of Byrd's religious commentary.

34. *Letters of Robert Carter, 1720–1727*, ed. Louis B. Wright (San Marino, Calif., 1940), *ibid.*, 87, 102; *William Fitzhugh and His Chesapeake World, 1676–1701*, ed. Richard Beale Davis (Chapel Hill. N.C., 1963), 198.

35. For William Byrd II's concern that his wife was resisting submission to God's will following the death of their infant son, see Wright and Tinling, eds., *Byrd's Secret Diary, 1709–1712*, pp. 188–91. This episode also is discussed in Michael Zuckerman, "William Byrd's Family," *Perspectives in American History*, XII (1979), 255–57.

36. "Jefferson's Extracts from the Gospels: 'The Philosophy of Jesus' and 'The Life and Morals of Jesus,'" *The Papers of Thomas Jefferson*, 2nd Ser., ed. Dickinson W. Adams (Princeton, N.J., 1983), Introduction by Eugene R. Sheridan; George Harmon Knoles, "The Religious Ideas of Thomas Jefferson," in Merrill D. Peterson, ed., *Thomas Jefferson: A Profile* (New York, 1967), 249. See also Charles B. Sanford, *The Religious Life of Thomas Jefferson* (Charlottesville, Va., 1984).

37. Thomas Jefferson to Horatio Gates Spafford, Jan. 10, 1816, *The Writings of Thomas Jefferson*, ed. Paul Leicester Ford (New York, 1899), X, 12–15. See also May, *The Enlightenment in America*, 293, 316, 400 n17. Jefferson's few criticisms of the Anglican clergy are mild compared with his denunciations of the Calvinists. For a recent discussion of the political context of Jefferson's anti-clericalism, see Constance B. Schulz, "Of Bigotry in Politics and Religion': Jefferson's Religion, the Federalist Press, and the Syllabus," *Virginia Magazine of History and Biography*, 91 (1983), 73-91.

38. Jefferson to Spafford, Jan. 10, 1816; Dumas Malone, *Jefferson the Virginian* (Boston, 1948), 109, 276; Julian P. Boyd, ed., *The Papers of Thomas Jefferson* (Princeton, N.J., 1950), II, 7–9; Knoles, "Religious Ideas of Jefferson," 244–45; "Jefferson's Extracts from the Gospels," ed. Dickinson W. Adams, Intro., 14–19.

39. *Minutes of the Vestry, Truro Parish, Virginia, 1732–1785* (Lorton,

Va., 1974); Elizabeth Bryant Johnston, *George Washington, Day by Day* (New York, 1895), 165; Paul F. Boller, Jr., "George Washington and Religious Liberty," in *George Washington: A Profile*, ed., James Morton Smith (New York, 1969), 163–85.

40. Irving Brant, *James Madison the Virginia Revolutionist*, 1751–1780 (New York, 1941), I, 113; Ralph Ketcham, "James Madison and Religion," *Journal of the Presbyterian Historical Society*, XXVIII (1960), 65–70; David Duncan Wallace, *The Life of Henry Laurens* (New York, 1915), 438.

41. *Journal & Letters of Fithian*, ed. Farish, Appx.

42. [Edward Synge], *A Gentleman's Religion: with the Grounds and Reasons of It* (London, 1693), 7, 17, 75–77, 121. The book was reprinted several times in an enlarged edition.

43. Louis Morton, *Robert Carter of Nomini Hall* (Williamsburg, Va., 1941).

44. *Journal & Letters of Fithian*, ed. Farish, 220; see, for example, Hermon Husband's description of a Maryland Anglican service around 1740 in *Some Remarks on Religion* (Philadelphia, 1761), in *Some Eighteenth Century Tracts Concerning North Carolina*, ed. William K. Boyd (Raleigh, N.C., 1927), 214.

45. Knoles, "Religious Ideas of Jefferson," 255.

46. Cotton Mather, *A Good Evening for the Best of Dayes* (Boston, 1708), p. 8; Robin, *New Travels Through North-America . . . 1781* (Philadelphia, 1783), 13.

47. Edward M. Cook, Jr., *The Fathers of the Towns: Leadership and Community Structure in Eighteenth-Century New England* (Baltimore, 1976). 122–31; Robert G. Pope, *The Half-Way Covenant: Church Membership in Puritan New England* (Princeton, N.J., 1969).

48. Robert Taylor *et al*, eds. *Papers of John Adams* (Cambridge, Mass., 1977–), I, 1, 49, 114n1, and *passim*; Howard I. Fielding, "John Adams: Puritan, Deist, Humanist," *Journal of Religion*, 20 (1940), 33–46; John R. Howe, Jr., *The Changing Political Thought of John Adams* (Princeton, N.J., 1966), 226 n36.

49. Bernard Bailyn, *The Ordeal of Thomas Hutchinson* (Cambridge, Mass., 1974), 21–23, 338–39; James K. Hosmer, *The Life of Thomas Hutchinson* (Boston, 1896), 341.

50. William Livingston, *The Independent Reflector*, ed. Milton M. Klein (Cambridge, Mass., 1963), 393, 396n6, 294; "Complete List of the Communicants of this [First Presbyterian] Church, Inserted by Order of the Session at their meeting Dec. 11, 1769," pp. 33–38, First Presbyterian Church Archives, New York City. For more on Livingston's special brand of anti-clericalism, see *The Independent Reflector*, pp. 203–5.

51. Leonard W. Labaree *et al.*, *The Papers of Benjamin Franklin* (New

Haven, Conn., 1960), II, 204; Paul Leicester Ford, *The Many-Sided Franklin* (1898; reprint ed., Freeport, N.Y., 1972), chap. 4.

52. Pauline Maier, "Coming to Terms with Samuel Adams," *American Historical Review*, 81 (1976), 30–31, 34–35; Rhys Isaac, *The Transformation of Virginia, 1740–1790* (Chapel Hill, N.C., 1982), chap. 8.

53. "Journal of Col. James Gordon, of Lancaster County, Va.," *WMQ*, 1st Ser., XI (1902), 98–112, 195–205, 217–36; *ibid.*, XII (1903), 1–12.

54. Michael J. Crawford, ed., "The Spiritual Travels of Nathan Cole," *WMQ*, 3d Ser., XXXIII (1976), 89–126; [Husband], *Some Remarks on Religion*; Muhlenberg, *Journals*, I, 146 and *passim*. On the devout poor, see *The Journal and Major Essays of John Woolman*, ed. Phillips P. Moulton (New York, 1971), 36–37.

55. Philip Greven, *The Protestant Temperament: Patterns of Child-Rearing, Religious Experience, and Self in Early America* (New York, 1977), 23–24; Julia Cherry Spruill, *Women's Life and Work in the Southern Colonies* (Chapel Hill, N.C., 1938), 246–47.

In Virginia's York Hampton Parish in 1758, women were significant contributors to the rector's salary; 33 women appear on a list of 184 persons paying the tithe. The Reverend John Camm, *A Single and Distinct View of the Act, Vulgarly entitled the Two-Penny Act . . .* (Annapolis, Md., 1763).

56. *The Letterbook of Eliza Lucas Pinckney, 1739–1762*, ed. Elise Pinckney *et al.* (Chapel Hill, N.C., 1972), 29.

57. *Ibid.*, 42, 70–71, xxi–xxii. For more on Eliza Pinckney see Nancy Woloch, *Women and the American Experience* (New York, 1984), chaps. 3–4.

58. Mary Beth Norton, *Liberty's Daughters: The Revolutionary Experience of American Women, 1750–1800* (Boston, 1980), 126; Elizabeth Delancey to Cadwallader and Alice Colden [parents], July 2, 1750, New-York Historical Society *Collections*, LIII (1920), 221; June 7, 1752, June 7, 1756, *ibid.*, LXVIII (1935), 112, 154–56.

59. Anne Grant, *Memoirs of an American Lady* (New York, 1901 [orig. publ. London, 1808]), I, 70–71; *Correspondence of Maria van Rensselaer, 1669–1689*, trans. and ed., A.J.F. Van Laer (Albany, N.Y., 1935), 87, 175. See also Alice P. Kenney, *The Gansevoorts of Albany: Dutch Patricians in the Upper Hudson Valley* (Syracuse, N.Y., 1969), 160–69.

60. See, for example, her comment about "a company of young Ladies from Trenton"; *The Journal of Esther Edwards Burr, 1754–1757*, eds. Carol F. Karlsen and Laurie Crumpacker (New Haven, Conn., 1984), 248; *ibid.*, 45, 53, 138, 250, 74.

61. Wright and Tinling, eds., *Byrd's Secret Diary, 1709–1712*, May 1, 1709, p. 29. Mrs. Carter had observed that certain authorities claimed women had no souls, a proposition which her daughter rejected with some

heat; *Journal & Letters of Fithian*, ed. Farish, 82, 111. *Life of Jarratt*, 31–36.

62. Laurel Thatcher Ulrich, "Vertuous Women Found: New England Ministerial Literature, 1668–1735," *American Quarterly*, XXVIII (1976), 20–40.

63. Mary Maples Dunn, "Women of Light," in *Women of America, A History*, ed. Carol Ruth Berkin and Mary Beth Norton (Boston, 1979), 115–33. For further information on the work and history of the Women's Meeting, see Milton D. Speizman and Jane C. Kronick, trans. "A Seventeenth-Century Quaker Women's Declaration," *Signs*, I (1975), 231–45.

64. William L. Lumpkin, "The Role of Women in 18th Century Virginia Baptist Life," *Baptist History and Heritage*, VIII (1973), 158–67. The religious activities of New England women of all ranks are discussed in Laurel Thatcher Ulrich, *Good Wives: Image and Reality in the Lives of Women in Northern New England, 1650–1750* (New York, 1982), esp. 215–26.

65. Muhlenberg, *Journals*, I, 125–27. For further case histories of pious women see *ibid.*, 144–149 and *passim*.

66. Mary Beth Norton, "'My Resting reaping Times': Sarah Osborne's Defense of Her 'Unfeminine' Activities, 1767," *Signs*, II (1976), 515–29.

67. Muhlenberg, *Journals*, I, 143.

68. Julius Friedrich Sachse, *The German Sectarians of Pennsylvania, 1742–1800* (Philadelphia, 1899–1900; reprint ed., 1971), I, 167.

69. *Ibid.*, II, 488, 492; I, 298. The hood must have been especially welcome after 1738, when Beissel inaugurated a plan whereby the sisters' hair was to be cut every three months and their crowns shorn in a tonsure; *ibid.*, I, 347.

70. *Ibid.*, II, chap. 8, p. 196. At least 76 sisters and 77 brothers have been identified as members of the two celibate orders; some hundreds of other men, women, and children were members of the larger Ephrata community; *ibid.*, II, 485–517.

71. *Ibid.*, I, 89–90, 254–58; *Chronicon Ephratense: A History of the Community of Seventh Day Baptists . . . [by] Lamech and Agrippa*, trans. J. Max Hark (Lancaster, Pa., 1889), 55–56.

72. Robert G. Pope, "New England Versus the New England Mind: The Myth of Declension," *Journal of Social History*, 3 (1969–70), 102; Mary Maples Dunn, "Saints and Sisters: Congregational and Quaker Women in the Early Colonial Period," *American Quarterly*, XXX (1978), 591.

73. Cotton Mather, *Ornaments for the Daughters of Zion* [Boston, 1692], Facsimile Reproduction, ed. Pattie Cowell (Delmar, N.Y., 1978), 48;

Greven, "Youth, Maturity, and Religious Conversion," 132; Pope, "New England Versus the New England Mind," 102.

74. Mather, *Ornaments for the Daughters of Zion*, 48–49; Ulrich, "Vertuous Women Found," 31–32; David D. Hall, *The Faithful Shepherd: A History of the New England Ministry in the Seventeenth Century* (Chapel Hill, N.C., 1972), 205.

75. Dunn, "Saints and Sisters," 590–93.

76. See, for example, *New York Quaker Records*, comp. John Cox, Jr. (New York, 1896–1920), II; *New Jersey Quaker Records*, comp. John Cox, Jr. (New York, 1910–1915), New York Public Library. In Pennsylvania monthly meetings, but 1.8 percent more women than men were disowned; Jack D. Marietta, *The Reformation of American Quakerism, 1748–1783* (Philadelphia, Pa., 1984), 28.

77. For a sampling see *Extracts from the Itineraries and Other Miscellanies of Ezra Stiles*, 9–19, 105, 344–50. Stiles seems to have listed single young men separately while listing single young women with their families. On widows, see *ibid.*, 14–17; and especially Heyrman, *Commerce and Culture*, 380–81 and 381 n13; Elaine Forman Crane, *A Dependent People: Newport, Rhode Island in the Revolutionary Era* (New York, 1985), chap. 6.

78. Lumpkin, "Role of [Baptist] Women." In the Germantown, Pa., Lutheran and German Reformed churches, female confirmands outnumbered male by 8 to 6 from 1747 to 1799; Lutheran communicant lists for October to December, 1769 show 69 women and 51 men taking the sacrament. Stephanie Grauman Wolf, *Urban Village: Population, Community, and Family Structure in Germantown, Pennsylvania, 1683–1800* (Princeton, N.J., 1976), 217. See also Susan Klepp, "Five Early Pennsylvania Censuses," *Pennsylvania Magazine of History and Biography*, CVI (1982), 483–514.

79. See his lists of confirmands in *Journals*, I, 505–6, 523–24; II, 70, 354–56; III, 481. Nor does Muhlenberg observe that women came to church or took communion more regularly than men.

80. Dr. Johnson to the Archbishop of Canterbury, Stratford [Conn.], Oct. 20, 1763, in *Documentary History of the Protestant Episcopal Church, . . . Connecticut*, eds. Francis L. Hawks and William S. Perry (New York, 1863) I, 53. Ministers' reports in the SPG and Fulham Papers do not differentiate between men and women. For a rare listing of communicants in which women slightly outnumber men, see A List of the Communicants of the Parish of St. Philip's . . . Charleston, S.C., July 1710–Aug. 1711, American Papers of the SPG, Lambeth Palace, XVII, 21–22 (World Microfilm Publications). See also Joan R. Gundersen, "The Non-

Institutional Church: The Religious Role of Women in Eighteenth-Century Virginia," *Historical Magazine of the Protestant Espicopal Church*, II (1982), 347–57.

81. Howe, "Accommodation and Retreat," 157–59. Men served as vestrymen and churchwardens, and noncommunicating male adherents bought pews and contributed to the ministers' salaries. But power in the Dutch church rested mainly in the hands of the domines; *ibid.*, 157, 164f.

82. Cole, ed., *First Record Book of the "Old Dutch Church of Sleepy Hollow," Organized in 1697.* For itinerant or supply preachers, see Weis, *Colonial Clergy of the Middle Colonies*, 43, 132, 168.

83. "Church Membership of Trinity Church (Lutheran) Corner of Broadway and Rector Street, Justus Falckner Pastor, who also officiated in other places" [1704–1723], transcripts, New York Genealogical Society; Weis, *Colonial Clergy of the Middle Colonies*, 51; "Records of the Round Top Lutheran Church, Pine Plains, New York," ed. Royden Woodward Vosburgh (New York, 1921), 31–46, New York Genealogical Society; Weis, *Colonial Clergy of the Middle Colonies*, 131.

84. For example, in 1769 the First Presbyterian Church of New York City, long served by a permanent minister, had 391 communicants, of whom 62 percent were women; "Complete List of Communicants." The Westfield, N.J., Presbyterian Church, gathered in the 1720s with a preponderance of male members, shared its minister with a congregation at Whippany. A full-time minister arrived in 1759; by the 1760s more women than men joined the church in most years, though couples predominated throughout the 18th century. William K. McKinney *et al.*, *Commemorative History of the Presbyterian Church in Westfield, New Jersey, 1728–1928* (1929), 350–54; Weis, *Colonial Clergy of the Middle Colonies*, 181.

85. *Life of Jarratt*, 16. School teachers supplied by the SPG often catechized both girls and boys. See, for example, Mr. Cleator to the Secretary, Rye, N.Y., Oct. 14, 1717, and Certificate on behalf of Mr. Huddleston, Oct. 15, 1717, [New York City], SPG Records, Letterbooks A, XII, 353–56, 408–10 (micro.).

86. John Calam, *Parsons and Pedagogues: The S.P.G. Adventure in American Education* (New York, 1971), especially chap. 4; Bonomi and Eisenstadt, "Church Adherence," 252, 254–55. That the Fundamental Constitution of Carolina required all settlers aged 17 and above to belong to some church suggests that 17 was considered the age of consent in religious matters; Bolton, *Southern Anglicanism*, 17.

87. Farish, ed., *Fithian's Journal & Letters*, 70, 96, and *passim*.

88. "Petition of the Presbytery of Hanover, 1775," in Charles F. James, *Documentary History of the Struggle for Religious Liberty in Virginia* (Lynchburg, Va., 1900), 44; Richard J. Hooker, ed., *The Carolina*

Backcountry on the Eve of the Revolution, 51. See also William Douglass, *A Summary, Historical and Political, of the . . . British Settlements in North America* (Boston, 1749–1753), II, 48.

89. David Humphreys, *An Historical Account of the Incorporated Society for the Propagation of the Gospel in Foreign Parts . . .* (London, 1730), 148.

90. Muhlenberg, *Journals,* I, 636.

91. *Ibid.,* 504–5, 648, 651–52; *Ibid.,* II, 92.

92. Ibid., I, 505–6, 632–33, III, 481–85; *Ibid.,* I, 144–49, 407, 419.

93. *Ibid.,* 327.

94. James Axtell, *The School Upon a Hill: Education and Society in Colonial New England* (New Haven, Conn., 1974), 37; Alice Morse Earle, *The Sabbath in Puritan New England* (New York, 1900), 55–61.

95. Alice Morse Earle, ed., *Diary of Anna Green Winslow, a Boston School Girl of 1771* (Boston, 1894). For a recent study which suggests that 14 to 16 years was about the youngest age at which New England children (especially boys) began serious study of the catechism, see Ross W. Beales, Jr., "In Search of the Historical Child: Miniature Adulthood and Youth in Colonial New England," *American Quarterly,* 27 (1975), 379–98.

96. Cotton Mather, *Ratio Disciplinae Fratrum Nov Anglorum* (Boston, 1726), 193. And see Charles E. Hambrick-Stowe, *The Practice of Piety: Puritan Devotional Disciplines in Seventeenth-Century New England* (Chapel Hill, N.C., 1982), 140–55.

97. Greven, "Youth, Maturity, and Religious Conversion," 122n6; Joseph Tracy, *The Great Awakening: A History of the Revival of Religion in the Time of Edwards and Whitefield* (Boston, 1842), 111; Mather, *Ratio Disciplinae,* 193.

98. Greven, "Youth, Maturity, and Religious Conversion," 126–27.

99. J. M. Bumsted, "Religion, Finance, and Democracy in Massachusetts: The Town of Norton as a Case Study," *Journal of American History,* 57 (1971), 817–31; J. M. Bumsted and John E. Van de Wetering, *What Must I Do To Be Saved?: The Great Awakening in Colonial America* (Hinsdale, Ill., 1976), 134.; Gerald F. Moran, "Religious Renewal, Puritan Tribalism, and the Family in Seventeenth-Century Milford, Connecticut," *WMQ,* 3d Ser. XXXVI (1979), 254 n52; Walsh, "The Great Awakening in Woodbury, Connecticut," 550–51.

100. John Demos, "Old Age in Early New England," in *Turning Points: Historical and Sociological Essays on the Family,* John Demos and Sarane S. Boocock, eds. (Chicago, 1978), 248–87; Rhys Isaac, "Evangelical Revolt: The Nature of the Baptists' Challenge to the Traditional Order in Virginia, 1765 to 1775," *WMQ,* 3d Ser., (1974), 353 n20; David Hackett Fischer,

Growing Old in America (New York, 1977), chap. 1; on elderly communicants see *Life of Jarratt*, 102.

101. Joy Day Buel and Richard Buel, Jr., *The Way of Duty: A Woman and Her Family in Revolutionary America* (New York, 1984), 226–28.

102. Robert J. Dinkin, "Seating the Meeting House in Early Massachusetts," *New England Quarterly*, XLIII (1970), 453–55; Earle, *Sabbath in New England*, 63.

103. Isaac, *Transformation of Virginia*, 61–65; Dix, *History of Trinity Church*, 217–18. In Truro Parish, Va., the magistrates, merchants, and "the most respectable Inhabitants" got the choice pews; *Minutes of the Vestry*, Feb. 24–25, 1774.

104. The holding of church offices and length of time associated with the congregation seem to have been the determining factors for seat assignment in Muhlenberg's Lutheran churches; see Muhlenberg, *Journals*, I, 586–591, II, 14–15, 26–27.

105. Mr. [Anthony] Gavin to the Bishop of London, St. James Parish, Goochland, Aug. 5, 1738, Fulham Papers, XII, 273–74 (micro.); Bolton, *Southern Anglicanism*, 108–15; Calam, *Parsons and Pedagogues*, 51–54; John C. Van Horne, "Impediments to the Christianization and Education of Blacks in Colonial America: The Case of the Associates of Dr. Bray," *Historical Magazine of the Protestant Episcopal Church*, L (1981), 243–69.

106. Francis LeJau, *The Carolina Chronicle of Dr. Francis LeJau, 1706–1717*, ed., Frank J. Klingberg (Berkeley, Calif., 1956); Peter H. Wood, *Black Majority: Negroes in Colonial South Carolina from 1670 through the Stono Rebellion* (New York, 1974), 131–43; Bureau of the Census, *Historical Statistics*, II, 1168.

107. Answers to the Bishop's Queries. 1724, Fulham Papers, IX, 160–71, quotation on p. 167. (micro.). Mr. Varnod of St. George's Parish, South Carolina, had close to 30 Negroes at his services in 1724, 17 of them communicants. This exception to the usual pattern occurred because all of the blacks were from two devout planter families. See Varnod to the Secretary, Jan. 13,–1724, SPG Records, Letterbooks Series A, XVIII, 70 (micro.).

108. Answers to the Bishop's Queries, 1724, Fulham Papers, XII, 41–84, III, 48–71 (micro.). Even where slaves were most heavily concentrated in Maryland, that is in Calvert, Charles, Prince George's and St. Mary's counties, "several" or "many" slaves were involved with the church. For slave distribution in Maryland, see Russell R. Menard, "The Maryland Slave Population, 1658 to 1730: A Demographic Profile of Blacks in Four Counties," *WMQ*, 3d Ser., XXXII (1975), 29–54.

109. The quotation is in Albert J. Raboteau, *Slave Religion: The "Invisible Institution" in the Antebellum South* (New York, 1978), 346 n36. In

1762 the Rev. Charles Martyn noted that in South Carolina only 500 of some 46,000 Negroes were Christians; Notes attributed to Charles Martyn, April 11, 1762, Fulham Papers, X, 153–54 (micro.).

110. "Journal of Josiah Quincy, Junior, 1773," *Massachusetts Historical Society Proceedings*, XLIX (1915–1916), 455.

111. Answers to the Bishop's Queries, 1724, Fulham Papers, IX, 160–71, XII, 41–84, III, 48–71 (micro.); Hugh Jones, *The Present State of Virginia*, 59–62.

112. Lorenzo J. Greene, *The Negro in Colonial New England* (New York, 1942, 1969), 260.

113. Sheldon Cohen, "Elias Neau, Instructor to New York Slaves," *New-York Historical Society Quarterly*, 55 (1971), 7–27. See also Faith Vibert, "The Society for the Propagation of the Gospel in Foreign Parts: Its Work for the Negroes in North America Before 1783," *Journal of Negro History*, XVIII (1933), 171–212; William Huddleston to the Secretary, New York, Nov. 24, 1722, SPG Records, Letterbooks A, XVI, 212–14 (micro.).

114. Thomas Barclay to the Secretary, Albany, Oct. 20, 1717, SPG Records, Letterbooks A, XII, 307–09; William Andrews to the Secretary, Mohawk Castle, April, 23, Sept. 26, 1717, *ibid.*, 310–12, 337–40 (micro.). And see James Axtell, *The Invasion Within: The Context of Culture in Colonial North America* (New York, 1985), 259–63.

115. Cotton Mather, *Advice from the Watch Tower* (Boston, 1713), 29; Stephen P. Sharples, ed., *Records of the Church of Christ at Cambridge in New England, 1632–1830* (Boston, 1906), 59, 108–9.

116. *Ibid.*; Earle, *Puritan Sabbath*, 62–63; Greene, *Negro in New England*, 262–67; Raboteau, *Slave Religion*, 109–10.

117. Rufus M. Jones, *Quakers in American Colonies*, 498, 521; Raboteau, *Slave Religion*, 110–11.

118. Bray to the Bishop of London, Oct. 28, 1723, Fulham Papers, XXXVI, 50–53; Carville V. Earle, *The Evolution of a Tidewater Settlement: All Hallow's Parish, Maryland, 1650–1783* (Chicago, 1975), 46; Edward Miles Riley, ed., *The Journal of John Harrower: An Indentured Servant in the Colony of Virginia, 1773–1776* (Williamsburg, Va., 1963), see entries for June 26, Aug. 21 and 28, Dec. 25, 1774, and *passim*.

119. Mr. Garden to Dr. Bearcroft, May 6, 1740, Papers Relating to the American Colonies, I, 18, Lambeth Palace Library, London.

120. Muhlenberg, *Journals*, I, 131, 660–61, and *passim*. For servants, see *ibid.*, I, 505–7; II, 354–56; III, 481.

121. Dunn, "Saints and Sisters," 599n26: J. William Frost, *The Quaker Family in Colonial America* (New York, 1973), 54.

122. Rectors of Anglican churches in Oxfordshire, England routinely observed in 1738 that those who absented themselves from Sabbath worship

were of the "lower rank," or of the "meaner sort." Some ministers ascribed the absences to laziness, others to poverty or the need to care for young children, and one allowed as how it might be "partly perhaps for want of decent apparel to appear in amongst their neighbours." Rev. H. A. Lloyd-Jukes, ed., *Articles of Enquiry Addressed to the Clergy of the Diocese of Oxford at the Primary Visitation of Dr. Thomas Secker*, 1738 (Banbury, 1957), quotation on p. 115. For a similar reference about clothing in New York, see Calam, *Parsons and Pedagogues*, 146.

123. [Thomas Prince, Jr.], *The Christian History, Containing Accounts of the Revival and Propagation of Religion in Great-Britain & America. For the Year 1743* . . . *1744* (Boston, 1744–1745), II, 97, 90, 238–39; I, 183; Walsh, "The Great Awakening in Woodbury, Connecticut," 544.

124. Bumsted and Van de Wetering, *What Must I Do To Be Saved?*, 131–34; Charles H. Maxson, *The Great Awakening in the Middle Colonies* (1920; Gloucester, Mass., 1958), 63. The surge of these two groups into the churches is one of the clearest indications, throughout the 18th century, that a revival was in progress. In addition to the sources cited above see Bumsted, "Religion, Finance, and Democracy in Massachusetts"; and Greven, "Youth, Maturity, and Religious Conversion."

125. Charles Chauncy, *Enthusiasm described and caution'd against. A Sermon Preach'd* . . . *the Lord's Day after the Commencement* . . . (Boston, 1742), in Alan Heimert and Perry Miller, eds., *The Great Awakening: Documents Illustrating the Crisis and Its Consequences* (New York, 1967), 241; John Caldwell, *An Impartial Trial of the Spirit Operating in this Part of the World* (Boston, 1742), 27.

126. William Wale, ed., *Whitefield's Journals* (London, 1905), 408.

127. Tracy, *The Great Awakening*, 184–91; Extracts from Wheelock's journal are in *ibid.*, p. 202.

128. William B. Sprague, *Annals of the American Pulpit* (New York, 1857–1869), III, 192–95; Cedric B. Cowing, *The Great Awakening and the American Revolution: Colonial Thought in the 18th Century* (Chicago, 1971), 83–85.

129. Mr. Honeyman to the Secretary, Newport, R.I., June 13, 1743, SPG Papers in Lambeth Palace Library, IV, 218 (micro.); Greene, *Negro in New England*, 269.

130. Carl Bridenbaugh, ed., *Gentleman's Progress: The Itinerarium of Dr. Alexander Hamilton, 1744* (Chapel Hill, N.C., 1948), 163.

131. For an example of such a response in Connecticut, see Harry S. Stout and Peter Onuf, "James Davenport and the Great Awakening in New London," *Journal of American History*, 70 (1983), 560–63.

132. Gary B. Nash, *Red, White, and Black: The Peoples of Early America* (2nd ed., Englewood Cliffs, N.J., 1982), 244–45. There is an

absence of specific comment about either Indians or young people in southern writings about the Great Awakening.

133. George W. Pilcher, *Samuel Davies: Apostle of Dissent in Colonial Virginia* (Knoxville, Tenn., 1971), 112; Farish, ed., *Journal & Letters of Fithian*, July 31, 1774, p. 199.

CHAPTER 5

1. The revivals touched off by Solomon Stoddard and Jonathan Edwards in Northampton, Mass., drew in some other towns along the Connecticut River Valley, but the generalization holds for most revivals. Jon Butler recently has argued that historians should discard the term "Great Awakening" as inadequate and imprecise. Though I am not inclined to accept this recommendation from his otherwise useful essay, my own use of the term is limited to events that took place in the Middle Colonies and New England from 1739 to 1745. Butler, "Enthusiasm Described and Decried: The Great Awakening as Interpretive Fiction," *Journal of American History*, 69 (1982), 305–25.

2. Edwin S. Gaustad, *George Berkeley in America* (New Haven, Conn., 1979), esp. chaps. 5 and 6; James Tanis, *Dutch Calvinistic Pietism in the Middle Colonies: A Study in the Life and Theology of Theodorus Jacobus Frelinghuysen* (The Hague, 1967).

3. Charles Chauncy, *Seasonable Thoughts on the State of Religion in New-England.* . . . (Boston, 1743), 325; Norman S. Fiering, "Will and Intellect in the New England Mind," *William and Mary Quarterly*, 3d Ser., XXIX (1972), 515–58. For more on pietism, see F. Ernest Stoeffler, *Continental Pietism and Early American Christianity* (1976).

4. See, for example, Frederick B. Tolles, "Quietism Versus Enthusiasm: The Philadelphia Quakers and the Great Awakening," *Pennsylvania Magazine of History and Biography*, LXIX (1945), 20–49. For a recent discussion of the part taken by ministers in leading parishioners to embrace the Awakening, see Harry S. Stout and Peter Onuf, "James Davenport and the Great Awakening in New London," *Journal of American History*, 70 (1983), 563, 570.

5. Like many other 18th-century denominations the Presbyterian congregations began as voluntary associations. The few Presbyterians resident in New York City in the first decade of the 18th century, for example, "having neither a minister nor a church, used to assemble themselves, every Sunday, at a private house, for the worship of God." But by the mid-18th century New York's First Presbyterian Church had two services each Sunday (with 60-minute sermons), catechism classes, a Thursday lecture, and a Friday evening service to prepare for communion. *The*

History of the Province of New-York, From the First Discovery to the Year 1732, by William Smith, Jr., ed. Michael Kammen (Cambridge, Mass., 1972), I, 125; Dorothy Ganfield Fowler, *A City Church: The First Presbyterian Church in the City of New York, 1716–1976* (1981), 26–28.

6. Jon Butler, *Power, Authority, and the Origins of American Denominational Order: The English Churches in the Delaware Valley, 1630–1730,* American Philosophical Society *Transactions,* 68, Part 2 (Philadelphia, 1978), 52–64; Guy S. Klett, *Presbyterians in Colonial Pennsylvania* (Philadelphia, 1937).

7. Klett, *Presbyterians in Pennsylvania;* Alfred Nevin, *Churches of the Valley* (Philadelphia, 1852), 82.

8. *The Paxton Papers,* ed. John R. Dunbar (The Hague, 1957), 249.

9. Manuscript Minutes of Donegal Presbytery, vols. I and II, Presbyterian Historical Society, Philadelphia; Klett, *Presbyterians in Pennsylvania,* chaps. 6–9.

10. Donegal Presbytery Minutes, July 19, 1733, I:10, PHS.

11. *Ibid.,* Oct. 16, 1734, Apr. 3 and June 12, 1735, May 27, 1736, I:49, 53, 65, 101–2, 125, 135.

12. *Ibid.,* I:45–48.

13. See note 28.

14. *Ibid.,* Sept., Nov. 1735, Apr. 14, 1736, I:70–75, 87–88, 92, 104–7, 115. Orr sailed for England that same year and was ordained a priest of the Anglican church by the Bishop of London. Early in 1737 he returned to Charleston, S.C., where he became assistant rector at the thriving St. Philip's Church; Frederick Dalcho, *An Historical Account of the Protestant Episcopal Church in South-Carolina* (Charleston, S.C., 1820), 127–28, 355–56.

15. Leonard J. Trinterud, *The Forming of an American Tradition* (Philadelphia, 1949), 73–74.

16. *Records of the Presbyterian Church in the United States of America, 1706–1788,* ed. William M. Engles (Philadelphia, 1904), 92–93. The 1729 act, which included a number of loopholes for those with scruples against subscription to the doctrinal statement written by the Westminster Assembly in the 1640s, was gradually tightened between 1730 and 1736; Bryan F. LeBeau, "The Subscription Controversy and Jonathan Dickinson," *Journal of Presbyterian History,* 54 (1976): 317–35.

17. *Records of the Presbyterian Church,* 139–40. Trinterud, *Forming of an American Tradition,* 74–75.

18. Douglas Sloan, *The Scottish Enlightenment and the American College Ideal* (New York, 1971), 22. A number of universities, but especially Leyden, had an influence on Scottish thought in these years (14–23).

19. *Records of the Presbyterian Church,* 51; Thomas C. Pears, Jr. and

Guy S. Klett, "Documentary History of William Tennent, and The Log College," *Jrnl. of Presb. Hist.*, 28 (1950): 37–64, 105, 128, 167–204.

20. Besides personally directing his sons' educations, Tennent entertained "some hopes" in 1725 of being made rector of Yale College; Pears and Klett, *ibid.*, 57, quote James Logan on this point. There is no evidence that Yale ever approached Tennent with an offer.

21. Trinterud, *Forming of an American Tradition*, chap. 3; Pears and Klett, "History of Tennent," 121–23.

22. *Records of the Presbyterian Church*, 141, 148, 187.

23. Gilbert Tennent, *Remarks Upon a Protestation Presented to the Synod of Philadelphia* (Philadelphia, 1741), 4; *An Examination and Refutation of Mr. Gilbert Tennent's Remarks . . . By Some of the Members of the Synod* (Philadelphia, 1742), 12–13; *Records of the Presbyterian Church*, 188; on the importance of Tennent to Presbyterian education, see Lawrence A. Cremin, *American Education: The Colonial Experience, 1607–1783* (New York, 1970), 324–25.

24. Pears and Klett, "History of Tennent," 195, 120–21.

That William Tennent was not bound by convention is suggested in the legend about the recruitment of one Log College student. Charles Beatty was 14 when he emigrated with his widowed mother from Northern Ireland; when of age he became a traveling peddler. One day Beatty was passing through Neshaminy, and "stopping at the Log College, he amused himself by surprising Mr. Tennent and his pupils with a proffer, in Latin, of his merchandise. Mr. Tennent replied in Latin, and the conversation went on in the same language, with such evidence of scholarship, religious knowledge and fervent piety, that Mr. Tennent urged him to sell what he had, and prepare for the ministry. This he consented to do." See Alfred Nevin, ed., *Encyclopedia of the Presbyterian Church* (Philadelphia, 1884), 61. Beatty was ordained in 1742 and had a successful career; Guy S. Klett, ed., *Journals of Charles Beatty, 1762–1769* (University Park, Pa., 1962).

25. Historians disagree on the number of Log College matriculants. For biographical information see Archibald Alexander, ed., *Biographical Sketches of the Founder and Principal Alumni of the Log College* (Philadelphia, 1851); George H. Ingram's three articles in *Jrnl. of Presb. Hist.*, 12 (1927): 487–511, vol. 13 (1928–29): 358–59, and vol. 14 (1930): 1–27; Richard Webster, *A History of the Presbyterian Church in America . . . until 1760 with Biographical Sketches of its Early Ministers* (Philadelphia, 1857).

For a list of the academies started by the revivalists, with at least six that were founded by Log College men, see Sloan, *Scottish Enlightenment*, 281–84. Finley's curriculum included Latin and Greek classics, logic, arithmetic, geography, geometry, ontology, and natural philosophy.

Ingram, "Story of Log College," 506; Klett, *Presbyterians in Pennsylvania*, 207.

26. This does not mean that the College of New Jersey was an outgrowth of the Log College, however, since other institutions were equally active in supplying its leadership. Jonathan Dickinson and Aaron Burr, first and second presidents of the college, were Yale men and leaders of the academy movement in New Jersey. Thomas Jefferson Wertenbaker, *Princeton, 1746–1896* (Princeton, N.J., 1946), 23–24, 27.

27. Trinterud, *Forming of an American Tradition*, 74, 82, 143; *Whitefield's Journals*, ed. William Wale (London, 1905), 351.

28. There is good evidence that at least a part of the congregation at Nottingham—not only in the Orr episode but for several years previously—had come under the influence of the Tennents' evangelical preaching. New Castle Presbytery supervised and supplied ministers for the congregation at least as early as 1730, and both Gilbert and John Tennent were associated with that presbytery in the later 1720s. In 1729 John Tennent was licensed by New Castle Presbytery; one year later he was criticized in the presbytery minutes for expressing "unsafe and ill grounded" opinions. "The Records of the Presbytery of New Castle upon Delaware," *Jrnl. of Presb. Hist.*, 15 (1932–33), 108, 114–16, 181–89, 193–97, 199–203.

29. Gilbert Tennent, *The Danger of an Unconverted Ministry, Considered in a Sermon on Mark VI.34* (Philadelphia, 1740), in Alan Heimert and Perry Miller, eds., *The Great Awakening: Documents Illustrating the Crisis and Its Consequences* (New York, 1967), 73–75. Here Tennent sounds like the pietistic sectaries of Pennsylvania who criticized the fixed salaries of the church clergy, insinuating that they looked upon the ministry as an office rather than a calling; see *Life and Letters of the Rev. John Philip Boehm . . . 1683–1749* (Philadelphia, 1916), 162.

30. Tennent, *Danger of an Unconverted Ministry*, in Heimert and Miller, eds., *Great Awakening: Documents*, 76–78, 86.

31. *Ibid.*, 84–90, 95–97.

32. Benjamin Franklin first published the sermon in Philadelphia in 1740, with a reprint appearing that same year; a second Philadelphia edition was published in 1741. The first Boston edition appeared in 1742 and was reprinted later that year. Christopher Sauer published a German edition in 1740. Charles Evans, *American Bibliography: A Chronological Dictionary of All Books, Pamphlets and Periodical Publications Printed in the United States . . . 1639–1800* (14 vols., 1903–59), vol. 2.

33. The synod repealed the rule that ministers were never to preach outside their own presbyteries on the ground that the original language was insufficiently flexible, though what exceptions would be allowed was not specified. The synod further confirmed that presbyteries were the main

licensing bodies, but it continued to assert that no minister could join the synod until his educational credentials had been approved by that organization. *Records of the Presbyterian Church*, 151–52.

34. But see note 38.

35. The Old Side ministers of the Philadelphia Synod included Francis Alison (1705–79), Adam Boyd (1692–1768), Robert Cathcart (?–1754), Samuel Caven (1701–50), John Craig (1710–74), Robert Cross (1689–1766), John Elder (1706–92), Robert Jamison (16??–1744), James Martin (16??–1743), Richard Sankey (1700?–1790), John Thomson (1690–1753), Samuel Thomson (1694–1787). Samuel Caven may have been as old as 36 when he arrived in the colonies.

Of the 12, Alison and Elder were educated at Edinburgh; Boyd, Cross, Martin, John Thomson, and possibly John Craig were educated at Glasgow. The others cannot definitely be traced through university registers, but as none attended Harvard or Yale all were presumably educated abroad. Charles A. Briggs, *American Presbyterianism, Its Origin and Early History* (Edinburgh, 1885); Nevin, ed., *Encyclopedia*; Webster, *History of the Presbyterian Church*; William B. Sprague, *Annals of the American Pulpit* (New York, 1857–69), vols. 3 and 4.

36. New Side ministers of the New York Synod included Charles Beatty (1715–72), John Blair (1720–71), Samuel Blair (1712–51), Aaron Burr (1716–57), Eliab Byram (1718–54), Jonathan Dickinson (1688–1747), Samuel Finley (1715–66), Azariah Horton (1715–77), Simon Horton (1711–86), Timothy Jones (1717–94), Joseph Lamb (1690–1749), James McCrea (1711–69), Charles McKnight (1720–78), Ebenezer Pemberton (1705–77), John Pierson (1689–1770), William Robinson (1700?–1746), Robert Sturgeon (?–1750), Charles Tennent (1711–71), Gilbert Tennent (1703–64), William Tennent, Jr. (1705–77), Richard Treat (1708–78), David Youngs (1719–52).

37. Besides the biographical sources cited above, information was drawn from Franklin Bowditch Dexter, *Biographical Sketches of the Graduates of Yale College, with Annals of the College History, October 1701–May 1745* (New York, 1885–1912), and Clifford K. Shipton, *Biographical Sketches of Those Who Attended Harvard College [Sibley's Harvard Graduates]* (Boston, 1873–).

38. Still, a more flexible approach to church government and presbyterial authority might have been forthcoming from the Philadelphia Synod had the Ulster side of its "Scotch-Irish" character outweighed the Scottish side before the split of 1741. The Irish practice of allowing each presbytery to set its own rules regarding creeds, ordination, and such had been followed in early 18th-century Pennsylvania. But as the struggle for power against the New Sides intensified in the early 1740s, the more orthodox

members of the Old Side staked out and defended increasingly conservative positions. These were not always approved by the Irish members, and probably would have been softened had not the contentions and emotionalism of the times forced the Old Sides to close ranks. Elizabeth I. Nybakken, "New Light on the Old Side: Irish Influences on Colonial Presbyterianism," *Journal of American History* 68 (1982): 813–32; Klett, *Presbyterians in Pennsylvania*, chap. 8. For further evidence that Scottish Presbyterianism was far from monolithic, see Ned Landsman, *Scotland and Its First American Colony, 1683–1765* (Princeton, N.J., 1985).

39. Klett, *Presbyterians in Pennsylvania*, 232.

40. Some conservative clergymen had urged in 1738 that the synod "fill our infant church with men eminent for parts and learning," thereby advancing its "honour . . . both at home and among our neighbors, who conceive a low opinion of us for want of such favourable opportunities." *Records of the Presbyterian Church*, 139. For a Pennsylvania matron's observation that "the English think fit sometimes to be very merry upon the ignorance and stupidity of our Presbyterian clerks," see *Gentleman's Progress: The Itinerarium of Dr. Alexander Hamilton*, ed. Carl Bridenbaugh (Chapel Hill, N.C., 1948), 27.

41. Richard Warch, *School of Prophets: Yale College, 1701–1740* (New Haven, Conn., 1973), 169–85.

42. Both groups came largely from middle-class circumstances; their fathers were ministers, magistrates, military officers, tradesmen, and merchants (see bibliographical sources above).

43. *A short reply to Mr. Whitefield's letter* . . . (Philadelphia, 1741) in Heimert and Miller, eds., *Great Awakening: Documents*, 144; Finley, *Christ Triumphing and Satan Raging* (Philadelphia, 1741), *ibid.*, 157, 163.

44. *Records of the Presbyterian Church*, 156; Donegal Presbytery Minutes, 1:258, 253, Presb. Hist. Soc. I have relied heavily on the Donegal Minutes because they are the most detailed of any presbytery. But patterns similar to those discussed here can be found in "Records of the Presbytery of New Castle upon Delaware," *Jrnl. of Presb. Hist.*, 14 (1930): 289–308, 377–84, and 15 (1932–33): 73–120, 159–68, 174–207, and in the Presbytery of Philadelphia Minutes in *Records of the Presbyterian Church*. The battery of charges against ministers recorded in the Donegal Minutes has led one Presbyterian scholar of New Side sympathies to conclude that the Donegal Old Sides were "morally and personally . . . the worst of the synod's clergy" (Trinterud, *Forming of an American Tradition*, 165), an interpretation that should be reconsidered. Charges of misconduct, especially sexual infractions, were a favorite device of those seeking to discredit ministers of any denomination.

45. Donegal Presbytery Minutes, 1: 206–10. Craighead later became a Cameronian Covenanter; he removed to Virginia in 1749, where he served a number of congregations until his death in 1766. Webster, *History of the Presbyterian Church*, 434–37.

46. Donegal Presbytery Minutes, vol. 1, entries for April and May, 231. John Thomson, *The Government of the Church of Christ*, and Samuel Finley, *Christ Triumphing*, in Heimert and Miller, eds., *Great Awakening: Documents*, 110–26, 152–67.

47. Arnold A. Dallimore, *George Whitefield: The Life and Times of the Great Evangelist of the Eighteenth-Century Revival* (London, 1970), I, 531; Joseph Tracy, *The Great Awakening: A History of the Revival of Religion in the Time of Edwards and Whitefield* (Boston, 1842), 87–105; *The Works of the Reverend George Whitefield, M.A. . . .* (London, 1771–1772), I, 220–221.

48. [John Hancock], *The Examiner, or Gilbert against Tennent* (Boston, 1743), quoted in Edwin Scott Gaustad, *The Great Awakening in New England* (New York, 1957), 36; *ibid.*, 30.

49. See the letter of "Anti-Enthusiasticus" in the *Boston Weekly News-Letter*, July 1, 1742; reprinted in Richard L. Bushman, ed., *The Great Awakening: Documents on the Revival of Religion, 1740–1745* (New York, 1970), 45–49.

50. *The Declaration of A Number of the associated Pastors of Boston and Charles-Town relating to the Rev. Mr. James Davenport, and his Conduct* (Boston, 1742); "Extracts from the Private Journal of the Rev. Ebenezer Parkman, of Westborough, Massachusetts," July 8, 1742 through July 20, 1742, in Tracy, *Great Awakening*, 209–210; *ibid.*, 247; *Boston Evening Post*, July 5, 1742, August 2, 1742.

51. *A Testimony . . . against several Errors in Doctrine and Disorders in Practice, which have of late obtained in various Parts of the Land* (Boston, 1743).

52. *The Testimony and Advice of an Assembly of Pastors of Churches in New-England, At A Meeting in Boston July 7, 1743* (Boston, 1743).

53. [William Rand?], *The Late Religious Commotions in New-England Considered* (Boston, 1743), 18. In Massachusetts, if not in Connecticut, New Light rhetoric was relatively restrained. For the best sampling, see [Thomas Prince, Jr.], *The Christian History, Containing Accounts of the Revival and Propagation of Religion in Great-Britain & America. For the Year 1743 . . . 1744* (Boston, 1744–1745).

54. [Charles Chauncy], *A Letter from a Gentleman in Boston . . . Concerning the State of Religion in New-England* (Edinburgh, 1742), in Bushman, ed., *Great Awakening: Documents*, 120; Stiles, *A Looking-glass*

for *Chang[e]lings* (New London, Conn., 1743), in Heimert and Miller, eds., *Great Awakening: Documents*, 312.

55. Charles Chauncy, *Seasonable Thoughts*, 366; *The Testimony and Advice of a Number of Laymen* (Boston, 1743), 6.

56. Jonathan Parsons, *Wisdom Justified of her Children* (Boston, 1742), 50, 54.

57. Thomson, *Government of the Church of Christ*, esp. 54–55; "The Wonderful Wandering Spirit," *The General Magazine*, I (Feb., 1741), in Heimert and Miller, eds., *Great Awakening: Documents*, 150.

58. George Gillespie, *A Sermon Against Divisions in Christ's Churches* (Philadelphia, 1740), 3, Appx., viii–xii; *Great Awakening: Documents*, ed. Bushman, 101. New England separatists frequently told their pastors that they were receiving greater edification elsewhere; *ibid.*, 101–103.

59. Gilbert Tennent, *Danger of an Unconverted Ministry*, 92–93; Finley, *Christ Triumphing*, 27, 28, 30.

60. See, for example, *Great Awakening: Documents*, ed. Bushman. 107.

61. *The Religion of Protestants A Safe Way to Salvation*, in *The Works of William Chillingworth* (London, 1704); *John Locke, A Letter on Toleration*, eds. Raymond Klibansky and J. W. Gough (Oxford, 1968), esp. 149–55 and note 69; Roland N. Stromberg, *Religious Liberalism in Eighteenth-Century England* (New York, 1954), 14–17.

62. Samuel Blair, *A Vindication of the Brethren who were unjustly and illegally cast out of the Synod of Philadelphia* (Philadelphia, 1744), 17, 21–30.

The Americans' use of "minority" was itself quite innovative as the word was just entering the language at this time in England (*Oxford English Dictionary* [Oxford, 1933], IX). I appreciate Professor Caroline Robbins's assistance in researching this point. The only earlier use I have found is in the 1719 Salter's Hall debate, whose voluminous literature includes but one pamphlet with the word "minority." Even then the context is a negative one: "For a *Minority* in any Assembly . . . to dispute the Legality and Force of any thing" approved by the majority "was never suffered in any civilized Community." *An Account of the late Proceedings of the Dissenting Ministers at Salters-Hall* (London, 1719).

63. Blair, *A Vindication of the Brethren*, 37; Gilbert Tennent, *Irenicum Ecclesiasticum, or A Humble Impartial Essay Upon the Peace of Jerusalem* (Philadelphia, 1749), 99, 117.

64. *Great Awakening: Documents*, ed. Bushman, p. 160; Williams, *The essential Rights and Liberties of Protestants. A seasonable Plea for The Liberty of Conscience, and the Right of Private Judgment* (Boston, 1744), 47–49.

65. *Ibid.*, 65. Williams refers specifically to Locke's second treatise on

4–5 and 30; John Dunn, "The Politics of Locke in England and America in the Eighteenth-Century," in *John Locke, Problems and Perspectives*, ed., John W. Yolton (Cambridge, 1969), 73.

66. See C. C. Goen, *Revivalism and Separatism in New England, 1740–1800* (New Haven, Conn., 1962), 96, and chap. 3.

67. [John Cleaveland *et al.*], *A Plain Narrative of the Proceedings which caused The Separation . . .* (Boston, 1747), 3–4, 16.

68. *Ibid.*, 15. It is difficult to determine how many Presbyterian churches divided, but a minimum of 20 to 30 seems reasonable; see Donegal Presbytery Records, vols. 1–2, Presb. Hist. Soc., and *Records of the Presbyterian Church*.

According to C. C. Goen, between 1741 and the Second Great Awakening there were at least 203 separations in Connecticut, Maine, Massachusetts, New Hampshire, Rhode Island, and Vermont; there were 25 in settlements of New Englanders in the Middle Colonies, mainly New York. Only eight of these were Old Light withdrawals. By decade the separations were as follows:

1740s	1750s	1760s	1770–1775	1776 on
87	41	19	22	50

(There was one separation in 1729; for eight no dates are provided.)

Source: Goen, *Revivalism and Separatism*, 300–327.

69. Gilbert Tennent, *The Necessity of Religious Violence in Order to Obtain Durable Happiness* (New York, 1735); Tennent, *Unconverted Ministry*, 86–92.

70. Finley, *Christ Triumphing*, 38; Tennent, *Unconverted Ministry*, 98.

71. Jonathan Edwards, *The Distinguishing Marks of a Work of the Spirit of God* (1741), in Heimert and Miller, eds., *Great Awakening: Documents*, 212–13.

72. Edmund S. Morgan, *Visible Saints: The History of a Puritan Idea* (New York, 1963), 88–94; David D. Hall, *The Faithful Shepherd: A History of the New England Ministry in the Seventeenth Century* (Chapel Hill, N.C., 1972), 96; Perry Miller, *The New England Mind: The Seventeenth Century* (New York, 1939), 443.

73. Gilbert Tennent, *The Duty of Self-Examination* (Boston, 1739), 133.

74. [Prince], *Christian History*, 1743, 126; Edwards, *An Humble Inquiry into the Rules of the Word of God*, in Heimert and Miller, eds., *Great Awakening: Documents*, 432, 434.

75. Ebenezer Frothingham, *The Articles of Faith and Practice, with the*

Covenant that is confessed by the Separate Churches . . . (Newport, R.I., 1750), in Heimert and Miller, eds., *Great Awakening: Documents*, 457. And see Richard Hofstadter, *America at 1750: A Social Portrait* (New York, 1971), 291–92.

76. Edwards, *An Humble Inquiry*, 427, 433–34; Solomon Williams, *The True State of the Question Concerning the Qualifications Necessary to lawful Communion* . . . (Boston, 1751), 142.

77. *America at 1750*, 216.

78. Shurtleff, *A Letter To Those of his Brethren In the Ministry Who refuse to admit The Rev. Mr. Whitefield Into their Pulpits* (Boston, 1745), 3, 10–11.

CHAPTER 6

1. Alan Heimert, *Religion and the American Mind: From the Great Awakening to the Revolution* (Cambridge, Mass., 1966). See reviews by Edmund S. Morgan in *William and Mary Quarterly*, 3d Ser., XXIV (1967), 454–59. and by Sidney E. Mead in *Journal of Religion*, XLVIII (1968), 274–88.

2. J. H. Plumb observes that by 1725 England possessed "an almost monolithic stability"; *The Growth of Political Stability in England, 1675–1725* (London, 1967), 188 and chap. 6.

3. From the election sermon of Joseph Fish, *Christ Jesus the Physician* . . . *May 8, 1760* (New London, Conn., 1760), p. 45.

4. Charles J. Hoadley, ed., *The Public Records of the Colony of Connecticut*, 8 (Hartford, Conn. 1874), 454–57, 521–22; William G. McLoughlin, *New England Dissent, 1630–1833: The Baptists and the Separation of Church and State* (Cambridge, Mass., 1971), I, 363; C. C. Goen, *Revivalism and Separatism in New England, 1740–1800* (New Haven, Conn., 1962), 195.

5. John W. Jeffries, "The Separation in the Canterbury Congregational Church: Religion, Family, and Politics in a Connecticut Town." *New England Quarterly*, LII (1979), 522–49; Goen, *Revivalism and Separatism*, 70–74, 81, 193–97.

6. Isaac Stiles, *A Prospect of the City of Jerusalem, in it's Spiritual Building, Beauty and Glory. Shewed in a Sermon Preach'd at Hartford* . . . *May 13, 1742* (New London, Conn., 1742), 42; Benjamin Trumbull, *A Complete History of Connecticut, Civil and Ecclesiastical* (New London, Conn., 1898), II, 191; Richard L. Bushman, *From Puritan to Yankee: Character and the Social Order in Connecticut, 1690–1765* (Cambridge, Mass., 1967), 237; Goen, *Revivalism and Separatism*, 62.

7. Bruce E. Steiner, "Anglican Officeholding in Pre-Revolutionary

Connecticut: The Parameters of New England Community," *WMQ* XXXI (1974), 381–82.

8. Bushman, *From Puritan to Yankee*, 235.

9. Trumbull, *Complete History of Connecticut*, II, 180–89.

10. *Ibid.*, 158–91.

11. Key pamphlets on either side of the question are Philemon Robbins, *A Plain Narrative of the Proceedings of the Reverend Association and Consociation of New-Haven County, against the Reverend Mr. Robbins of Branford, Since the Year* 1741 (Boston, 1747), and Jonathan Todd, *A Defence of Consociation* (New London, Conn., 1748).

12. Trumbull, *Complete History of Connecticut*, II, 191; Goen, *Revivalism and Separatism*, 197–99, 66; McLoughlin, *New England Dissent*, I, 367–68.

13. On this subject Richard Bushman quotes Dr. Benjamin Gale as follows: "'The several Factions wh. have subsisted in this Colony, originating with the N London Society—thence metamorphisd into the Faction for paper Emissions on Loan, thence into N Light, into the Susquehanna and Delaware Factions—into Orthodoxy,' and finally (he added to bring the progeny up to date) 'now into Stamp Duty.' 'The Actors,' he said were the same throughout, 'each Change drawing in some New Members,'" *From Puritan to Yankee*, 259.

14. Johnson to J. Beach, as quoted in Edmund S. and Helen M. Morgan, *The Stamp Act Crisis: Prologue to Revolution*, rev. ed. (New York, 1962), 289; Jonathan Lee, *A Sermon . . . At Hartford on the Day of the Anniversary Election, May* 8, 1766 (New London, 1766), 23; Oscar Zeichner, *Connecticut's Years of Controversy, 1750–1776* (Chapel Hill, N.C., 1949), 72–77.

15. The quotation appears in Robert Sklar, "The Great Awakening and Colonial Politics: Connecticut's Revolution in the Minds of Men," Connecticut Historical Society *Bulletin*, 28 (1963), 94–95.

16. Louis Leonard Tucker, *Puritan Protagonist: President Thomas Clap of Yale College* (Chapel Hill, N.C., 1962), 208–11; Bushman, *From Puritan to Yankee*, 255; Zeichner, *Connecticut's Years of Controversy*, 252n36.

17. [Benjamin Gale], *A Reply to a Pamphlet, Entitled, The Answer of the Friend in the West* (New London, Conn., 1755), 27.

18. Gale to Silas Deane, February 27, 1775, Connecticut Historical Society *Collections*, 2 (1870), 202.

19. Carl and Jessica Bridenbaugh, *Rebels and Gentlemen: Philadelphia in the Age of Franklin* (New York, 1942), 237–41.

20. Quietistic sects like the Mennonites and Amish shunned involvement in secular affairs.

21. Rufus M. Jones, *The Quakers in the American Colonies* (1911;

reprint edition, New York, (1966), 522–24; Hermann Wellenreuther, "The Political Dilemma of the Quakers in Pennsylvania, 1681–1748," *Pennsylvania Magazine of History and Biography*, XCIV (1970), 135–72; James T. Lemon, *The Best Poor Man's Country: A Geographical Study of Early Southeastern Pennsylvania* (Baltimore, 1972), 49–51.

22. William Smith, *A Brief State of the Province of Pennsylvania* (London, 1755; New York, 1865), 28. An excellent brief discussion of the meeting structure is in Richard Bauman, *For the Reputation of Truth: Politics, Religion, and Conflict Among the Pennsylvania Quakers, 1750–1800* (Baltimore, 1971), Appx. I.

23. *The Journal and Major Essays of John Woolman*, ed. Phillips P. Moulton (New York, 1971), 84, For a copy of the letter see pp. 85–86; for a sample of the debate see 75–93.

24. Bauman, *For the Reputation of Truth*, 73–74.

25. *Ibid.*, 104–5; James Pemberton to John Fothergill and Hinton Brown, Dec. 17, 1765, quoted in *ibid.*, 123–24. Even after 1756 the Quakers comprised half or more of the assemblymen until 1773, when their proportion of members dropped off sharply; Wayne L. Bockelman and Owen S. Ireland, "The Internal Revolution in Pennsylvania: An Ethnic-Religious Interpretation," *Pennsylvania History*, XLI (1974), 125–59, Appx. II.

26. Smith, *Brief State of Pennsylvania*, 28–30. For the Quaker "politiques," see Bauman, *For the Reputation of Truth*, 106.

27. Guy Soulliard Klett, *Presbyterians in Colonial Pennsylvania* (Philadelphia, 1937), 235; Brooke Hindle, "The March of the Paxton Boys," *WMQ*, 3d Ser., III (1946), 461–86. These calculations are based on the data in *ibid.*, note 5, p. 463. Lancaster County sent four representatives.

28. In addition to the Hindle article cited above, an excellent summary of the Paxton episode appears in the introduction to *The Paxton Papers*, ed. John R. Dunbar (The Hague, 1957).

29. Dunbar, ed., *Paxton Papers*, 101, 104; *The Quaker Unmask'd: Or, Plain Truth: Humbly address'd to the Consideration of all the Freemen of Pennsylvania* (Philadelphia, 1764, 2nd ed.), in *ibid.*, 210, 212, 214.

30. The Society of Friends itself offered a restrained response to the attack through its Meeting for Sufferings, reiterating that devout Quakers should withdraw from government rather than act against their beliefs. Bauman, *For the Reputation of Truth*, 113–14.

31. *Minutes of the Provincial Council of Pennsylvania* [Pennsylvania Colonial Records] (Philadelphia, 1838–1853), IX, 126.

32. *The Paxton Boys, A Farce* (Philadelphia, 1764), and *A Looking–Glass For Presbyterians* (Philadelphia, 1764) in Dunbar, ed., *Paxton Papers*, 158, 248, 246, 250, 255.

33. James H. Hutson, *Pennsylvania Politics, 1746–1770* (Princeton, N.J., 1972), chap. 2 and pp. 152–53. For a description of the multilayered character of the colonial Presbyterian Church, see *A Declaration of the Presbyteries of New-Brunswick and New-Castle, judicially met together at Philadelphia, May 26,* 1743 (Philadelphia, 1743), esp. 9ff.

34. Copy of a Circular Letter, March 30, 1764, [Manuscript] Documents Relating to the Province of Pennsylvania and to the American Revolution, American Philosophical Society, Philadelphia. The letter is also reproduced in *A Looking-Glass for Presbyterians*, Dunbar, ed., *Paxton Papers*, 311–12.

35. The letter is reprinted in the *Pennsylvania Chronicle*, September 18, 1769, as "The Circular Letter and Articles of 'some Gentlemen of the Presbyterian Denomination' in the Province of Pennsylvania, March 24, 1764," as well as in [Joseph Galloway], *Historical and Political Reflections on the Rise and Progress of the American Rebellion* (London, 1780), 49–53.

36. *The Scribbler, Being a Letter from a Gentleman in Town to his Friend in the country* (Philadelphia, 1764), 17. Also see the correspondence between Samuel Purviance, Jr., and Col. James Burd for 1764 and 1765 in the Shippen Papers, vol. 6, Historical Society of Pennsylvania.

37. *The Substance of a Council Held at Lancaster August the 28th 1764. By a Committee of Presbyterian Ministers and Elders deputed from all Parts of Pennsylvania, in order to settle the ensuing Election of Members for the Assembly* ([Philadelphia], 1764), 6, 2, 13–14, 17–18.

38. *The Scribbler,* 15–17; *Observations on a late Epitaph* (Philadelphia, 1764), 3–4. During 1764 and 1765 between 10,000 and 15,000 people signed petitions opposing a royal charter; Hutson, *Pennsylvania Politics,* 168.

39. Dietmar Rothermund, *The Layman's Progress: Religious and Political Experience in Colonial Pennsylvania, 1740–1770* (Philadelphia, 1961), 98–100; Hutson, *Pennsylvania Politics,* chap. 3.

40. Purviance to Burd, Philadelphia, Sept. 10, 1764; see also [Burd] to Purviance, September 17, 1764, Shippen Papers, vol. 6, HSP; Allen to Penn, Oct. 21, 1764, Penn Papers, reprinted in Rothermund, *The Layman's Progress,* 188.

41. Benjamin Marshall to Joseph G. Wanton, Philadelphia, Oct. 5, 1764, in "Extracts From the Letter-Book of Benjamin Marshall, 1763–1766," *The Pennsylvania Magazine of History and Biography,* XX (1896), 207. Franklin lost by 18 votes and Galloway by 7; Hutson, *Pennsylvania Politics,* 175. The proprietary party won 11 of 36 seats including Cumberland, York, and Northampton Counties, and one seat in Lancaster County: William S. Hanna, *Benjamin Franklin and Pennsylvania Politics* (Stanford, Calif., 1964), 167.

42. Muhlenberg, *Journal*, II, 18–19, 21.

43. A remarkably detailed description of these negotiations is in Muhlenberg, *Journal*, II, 22–23.

44. *Ibid.*, 55.

45. *Ibid.*, 55–56, 102–3, 107.

46. *Ibid.*, 122. (For a good description of the election of 1764 see Hutson, *Pennsylvania Politics*, 170–76.) Franklin to Richard Jackson, Philadelphia, Oct. 11, 1764, *The Papers of Benjamin Franklin*, ed. Leonard W. Labaree (New Haven, Conn., 1967), XI, 397.

47. Muhlenberg, *Journal*, II, 123.

48. Purviance to James Burd, Sept. 20, 1765, Shippen Papers, vol. 6, HSP.

49. In my reading of 18th-century political comment, I have found this usage nowhere else. Purviance had a remarkably modern conception of political organization and electioneering.

50. Purviance to Burd, Sept. 20, 1765, Shippen Papers, vol. 6, HSP. Most of this letter is reproduced in Rothermund, *Laymen's Progress*, 185–88.

51. Muhlenberg, *Journals*, II, 190–92. Muhlenberg also noted during this conversation that "our German inhabitants have been previously prepared and instructed every year in the public newspaper by the German newspaper publisher, the late Mr. Sauer [Sr.], as to how they should vote and whom they should elect" (191). With Sauer's death in 1758, political leadership of the German community seems to have been taken up more directly by religious leaders, both clerical and lay.

52. Muhlenberg, *Journals*, II, 192, 167–68, 271; John Penn to Thomas Penn, Oct. 14, 1765, quoted in Rothermund, *Layman's Progress*, 104n63.

53. Muhlenberg, *Journals*, II, 273.

54. Wesley M. Gewehr, *The Great Awakening in Virginia*, 1740–1790 (Durham, N.C., 1930), 45–46.

55. George William Pilcher, *Samuel Davies: Apostle of Dissent in Colonial Virginia* (Knoxville, Tenn., 1971), 54, 34.

56. William Henry Foote, *Sketches of Virginia, Historical and Biographical*, 2 vols. (Philadelphia, 1850–1855), I, 176–77; Pilcher, *Samuel Davies*, 121.

57. Foote, *Sketches of Virginia*, I, 183–86, 177, 203.

58. Pilcher, *Samuel Davies*, 58, 56–7.

59. Foote, *Sketches of Virginia*, II, 32–33; 16, I, 283; Pilcher, *Samuel Davies*, 164.

60. Charles F. James, *Documentary History of the Struggle for Religious Liberty in Virginia* (Lynchburg, Va., 1900), 40; Pilcher, *Samuel Davies*, 169; Gewehr, *Great Awakening in Virginia*, 89.

61. Rhys Isaac, *The Transformation of Virginia,* 1740–1790 (Chapel Hill, N.C., 1982), 161–70.

62. L. F. Greene, ed., *The Writings of the Late Elder John Leland* (New York, 1845), 117.

63. Madison to Bradford, April 1, 1774, in James, *Documentary History,* 37.

64. Robert B. Semple, *A History of the Rise and Progress of the Baptists in Virginia* (1810; rev. ed., Philadelphia, 1894), 43; James, *Documentary History,* 33–35; Isaac, *Transformation of Virginia,* 280, 401–2 n11.

65. The quotation is from William Fristoe, *A Concise History of the Ketocton Baptist Association* (Staunton, Va., 1808), 90. Gewehr, *Great Awakening in Virginia,* 193 and note 22; Isaac, *Transformation of Virginia,* 166.

66. Petition from "a Baptist Church at Occaqon, Pr. William Coun[ty]," cited in Isaac, *Transformation of Virginia,* 404n29.

67. As one early commentator observed, the Baptists were "to a man favorable to any revolution by which they could obtain freedom of religion." Semple, *History . . . of the Baptists in Virginia,* p. 62.

68. *Observations on a late Epitaph,* 4.

CHAPTER 7

1. *Speech of Edmund Burke, Esq. on Moving His Resolutions for Conciliation with the Colonies, March* 22, 1775, ed. Thomas Arkle Clark (New York, 1908), 18–21. Among the many Englishmen making similar comments was William Blackstone, who, as Caroline Robbins writes, observed that "the spirit, doctrine and practice of the dissenters were not likely to make them good subjects"; *The Eighteenth-Century Commonwealthman: Studies in the Transmission, Development and Circumstance of English Liberal Thought from the Restoration of Charles II until the War with the Thirteen Colonies* (Cambridge, Mass., 1961), 349.

2. (New York, Johnson Reprint Corporation, 1972), 54 and *passim.*

3. Quentin Skinner traces the development of resistance ideology in Europe, Scotland, and England during the 16th century in *The Foundations of Modern Political Thought* (Cambridge, 1978), esp. vol. II, Pt. 3.

4. *Speech of Edmund Burke,* 29. Bernard Bailyn, *The Ideological Origins of the American Revolution* (Cambridge, Mass., 1967), while sensitive to religious issues and writings, takes a predominantly secular view of opposition thought. See, however, Bailyn, "Religion and Revolution: Three Biographical Studies," in *Perspectives in American History,* 4 (1970), 85–169. Alan Heimert, *Religion and the American Mind: From the*

Great Awakening to the Revolution (Cambridge, Mass., 1966), explores opposition ideas mainly from the perspective of New England evangelical Calvinism. A recent study of the influence of rationalism in all colonies is Henry F. May, *The Enlightenment in America* (New York, 1976).

5. For a sense of how ambiguous the constitutional issues were, see Jack P. Greene, "From the Perspective of Law: Context and Legitimacy in the Origins of the American Revolution," *The South Atlantic Quarterly*, 85 (1986), 56–57.

6. J.G.A. Pocock, *The Machiavellian Moment: Florentine Political Thought and the Atlantic Republican Tradition* (Princeton, N.J., 1975); Robbins, *Eighteenth-Century Commonwealthman*.

7. *Pro Populo Anglicano Defensio* (London, 1651), in *The Works of John Milton* (New York, 1931–38), VII, 111, 115. See also *Eikonoklastes* (London, 1649), esp. 209–35, in *ibid.*, vol. V.

8. *Of Reformation Touching Church Discipline in England* (London, 1641), in *Works of Milton*, III, 46–49.

9. J. R. Jones, *The First Whigs: The Politics of the Exclusion Crisis, 1678–1683* (London, 1961); John Neville Figgis, *The Divine Right of Kings* (Cambridge, 1934).

10. *An Account of Denmark, as it was in the Year 1692* (London, 3rd ed., 1694), esp. chap. 16.

11. W. A. Speck, *Tory & Whig: The Struggle in the Constituencies, 1701–1715* (London, 1970), 7, 42, and *passim*; Geoffrey S. Holmes, *British Politics in the Age of Anne* (London, 1967), 42–47.

12. Benjamin Hoadly, *Some Considerations Humbly offered to the Right Reverend the Lord Bishop of Exeter* (London, 1709), 2, 13, 16. And see Norman Sykes, "Benjamin Hoadly, Bishop of Bangor," in F.J.C. Hearnshaw, ed., *The Social & Political Ideas of Some English Thinkers of the Augustan Age, A.D. 1650–1750* (London, 1928), 112–56.

13. That the sermon was to mark Guy Fawkes's Day apparently inhibited Sacheverell not at all, and may even have appealed to whatever perversity there was in his character.

14. (London, 1709), 7–9, 18, 12, 15. Norman Sykes believes that with the rise of Sacheverell the doctrines of divine right and passive obedience reappeared in all their "pristine vigour"; *Social & Political Ideas*, ed. Hearnshaw, 117.

15. Holmes, *British Politics in the Age of Anne*, 106, 183–84, chap. 10, and p. 238. See also Holmes, *The Trial of Dr. Sacheverell* (London, 1973); Abbie Turner Scudi, *The Sacheverell Affair* (New York, 1939), 11–16 and chap 6.

16. For a discussion of the permutations of English politics from 1688 to 1776 and a review of recent historiography, see J.G.A. Pocock, "Radical

Criticisms of the Whig Order in the Age between Revolutions," in *The Origins of Anglo-American Radicalism*, eds. Margaret Jacob and James Jacob (London, 1984), 33–57. For the fortunes of divine right in the 18th century, see Linda Colley, *In Defiance of Oligarchy: The Tory Party, 1714–60* (Cambridge, 1982.)

17. *The Independent Whig* (London, 8th ed., 1753), No. 1; J. M. Bulloch, "Thomas Gordon, The 'Independent Whig'," *Aberdeen University Library Bulletin*, 3 (1915–18), 598–612.

18. *Independent Whig*, Dedication and Nos. 2, 12,

19. *Ibid.*, Nos. 14, 15, 41.

20. *Cato's Letters* (London, 3rd ed., 1733; reissued New York, 1969), No. 66, No. 138.

21. Robbins, *Eighteenth-Century Commonwealthman*, 221–33; Roland N. Stromberg, *Religious Liberalism in Eighteenth-Century England* (London, 1954), chap. 9.

22. Bailyn, *Ideological Origins*, 34–35; *Pamphlets of the American Revolution, 1750–1776*, ed. Bernard Bailyn (Cambridge, Mass., 1965), 204–11.

23. *The Independent Whig* appeared in a Philadelphia edition in 1724 and again in 1740; David L. Jacobson, ed., *The English Libertarian Heritage: From the Writings of John Trenchard and Thomas Gordon in "The Independent Whig" and "Cato's Letters"* (New York, 1965), lxii. Milton's pamphlet, *An Old Looking Glass for the Laity and Clergy . . .*, was republished in Philadelphia in 1770. The colonial newspapers, of course, regularly published excerpts from the radical satirists. For a comment about how the ordinary inhabitants of the town of Oyster Bay, New York, read *The Independent Whig*, see Thomas Keble to the Secretary, April 4, 1743, SPG Records, Letterbooks Ser. B, XI (Micro Methods Ltd.). For a similar comment from Cecil County, Md., see William S. Perry, *Historical Collections Relating to the American Colonial Church* (New York, AMS reprint, 1969), IV, 321–22.

24. *New-York Weekly Journal*, January 21, 1734.

25. Jonathan Mayhew, *A Discourse Concerning Unlimited Submission and Non-Resistance to the Higher Powers* (Boston, 1750), Pref. 11–13, 20, 29, 45.

26. *Ibid.*, note, 37–39.

27. *Ibid.*, 40, 45–6, 54. That there was actually very little divine-right preaching in colonial America (Bailyn, ed., *Pamphlets*, 696n5) accords with the suggestion made here that the growth of Anglicanism, especially in New England, had stirred up Mayhew on this subject. The best brief discussion of Mayhew's sermon is in Bailyn, *Pamphlets*, 204–11, 695–99.

28. Bailyn, ed., *Pamphlets*, 207–9; quotation on 209.

29. Milton M. Klein, ed., *The Independent Reflector, or Weekly Essays on Sundry Important Subjects More particularly adapted to the Province of New-York, by William Livingston and Others* (Cambridge, Mass., 1963), 27–28, 326, 320.

30. [Bland], *The Colonel Dismounted: Or the Rector Vindicated* (Williamsburg, Va., 1764), in Bailyn, ed., *Pamphlets*, 323–24; Landon Carter, *A Letter to the Right Reverend Father in God, The Lord B——p of L——n* (Williamsburg, Va., 1759 [?]), 47–49; Adams, *A Dissertation on the Canon and Feudal Law*, in *The Works of John Adams*, ed. Charles Francis Adams, III (Boston, 1851), 454.

31. For a discussion of this issue see Anne Young Zimmer and Alfred H. Kelly, "Jonathan Boucher: Constitutional Conservative," *Journal of American History*, 58 (1972), 897–922.

32. Richard Hofstadter, *The Idea of a Party System: The Rise of Legitimate Opposition in the United States, 1780–1840* (Berkeley, Calif., 1970); the quotation is from Swift, *ibid.*, 2. Pauline Maier, *From Resistance to Revolution: Colonial Radicals and the Development of American Opposition to Britain, 1765–1776* (New York, 1972), chap. 2.

33. *Cato's Letters*, No. 14; Peter Laslett, ed., *John Locke, Two Treatises on Government: A Critical Edition* (Cambridge, Mass., 1960); *Second Treatise*, paras. 204, 207, 215; Robbins, *Eighteenth-Century Commonwealthman*, 7–8 and *passim*.

34. John Locke, *A Letter on Toleration*, ed. Raymond Klibansky and J. W. Gough (Oxford, 1968), 127.

35. See especially Carl Bridenbaugh, *Mitre and Sceptre: Transatlantic Faiths, Ideas, Personalities, and Politics, 1689–1775* (New York, 1962).

36. Arthur Lyon Cross, *The Anglican Episcopate and the American Colonies* (New York, 1902); Frederick V. Mills, Sr., *Bishops by Ballot: An Eighteenth-Century Ecclesiastical Revolution* (New York, 1978). Concerning the absence of support in England for a colonial bishop, see Herbert Schneider and Carol Schneider, eds., *Samuel Johnson, President of King's College, His Career and Writings* (New York, 1929), III, 256–60, 277–78, 286–88.

37. Patricia U. Bonomi, *A Factious People: Politics and Society in Colonial New York* (New York, 1971), 248–54. For the earlier history of Anglican-dissenter disputes in New York, see Donald F. M. Gerardi, "The King's College Controversy 1753–1756 and the Ideological Roots of Toryism in New York," *Perspectives in American History*, XI (1977–1978), 147–96.

38. Klein, ed., *Independent Reflector*, 25–26, 267–77; William M. Hogue, "The Religious Conspiracy Theory of the American Revolution: Anglican Motive," *Church History*, 45 (1976), 277–92.

39. Adams to Dr. J. Morse, Quincy, Dec. 2, 1815, in *Works of Adams*, ed. C. F. Adams, X (1856), 185; Alison to Ezra Stiles, Aug. 7, 1766, cited in Bridenbaugh, *Mitre and Sceptre*, 272; see also 305n32, 321.

40. Mayhew to Thomas Hollis, Boston, April 6, 1762, Massachusetts Historical Society *Proceedings*, LXIX (Boston, 1956), 128–29; Edmund S. Morgan, *The Gentle Puritan: A Life of Ezra Stiles, 1727–1795* (New Haven, Conn., 1962), 221–25; Mills, *Bishops by Ballot*, 111–13. For a Dissenter's evaluation of North Carolina's Governor Dobbs, see Elizabeth I. Nybakken, ed., *The Centinel: Warnings of a Revolution* (Newark, Del., 1980), 214.

41. On Pennsylvania see *The Journals of Henry Melchior Muhlenberg*, trans. Theodore G. Tappert and John W. Doberstein (Philadelphia, 1942), II, 191–92. John Webb Pratt, *Religion, Politics, and Diversity: The Church-State Theme in New York History* (Ithaca, N.Y., 1967), 74, 76.

42. Stiles to Jonathan Mayhew, April 15, 1763, in Bridenbaugh, *Mitre and Sceptre*, 224; Cooper to William Livingston, April 18, 1768, in *ibid.*, 298.

43. Smith, "A Brief Account of the State of the Church of England in the British Colonies in America, 1762," American Papers of the SPG, Lambeth Palace Library (World Microfilm Publications), X, 166, 146. Many Americans linked the growth of the Church of England with support for British authority. See Gov. Joseph Martin to Dartmouth, Nov. 4, 1774, in *The Colonial Records of North Carolina*, ed. William L. Saunders (Raleigh, N.C., 1886–1890), IX, 1086–87; Nybakken, ed., *The Centinel*, 92–93 and *passim*.

44. Mayhew, *Remarks on an Anonymous Tract, entitled An Answer to Dr. Mayhew's Observations On the Charter and Conduct of the Society for the Propagation of the Gospel in Foreign Parts* (Boston, 1764), 62; Bridenbaugh, *Mitre and Sceptre*, 220–29, 240–41.

45. Adams, *Dissertation*, 451, 464; A Letter from the Clergy in Convention, Perth Amboy, October 3, 1766, SPG Records, Letterbooks Ser. B., XXIV, 314, London (micro.).

46. "It is a certain Truth," they stated, "that Dissenters in general, and particularly Presbyterians and Congregationalists were the active Promoters of the Rebellion." Clergy of New York to [?], Oct. 28, 1780, American Papers of the SPG, Lambeth Palace Library, X, 189–96 (micro.).

47. Chandler, *Appeal* (New York, 1767), 58, 79–81, 110–11, 107. For dissenter reaction to Chandler's effort see Nybakken, ed., *The Centinel*, p. 173.

48. *A Sermon Preached before the Incorporated Society for the Propagation of the Gospel . . . On Friday, February 20, 1767, by John Lord*

Bishop of Llandaff (London, 1767; reprinted New York, 1768), 5–6; Livingston to Noah Welles, April 23, 1768, cited in Bridenbaugh, *Mitre and Sceptre*, 304.

49. Charles Chauncy, *A Letter to a Friend* (Boston, 1767), 51; Bridenbaugh, *Mitre and Sceptre*, 294–95.

50. (New York, 1768; reprinted in Boston, 1768); Bonomi, *A Factious People*, 248–51; Nybakken, ed., *The Centinel*, Introduction; Bridenbaugh, *Mitre and Sceptre*, 300.

51. *Ibid.*, 31, 264–65. For a detailed look at how one moderate and rational American grew increasingly uneasy over this prospect, see Morgan, *The Gentle Puritan: Ezra Stiles*, esp. chap. 16.

52. Ezra Stiles, *A Discourse on the Christian Union* . . . (Boston, 1761), in *The Great Awakening: Documents Illustrating the Crisis and Its Consequences*, eds. Alan Heimert and Perry Miller (New York, 1967), 605; Franklin Bowditch Dexter, ed., *Extracts from the Itineraries and Other Miscellanies of Ezra Stiles* . . . (New Haven, Conn., 1916), 427, 467–68, and *passim*; Morgan, *The Gentle Puritan: Ezra Stiles*, 241–46.

53. "Minutes of the General Convention of Delegates Appointed by the General Association of Connecticut, 1766 to 1775," in *Records of the Presbyterian Church in the United States of America, 1706–1788*, ed. William M. Engles (Philadelphia, 1904), Appx. 18–19, 26.

54. *Ibid.*, 22–23, 32. If, however, the bishop proposal were to gain ground, the men from Massachusetts would unite with the others to fight it; p. 24.

55. The Hart quotation is in *Stiles Itineraries*, ed. Dexter, 496; Stiles's rising concern about mixing religion and politics is discussed in Morgan, *Gentle Puritan*, 248–54; for a more activist view of Stiles's participation in religious politics see Bridenbaugh, *Mitre and Sceptre*, 276–77.

56. "Minutes of the Convention of Delegates," 27–30.

57. *Ibid.*, 33. The committee network described here, as well as that established earlier by Pennsylvania Presbyterians (see pp. 174–75), was undoubtedly a model for the American Revolutionaries. See also Bridenbaugh, *Mitre and Sceptre*, 202–4.

58. Ebenezer Jessup to Dr. Auchmuty, Feb. 22, 1773, SPG Papers, Ser. C, Box 2 (New York and New Jersey), 1730–1791, no. 65, USPG Archives, London. Whitehall apparently instructed that any conveyance of the land to St. Peter's be delayed.

59. London instructed Governor Tryon to reverse the decision regarding the Dutch Reformed Church; Earl of Dartmouth to Tryon, May 4, 1775, *Documents Relative to the Colonial History of the State of New York*, eds. Edmund B. O'Callaghan and Berthold Fernow (Albany, N.Y., 1853–1887), VIII, 572–74. Boucher was no 18th-century Filmerite, but he should not

have been suprised that in 1775 no colonial press would print a sermon advising Americans "to be quiet, and to sit still" before their governments. Bailyn, *Ideological Origins*, 317; Zimmer and Kelly, "Jonathan Boucher," 897–922.

60. The characterization is Alan Heimert's, in *Religion and the American Mind*, 367.

61. *Ibid.*, 351–52.

62. North Carolina Delegates to Elihu Spencer, Philadelphia, Dec. 8, 1775, in Paul H. smith *et al.*, eds., *Letters of Delegates to Congress, 1774–1789* (Washington, D.C., 1976–), II, 461; Jonathan Sewell to General Frederick Haldimand, May 30, 1775, in Jack P. Greene, ed., *Colonies to Nation, 1763–1789; A Documentary History of the American Revolution* (New York, 1975), 267; the Serle quotation is in Charles Royster, *A Revolutionary People at War* (New York, 1979), 19.

63. [John Adams], *Novanglus: or A History of the Dispute with America* (1774), in C. F. Adams, ed., *Works of John Adams*, IV, 55–56.

64. See, for example, Jonathan Mayhew, *A Sermon Preach'd . . . May 29, 1754, Being the Anniversary for the Election* (Boston, 1754). On the general subject of clergymen's influence in New England communities, see Richard D. Brown, "Spreading the Word; Rural Clergymen and the Communication Network of 18th-Century New England," *Proceedings of the Massachusetts Historical Society*, XCIV (1982), 1–14.

65. John Adams to Abigail Adams, July 7, 1775, in Smith, ed., *Letters of Congress*, I, 602; Adrienne Koch, ed., *The American Enlightenment* (New York, 1965), 288–89; *The Diary of Colonel Landon Carter of Sabine Hall, 1752–1778*, ed. Jack P. Greene (Charlottesville, Va., 1965), II, 818.

66. John Elder to Col. James Burd, Paxton, Nov. 24, 1774, Shippen Papers, VII, 107, Historical Society of Pennsylvania; [John Witherspoon], *A Pastoral Letter from the Synod of New-York and Philadelphia to the Congregations Under Their Care; to be read from the Pulpits on Thursday, June 29, 1775, being the Day of the General Fast* (New York, 1775). The pastoral letter recommended continuing loyalty to the king, who it suggested was being misled by his councillors. For Virginia, see Philip Davidson, *Propaganda and the American Revolution, 1763–1783* (Chapel Hill, N.C., 1941), 90 n15.

67. David L. Holmes, "The Episcopal Church and the American Revolution," *The Historical Magazine of the Protestant Episcopal Church*, XLVII (1978), 267–68, 280–83; Otto Lorenz, "The Virginia clergy and the American Revolution, 1774–1799" (unpublished Ph.D. Diss. University of Kansas, 1970); S. Charles Bolton, *Southern Anglicanism: The Church of England in Colonial South Carolina* (Westport, Conn., 1982), 79.

68. Charles W. Akers, *The Divine Politician: Samuel Cooper and the*

American Revolution in Boston (Boston, 1982); Alice M. Baldwin, *The New England Clergy and the American Revolution* (New York, 1958), 94–95, 159–61, and chaps. 8–9; *Peter Oliver's Origin & Progress of the American Rebellion: A Tory View*, eds. Douglass Adair and John A. Schutz (Stanford, Calif.; paperback reprint, 1967), 104; Christopher M. Jedrey, *The World of John Cleaveland: Family and Community in Eighteenth-Century New England* (New York, 1979), 135.

69. Elihu Spencer, pastor of the church at Trenton, New Jersey, and the Rev. Alexander McWhorter of Newark (both of whom were active in the annual dissenter conventions) spent the early months of 1776 on the frontier, for which they were paid $261 each by the Congress. North Carolina Delegates to Spencer, Philadelphia, Dec. 8, 1775, in Smith, ed., *Letters of Congress*, II, 459–61, and note 2.

70. Witherspoon, *The Dominion of Providence over the Passions of Men: A Sermon Preached at Princeton, On the* 17th *of May, 1776, Being The General Fast appointed by the Congress through the United Colonies. To Which is added, An Address to the Natives of Scotland residing in America* (Philadelphia, 1776); North Carolina Delegates to the Presbyterian Ministers at Philadelphia, July 3, 1775, in Smith, ed., *Letters of Congress*, I, 575; Joseph Hewes to Samuel Johnston, July 8, 1775, *ibid.*, I, 613.

71. "A Fragment of a Journal Kept by Rev. William Tennent . . . [Aug. 2, 1775–Sept. 15, 1775]," and miscellaneous correspondence, in R. W. Gibbes, *Documentary History of the American Revolution* (New York, 1855); *Philip Vickers Fithian: Journal, 1775–1776*, eds. Robert G. Albion and Leonidas Dodson (Princeton, N.J., 1934), 64.

72. Alexis de Tocqueville, *Democracy in America*, ed. Phillips Bradley (New York, 1945), I, 317.

73. For the importance of radical whig as opposed to millennial themes in the sermon literature, see Melvin B. Endy, Jr., "Just War, Holy War, and Millennialism in Revolutionary America," *WMQ*, 3d Ser., XLII (1985), 3–25. No more than about one-sixth of the patriotic writings by ministers in the Revolutionary era stressed millennial motifs; *ibid.*, 17.

74. Langdon, *Government corrupted by Vice; a Sermon preached before the Honorable Congress of the Colony of Massachusetts Bay, on the* 31st *of May, 1775*, in Frank Moore, ed., *The Patriot Preachers of the American Revolution* (New York, 1860), 52; Stillman, *A Sermon preached before the Honorable Council, and Honorable House of Representatives of the State of Massachusetts Bay, May* 26, 1779, *ibid.*, 275; Griffith, *Passive Obedience Considered in a Sermon Preached at Williamsburg, December* 31, 1775 (Williamsburg, Va., 1776), 22.

75. Witherspoon, *Dominion of Providence*, 40–41; William Foster, *True Fortitude Delineated: A Sermon Preached at Fags Manor to Captain*

Taylor's Company of Recruits on the Lord's Day, February 18, 1776
(Philadelphia, 1776), 12; William Smith, *A Sermon on the Present Situation
of American Affairs, preached in Christ Church, Philadelphia, June* 23d,
1775, in Moore, ed., *Patriot Preachers,* 105.

76. Duché, *The Duty of Standing Fast in our spiritual and temporal
Liberties* . . . (1775), in Moore, ed., *Patriot Preachers,* 80; Whitaker, *An
Antidote against Toryism, or the Curse of Meroz* (1777), *ibid.,* 197–200;
Griffith, *Passive Obedience Considered,* 25; William Gordon, *A Discourse
Preached December* 15, 1774, *Being the Day Recommended by the
Provincial Congress; and Afterwards at the Boston Lecture* (Boston, 1775),
11–12.

77. Whitaker, *Antidote against Toryism,* in Moore, ed., *Patriot Preachers,* 206; Carmichael, *A Self-Defensive War Lawful, Proved in a Sermon,
Preached at Lancaster, before Captain Ross's Company of Militia, in the
Presbyterian Church on Sabbath Morning, June* 4, 1775 (Lancaster, Pa.,
1775), 10–11; Howard, *A Sermon Preached To the Ancient and Honorable
Artillery-Company, in Boston, New-England, June* 7, 1773 (Boston, 1773),
14.

78. Duché, *The American Vine, A Sermon, Preached in Christ-Church,
Philadelphia, Before the Honorable Continental Congress* . . . , *July* 20,
1775 (Philadelphia, 1775), 27; Langdon, *Government corrupted by Vice,* in
Moore, ed., *Patriot Preachers,* 65; Oliver Hart, *Dancing Exploded, A
Sermon showing the unlawfulness, sinfulness, and bad consequences of
Balls, Assemblies, and Dances in general* (Charleston, S.C., 1778), in
Moore, ed., *Patriot Preachers,* 232–57; Charles Chauncy, *The Accursed
Thing . . . A Sermon Preached at the Thursday Lecture* (Boston, 1778). Alan
Heimert agrees that Chauncy's sermon was a jeremiad, though "a reason-
able one"; *Religion and the American Mind,* 487.

79. Smith, *A Sermon on the Present Situation,* in Moore, ed., *Patriot
Preachers,* 108, 111; Witherspoon, *Dominion of Providence,* 69.

80. John J. Zubly, *The Law of Liberty, A Sermon on American Affairs,
preached at the opening of the Provincial Congress of Georgia* (1775), in
Moore, ed., *Patriot Preachers* 128; Griffith, *Passive Obedience Considered,*
14, 17–19; William Foster, *True Fortitude Delineated,* 11–12.

81. Witherspoon, *Dominion of Providence,* 28, 40–42, 68; Langdon,
Government corrupted by Vice, in Moore, ed., *Patriot Preachers,* 362; and
see also William Gordon, *A Discourse Preached December* 15, 1774, 5–11.
The theme was familiar from at least 1750, with Jonathan Mayhew's
Discourse on Unlimited Submission. It was renewed during the Stamp Act
crisis by such as Stephen Johnson of Connecticut (see Richard L. Bushman,
From Puritan to Yankee: Character and the Social Order in Connecticut,
1690–1765 [Cambridge, Mass., 1967], 266 and chap. 16, and Bernard

Bailyn, "Religion and Revolution: Three Biographical Studies," *Perspectives in American History*, 4 [1970], 85–169). By the 1770s the nonresistance theme was a commonplace of Massachusetts election sermons (A. W. Plumstead, ed., *The Wall and the Garden: Selected Massachusetts Election Sermons*, 1670–1775 [Minneapolis, Minn., 1968]) and of patriot sermons throughout the colonies.

82. William Gordon, *The Separation of the Jewish Tribes, after the death of Solomon, accounted for, and applied to the present day* (1777), in Moore, ed., *Patriot Preachers*, 158–85; Peter Thacher, *Oration Delivered at Watertown, March 5, 1776* (Watertown, Mass., 1776), 14; William Linu, *A Military Discourse Delivered in Carlisle [Pennsylvania], March 17, 1776, To Col. Irvine's Battalion of Regulars and a very respectable number of Inhabitants* (Philadelphia, 1776), 15.

83. David Jones, *Defensive War in a just Cause Sinless, A Sermon, Preached on the Day of the Continental Fast, at Tredyffryn, in Chester County* (Philadelphia, 1775), 6–19. For a particularly good example of this class of sermon, see Carmichael, *A Self-Defensive War Lawful*. For the origins of this notion in 16th-century thought, see Skinner, *Foundations of Modern Political Thought*, II, 309.

84. Linn, *A Military Discourse*, 14–15; Peter Laslett, ed., *Locke . . . Second Treatise*, para. 21, 168, 241, 242; Klibansky and Gough, eds., *Locke . . . Letter on Toleration*, 129; *Cato's Letters*, No. 59.

85. Royster, *A Revolutionary People at War*, 171.

86. David Tappan, *A Discourse delivered in the Third Parish in Newbury, Massachusetts . . . 1783*, in Moore, ed., *Patriot Preachers*, 302; George Duffield, *A Sermon preached in the Third Presbyterian Church in the City of Philadelphia . . . 1783, ibid.*, 362, Robert Smith, *The Obligations of the Confederate States of North America . . . 1781* (Baltimore, 1783), 14–15.

CHAPTER 8

1. *Democracy in America by Alexis de Tocqueville*, ed. Phillips Bradley (New York, 1945 [orig. publ. Paris, 1835–1840]), I, 319; *Domestic Manners of the Americans by Frances Trollope*, ed. Donald Smalley (New York, 1949 [orig. publ. London, 1832]), 111ff; George E. Probst, ed., *The Happy Republic: A Reader in Tocqueville's America* (New York, 1962), 225. And see Eric L. McKitrick and Stanley Elkins, "Institutions in Motion," *American Quarterly*, 12 (1960), 188–97.

2. Mr. Hunt to the Secretary, May 6, 1728, Records of the SPG, Letterbooks Series A, XXI, 97–104 (Micro Methods, Ltd.); J. Hector St. John Crèvecoeur, *Letters from an American Farmer* (Garden City, N.Y.,

n.d. [orig. publ. London, 1782]), 54–56. For denominationalism, see Sidney E. Mead, *The Lively Experiment: The Shaping of Christianity in America* (New York, 1963), chap. 7.

3. *Democracy in America*, ed. Bradley, I, 319, II, chap. 15; Probst, ed., *Happy Republic*, 213; Harriet Martineau, *Society in America*, ed. Seymour Martin Lipset (Garden City, N.Y., 1962 [orig. publ. New York, 1837]), 344. The Bryce quotation is in Michael McGiffert, ed., *The Character of Americans: A Book of Readings* (Homewood, Ill., 1964; rev. ed., 1970), 75.

4. Patricia U. Bonomi and Peter R. Eisenstadt, "Church Adherence in the Eighteenth-Century British American Colonies," *William and Mary Quarterly* 3d Ser., XXXIX (1982), 245–86.

5. Henry F. May, *Ideas, Faiths, and Feelings: Essays on American Intellectual and Religious History, 1952–1982* (New York, 1983); Christine Leigh Heyrman, *Commerce and Culture: The Maritime Communities of Colonial Massachusetts, 1690–1750* (New York, 1984), chaps. 3, 5, 8, 11, and *passim*; Darrett B. Rutman and Anita H. Rutman, *A Place in Time: Middlesex County, Virginia, 1650–1750* (New York, 1984), 52–59, 122–25, and *passim*.

6. *Democracy in America*, ed. Bradley, I, 314.

Index

Adams, John, 197, 209; religious
  beliefs of, 103; on Anglican bishop,
  200, 202
Adams, Samuel, 104
Alison, Francis, 142, 173, 200, 206,
  207
Allen, John, 174
Allen, William, 173, 174, 175
American Revolution: and the Great
  Awakening, 152, 160, 161, 167; and
  religious politics, 172, 185–86,
  187–216; political ambiguity of, 188,
  270 (n5)
Anabaptists, 19, 20, 58, 73
Andrews, William, 121
Anglican bishop, 54, 189–90; for the
  colonies, 30–31, 41, 42–43; in
  Revolutionary politics, 199–209, 222,
  274 (n54)
Anglicans, 40, 41–61, 91–92, 219; and
  colonial governors, 16, 43–44, 46,
  49, 50, 51–54, 200–201; in Virginia,
  16–17, 42–46, 48–49, 57, 59, 89,
  97–102, 119–20, 181–82, 184–85,
  210; in Maryland, 24, 46–49, 119–20,
  232 (n20); and the Restoration,
  30–31, 41–42, 229 (n42); in Georgia,
31, 32–33, 50; in South Carolina,
  32, 49–50, 55, 58, 60–61, 92,
  106, 119, 210; in North Carolina, 32,
  50, 98, 200; in Carolina, 32, 250
  (n86); in New Jersey, 35, 50, 53,
  54, 56–57; and commissaries, 41,
  43–44, 46, 47, 49–50, 122;
  expansion of, 41, 54, 61, 81, 195,
  201; financial support of church, 42,
  46–47, 48–50, 51–54, 100; in
  New England, 50, 62, 64–65, 68,
  202, 205; in New York, 51–54,
  56–57, 58, 81, 90, 93, 120–21,
  205–8, 233 (n38); in Pennsylvania,
  53, 54, 58, 89, 93, 175, 178,
  200–201, 205; in Connecticut, 54,
  56, 66, 164–65; in Massachusetts, 54,
  62, 93, 202; catechism and
  communion, 56, 58, 88–89, 100–101,
  115–16, 119–22, 250 (n85); clergy
  and laity, 58, 60–61; social
  composition of, 92–94, 96–97, 252
  (n103), 253 (n122); and Indians,
  119–21; and blacks, 119–21, 125, 252
  (nn107–9); and Glorious Revolution,
  190–91, 192; in the 18th century,
  191–95; and the American

Anglicans (*continued*)
    Revolution, 199–208, 210, 222; in
    the Middle Colonies, 202–3, 206.
    See also Anglican bishop; Clergy;
    Society for the Propagation of the
    Gospel
Anglicization: in New York, 93; in the
    Revolutionary era, 200–203, 206, 273
    (n43)
Anne, queen of England, 36
Anticlericalism, vii, 100, 103, 245
    (n37); absence of, in America, 222
Antis, Frederick, 178
Apthorp, East, 202
Armstrong, John, 175
Atheism, rarity of, in 18th century, 73,
    88, 90, 241 (n4)

Bacon's Rebellion, 42
Baptists, 92, 125; in New England, 29,
    65, 229 (n39); in Carolina, 32; in
    New Jersey, 35; in Virginia, 45,
    184–86; and social rank, 94–95, 97;
    and women, 108, 112–13; in
    Pennsylvania, 175, 179; and
    American Revolution, 185, 208, 269
    (n67). *See also* Anabaptists
Barnard, John, 117
Barnes, Mary, 137
Bartow, John, 56
Beatty, Charles, 257 (n24)
Becket, William, 55–56
Beissel, Conrad, 109
Berkeley, George, 131
Berkenmeyer, William, 76
Bernard, Francis, 200
Blacks, 49, 99; as churchgoers, 108,
    119–22, 124–26, 252 (nn107–9);
    proportion of, in population,
    119–20; and the Great Awakening,
    124–26
Blackstone, William, 269 (n1)
Blair, James, 43–44, 46, 57
Blair, Samuel, 142, 155
Bland, Richard, 197
Boehm, John Philip, 75, 78

Boschi, Charles, 60–61
Boston, 20, 27, 197, 201; sabbath
    practice in, 5–6, 102; and Quakers,
    27, 28; number of churches in, 90;
    congregations, 93–94; and the Great
    Awakening, 149–51; and American
    Revolution, 210
Boucher, Jonathan, 208, 274 (n59)
Boyle, Robert, 106
Bradford, William, 18
Bradstreet, Simon, 63
Brainerd, David, 124
Brattle Street Church (Boston), 62, 68,
    93, 210
Brattle, Thomas, 68
Bray, Thomas, 122
Bryce, James, 220
Brycelius, Paul, 176–77
Burd, James, 175
Burke, Edmund, 187, 188
Burr, Aaron, Sr., 107
Burr, Esther Edwards, 107
Bushman, Richard, 165
Byrd, William, II, 98–99, 102, 107,
    116, 245 (n35)

Calvert family, 21–22, 23–24
Cambridge University, 45, 56
Camm, John, 197
Carmichael, John, 212–13
Carolina (colony), 31–32
Carter, Frances, 107
Carter, John (of Shirley), 98
Carter, Landon, 5, 44, 197, 210
Carter, Robert ("King"), 99
Carter, Robert (of Nomini Hall), 101,
    104, 115, 126
Catechization, 89, 115–18; of children
    and servants, 106, 122, 250 (n85); of
    blacks, 122
Catholics, 30; in Maryland, 21–24, 46;
    in Carolina, 32; in Georgia, 33; in
    Pennsylvania, 36, 230 (n54)
Cato's Letters, 194–95, 216
Chandler, Thomas Bradbury, 203, 205,
    207–8

Charles I, king of England, 21, 172, 189, 196, 214
Charles II, king of England, 30, 31, 36, 179
Charleston, South Carolina, 58, 59, 60; number of churches in, 92
Chauncey, Charles, 123–24, 205, 210, 213
Chevalier, Michel, 220
Children and youths: as churchgoers, 69, 115–18; catechization of, 106, 115–18, 250 (n85)
Chillingworth, William, 154–55
Church adherence, vii, 56, 81–82, 87–92, 102, 235 (n60); decline of questioned, 7–8, 220–21; and the Great Awakening, 123–26; *See also* Churchgoing; Congregations
Church and state, 13–15, 200; changing attitudes toward, 15, 21–23, 24–26, 28–29, 33–37, 60–62; in Virginia, 15–17; in New England, 17–19, 26–29, 61, 64, 66, 237 (n71); in New Netherland, 24–25; in Restoration England, 30–31; separation of, 35; in New York, 51–54. *See also* Anglicization
Churches; size and description of, 8, 55–57, 59–60, 67–68, 75, 77, 84–85, 90–92, 235 (nn56, 58); and moral oversight, 16, 40, 60–61, 80, 135–38, 240 (n110); and ecclesiastical consolidation, 40, 44, 58, 61–66, 82–85, 133–34; as voluntary associations, 50, 72, 74–80, 82–84, 135, 156, 217, 220, 255 (n5); destruction of, 58; as community centers, 67, 74, 87–88, 134, 186, 218; feminization of, 111–15, 123, 249 (nn78–80), 250 (n84). *See also individual denominations*
Churchgoing: motives for, 87–92, 105; among children and youths, 88, 108, 115–18, 122, 123; obstacles to, 88–89, 115–16, 122; and social rank, 92–97, 122–23, 125; and men,

97–105, 111–12, 123, 125, 250 (n81); and women, 105–15, 116, 123–24, 125; among blacks, Indians, and indentured servants, 116, 119–23, 124–26; and the aged, 118–19; effect of the Great Awakening on, 123–26; in American culture, 220–21. *See also* Church adherence
Clap, Thomas, 167
Clark, Jonas, 210
Clarke, Samuel, 4
Cleaveland, John, 211
Clergy, 31, 39–85; shortage of, 7, 15, 16, 18, 23, 36, 40, 42, 50, 72, 74–79 *passim*, 82, 84, 89; numbers grow, 8, 19, 58, 59, 70, 84, 126, 231 (n5), 238 (n86); professionalization of, 39, 40–41, 44–45, 58, 62–66, 70–71, 78–80, 82–84, 133–34, 139–49, 155, 156; in comparative perspective, 39–40, 46, 48, 54–55, 61, 70, 72–73, 79–81, 84, 140, 260 (n40); criticism of, evaluated, 39, 41, 45–46, 47–49, 77, 80, 231 (n14), 232 (nn23, 24), 238 (n82), 260 (n44); social and cultural role of, 39, 71–72, 134–35, 137, 162, 201; and tenure in office, 42–49 *passim*, 56, 71, 79, 80, 82–83; Scottish, 43, 47, 48, 133–35, 145–46; education of, 45–46, 48, 70, 134, 139–42, 144–47, 184, 232 (n25), 238 (n87), 259 (n35), 260 (n40); daily life of, 54–61, 66–72, 75–80, 82–84, 134; as itinerants, 55–57, 58, 70, 75–76, 90, 113, 125, 134, 135, 142–44, 163, 181–82; licensing of, 64, 66, 70, 77, 78, 79, 139–40, 141, 144, 146, 239 (n106); financial support of, 70–71, 73, 80, 165–66, 232 (n17), 233 (n34), 238 (n91); and feminization of churches, 112, 113–15; in the American Revolution, 209–16, 222. *See also individual denominations*
Clergy and laity, 40, 43, 44–45, 46–47, 60–61, 63, 75–80, 82–84, 112–15; Presbyterians, 134–38, 147–49,

Clergy and laity (*continued*)
173–75, 183–84; in the Great
Awakening, 152, 157–60; in
Connecticut, 165–66, 236 (n64);
Quakers, 169–71; in Pennsylvania,
176–77, 240 (n119); and German
churchpeople, 176–80; in Virginia,
184–86. *See also* Leadership; Parish
life
Coddington, William, 20
Cole, Nathan, 105
Coleman, Benjamin, 71, 111
Committees of correspondence, 186;
Presbyterian, 174–75; and
convention of dissenters, 206–7; in
the American Revolution, 210, 274
(n57)
Communicants, 88–89, 111, 115–18,
241 (n6)
Congregationalists, 40; in New Jersey,
35; and ecclesiastical reform, 61–72,
84, 236 (nn64, 68); in New England,
61–72, 84, 90, 149–54, 156–57,
158–60, 184, 206–7, 209; and Church
of England, 62, 64; communion and
catechization, 62, 67, 69, 71, 88;
financial support of clergy, 65, 66,
103; and Saybrook Platform, 65–66,
164–65; and singing reforms, 67, 68;
expansion of, 67, 70, 72; and musical
instruments, 68, 237 (n79); social
composition of, 93–94, 96; ages of
members, 94, 117–18, 251 (n95);
feminization of, 111–13; children and
youths, 117–18; and elderly
parishioners, 118; blacks and
Indians, 121–22, 124; and the Great
Awakening, 149–52, 156–60, 163–66,
262 (n58); and the American
Revolution, 187, 206–8, 273 (n46);
and convention of dissenters, 206–7.
See also Churchgoing; Clergy; Parish
life
Congregations: numbers of, 61, 72;
compared with town meetings, 186,
218; organization of, 220–21

Connecticut, 62; Quakers in, 26, 66;
and Church of England, 54, 56, 66,
164–65; General Court and religion,
65, 66, 163–67; and ecclesiastical
reform, 65–66; attitude toward
dissenters, 66, 163; and Baptists, 66,
165; religion and politics in, 162–68,
206–7. *See also* New England
Cooper, Samuel, 201, 210
Cornbury, Lord, *see* Hyde, Edward
Cotton, Elizabeth, 107
Cotton, John, 18
Craig, John, 183
Craighead, Alexander, 148, 261 (n45)
Crèvecoeur, Hector St. John de, 219

Dale, Thomas, 16
Dartmouth College, 124
Davenport, James, 124, 150, 163
Davies, Samuel, 125–26, 142, 181–83
Deference, and the Great Awakening,
133, 139, 152–53
DeLancey, Elizabeth Colden, 106
Denominational networks, 9, 168–70,
173–75, 176–81, 184–86, 267 (n33)
Denominationalism, 73; and religious
competition, 7, 9, 39, 40, 57–58,
72–74, 75, 80–81, 92, 132, 219; and
politics, 162–68. *See also* Great
Awakening, and church schisms
Devotional literature, 4–5, 223 (n2)
Dissenters: as vestrymen, 49, 50; in
New York, 51–53; and tradition of
political resistance, 172–73, 187–89,
193, 195–99, 208, 216, 269 (n1); and
the American Revolution, 185–86,
187–216; in England, 195;
convention of, 206–7. *See also*
individual denominations
Divine Right, doctrine of: in colonial
America, 188–89, 195–99, 214; in
England, 188–93, 194, 270 (n14);
rarity of, in colonies, 271 (n27)
Doddridge, Philip, 4
Drayton, William Henry, 211
Duché, Jacob, 212, 213

Dunster, Henry, 19
Dyer, Mary, 28, 108

Ecclesiastical courts, 16, 43, 135–38,
140, 200, 203
Edinburgh, University of, 140, 146
Edwards, Jonathan, 107, 117, 158–60,
255 (n1)
Elder, John, 210
Eliot, Andrew, 205
Emerson, William, 208
Endicott, John, 27, 28
Ephrata Cloister, 109–11, 248
(nn69–70)
Ethnicity, in the colonies, vii, 168
Evangelical religion: style of, 104–5,
108–9, 124–27, 131–33, 138n,
142–45, 147–49, 184; defined, 138n;
and New Side Presbyterians,
139–49, 153–55; and New Light
Congregationalists, 150–52, 156–57,
158–60, 163–67; and the American
Revolution, 188, 208, 211; in
American culture, 219–20. *See also*
Great Awakening
Ewer, John, 203–5
Ewing, John, 173

Factions, 153; political and religious,
compared, 154; in Connecticut,
162–68, 265 (n13); in Pennsylvania,
168–81; in Virginia, 181–86; in
18th-century Anglo-America, 198–99
Falckner, Justus, 76
Fauquier, Francis, 183
Finley, Samuel, 142, 154, 158, 163
Fithian, Philip, 5; on Virginia, 97–98,
101, 107, 115; on black piety, 126;
and the American Revolution, 211
Fitzhugh, William, 4, 99
Fletcher, Benjamin, 51
Franklin, Benjamin, 103–4, 176, 177,
178
Frelinghuysen, Theodore, 131
French and Indian War, 183

Gale, Benjamin, 167, 265 (n13)
Galloway, Joseph, 176, 187, 207
Garden, Alexander, 122
Gardiner, Horred, 27–28
Gavin, Anthony, 119
George I, king of England, 195
George II, king of England, 197
Georgia, and Anglican establishment,
31, 32–33, 50
Germans: in the Middle Colonies,
72–85, 134, 135; in Pennsylvania
politics, 169, 175, 176–80. *See also*
Lutherans; Reformed
Glasgow, University of, 145, 146
Goetschi, Henry, 77
Gooch, William, 181–82
Gordon, James, 104–5
Gordon, Thomas, 193–95, 198, 216
Gordon, William, 212
Gorton, Samuel, 20
Great Awakening, 37, 213; causes of,
8, 133, 255 (n4); and church schisms,
8–9, 132–34, 138–40, 143–45,
147–49, 150–57, 160, 164–65, 263
(n68); in New England, 66, 149–54,
156–60, 162–66; and the Middle
Colonies, 73, 81, 131–49; effect of,
on churchgoing, 123–26; and
Presbyterians, 133, 138–49, 153–55,
157–58; in Pennsylvania, 133,
139–49; and social rank, 147, 150; in
Boston, 149–51; and the American
Revolution, 152, 160, 161, 167, 186;
and individualism, 157–60; defined,
225 (n1). *See also* Evangelical
religion
Griffith, David, 212, 213–14
Gumby, Dadda, 126

Hager, John Frederick, 76
Hamilton, Alexander (of Maryland),
125
Hamilton, Thomas, 218
Harrison, Sarah, 43
Harrison, William, 56–57
Harrower, John, 122

Hart, Oliver, 213
Hart, William, 207
Harvard College, 19, 52, 70, 146–47,
    150, 202
Henderson, Jacob, 57
Higginson, Francis, 18
Hoadly, Benjamin, 191, 193, 200
Hofstadter, Richard, vii, 160
Hooker, Thomas, 18
Howard, Simeon, 213
Hughes, John, 179
Huguenots, 32
Hunt, Brian, 60
Hunter, Robert, 75
Husband, Hermon, 105, 246 (n44)
Hutchinson, Anne, 18, 19, 20, 103,
    108
Hutchinson, Thomas, 103
Hyde, Edward (Lord Cornbury),
    52–53

Ideology of dissent, 188, 198–99, 208;
    roots in England, 188–95
Independent Whig, The, 193–94;
    influence of, in the colonies, 195,
    197, 271 (n23)
Indians: and frontier settlers, 58,
    171–72, 176; as churchgoers, 119–22,
    124–25
Ingersoll, Jared, 166
Inglis, Charles, 57, 205

James II, king of England, 24, 192,
    214, 229 (n42)
Jarratt, Devereaux, 89, 107, 115
Jefferson, Thomas, 81, 210; religious
    beliefs of, 100, 102, 245 (n37)
Jews, 23, 108, 143–44; in New
    Netherland, 25, 227 (n28); in
    Carolina, 32; in Georgia, 33; in
    Pennsylvania, 36, 230 (n54);
    Maryland, 227 (n22)
Johnson, Nathaniel, 49
Johnson, Samuel (SPG clergyman), 56,
    61, 113
Johnson, Stephen, 277 (n81)

Johnson, William (of New York), 206
Johnson, William Samuel, 166
Jones, Hugh (of Virginia), 46

Kay, William, 44
Keppel, Henry, 178
King George's War, 58, 104
King's Chapel (Boston), 61, 68, 93, 103
King's College (New York), 197
Kocherthal, Joshua, 76
Kraft, Valentin, 79

Laity, *see* Churchgoing; Clergy and
    laity; Parish life
Langdon, Samuel, 212, 213, 214
Latitudinarianism, 8, 57–58, 73–74;
    resisted, 74; English writers on,
    154–55; in American culture, 217,
    218–19
Laurens, Henry, 101
Lay preachers, 18, 20, 75, 105; and the
    sects, 74; and German churchpeople,
    75–79; and the Great Awakening,
    126, 164
Leadership, in the colonies:
    consolidation of, 37, 40, 42; by laity
    and clergy, 75, 77–78, 82; female,
    108–9; and the Great Awakening,
    133, 139, 161–62, 168; clerical, 162,
    168, 186, 218 275 (n64)
Lee, Jonathan, 166–67
Leyden University, 256 (n18)
Livingston, Gilbert, 6
Livingston, William; religious beliefs
    of, 103; on passive obedience, 197;
    and Anglican bishop controversy,
    200, 203, 205
Locke, John, 5, 98, 106, 154, 156, 198,
    199, 212, 216
Log College, 140–42, 146, 257 (n25)
Logan, James, 5, 171
Lumbrozo, Jacob, 227 (n22)
Lutherans, 40, 72–73, 77; in New
    Netherland, 25; in Georgia, 32, 77;
    and voluntary association, 72, 74,
    76–77, 81; in Pennsylvania, 74,

76–79, 175, 176–80, 252 (n104); and clerical professionalism, 74, 79, 219; in New York, 76, 78–79; in New Jersey, 76, 79; and feminization of the church, 113–15; children and youths, 116–17; and politics, 176–80; and the American Revolution, 211

Madison, James, 101, 184
Maine, 151–52
Martineau, Harriet, 220
Maryland: and religious toleration, 13, 21–24, 226 (n20); Catholics in, 21–24; and religious diversity, 22–24; Quakers in, 23; Church of England in, 24, 46–49, 119–20, 232 (n20)
Massachusetts: General Court and religion, 18, 63, 65; establishment of religion in, 18–19, 64; and Quakers, 26–29; and Church of England, 54, 62, 93, 202; and Congregational churches, 61–65, 68–72, 102; and the Great Awakening, 149–52, 156–57, 158–60. *See also* New England
Mather, Cotton, 62, 64, 68–69, 71, 90, 102; and female churchgoers, 111; describes youth group, 117; and blacks, 121
Mather, Increase, 62, 68, 71, 237 (n76)
Mather, Richard, 18
Mayhew, Jonathan: on divine right and passive obedience, 196–97; on Anglican bishop, 200; and Church of England, 202
Men, as churchgoers, 97–105, 111–12, 123, 125
Mennonites, 74, 95, 176, 178–79
Methodists, 125
Middle Colonies, 8, 10; and religious voluntarism, 72, 82–84; Germans in, 72–85; character of religion in, 80–84, 90, 93, 102, 103–4, 106–7, 121–22; population growth in, 90; and the Great Awakening, 131–49

Millennialism, and the American Revolution, 9, 188, 276 (n73)
Milton, John, 106, 189–90, 195, 200
Minorities, rights of, 153–57, 188, 262 (n62)
Molesworth, William, 190–91
Montesquieu, 198
Moravians, 32–33, 176, 178, 240 (n109)
Monson, Samuel Eliot, 19
Morris, Lewis, 53, 81
Muhlenberg, Henry Melchior, 79–80, 84, 105; and female parishioners, 108, 109, 113; and catechization of the young, 116–17; and indentured servants, 122; in Pennsylvania politics, 176, 177–80, 268 (n51)

Neau, Elias, 121
New England, 40; and establishment of religion, 17–19; number of ministers in, 18, 19, 70–71; denies religious toleration, 26–29, 66; and Church of England, 50, 62, 64–65, 68, 202, 205; and half-way covenant, 62, 102; Great Awakening in, 66, 149–54, 156–60; best churched section, 90; clergy and the American Revolution, 209–210. *See also* Congregationalists; Connecticut; Massachusetts
New Jersey: and the Quakers, 35; and the Church of England, 35, 50, 53, 54, 56–57; Lutherans in, 76, 79
New Hampshire, 54, 151
New Netherland: and religious diversity, 24; church and state in, 24–26; and Jews, 25; Quakers in, 25–26; and Lutherans, 25, 76
New York (colony), 106–7; and Reformed Church, 24–25, 75–76, 78, 91, 208; and Church of England, 51, 58, 81, 90, 93, 120–21, 205–8, 233 (n38); Anglicans in Queens, Richmond, and Westchester counties, 51–54, 56, 57; Trinity Parish, 52, 90, 93; St. Peter's

New York (colony) (*continued*)
Church (Albany), 58, 208; conversion
of blacks and Indians in, 120–21
New York City, 6, 51–54, 90, 255 (n5)
North Carolina, 84; and Church of
England, 32, 50, 98, 200; and the
American Revolution 209, 211
Nunez, Samuel, 33

Occum, Samson, 124
Oehl, John Jacob, 76
Oglethorpe, James, 33
Oliver, Jerusha Mather, 107
Orr, William, 137–38, 256 (n14)
Osborne, Sarah Hagger, 108–9
Oxford University, 45

Paine, Elisha, 164
Paine, Solomon, 156
Parish life, 59; in Virginia, 16–17, 55,
57, 92–93, 97–102, 104–5, 115–16,
125–26; in Massachusetts, 18–19,
67–72, 93–94, 102–3, 105, 117–18,
150–52, 158–60; in Maryland, 46–47,
92–93; in South Carolina, 49–50, 55,
58, 60–61, 89–90, 92–93; in Georgia,
50; in New York, 52–53, 56, 57, 58,
75–76, 93; on the southern frontier,
54–55, 60–61, 115–16, 119, 183–86;
in Pennsylvania, 55–56, 57, 58,
74–78, 89, 93, 109, 116, 134–38,
147–49, 169–70, 173–75; in
Connecticut, 56, 93, 164–66; in New
Jersey, 56–57; on the northern
frontier, 70, 75–76, 121, 134–38; in
North Carolina, 89; in Rhode Island,
108–9; in cities, 116–17, 218; in the
American Revolution, 211. *See also*
individual cities; Churchgoing;
Sabbath
Parrington, Vernon L., 9, 221
Parsons, Jonathan, 152
Passive obedience, 188–90, 192–97,
208, 212–14
Pawling, Henry, 179
Pemberton, James, 170

Penn, John, 173, 180
Penn, Thomas, 93, 175
Penn, William, 35–36
Pennsylvania (and Delaware): freedom
of conscience in, 33, 35–37, 81; and
Quakers, 35–36, 57, 88, 91, 168–74,
176–81; and Anglicans, 50, 53, 54,
58, 89, 93, 175, 178, 200–201, 205;
Reformed in, 74–75, 78, 175,
176–80; and Lutherans, 76–80, 175,
176–80; Great Awakening in, 133,
139–49, 258 (n29); Presbyterians in,
135–49, 171–77, 178, 179;
representation in, 171
Peter, Hugh, 18
Philadelphia, 168; Christ Church, 58,
104; number of churches in, 90;
St. Peter's Church, 91, 93; and
Lutherans, 116, 176–78; 180; and
the Paxton Boys, 171, 176–77;
religion and politics in, 173–74,
176–80, 209
Pietism (continental), 131–32
Pinckney, Eliza Lucas, 106
Plymouth Colony, 18, 20
Politics, moderation of, in 18th
century, 161–62
Pontiac's War, 171
Popery, 190; as high-church
Anglicanism, 191, 194
Prentice, Solomon, 156
Presbyterians, 19, 30, 40, 92; in
Carolina, 32; in Georgia, 32; in New
Jersey, 35; in Virginia, 45, 57,
104–5, 181–84; in New York, 52–53,
255 (n5); in Pennsylvania, 57,
135–49, 171–77, 178, 179, 259 (n38),
260 (n42); in South Carolina, 58; and
social rank, 95–97; and the Great
Awakening, 133, 138–49, 153–55,
157–58, 258 (n33); and ecclesiastical
structure, 133–35, 139, 146–47, 256
(n16); Donegal, Presbytery of,
135–38, 148–49, 260 (n44); and
frontier warfare, 171–72; in politics,
171–79; and the American

Revolution, 187, 206–7, 209–11, 212–16, 273 (n46) 276 (n69); in North Carolina, 209, 211
Price, Richard, 212
Prince, Sarah, 107
Princeton, College at, 107, 142, 258 (n26)
Professionalization, *see* Clergy, professionalization of
Puritans, 66, 88, 104, 203–4; as problem in historiography, 6–7; on church and state, 17–19, 26–29, initial disarray of, 18–19; and church admission, 19, 29; in Maryland, 21; and Quakers, 26–29, 65, 228 (nn31–34, 36–37); oppose toleration, 26–29, 202. *See also* Congregationalists
Purviance, Samuel, Jr., 174, 175, 179, 181, 206, 268 (n49)

Quakers, 6, 21, 40, 51, 122; in Maryland, 23; in New Netherland, 25–26; in Massachusetts, 26–29, 65; in Carolina, 32; and freedom of conscience, 33, 36; in New Jersey, 35; and Roger Williams, 35, 229 (n49); in Pennsylvania, 35–36, 57, 88, 91, 168–74, 176–81; in South Carolina, 58; London Yearly Meeting of, 65; in the Middle Colonies, 73; and social rank, 94–97; and women, 108, 112; attitudes toward blacks, Indians, and indentured servants, 122–23; and politics, 168–74, 176, 178–81, 266 (n25), 266 (n30); peace doctrine of, 169–72, 176

Randolph, Peyton, 182
Reformed (church and churchgoers), 40, 72–73, 80; in New Netherland, 24–25; as voluntary association, 72, 74, 81; and clerical professionalism, 74, 78; sacraments and catechization, 74, 75, 78; in Pennsylvania, 74–75, 78, 175, 176–80; in New York,

75–76, 78, 91, 244 (n26), 274 (n59); social composition of, 95–96; and feminization, 113, in the Revolutionary era, 206, 208, 211
Regulators, 209
Religion: in colonial culture, vii–viii, 3–6, 9–10, 39, 67, 69–70, 71–72, 84; decline of questioned, vii–viii, 6–8, 15, 37, 69, 71, 72–73, 81, 85, 126, 220–21; folk, 7, 8, 14, 19, 137, 224 (n12); and the American Revolution, 9, 102, 187–216; of radical sects, 14, 19, 20–21; and immigration, 26, 31, 32–33, 73–74, 132, 134; as a source of radicalism, 162; in American culture, 217–22; and modernism, 221
Religion and politics, vii–viii, 9; in the North, 34–35, 102, 162–68, 168–81; 195–96; in the South, 43, 49, 50, 181–86; effect of the Great Awakening on, 132–33, 152–60; in the Revolution, 187–216; and the bishop controversy, 199–209, 222; and the clergy, 209–16
Religious identity, vii, 74, 82
Religious liberty, 222; in Rhode Island, 20–21, 23, 33–35, 37; in Georgia, 32–33, 50; in New Jersey, 35; in Pennsylvania, 35–36; and vitality of churches, 81, 84, 240 (n115). *See also* Church and state
Religious rationalism, 9, 97–104, 106, 131–32, 147, 161, 188, 208, 211–12, 219, 221
Religious sociology, viii, 217–18, 221–22
Religious toleration, 15; in Maryland, 21–24; in New Netherland, 24–26; in New England, 29, 61, 64, 65; in the Restoration colonies, 31–37. *See also* Church and state
Rhode Island, 26; chaotic beginnings of, 19–21; freedom of conscience in, 20–21, 23, 33–35, 37; and Church of England, 54
Robbins, Philemon, 165

Robin, Abbé, 102
Robinson, Mrs. (of Pennsylvania),
    137–38
Robinson, William (Quaker), 28
Robinson, William (Presbyterian),
    145–46
Ross, Elizabeth, 136–37
Ross, John, 136–37
Rowland, John, 140, 142

Sabbath: in Virginia, 5, 59, 98, 101; in
    Boston, 5–6; in Charleston, 59; in
    New England, 67–69; on the
    frontier, 135; political uses of, 173,
    178, 186. *See also* Churchgoing;
    Parish life
Sacheverell, Henry, 191–93, 194, 197,
    270 (nn13–14)
Saltonstall, Guerdon, 65
Sauer, Christopher, Sr., 110, 268
    (n51)
Sauer, Maria Christiana, 110
Schlatter, Michael, 80, 96
Schwenckfelders, 176, 178
Scots, 43, 47, 48, 81; and the
    Enlightenment, 98; and the Great
    Awakening, 133–35, 139–40, 145–46,
    259 (n38); in Pennsylvania politics,
    171–73; in the American Revolution,
    211
Secker, Thomas, 61
Sectaries, 74, 95, 109–11, 176, 178
Serle, Ambrose, 209
Sermons: printing of, 4; as public
    attractions, 4, 69, 77; frequency of,
    56, 58, 67; in Congregational
    churches, 67, 68–69, 209, 223 (n2);
    in the Church of England, 101–2;
    and the Great Awakening, 143–44,
    157–58; themes of, in the American
    Revolution, 209–16, 276 (n73), 277
    (n81)
Servants, as churchgoers, 69, 122–23
Sewall, Samuel, 67
Seymour, John, 46
Shepherd, Thomas, 18

Sherman, Roger, 167
Shippen, Edward, Jr., 175
Shippen, Edward, Sr., 175
Shurtleff, William, 160
Silliman, Mary Fish, 118
Smith, William (of Pennsylvania), 169,
    173, 178, 201–2, 213
Smith, William, Jr. (of New York), 53,
    81
Social religion, 218
Society for the Propagation of the
    Gospel (SPG), 46, 60, 65, 89, 203;
    founded, 41, 42–43; and clerical
    salaries, 48–50; in South Carolina,
    49–50, 58, 91; in Georgia, 50, 92; in
    New York, 52–54, 56, 239 (n102); in
    North Carolina, 92; conversion of
    blacks and Indians, 119–21, 125; in
    New England, 202. *See also*
    Anglicans
South Carolina, 5; and the Church of
    England, 32, 49–50, 55, 58, 60–61,
    92, 106, 119, 210; dissenters in, 49;
    St. Philips Church (Charleston), 59,
    60, 92; rising number of churches in,
    92
South, the, 90; church adherence in,
    92
Spotswood, Alexander, 44
Stevenson, Marmaduke, 28
Stiles, Ezra, 112, 124–25, 201, 206–7,
    274 (nn51, 55)
Stiles, Isaac, 151, 164
Stillman, Samuel, 212
Stoddard, Solomon, 62, 63, 69, 71, 255
    (n1)
Stone, William, 22
Stuyvesant, Peter, 25–26, 76
Synge, Edward, 101

Talbot, John, 57
Tempelman, John Conrad, 75
Tennent, Charles, 139, 141, 145
Tennent, Gilbert, 132; and the Great
    Awakening, 139–44, 145, 149–50,

154–55, 157–58, 258 (n28); and the
politics of the 1760s, 173–74, 177
Tennent, John, 139, 258 (n28)
Tennent, William, Jr., 139, 145, 207,
211
Tennent, William, Sr., 139–42, 257
(n24)
Thatcher, Peter, 123
Tillotson, John, 4, 98–99, 154
Tocqueville, Alexis de, 211, 218, 220,
222
Toleration Act of 1689, 30, 156, 166,
182, 183, 185
Trenchard, John, 193–95, 198, 216
Trinity College (Dublin), 45
Troeltsch, Ernst, 97
Trollope, Frances, 218

Van Dieren, John Bernhard, 78–79
Van Rensselaer, Maria, 106
Vesey, William, 52, 233 (n34)
Vestries: in the South, 17, 42–44, 46,
49, 50, 230 (n4); resist ecclesiastical
consolidation, 41–42, 43; choosing of,
42, 46, 49; duties of, 42, 46, 49; in
the North, 51–53, 93; composition
of, 92–93, 102
Virginia, 22, 197; establishment of
religion in, 15–17; Church of
England in, 16–17, 42–59 *passim*,
89, 97–102, 119–20, 181–82, 184–85;
and the Baptists, 45, 184–86;
Parsons' Cause in, 49, 197; Great
Awakening in, 125–26, 181; and the
Presbyterians, 181–84; and the
Revolution, 210

Wagner, Tobias, 80
Walpole, Robert, 195
Ward, Nathaniel, 19
Washington, George, 100–101, 214,
216

Watts, Isaac, 4, 5
Weber, Max, 97
Wheelock, Eleazer, 124
Whitaker, Nathaniel, 212
Whitefield, George, 105, 124; and the
Great Awakening, 132, 142, 144,
149–50, 181
Wilkie, Thomas, 136–37
Wilkinson, Christopher, 47
Willard, Samuel, 71
William and Mary, king and queen of
England, 24, 36, 190
William and Mary College, 43, 44,
45–46
Williams, Elisha, 156, 164
Williams, Roger, 18; and Rhode Island,
20, 34–35; and freedom of
conscience, 34–35; and the Quakers,
35
Williams, Solomon, 160
Winslow, Anna Green, 117
Winthrop, John, 18, 19, 20
Wise, John, 63–64, 71
Witherspoon, John, 207, 211, 213, 214
Women, 16, 186; as churchgoers, 5,
60, 69, 105–15, 121, 123–24; and
Quakers, 25–26, 27–28, 108, 112,
248 (n63), 249 (n76); in rural
parishes, 60; and church politics,
107, 108; souls of, 107, 247 (n61);
and feminization of the church,
111–15, 249 (nn78–80), 250 (n84);
widows, 112; and accusations against
the clergy, 136–37; contribute to
rector's salary, 247 (n55)
Woodmason, Charles, 61
Woolman, John, 169
Wrangel, Charles, 176, 177, 178

Yale College, 70, 146–47, 150, 163–64,
167, 257 (n20)
Yamasee War, 58